A Commentary on
1 & 2 CORINTHIANS

UNLOCKING THE NEW TESTAMENT

A Commentary on

1 & 2 CORINTHIANS

David Pawson

Anchor Recordings

First published in Great Britain in 2016 by
Anchor Recordings Ltd
72 The Street, Kennington, Ashford TN24 9HS

**For more of David Pawson's teaching,
including DVDs and CDs, go to
www.davidpawson.com**

**FOR FREE DOWNLOADS
www.davidpawson.org**

**For further information, email
info@davidpawsonministry.org**

ISBN 978-1-909886-95-7

Printed by Lightning Source

Contents

This book is based on a series of talks. Originating as it does from the spoken word, its style will be found by many readers to be somewhat different from my usual written style. It is hoped that this will not detract from the substance of the biblical teaching found here.

As always, I ask the reader to compare everything I say or write with what is written in the Bible and, if at any point a conflict is found, always to rely upon the clear teaching of scripture.

David Pawson

INTRODUCTION

1. Mixture: sordid – depths to which men sink
                    sublime – heights to which God can raise
2. Background:
   a. World – human b. Empire – Roman c. Country – Greek
   d. City – mentally proud; materially prosperous; morally perverted
3. Church and Paul
   VISIT 1 (original = 18 months) Paul fearful
        LETTER 1 ("previous")
        LETTER 2 (our FIRST) Questions and bad reports
   VISIT 2 ("painful") Paul unwelcome
        LETTER 3 ("severe") Paul critical
        LETTER 4 (our SECOND) Paul defensive
   VISIT 3 (final) Paul joyful
4. Themes
   a. BASIC STRUGGLES
        Corporate: Church v. world
        Individual: Spirit v. flesh
   b. BALANCED SPIRITUALITY
        Emotional – heart
        Intellectual – mind
        Moral – will

Is Christianity intellectually acceptable? What is the Christian attitude to sex and marriage? Will we survive death? Will we have bodies on the other side of the grave? Should women wear hats in church? Should men have long hair? What about speaking in tongues? What is the job of the minister? Ought a Christian ever to go to law? What is the actual evidence for the fact of the resurrection of Christ from the dead? What is real love? Does it matter if I dabble in the occult? What do Christians believe? How do they behave? Sordid behaviour – and heights to which God can lift us. The dark background of human sin and the light of the gospel.

These and many other matters of belief and behaviour are dealt with in Paul's first letter to the Corinthians.

Corinth, situated in Greece, was founded just fifty years before Jesus' earthly ministry, after a gap of a century from the previous city in its place. It was part of the Roman Empire. With its fine system of administration and justice, the empire had brought peace and safety to the Mediterranean world. With that peace came permissiveness and complacency. The empire had already begun to fragment through moral corruption, family life breaking up, unwanted children, divorce.

In the 1960s there were sweeping changes in education, departing from Greek influence, but for two thousand years Western education was founded on Greek culture and thinking. Greeks were great thinkers and talkers. Entertainment was "travelling speakers" and novelty was the order of the day – "if it is new, it is good." Philosophy was important – the development of the mind and thought – as was developing the body in physical exercise. The Olympic games, and Isthmian and other lesser games, were known throughout Greece. Corinth, with its massive stadium, was the centre of the Isthmian games. Here were people worshipping the mind and the body of man. The reckless development of the individual – in whatever direction he chose – was the religion of the day.

Corinth was a sea port situated where the peninsula of Greece is nipped almost in half by two gulfs of the sea, and almost cuts off the southern part from the north. There is only a four mile gap across, and Corinth was at the western end of this narrow neck of land. Since the route round the coast and the cape of the south was terribly dangerous, ships from the west would come to Corinth, their cargo would be unloaded, transported overland four miles, loaded onto another ship and taken further east. So Corinth became the way from east to west and west to east.

It was also the main road from the north (Europe) to the south of Greece. In this crossroads and sea port you had people from east and west living alongside each other. Every race was represented. Every religion was represented. There were Jews, Egyptians, Syrians, Greeks, Romans – a cosmopolitan crowd. So "everything went". You could do anything in Corinth and nobody would raise an eyebrow. It has been called the "Piccadilly Circus" of the Roman Empire. People drifted through this cross-roads believing what they wished and behaving as they wished. There was a saying equivalent to our modern phrase about "going to the devil" – it was said that he or she was being "Corinthianised". That is the town to which this letter was sent.

The church at Corinth had no building in those days. They had not developed far enough to ask permission for a building. That was to come later. In packed rooms in private homes there was a lively church, full of all kinds of people. The first impression would have been of excitement, certainly not dull services. (People getting drunk at the Lord's Supper is not dull). Languages known and unknown were spoken. People came and ate, and went home again.

Just twenty years after the death and resurrection of Jesus, this was a church that was some eighteen months old. It had started when Paul was told by Jesus to go and plant churches throughout the Gentile world, and he did. His strategy was to go to every key centre and establish a work that would spread out into that district, and then he moved on as soon as it was established. In some places it took three weeks, in other places longer. In some places he was thrown out. In Corinth it took eighteen months, and then Paul returned to Ephesus. Reading carefully between the lines of the first and second letters to the Corinthians, we find that Paul went three times to Corinth. In between these visits he wrote two letters between the first and second visits and two letters between the second and third visits. Of Paul's four letters we have two left and the other two were lost.

To summarise: on his first visit, Paul went for eighteen months, founded the church, and left. He wrote the first letter, and the reason for it is unknown. It was a letter to the converts. He refers to it in 1 Corinthians. Then he wrote a second letter which we call 1 Corinthians. It was written to reply to their questions. For example: should a Christian who is married to a non-Christian separate from them? He wrote it having heard some disturbing reports about what was going on.

Then he heard things were going from bad to worse, and the second visit took place. This was a painful visit. He was not welcome. The church he had founded did not want him. He had to leave, and he returned to Ephesus.

He called his third letter a "severe letter". That one is lost. The third letter did what his second visit had failed to do: it brought them to repentance. Thrilled to hear this, he wrote a fourth letter, which is our 2 Corinthians. On his third visit there was renewed happy fellowship.

Intellectually proud, materially prosperous and morally corrupt – that sums up Corinth. Then people wonder why we read the Bible! Isn't that an amazing parallel to the society in which we live?

Consider the theme of 1 Corinthians. The main thrust of the letter is how the church can be seen in many different pictures – as a bride, as a body, as a building, a family, a flock. There is one good picture of the church that is not mentioned in the Bible, namely a lifeboat for the purpose of getting people saved, for those who cry "SOS" – "save our souls". The church should go out and save such people. The lifeboat to save people must be in the sea. It is of no use in the lifeboat house. But if the sea gets into the boat, that is disaster. Lifeboats are built to avoid that. In the same way, the church must be right in the world – in the middle of Corinth. The church must be where it is needed, in the thick of life, but when the world gets into the church, it is finished. Corinth's real problem was that not only was the church in the midst of it, the world was right in the church. The kind of attitudes and thinking, activities and behaviour, that went on in Corinth, was happening inside the church too. There was no difference. The church was being submerged in society.

The real problem was that some of those who were called to live in the Spirit were "living after the flesh". Here are the two tensions in 1 Corinthians: the church versus the world, and the spirit versus the flesh. And the church was fighting a losing battle. Every church in every generation has to fight this battle and win it, or it will be quite ineffective to save people. Balanced Christianity must meet the needs of your heart, your mind and your will – the emotional, intellectual and moral. All three should go together. You can get so excited emotionally and services were exciting, but mentally they had wrong, confused beliefs about the resurrection, and morally their wills were weak – there was even a case of incest known among the membership and not dealt with. That is the kind of imbalance they had. They had majored on the heart, on the emotions, and were too excited. Their mental grasp of the truth had been lost and their moral grasp of Christ was slipping, and Paul wrote 1 Corinthians to plead with them to get rid of this carnality, this "fleshiness", this "old life" and get back to Christ.

You may be shocked by the laxity of that church and if all that went on in a church in your home town you might be tempted to deny it was a Christian church at all – but it was, and the problems here were problems of life, and wherever you get a live church, and where you get new people coming into the church, these are the problems you will get.

You can have the order of a cemetery. Corinth was disordered because it had life. Which would you rather have? A church with life and problems like this, or a dead church? Every corpse I have known has been very well behaved, staying exactly where put, never doing or saying anything wrong, beautifully ordered and you can make a church into a place where every service has the decorum of a funeral. Or you can have the life and vigour and excitement at Corinth, with all its problems. I would rather have that and do what Paul did – and say: I thank God that you are not lacking in any spiritual gift; I thank God that you have this life, but I am going to teach you how to keep it right and how to balance the gifts of the Spirit with the fruit of the Spirit and how to put tongues and love together, which is where they belong; and how to look forward to the resurrection as something even more wonderful than this life.

PAUL AND CORINTH
Read 1 Corinthians 1:1–17

A. HIS GREETING – grace and peace (1–3)
 1. WHO HE INCLUDES (1–2)
   a. Paul and Sosthenes
   b. Corinthians and Christians
   c. Father and Son
 2. WHAT HE INCLUDES (3)
   a. Grace (Greek "charis")
   b. Peace (Hebrew "shalom")

B. HIS GRATITUDE – grace kept (4–9)
 1. THEIR PAST GIVEN (4–5)
 2. THEIR PRESENT GIFTED (6–7)
 3. THEIR FUTURE GUILTLESS (8–9)

C. HIS GRIEF – peace lost (10–17)
 1. CAUSE – human attachment (10–12)
   a. Paul
   b. Apollos
   c. Cephas
   d. Christ
 2. CURE – divine atonement (13–17)
   a. Belonging
   b. Baptised

They had a sensible habit in those days when they wrote letters. They put the name of the writer at the beginning. They started with who wrote it, who is going to read it and where it is going to. It was often written on a rolled up piece of paper, so you rolled it up from the end, therefore the address was at the beginning. His greeting is to Corinth, and was a fairly normal sort of greeting for those days, yet it was different. Somehow a letter from a Christian is different. There is a tone, something added.

Paul would always bring as many people as he could into his correspondence. He loved to make it a letter to the family and from the family. We don't know who Sosthenes was, what he was there for and why he was included, but Paul writes "Paul and Sosthenes" – both of us. There is something profoundly against individualism in the New Testament. We are taught to use the word "our", not "my"; Jesus sent his disciples out two by two. The letter is to "us", so we are included. It is a big greeting. The letter is really from God and Christ – grace and peace are from him – so let us take this as a letter from Christ. That is precisely how we do take it. It is the Word of God. It is not just from Paul and Sosthenes. It is not just for the Corinthians. It is to all Christians – everyone comes into this letter.

"Grace and peace" – when the Greeks wrote a letter they used a word very much like "grace" but not quite. Their usual word meant "good wishes". When the Hebrews wrote a letter they began with the word "peace" [Shalom] which meant: I hope you will have a harmonious life; be at peace with yourself, other people and God. But when Christians write a letter they bring together the Greek world and the Jewish world and they transform it to say: "grace and peace" – everything that people wish each other is really to be found in God and in Christ. That is the greeting.

They have kept their "grace" that they had received. "Grace" is one of the loveliest words in the Bible. Someone has made a neat acrostic from the five letters – "**G**od's **R**iches **A**t **C**hrist's **E**xpense". That is one meaning. "Grace and favour" houses are homes given by the Queen to her relatives or friends free of rent, and my Lord and Saviour has prepared a home, free of rent, for every person who believes in him. "Grace" simply means it is *free*, but that is a word which is so overdone today that I hardly dare use it. Everywhere I look I see something that is free but I know perfectly well I have to pay for it. "Free gift included in this magazine"; "send for this free" on the back of a cereal packet! Who is giving it all to me? I am. Giving for nothing? Don't believe it. There is only one thing finally that is free, and it is *grace*.

"You have kept this grace...." Paul isn't starting this letter with thanksgiving as a kind of deliberate policy to pat them on the back to keep them happy for what is coming, but because he is genuinely glad about this. He gives thanks for their past, their present and their future. It is lovely that a Christian can look in all three directions at once and be grateful for them all.

First, the *past* (vv. 4–5): one of the first signs that a person has received the grace of Christ is that they start talking – speech. I know some are born talkers but when you are full of the Lord, the lips are the God-provided overflow. You want to tell others. You were enriched in speech. If people don't talk about the Saviour you wonder if they really know him. "I thank God you were enriched in speech and in knowledge." This is speech worth listening to! You know the one you are talking about now. You know the Lord.

Now the *present* (vv. 6–7). "I give thanks...." This testimony of Christ was confirmed in you so that you come short in no gift – "you have them all". There are very few churches today that have all the spiritual gifts. We shall come across lists of them later in this letter. Paul thanks God that now they are not lacking in any. Of course, they were lacking in graces, but they didn't lack gifts. I think today we find more churches where the graces are present and the gifts are lacking. God wants us to have both.

Then the future (vv. 8–9). He gives thanks for their future. He says: "One day you will stand guiltless before God when

Christ comes again, and I can give thanks that you are going on to perfection." Why is he so confident? He says, "I am confident because God is faithful". I am not confident in you. I hope you are not confident in me. Our confidence is in the fact that God is faithful and he will see us right through.

That is a wonderful tone of gratitude with which to begin the letter. I thank God that he graced your past, that he gifted your present and that he will present you guiltless in the future.

Now comes the rub, a tender and strong appeal: Brethren, I appeal to you, I plead with you. What is this I hear? ... quarrelling, dissensions, the church is dividing into cliques, what is all this?

The first cause of his grief was that they were no longer one happy family. They had almost started holding placards over each group, and they had dared to start the first denominations recorded in the Bible, for the word "denomination" simply means a new name. This is the beginning of denominational labels and the first were based on the names of human beings who were ministers of God – "Paul, Apollos, Cephas, and we are of Christ". Paul condemns using each name as a label in this way. He starts with his own name – never say I belong to Paul. Apollos – an eloquent preacher and gifted in the scriptures – don't say you belong to him. Cephas (Peter) – had he preached in this church too? What a succession! "I am of Christ" – what is wrong with that? It implies two things: first that you are superior to the others and, secondly, it implies the others are not of Christ. I remember seeing a whole list of churches in an area in the north of England and noticed a church calling itself "The Christian Church" – and the very use of that title implied that others were not. It is difficult to know what name to give a church without implying something misleading, something partial or something exclusive. It is almost better not to have denominational labels at all.

Let us bring this right up to date: Wesleyans, Lutherans – here is the same kind of label. Wesley and Luther were just men of God, as were Paul, Cephas and Apollos. Have you ever heard or said "I go to Mr So-and-so's church"? Rebuke it delicately and lovingly. Coming closer to ordinary church life, do you hear people comparing one servant of God with another? "I like Mr So-and-so better." You may have fallen into this same trap. And if you proudly say, "I belong to no denomination, no church, I belong to the Christian church" that too can be a form of spiritual pride. "I thank you that I am not as the Baptist, the Methodist...."

Let us take these scriptures to our hearts and have done with all confusion between God and Christ and his servants. His servants are nothing and nobody without him.

How does Paul deal with this dreadful thing, ministerial fan clubs? He deals with it by pointing to three simple things:
1. You can't divide Christ. You can't split him up into bits and say "We belong to this bit." There is only one Christ. Is Christ divided? Don't divide yourselves.
2. Was Paul crucified for you? The cross cures most of this kind of trouble. The death of Christ atones. Therefore you should never look to a man as if he saved you, forgave you, died for you, bled for you. Christ was crucified.
3. You were baptised into the name of Jesus. Again, let me be quite specific, and I may appear to be tough in this, but it really goes through me when I hear somebody say "I was baptised by Mr So-and-so". You were baptised by the church into Christ. That is all. And one of the reasons I prefer to have somebody baptising with me is so that no-one can say "Mr So-and-so baptised me". You don't belong to the minister who baptises you. It honestly doesn't matter who baptised you. You belong to Christ, and Paul says: "I am thankful that even though I started your church, I didn't do

the baptising." He left someone else to do that. He was the evangelist.

One of the reasons Billy Graham, who was a Baptist pastor, did not baptise people was precisely so that no-one could go around saying "I was baptised by Billy Graham." He was an evangelist and he left the pastors and teachers to do the baptising, as Paul did here. And Paul is saying: My friends, Christ is One, Christ was crucified for you, it was the name of Christ at your baptism, you belong to him. Never talk of belonging to anyone else.

In seventeen verses Christ has been specifically mentioned fifteen times – and that is just the beginning of the letter! Christ, Christ, Christ, Christ.... There is no doubt about what is the centre of Paul's religion. It is the person called Christ. What Paul is saying in all this letter is this: the closer you get to Christ, the fewer of these problems you will have. The closer you draw to other people (and people whom you have chosen to follow), the more problems you will get. So come to Christ. Christ must have the pre-eminence in the Church. It is his and he must be in the centre of it.

So when we baptise people, we baptise them into the name of Christ. They belong to him and to no-one else.

We can see our own weaknesses. We find it much easier to get attached to someone we can see than someone we can't see, but we know this is of the flesh and not of the Spirit. May this letter be to us, as we study it, a surgeon's knife cutting out all harmful growth and that which spoils and hinders our lives, and when we boast may it be in the Lord.

CROSS AND CHRISTIANS
Read 1 Corinthians 1:18–31

A. WORD OF CROSS: no proof (18–25)
 1. WORLD – seeing (18–23)
   a. Jews want evidence
   b. Greeks want eloquence
 2. CHURCH – believing (24–25)
   a. Practical – saves
   b. Intellectual – satisfies

B. WEAKNESS OF CHRISTIANS: no pride (26–30)
 1. WORLD – embarrassed (26–29)
   a. Nobodies to somebodies
   b. Something to nothing
 2. CHURCH – emboldened (30–31)
   a. Somebody with everything
   b. Everybody with nothing

In a West country village there was a man who was known as the village fool, and he was called this because if you offered him a pound note or a sixpence he always took the sixpence. Hundreds of people had tried this on him and he went on doing it.

The Rev. Dr Soper was used to answering thousands of questions at Hyde Park Corner, but he confessed that there was one man he could not deal with, who accused him of being insane.

Dr Soper said, "I am as sane as you are."

"You are not, the man responded, "I can prove I am sane, but you can't prove you are sane."

So Dr Soper said, "Well, you prove you are sane first then."

Then the man pulled out of his pocket a discharge certificate from a mental hospital – which finished Dr Soper off!

A young man danced through the streets of Manchester dressed as a clown, wearing a placard on his front which said "I am a fool for Christ". People looked at him and thought he was a bit "touched" – until they noticed that on his back he wore another placard which said: "Whose fool are you?" We are concerned here with who is foolish and who is wise – because a burning question in ancient Greece, their main entertainment, was to discuss who is the biggest fool. Some would say "this man is a fool" and some would say "that man is a fool" and they would argue about who was wise and who was a fool.

There were some, the Epicureans, who said that the wise person is the one who indulges passion, every lust, every feeling, lives it up and enjoys himself, for it is later than he thought, and tomorrow he is going to die anyway. Then there were the Stoics, who said that a man who does that is a fool – he will become the victim of his own passions – and that the really wise man is the one who rises above feelings, above being moved to tears or joy, and achieves a spiritual attitude that lives up on a mountain top and is unmoved by life.

One of the favourite places for discussing this was on Mars Hill, in the centre of the city of Athens. It was the Hyde Park Corner of the ancient world. Here, men would get up and debate who was wise and who was foolish. One day, a new speaker, a Jew called Paul, got up on that hill. As far as we know he was bald, small, bandy legged – not prepossessing in appearance. He told these great thinkers and philosophers and debaters the truth about God.

They just laughed, and he came away from Athens feeling somewhat discouraged but having learned one of the biggest lessons of life, and it is one of the hardest lessons to learn: that what to God is wise is foolish to men, and what to men is wise is foolish to God, for the simple reason that God's ways and thoughts are so much higher than ours. Each seems foolish to the other. When I think I am being clever, God says I am being a fool, and when God reveals his wisdom, men think he is being foolish. This is the theme of the passage.

Paul gives two examples of things which God has done which might appear nonsense to thinking people, and yet are God's wise way of dealing with people. One is the word of the Cross; the other is the weakness of Christians. Both are true and effective! Let us take the first – the message of Christianity – for the two things that seem nonsensical to the world are the message we preach and the people who preach it. This is the extraordinary "foolishness of God" that demonstrates his wisdom: that he chose the message of the Cross to save people, and that he chose foolish men and despised men to give that message.

The heart of Christianity is this message: the news that two thousand years ago a young man in his mid-thirties was executed as a common criminal in an obscure province of the Roman Empire, and that this single event is the most important thing that ever happened in human history. That is the first "nonsense" of the Christian gospel. And we preach this event – it is the height of our faith, so much so that the Cross has almost become the visual aid, the symbol of our religion, though before it was a visual symbol it was a verbal one in words. We preach the cross for three reasons. I am sure you know there were hundreds of other people who died on crosses in that same period. We preach this one for these three reasons:

Reason 1 *What* **this man was**

The answer was that he was the only perfect man who ever lived. He was not a common criminal. Everybody who has studied his life has said: that is human life at its peak; that is the finest life I have ever read; that is the finest character I have ever heard about. Yet this perfect man – who claimed to be perfect (which is astonishing) and got away with that claim because nobody could disprove it – was put to death as a criminal.

Reason 2 *Who* **this man was**

The only crime they could finally pin on him was what they called "blasphemy" because he claimed to be the Son of God, and they said that was untrue – "Away with Him!" But he died appealing to God to release him from the verdict and the sentence, and he said: If I am the Son of God you will not be able to get rid of me by killing me.

Reason 3 The reason *why* **he died**

He was allowing himself to be treated as a criminal, even though he was innocent, because he wanted to redeem people – not just to influence them, not just to help them, not just to teach them or to heal them but to *redeem* them!

I want you to imagine that you are the son or daughter of a very wealthy man, and that you have been kidnapped and that your father has been told that unless he pays a certain sum of money then you will be killed. If he pays that money then, quite frankly, he has redeemed you. That is all. He has paid a price to set you free. That is all that "redeem" means.

Going back to days that most of us can hardly remember, if I went to pawn my suit and later redeem it, I would pay the price to set it free from the clutches of someone else.

But now I want to take this illustration a little further. Supposing your kidnappers said to your father: "If you send in someone else we will let this child of yours go free." Then the price being paid for you would not be money but would be a person. In utterly simple terms, Jesus said he died as a ransom for many. It is not silver or gold, but his own life, and that is why we preach the Cross. The word of the Cross is as simple as that. And wherever people preach it, people get set free from evil, from self, from pride and from sin. That is the amazing truth of the gospel.

Now this is the word of the Cross which Paul preached when they laughed at him. It is the word of the Cross which he took round the Roman Empire, challenging everybody to believe it to be the truth. Wherever he preached it, things happened and lives got changed.

In the early days of Billy Graham's ministry he was quite a well-known preacher, and reasonably effective, yet he realised that he wasn't being as effective as he ought to be. He went to a dear saint of a man who really walked with the Lord for some forty or more years and said, "Would you tell me what is wrong with my preaching that it is not having more effect on people?"

The old man said: "There is just one thing, Billy. There's not enough of the Cross in it." Billy made a resolution then that he would never preach once without including the Cross, and that is why he was blessed as one of the greatest evangelists of his day. It is the word of the Cross – not because of Billy. People who had been to hear him said: "Well, I've heard better sermons than that elsewhere" – but it was because he preached this simple word: Jesus died in your place, for your sin, that you might be free. This is the message that is utter nonsense to people, and Paul mentions two groups of people who find it utterly ridiculous and even offensive – the idea of a man whose dying years ago can set me free! He mentions "Jews" and "Greeks". These were two groups of people representing our world who want to see before they believe. And this is one of the greatest barriers to a person becoming a Christian. There are those who say "Until I see, I will not believe", but the simple truth is that seeing is not believing! Once you have seen, you don't need to believe. And the two are contrary to one another. If you see, you don't believe. If you believe, you have believed without seeing. Faith and sight are contradictory.

Those who want to see before they believe want to see in two ways – either with their eyes at a practical level or with their minds at an intellectual level. The Jews said, "We want to see with our eyes! We want miracles, we want proof before our eyes, that this thing works." The Greeks said, "We want proof for our minds! We want logic, rational argument that will persuade our minds that this is true."

But they were both saying they wanted to see before they would believe. God, in his great wisdom, will have none of that. He says to the Jew "no miracles"; and he says to the Greek "no arguments", and he says to the whole world: the word of the Cross – Christ died for your sins!

So when we turn from the world (that wants to see) to the Christians who had believed this, and though they cannot understand, they say, "I only know at his right hand stands one who is my Saviour" – they can't explain it, they can't confound the clever brains of the critics and the scholars, they can only say, "I just know!" – I believe two things happen. First, to the Jew who wants practical proof, I say: Once I believed, I got practical proof! It worked. The Cross became the power of God to me! To the Greek who says "I want mental proof before I believe," I say as a Christian: "I believe, and then I get my mental proof! I understand it now. It is logical. It is rational. I can see it to be true!"

But notice the order. Some people say "Show me proof" and God says, "No proof – only a Cross"; and others say, "Lord, I believe that Cross" and God then says, "Right, now that cross will save you and satisfy you." It will meet your practical needs and it will harmonise your intellectual thinking. That is how it always has been.

Now to the world this is a ridiculous way of going about saving it. To go round the world telling people today that Christ died on a cross two thousand years ago and you can be saved is ridiculous. But it is so wise of God to have done it this way, and now that I am a Christian it doesn't seem silly any more. It seems so sensible, and I will tell you why.

First of all, it means that nobody is forced to believe. Wasn't that wise of God? If God had given proof to people before they believed, then everybody would have to believe. They would have no choice. But God in his wisdom doesn't force anyone to be a Christian. He never will. He loves people too much to force them, and so presents a message that leaves them entirely free to say "no – that is not true", or to say "yes, I believe it to be true."

The second thing I am glad about concerning the wisdom of God in the cross is this: there is no premium on intelligence. If men could find God by using their brains then I am afraid it would be the brainy ones that would get to heaven before the rest of us. And if God had chosen to let human wisdom and cleverness discover the truth, then quite frankly that would have been totally unfair to people. Those who failed academically wouldn't get to glory. You can see how sensible it was of God to ignore intelligence. Indeed, according to the Bible which Paul knew, and he quotes it at this point, God's intention is to destroy the brilliance of men's brains, to thwart it, to wreck it – and that is the answer to those who have asked me why it is that some of the most brilliant intellects in the world are atheists. The answer is because God has chosen to thwart the cleverness of men, and in his wisdom he has revealed the truth to the simple, child-like person.

Jesus once thanked his Father in these terms: "My Father,

I thank you that you have hidden these things from the wise and revealed them to babes and sucklings." In other words, you have got to become like a little child, not with brains but with trust. Quite simply, to come to the Cross, and right there to believe that Jesus died for you.

That is the first example of the wisdom of God which makes all men's brains ridiculous because the greatest brains that have been exercised have failed to prove God's existence and have failed to find man's happiness. And no brain will ever be great enough to do those two things. But God in his "foolishness" brings people to salvation, to himself, through a Cross.

Now what about the second thing mentioned here – the weakness of Christians? Take a look at the people who have found the power of God in the Cross. There are now a large number. For quantity it is quite impressive. Millions living today believe in the Cross of Christ. But when you look at the quality of the people who have believed it is not very impressive and it never will be. When you look at a typical church you don't see all the brains, you don't see all the nobility, you don't see all the aristocracy, you don't see all the top powerful people. You see very ordinary men and women for the most part. "Not many wise, not many noble" ... God has chosen ordinary folk. As Abraham Lincoln used to say, "God must love common people. He made so many of them!" – and he understood this truth. Here again is the utter folly of God's way of going about things. Why didn't he go for the "key" people, the brilliant people, the powerful people and get hold of them? They would influence others. That is how human wisdom talks. Alas, if we are not careful, we can fall into that very trap ourselves. But God in his wisdom said: I am going to choose nobodies, I am going to choose ordinary people, and I am going to make them extraordinary. People who are despised and overlooked and you pass them in the street – God takes a person like that and makes them an extraordinary person.

The second thing he says he will do is to bring to nothing the "somethings" that men have built, through these nobodies who are now somebodies, so he takes nobodies and he makes somebodies that they may take something that men have made and bring it to nothing. I will give you an illustration of that. There was a famous explorer and geographer living in London who was recognised by the world as brilliant, and he explored the continents. One day he engaged a girl as a parlour maid, a nobody. Gladys was to be the parlour maid to the great explorer. I remember Gladys's name now, and so do many others. She has gone right round the world. Gladys Aylward went out to China alone – that parlour maid, a nobody – and when she got there, she was faced very early with the cruel and horrible practice of binding the feet of the women so they didn't grow beyond the size of children's feet, a painful habit imposed on them by the men who liked that, with some perverted desire in them. And little Gladys Aylward, the parlour maid, brought that "something" – bringing to an end a practice that had lasted for centuries. She brought it to nothing by herself.

This is God's "foolishness". This is the way God does things, taking "nobodies", ordinary people. Christianity is not a religion for the elite. It is the religion for everyone. God makes people somebodies to take the things that men erect and bring them to nothing and show that he is God, and therefore, when he does this, the world is ashamed of itself – it is bound to be. And the world will one day be terribly ashamed of all its achievements, when it sees that the people who really did things that lasted were ordinary people whom God touched by his Spirit.

Now you can see how sensible this is of God. I suppose if you or I were told to choose twelve people to start a new

29

world religion, we would choose a brilliant man here and a great man here and a powerful man there, and we would say, "Now we've got a really good team." I don't think we would choose fishermen or a tax collector. No, we would go for important people. But Jesus didn't. How sensible he was.

I will give you two reasons why it was so wise. First, it made it utterly clear all along that what happened was God's doing and not man's, so that nobody could say "It's this brilliantly clever man." It is God who has done it. It must be! There's no other explanation. And he would get the glory! And men would know that he is the Creator and can take a nobody and create somebody out of that nobody.

The second sensible reason for doing this is that it cuts out all pride. The basic and most offensive sin in anybody is pride. We don't like it even in each other. Somebody who is a name dropper, or whose nose is carried high, and somebody who thinks more of themselves than they should – they are offensive even to men. What do you think they are like to God? And God is going to cut out every bit of pride in men. He chose to do it by choosing ordinary people so that no man should boast in the presence of God.

But the church can boast. Christians are the only people in the world who are allowed to boast, according to my Bible. However, they must be careful what they boast about. And now Paul turns to the Christians. Pride in yourself is as offensive, and even more so, when you are a Christian than before you were a Christian. The pride that we are allowed is this sort of pride: that we know somebody who has got everything. God has made Christ our wisdom, our righteousness, our sanctification, our redemption.

To put it in simple English: Do you want to be wise? Then you have got all the wisdom you need in Jesus. Do you want to be good? Then you have got all the righteousness you need in Jesus. Do you want to be different? Then you have got all the sanctification you need in Jesus. Do you want to be free? Then you have got all the redemption you need in Jesus. Therefore a Christian can boast: "I've got everything because he has got everything", and that is a tremendous thing to be able to say. But it must be because he has got everything. Everybody has nothing and that is the other side of the coin. Christ is my all. Everything I have is his. If I can do anything in this world of lasting value, it is because he did it through me, and therefore if I boast, I boast in the Lord, and every Christian has the biblical authority and right to boast in the Lord and to say: "I am proud of him"; "I'm proud of my Lord. I am proud to introduce him to you". "I'm just thrilled to know that my best friend is the greatest person who has ever lived." That is boasting in the Lord.

So "foolish" is God to choose the word of the Cross to save people, and to choose the weakness of Christians to pass it on to others – and yet how sensible.

The same thing runs through baptism. We baptise those who have believed that Jesus died for their sins. There was a time when it was nonsense to them, there was a time when they didn't understand, they didn't see, and then they believed and now they do see. Then they do something which in the world's eyes is silly – nonsense.

I was introduced to an ecclesiastical dignitary by someone who said, "This man actually goes into the water in his suit at baptisms; I think that is going a bit far, isn't it?" To the world what we do seems nonsense. It is an undignified thing to do. It is a silly thing to get all wet in front of a lot of staring people. Yet it's God's wisdom. It is God's way of doing things.

If it seems folly and nonsense to the world, those who do it say after they have done it: "It was right. It was God's way of bringing me to utter obedience to himself. It was God's way of sealing to me that he has cleaned my conscience. It was God's way of burying my old self and holding a funeral over my old life and it is not silly at all. It is the most sensible thing I ever did." This is the Christian life. We are called to be fools for Christ's sake. We are called to be clowns for his sake. We are called to be despised and to suffer contempt in the eyes of others.

"What, have you got this too? Have you become a Christian also? Oh you are mad, Paul," said Festus, when he heard what Paul had to say about Jesus – and the world will think we are mad.

If this is madness, I wish we were all mad! If this is insanity, then I feel utterly sane in doing it! If this is foolish then it is the wisdom of God to bring us so low that we can only look up and see his glory.

GOD AND MAN
Read 1 Corinthians 2

A. DEMONSTRATION OF GOD'S POWER (1–5)
 1. DIVINE TRUTH – THOUGHTS
   a. Christ – a person
   b. Cross – an event
 2. HUMAN TREMBLING

B. DECREE OF GOD'S PURPOSE (6–13)
 1. HIDDEN WISDOM
   a. Investigation – present
   b. Instruction – past
   c. Imagination – future
 2. REVEALED WORDS
   a. Our own spirit
   b. World's spirit
   c. God's Spirit

C. DISCERNMENT OF GOD'S PEOPLE (14–16)
 1. NATURAL MAN
 2. SPIRITUAL MIND
   a. Judges all
   b. Judged by none

How did Paul learn all that we have seen in this letter so far? Who taught him? The answer is that he learned in the hard school of experience so he was able to wear those school colours of black and blue. Where did he learn it? We learn the answer to that in the first phrase of chapter 2.

"When I came to you" – we must go back to the book of Acts and ask when this was. Where did he come from? What had happened just before he got to Corinth? The answer is that he had been in Athens, which in the Roman Empire was the seat of brilliant intellects. It was the place where all the famous scholars and lecturers came. It was the place where you went to have your mind stretched. It was the place where you went to be entertained by all the latest lecturers and philosophers. You went there to hear some new thing. It was intellectually exciting and stimulating.

Athens was just a few miles away from Corinth and the two cities between them represented the greatest intellectual centre the world had ever seen. Here were architecture and philosophy, here were the debaters, and Paul had just been to Athens with the gospel. And he had learned a profound lesson. When he saw Mars Hill on the Areopagus at Athens (and I have stood on that hill, and have seen groups of students gathered around, talking together about the things of the mind) he thought: what an opportunity to preach the truth! Here they all are – searching, seeking. Indeed, when you talk to the brilliant brains of this world, you find they are all seeking. So very few of them, if they are honest, will admit that they have found what they are looking for. Paul saw this opportunity. He had studied the religious life of that city as he walked through it, and he discovered how confused were their ideas about God. The place was littered with altars and temples to every conceivable named 'god' you could imagine, but at the end of the road, he came across a most unusual altar "To an unknown God".

The story behind that altar is extraordinary. About 150 years earlier, the city of Athens had been ruined in an earthquake and everybody said "the gods are angry" or at least "one of the gods must be angry" to have done this. Which one? That is part of the problem when you worship so many – you don't know which one to get right with. So they let loose a flock of sheep and they said, "Wherever the sheep lie down, the deity of the nearest altar to the sheep is angry and we will sacrifice the sheep on the altar and get the god happy again." That is how they used to think in those brilliant, intellectual days – and in our brilliant and scientific age superstition goes along with the most brilliant science. The computer is now being used to produce horoscopes! This is what happens when brilliant brains do not acknowledge truth. Superstition and science get all mixed up in society.

So they let the flock of sheep loose and the sheep wandered around. One of the animals decided to sit down by the altar of Jupiter and promptly paid for that. Another went down the road and sat down at the altar of Mercury and lost his head in a crisis too, and they went down the road like this. But the majority of sheep went past all the altars and sat down in the middle of a field. I could give you a sound biological reason why they did! But the Greeks, in their superstitious darkness, with all their brilliance, said, "There must be another god. We had better get another altar up quick. We don't know his name." That is how it was done.

Paul got up on Mars Hill and said: "There is another God. In fact, there is only one, you just don't know him" and he quoted their poets. He tried every way he could to get them to listen. He argued closely, he quoted from their literature, showed an awareness of their society and did everything he could to get through to these brilliant men – and they laughed as soon as he mentioned anything Christian. They listened to him well as long he stuck to their thoughts, their prophets, their world, their life, but as soon as he started on anything which was specifically God's truth, they stopped him and cut him off like that.

The result was that there were two things he never got out in that speech on Mars Hill. He only got through to the phrase "a man raised from the dead" and they stopped him, so he never got through to the name of Christ – and he never got through to mentioning the Cross. They wouldn't listen any more, and the speech ended like that.

Now it is true that it was not a complete failure. One man called Dionysius wanted to know more. A woman of the streets wanted to know more, and a handful of others, and privately he talked to them about Christ and his Cross. They believed and they became Christians, but as far as the public preaching of the truth went, that was it at that time.

Paul had been thrown out of every previous city that he had preached in – Philippi, Thessalonica, Berea – but Athens was the first city which he left voluntarily, and he left straight after this. As he walked over from Athens to Corinth he was worried, he was discouraged, he was afraid – though not of men. I will tell you what he was afraid of in a moment. He was downcast. He was on his own. Timothy and Silas had been left away up in the north, and as he trudged across that narrow isthmus that cuts Greece in two, he was thinking, "How do you get hold of the intellectual? How do you establish the church in a city that gives the brain the place of God?" That was his problem. He had not left a church behind at Athens and there is no record of a church at Athens in the whole of the New Testament. So how can you do it? And as he trudged down the road he came to certain conclusions about his strategy at Corinth. He decided to try something quite different and to see if it worked. He didn't know if it would. It was an experiment, and when you try something new you are always nervous, afraid that it might be a failure, that it might flop, that it won't do any good. But he came to Corinth determined to try a different strategy and to see if he could leave a church in brilliant intellectual Corinth. The first five verses of Chapter 2 tell you the thoughts and the feelings of his mind and his heart as he came to Corinth.

The first basic thing that he decided in his strategy was that he would let the Greeks *see* rather than *hear* the gospel. Let us pick up another thread from our earlier study. He said: "The Jews want to see with the eyes. They want visible evidence. The Greeks don't want to see with the eyes. They want to see with the mind. They want verbal eloquence.

So the Jews want visible evidence, the Greeks want verbal eloquence – I am going to change them round and give the Greeks the opposite of what they want. I will give them the visible evidence." It had been Paul's strategy to give the Jews not what they wanted but verbal eloquence. He had argued with them out of the scriptures. So he simply switched around the strategy and gave man the exact opposite of what he wanted. Again, the "foolishness" of God. The wisdom of men would say "If people want visible evidence, give it to them. If people want verbal eloquence, give it to them." Paul says: "I am going to swap them round and I will come to the Greeks with a demonstration of God's power." The word "demonstration" means visible, incontrovertible evidence. "I am going to let them see it rather than hear it. How can I do that?" Then he goes a little further in his strategy and he asks God: "How can I let them see your power?" – and God told him. So when Paul came to them he decided to come with a plain, unvarnished "no frills" presentation of the divine truth of the gospel pared down to its utter simplicity. In fact he decided only to tell them two little things. He wasn't going to argue with them. He wasn't going to try and be brilliant. He wasn't going to try and begin with all their thoughts and philosophies. He was not going to try and say these two things in a clever way, he was just going to say them.

One word was "Christ" and the other was "crucified". This was how he was going to tackle the brilliant intellects of Corinth. So he came along and this is what he did. He was going to present these before they had a chance to laugh, before they cut him off mid-stream in the middle of his address. Straight away: Christ and his cross.

Now I want you to notice first of all that he was going to start with a *person*. In the face of those who were always looking for a method of success or a system of thought, or a pattern of living, he was going to present the person who is the Way, the Truth and the Life. These are the ways you might talk to people. You can either say that Christianity is a method of success ("Do you want to succeed in life? – then this is the method") or you can present Christianity as a system of thought: ("Do you want to know what to believe? This is the system of thought – become a theologian.") Or again you might present Christianity as a pattern for living, which is the commonest idea of Christianity in England. It is *behaving* like this, that and the other.

But Paul said: no, I am going to present a person – and when you present a person, you find the method of success for he is the Way; you find a system of thought because he is the Truth; you find a pattern for living because he is the Life, but you find all three after you have found the person. The real way to get through to a world that is brainy and proud of its brains is to say: "I present you with a person you don't know – *Jesus*."

The second thing is so important also – not just to present a person, not just to say "Come to Jesus, and you will have this", but to present a person who has been crucified. Now here I must tell you that the Greek verb translated "crucified" is in a peculiar tense. If I translated it quite literally into English, I would have to say: "I decided to know nothing among you except Jesus Christ and him having been crucified."

What did that mean? It means that you are preaching someone who is alive now who was killed. I mention this because it is so important – not to preach a person was alive and was then crucified, but a person who is alive who has been crucified. Have you got the difference? Not to "preach Jesus" as a past figure who finished up on a cross but a Jesus who is alive now who started his work on a cross. In other words, to Paul the resurrection is more fundamental than the Cross. To preach Christ and him having been crucified is to preach the resurrection! Many preachers unfortunately have misunderstood this text and thought that all you need to preach about is the Cross. But Paul is not saying "I'm going to preach nothing but the Cross" but "I'm going to preach nothing but the risen Jesus" – and that is different. So let us not think that it is preaching a crucifix that is going to save people. It is preaching the risen Jesus who was dead and is alive. That is the meaning of this phrase. To preach Christ, and him *having been* crucified. That is the order. A living Saviour who was crucified for our sins.

So Paul came to Corinth determined to do those two things – to preach the resurrection and the Cross in the light of it. That is the way to preach the Cross: in the light of the resurrection.

Paul is concentrating on the message and not on the method. He is going to eschew all methods of oratory, all the rules of logic and eloquence. He is going to sweep them aside and say: "I have come to tell you about a person who is alive, who was put to death." Now that in a sense is an "incredible" gospel. The world will accept Jesus as a person who was alive and who finished dead. You ask a brilliant man who is not a Christian, what he thinks of Jesus and he will say "I think he was such-and-such" and will go a long way towards accepting him as a great person who *was*, and who finished dead. But that is not the gospel. The gospel is "He who is – or who was crucified". That is the message that saves. Because a dead Christ couldn't save anybody.

Now having shared his thoughts with the Corinthians, Paul shares his feelings, and he says: These are my thoughts, but I will tell you what my feelings were. I really was nervous! I trembled because I hadn't tried this before and I didn't know if it would work, and having had something of a fiasco at Athens I couldn't face another situation like that at Corinth. I came very nervous. I came trembling. I came wondering what on earth would happen, but I came to you trusting in God.

What happened at Corinth? When Paul presented quite simply a straightforward, certain proclamation of Jesus alive and having been crucified, lives changed. Old people became new. A church began and the gospel succeeded. He said: "This is what happened. You saw lives changed. You had a demonstration to your eyes and all your brains couldn't argue against that." Do you know the best argument to someone who is more brilliant than you are, someone who has got a greater intellect than you have, who has studied more than you have? The best argument that they can possibly face is the argument of a changed life. They have no argument against that.

Edgar Wallis, the writer of detective mystery novels, lived in the same road as a lovely humble Christian man. Edgar said, "I can never be an atheist as long as I live in the same road as that man." It is the one argument that they can't deal with. They can argue logically. They can present all their philosophy and all their wonderful reasoning. But they just can't deny that the gospel changes people and that it works. That gets right through their brain, it gets underneath all their brilliance, and they have no answer. Paul said: "You had a visible demonstration of the power of the Holy Spirit. That is what happened. And you believe."

It was reported of two famous preachers in London that when you went to hear one you came away saying "What a wonderful preacher" but when you came away from the other you said "What a wonderful Saviour." This is what Paul was doing to the Corinthians. He didn't care what they thought of him as a speaker. He didn't care what they said of the sermon. He didn't care if they had "roast preacher" for Sunday lunch. All he was concerned about was that they saw God's power at work – and they did.

Christians who are called to serve the Lord know that this principle applies to more than preaching. It applies to me, and I have got to fight this battle and I must not put my trust in brilliant eloquence or in logic or reason. It is a battle between putting your trust in human ways and God's ways. But let me mention at least four other areas of Christian service where this same difficult lesson has to be learnt.

The first concerns church organisation. You might have a brilliant organisation. You may have a business acumen applied to church affairs that is as good as any commercial business in the world, and yet you may still fail as a church. God does not honour brilliant organisation for its own sake. He doesn't use it. So I get tired of denominations talking of re-structuring and re-organising, and thinking that re-organising departments is going to bring the kingdom in. It doesn't! We still go on reporting a decline of membership every year. We mustn't trust in organisation.

Secondly, in our children's work we could say we must copy all the methods that schools use. But sometimes a Sunday school teacher with hardly any visual aids just leads people to Christ.

Thirdly, there is architecture. We think that if we put up a magnificent building this will make people religious. We think: "Isn't that beautiful – that is going to make them worship" so we trust in architecture, and down the road in a little tin hut there are people nearer to God.

Fourthly, music is another area in which this applies. We can have brilliant, marvellous music and sometimes God uses a simple doggerel ballad to get right through to the heart of somebody.

I must not trust in eloquence as a preacher, I must offer a simple, straightforward presentation of the gospel, and if people say, "Well, he is not very brilliant and that's not a great speech", that must not trouble me. The musicians must trust simple music that conveys the power of the Spirit of God so that people don't go away saying "What a marvellous choir; what marvellous music" – but "What a wonderful Saviour those people must have!" Sunday school teachers must so love their children that the children go away loving the Lord and not just talking about the lesson. In our organisation, it may seem a bit haphazard and the life of the church may spring up here and die down there – and the organisation may go and things we have organised may collapse. Who cares? As long as God's power is demonstrated.

This is a radical lesson to learn, and one of the hardest, because we think that great music, great eloquence and great organisation are really what is going to get through to the human mind. They will, but people will give glory to man and put their faith in men! We want them to put their faith in God.

Now why did Paul tell them about this? For the simple reason that in Corinth the Christians were falling back into their old ways of thinking. They were comparing and contrasting preachers. Some of them liked Paul with his simple gospel of Christ and his Cross. Then came another minister to the church. His name was Apollos. In Acts 18 it says that he was an eloquent man, well versed in scriptures. So some people preferred him and might say: "I prefer to get away from the simple gospel, I want deeper teaching." They said "We are of Paul", "We are of Apollos." Paul says: "Don't you see that both are needed?" If you are going to win people for Christ it must be simple, and be pared down to the essentials, but then if you are going to grow in Christ there has to be much deeper teaching. You must have your brain stretched then. You must get into deeper things. Now you need both.

Paul could do both. He could preach simply to the unconverted and he could go very deep to the converted, as his letters testify. But he didn't do this in Corinth – he moved on to plant another church and he left Apollos to take them deep. This is important. It takes the simple presentation of the gospel to plant; it takes a much deeper rational presentation of Christian truth to make a person grow and to be watered, though all the time it is God who enables the whole thing to grow. We must never set preachers against one another.

To be quite frank, I think my own ministry which God has given me is nearer to Apollos than Paul in this regard. Sometimes people have said to me, "I wish you would just give us the simple gospel every Sunday night – about the Cross." It is not my ministry. I want people to grow. I want to water their faith and see it mature, and help Christians to grow up. God has given others the ministry of a simple word that helps them to come to the faith, but you must never line up with one of these two kinds of ministry. You must never say "I am of this" or "I am of that" – "I am of the simple gospel."

There is a simple gospel for the beginner, but it gets more and more complicated for the mature Christian as he grows and stretches his understanding of it and learns to love God with all his mind. Both are needed, which is why Paul goes on to the second point he wants to make, which is this: I can give wisdom. I do give wisdom. I am prepared to stretch the mind. I am prepared to be rational and to argue, with two qualifications.

Firstly, I will do it with the mature, not with babies. Secondly, even when I do this, it will still not appeal to the brains of this world because it is a wisdom and mind-stretching and a rational intelligence that they cannot recognise, and therefore that is why it is not appropriate.

After a debate on humanism, one or two in my church said to me: "Why didn't you argue, instead of just presenting Christian beliefs? Why didn't you present all the intellectual reasons?" The answer is very simple: because to the unconverted the intellectual reasons which convinced Christians would not hold any validity at all. The wisdom that I know, which I would use to stretch your brains as far as I can, is a wisdom that leaves the unbeliever stone cold. His basic premises on which he builds, from which he argues, are so different that the wisdom of the mature Christian will never appeal to the brains of the worldly man. If it did, and if God's wisdom could be made intelligible to the unbeliever, they would never have crucified the Lord of glory. They would never have so misunderstood God's purpose in sending Jesus that they stopped it dead on the Cross. The Cross is the proof that man, with all his brains, can't understand God's ways of doing things.

So there is a wisdom that is not worldly wisdom for a Christian to go on to. Let me put it this way: a Christian must start the Christian life by being a "fool", by submitting his intelligence to God – but as a Christian he must not go on being a fool; as a Christian, he must then learn.

Then we impart to mature people the wisdom that comes from a hidden secret of God. Things that are utterly inaccessible to the human brain become revealed to the mature Christian as God's wisdom. Now I am going deeper and I am afraid I am going to leave behind those who are not mature. Because we are now going into the kind of wisdom of which Paul speaks. He says that God decided before the world began, he decreed before the ages, what he was going to do in the future, and nobody can discover that. There are three ways in which human beings discover things that are true. There is investigation into the present, instruction from the past and imagination about the future. This is the scientific method. You investigate the present with your eye – you observe. You get instruction from the past as the knowledge of former generations comes down to you. Then you project into the future by imagination, and you envisage what is going to happen next.

What Paul is teaching here, quoting the Old Testament, is this: What eye has not seen (by investigation), what ear has not heard (by instruction), what the mind has not seen (by imagination) God has revealed to us through the Spirit. There may be people in your church who know more about the future than the most brilliant intellects in the human race – yet it is revealed to the simple. God has revealed to us what he is going to do. I know how history is going to end. I know what it is all going to lead to.

Futurologists think they can tell us what is going to happen. But I go back to the book of Revelation and can say: "Now I will tell you what is going to happen in the future." We can witness to what God is going to do in the future – what he decreed from all ages. He has revealed it. How has he revealed it? By words. The only way you can understand a person's inmost thoughts is by his expressing those thoughts in words. What makes a person tick? You see people look at you in church. They wonder what you are like. Maybe they wonder what sort of a week you have had. They will never know unless you talk to them and tell them. They don't know what secret burdens you carry. As a minister I don't – unless you tell me. You can never get to know a person unless you listen to the words they utter. Of course, they can utter words that don't reveal their thoughts. They can talk about the weather and be polite, reserved and formal. But if a person is prepared to put their innermost thoughts into words, you can know them. As they talk to you, then you can know what they have decided to do with their life. Any psychiatrist will tell you this. You can't possibly help them unless they are prepared honestly and frankly to put their innermost thoughts into words and tell you, and that is the beginning of all helping people.

If that is true of all people, isn't it true of the divine Being? No-one knows the thoughts of God. How can you? They are God's thoughts. Just as we don't know each other's thoughts – and I don't really know what another person is thinking. Sometimes I can have a good guess, but I still might be miles out. You might be thinking "Did I leave the gas on?" or, "Wasn't it a good football match yesterday" for all I know. I wouldn't know unless you told me. And how can you possibly know God whom you can't even see? I might guess the thoughts of another human being sometimes because I can see their face, but how can I guess God's thoughts when I can't even see his face? The answer is this: the Spirit of God himself knows what God thinks and what he has decided to do. And that Spirit of God has been given to human beings, and with the Spirit of God has come the gift of words which express God's thoughts.

That is why I believe in what is called *verbal inspiration*. The Bible is not a book of inspired *ideas*, it is a book of inspired *words*. That is what makes it the *Word of God*, not *the thought of God*. Jesus, too, is called the Word of God. Though he was the expression of God's total godhead and in him you see the express image of the godhead, he is the Word of God because he talked and he spoke, and God in his amazing wisdom has taken his thoughts and, through the Holy Spirit given to men, turned it into words and we have words inspired by the Spirit of God. I believe in the verbal inspiration of the Bible because God has put words into man's mouth that declare God's truth. That is the meaning of prophecy.

So I come to the final point mentioned here. Why is it then, if God's thoughts have been put into words and the truth is now available to men and women, that they still don't all believe it? This can be the most frustrating experience in life. When brilliant minds cannot see it, the temptation is to get impatient and to say "Why? – you must be terribly perverted to refuse to believe the truth!" Oh, no. I came to see one day that in fact the unbeliever cannot see. It is not that he won't. He can't help it. He can't see. And Paul says that wherever the truth is preached there are two sorts of people: the natural man and the spiritual man.

Consider first the natural man. The word translated "natural" is the Greek word *psuchikos*, which here simply means physical life. An animal has this *psuchikos*, and you can have the psychology of chimpanzees as you can have the psychology of human beings. This psychology cannot see the truth of God. So you must not blame a person for not seeing the truth.

In other words, a natural man listening to the gospel will understand no more of it than my dog. The natural man cannot accept the things of God. But the "spiritual man", which means a person who has received the Holy Spirit – the person who is sensitive to the Spirit, whose eyes have been opened by the Spirit, whose ears have been unstopped – that man has within himself the point of reference by which to judge all things. He can listen to the most profound intellectual philosopher and in his heart, even though he doesn't understand what has been said, he knows when what he hears is wrong. He judges all things. And he is to be judged by no-one, because no-one else has the power to judge him since he has got spiritual understanding.

"You are the body of Christ" is a remarkable statement, but even more astonishing is this other statement in this same letter: "We have the mind of Christ." We are not just the body, we have the *mind* of Christ. God is able to take any simple person and give them the most brilliant mind there has ever been – the mind of Christ! Nobody ever won an argument with Jesus because his mind could leave anybody else at the starting post. And we have our brain stretched.

We can say two simple things at this point:

1. The sin of man includes his reason. Man has fallen mentally as well as morally. It is not just that he can't help doing wrong morally, he can't help thinking twisted thoughts. The Fall of man dragged his brain down as well as his heart. That is why you have such difficulty persuading men to think God's thoughts.

2. Salvation includes man's reason and lifts his brain up until he is able to use his brain rationally, stretch it to the utmost limit using all his intellectual powers and still finding that there is more to discover. Some atheists would say, wrongly, that a believer has committed intellectual suicide, that we have become credulous fools, and that Christianity is a creed for the credulous. I cannot persuade them that I have never had to do so much thinking since I surrendered my thoughts; I have never had to use my brain so much as when I accepted the Bible as being true. I have never had to give myself to such study as I have to since I agreed not to be my own judge in intellectual matters.

Sin includes dragging the brain down, but salvation includes lifting the brain up and dedicating the intellect. There is a wisdom for the mature to go on to. You became a "fool" to become a Christian, but don't stay a fool afterwards! Go on to the wisdom and the maturity. Don't let your teachers have to feed you with milk as a baby, but go on to meat that you can get your teeth into and chew over – into sermons that stretch the brain. Get into those deep truths of God which he decreed before the ages.

REAL CHURCH
Read 1 Corinthians 3

A. A SQUABBLING FAMILY (1–4)
  1. MILK
  2. MALICE

B. A SPROUTING FIELD (5–9)
  1. LABOUR
  2. LIFE

C. A SURE FOUNDATION (10–15)
  1. BASE
  2. BUILDING

D. A SACRED FABRIC (16–17)
  1. DIVINITY
  2. DESTRUCTION

E. A SENSIBLE FOOL (18–23)
  1. WISDOM
  2. WEALTH

The world has many divisions in the human race, but the Bible splits the whole human race into just two groups – the saints and the sinners; the believers and the unbelievers; the sheep and the goats – and one lot are going to heaven and the other lot are going to hell.

In the terms of 1 Corinthians 2, there are the spiritual people and the natural people; people of the Spirit and people of the flesh. This division into two groups, and only two, is offensive to many people, especially because observed behaviour does not seem to bear out the truth of this division. For, as one person put it to me, quoting a cliché, it seems as if, "there's so much good in the worst of us and so much bad in the best of us that it ill behoves any of us to criticise the rest of us" – and in fact people are such a mixture of good and bad, of spiritual and natural, that it is really a graded variety all the way across the spectrum.

Who is right? Is our observation of human behaviour correct – that people are graded right across the scale from good to bad, with most of us in a mixture in the middle – or are people in fact sharply divided into saints and sinners, Christians and the rest, believers and unbelievers, natural men and spiritual men?

The first thing I want to state is that behaviour is not an infallible guide to a person's real nature. You might behave in a way that is out of character with the real "you". When I was a boy, there was a Baptist minister in the North of England who used to come and visit our home – The Reverend Ralph Mitchell. A little Scotsman with a little Scots wife, he rolled up in a very elderly car. They were simple, honest, down-to-earth folk. But I remember them coming to visit our home many years later. They drove up in a big American car which had a half-acre bonnet and a half-acre boot, and they stepped out and we just gasped. They really looked as if they had come straight from Detroit and that he was Henry Ford Jnr., twice removed, or whatever. He looked so different. He was wearing one of those Stetson 10-gallon hats, and if you had taken one look at him you would have said that he was an American tourist. But he was the same little Scotsman. He finished up by becoming chaplain to one of the largest hotels on Miami Beach, Florida and they made him the Managing Director. He was one of the Billy Graham team at one stage of his life. Looking at his outward behaviour you would have said: "Now there is an American if ever there was one." But you would have been absolutely wrong. He lived and died a Scotsman, and his behaviour would have been a complete contradiction, in a sense, of what he really was. Similarly there was a well known and wealthy American living not far from Guildford who behaved very much like an Englishman. You would have been quite mistaken if you thought he was English. He was not. There are two deductions I can make from this. Firstly, a person who behaves like a Christian isn't necessarily a Christian. It is possible to give a very passable imitation of a Christian and not be one. Christians do good – but then other people do good as well. Christians go to church. So do people who are not Christians, though not so many of them nowadays. It is possible to give in your behaviour an impression to someone else that you are a Christian when you are not. Secondly, it is also very sadly possible for a person who is a Christian to behave as if they are not. It is terribly damaging. It damages God's reputation because people say "Well, if that's a Christian, I am not interested." It damages a church and people say "Well, if he or she goes to that church, I'm not going." It damages a person's own spiritual life, and above all it pleases the devil tremendously when a Christian behaves as if he were not one. But it is possible.

Also, the Bible says quite clearly that everybody is either a natural man (doing what comes naturally) or a spiritual man. But within the category of spiritual men, there are two further sub-divisions. There are the spiritual people who do what comes naturally and there are the spiritual people who do what comes spiritually. So in fact, we may divide the world now into three groups. There is the natural man who does what comes naturally, who thinks what comes naturally, who as far as God is concerned is spiritually dead, who doesn't know God, who doesn't accept the truth of God and who doesn't want to. Then you have the spiritual man who has known God, who has become a Christian, and yet who reverts to his former behaviour and behaves just like an ordinary man.

Then you have the spiritual man, the Christian who goes on to let the Lord direct his life.

We are going to consider the group in the middle. Paul calls them carnal people. There are natural people who can't help behaving that way. There are carnal people who know Christ and could behave differently, and there are spiritual people who do behave differently. Carnal people are those who know Christ but who know that they are not living a fully Christlike life, and that there are times when others could point at them and say: "You are behaving and talking and acting just as if you were any ordinary man. I can see no difference between you and other people."

I am sure you will have heard parents have this kind of discussion with their teenage children. A teenager says to his parents "When are you going to treat me like a grown-up?" – and the parent says, "When you behave like one." In other words, you can't treat people as adults if they don't behave like adults. Paul is going to say to the Christians at Corinth that he can't treat them as mature Christians, he can't treat them as grown up because they behave like babies, so he is going to go on treating them with the bottle. Sometimes, alas, you have got to say to Christians: "I wish I could treat you as mature Christians, but I have got to teach you as little babies, because you are still behaving as babies in Christ. You are spiritual by nature, but in behaviour you are still natural. You are behaving, as Paul says here, as ordinary people, as if you had no-one to help you live any better, as if you had to do this all on your own. That is to be a spiritual baby. He does this by giving a series of pictures of the Corinthians as they are, of Paul as he is, and of what they all ought to be. I am going to take you through these five little portraits he gives.

Now Paul had never been a father, so he should have known nothing about babies. I am sure he never changed a nappy in his life. He had loads of spiritual babies so he did know a little about them, and he was saying that his spiritual babies often behaved just like physical babies. He must have been with sufficient families to observe what happens to little babies. In particular there are two things about babies concerning their diet and their relationships which come out in the spiritual behaviour of the Corinthians. Firstly, babies have no teeth. Therefore they can only swallow, they can't chew. You must only give them liquid rather than solids and you must feed a baby little and often. When you first become a Christian, you can't chew. You can't get your teeth into much. You have to be fed little and often and a young new Christian needs someone to see them very frequently and just give them a little bit more of the Christian life, and they must simply swallow that, take it into their system and feed on it. But we mustn't stay there.

Now a dear lady once said to me – when I was in a position when I had to give regular children's addresses as well as sermons (and I never found that easy) – that she much preferred my children's addresses to my sermons! Which is fair enough, except that she had been a Christian for at least forty years. One wanted to say "Grow up!", though I never dared to. Leave children's addresses behind and grow up. Get beyond milk and get meat. Because a person who has studied their Bible as they should, even for two years, is ready for meat, ready to get their teeth into something, to chew something, to work it over in their mind, to digest it. Do as the Collect in the Book of Common Prayer tells us to do: "...to read, mark, learn and inwardly digest" the same, get down to real study. I do hope that you have got to the stage when you can do just that and not feed on the milk of an odd text, but feed on the meat of the whole of God's Word. I hope that you will make up your mind to read the Bible right through. Three chapters every day and five on Sunday and it will take you one year. But don't just rush through it.

Sit down to the meat of it, chew it over and chew and chew. How nourishing it becomes.

That is the first thing in which, I am afraid, they showed that they were babies. Paul had to give them little simple things, and often, and spoon-feed them. Now let me illustrate this another way. I have heard some people say that they love the teaching of Jesus, they can't stand Paul. They love the simple stories that Jesus told, but Paul – he gets so theological, and they say "Can't we go back to the simple teaching of Jesus?"

Remember that when Jesus was giving the parables he was speaking to natural men and spiritual babies. He wanted them to grow up out of that and to go on. So, when he got his disciples a bit further, he began to go much deeper. The little stories got left behind and long discourses came, and alas many walked no more with him because they said "these things are too hard for us" – can't understand this; can't grasp this.

Paul is only taking the simple gospel of Jesus to its mature level. The letter to the Romans says nothing that Jesus had not said simply before, but it is in the form of meat, not milk. I hope that every Christian will go on as Christ intended them to – from the simple stories of Jesus to the meat of the letter to the Romans.

The other thing in which you can be a baby is to fight. Isn't it worrying how early children can fight? They look so peaceful lying in their cots at night, yet I was in a home where there were two children and they were fighting like "cat and dog". The boy was pulling the girl's hair and the girl was slapping his face as hard as she could, and the boy was three and the girl was about a year younger. I asked the mother why, and she said, "Well, you see, the boy is jealous of the girl; ever since the little girl arrived the boy has shown jealousy." Paul, writing to the Corinthians, said:

"You babies...." Are you not babies when there is jealousy and strife among you, when Christians are jealous of one another and striving against one another? That is to be a baby. It is what babies do. So we have the first little snapshot. He says: you are a squabbling family, just like a lot of little infants fighting each other.

How did they do it? They didn't do it with their fists. Grown-ups don't fight with their fists unless they are pushed. They fight with their tongues. That is how you do it. You learn the art of how to use your words as weapons when you grow up. It is much more dignified, isn't it, to let somebody have a piece of your mind this way, than a piece of your fist? So you fight with words. Paul said, "Can't you see that you are just little babies when you say "I am of Paul", "I am of Apollos"? You are fighting each other, you are creating jealousy among each other. Grow up.

Now he goes on to the next thing and says: you are fighting over something you shouldn't fight about. You are fighting over Christian preachers and Christian ministers and you are saying "This one is best" and, "That one is best". We are now given another little picture of what we are: it is of a field and it is rather surprising because Paul was a town-dweller, a city man, and most of his illustrations are from town life, but he had obviously seen enough of agriculture or horticulture to use this picture. There are two points he wants to make.

First, if you see a field full of growth, plants springing up, you know that somebody has put a lot of hard work into that. Somebody has put the plants in and someone else has looked after the plants since then – watering them. This is, of course, a Middle East picture where irrigation is needed. Somebody has been doing the work. And wherever you see a church which is growing, somebody has been putting a lot of work into that church. Somebody has been planting and somebody has been watering, looking after what is growing. But here is the point he wants to make: It doesn't matter at all to the plant who planted it. It doesn't matter at all to the plant who waters it – the plant is only concerned about getting the water. It isn't the slightest bothered whether you water your plants or somebody next door waters them while you are away. The plant is only interested in water. Why then should Christians get so interested in the person who planted the seed of the gospel in their heart? "Mr So-and-So was the one who led me to the Lord." Why should we get so bothered? Who cares who planted that seed? It doesn't matter in the slightest. The important thing is that there is a plant that is growing. It doesn't matter who converted you. It doesn't matter who baptised you. It doesn't matter who taught you. It doesn't matter in the slightest, as long as you are a growing Christian in a sprouting field.

So Paul and Apollos were just the workmen. Every Christian minister should say: "Don't mind me, I just work here." Quite literally we are slaves for God. He told us to do something in his field, that there might be growth, and he would give wages – not according to status or according to particular function, but according to labour. That is all. Therefore Christians can learn from their own garden how to behave towards Christian ministers.

The second lesson Paul wants to bring from the picture of a field is this: not only does it not matter where the labour comes from, as long as the job has been done, but more important than labour is the *life* that there is in that field. And no man can do that. Even if I were to talk for the rest of my life, nothing would happen at all unless God did something. It is he who gives the growth. My wife and I went to a garden party on a lovely evening in October, and when we went into the garden it was a blaze of colour. We said, "Oh Mrs So-and-so, what a beautiful garden" – and then we thought "hyacinths in October?" We looked more closely and saw that she must have bought the entire stock of Woolworth's plastic flowers and they were planted in every flower bed! They didn't need watering. They were planted. There was no growth there. And you can have a church with rows of people in the pews just like those plastic hyacinths – it may look very good, but there is only life if God is busy.

I may put a plant in my garden, I may weed and water it, but only God can make my garden. Only God can make those things grow. Mind you, I don't know who looks after my weeds so well when we have been away! But only God can give that life, that growth, and therefore to learn the lesson from the field, take your eyes altogether away from whoever was used of God to minister to you, and say: "God gave me the life." This man may have planted the seed of the gospel in my heart, that man may have watered it, but it was God who gave the life and the increase. Therefore Paul and Apollos are just two fellow workmen. One translation says that we are fellow workmen *for* God. It is not good to say we are fellow workmen *with* God – that gives us a status that Paul is anxious not to give us here. We are not fellow workmen with God, we are fellow workmen with each other for God. No preacher can do a thing unless God is busy.

Paul then changes the picture again and we are now looking at a building. He sometimes feels like a labourer in a field and sometimes like an architect, or in today's language a structural engineer. Many years ago I was talking to the structural engineer for a Church Centre we were building at that time, and his job was to get the frame right so that it would support everything else. His role was to get the foundations and the hidden reinforcements strong enough so that the whole thing would hold up. If that building had collapsed on our congregation, it would have been to that structural engineer that I would have gone first! Paul is saying: I regard myself as a structural engineer; I go from place to place, getting that foundation in, getting that unseen reinforcement in, on which others are going to build, on which everything is going to be supported later. I want to get a good base to the building of the church. In fact he said that no other foundation can be laid, but only Jesus. So every church that there has ever been started with Jesus, but now Paul takes us further up the building. He says: I always laid that base because there is no other you can lay, but I get worried about what men build on the base I have laid.

You can build almost anything on Jesus. That may sound an extraordinary statement, but you can, and whether you build something good or bad depends on a lot of things. Paul says that it depends on the material you build with. You can build with gold, silver and precious metal or stone, and chip and carve the stone, or you can build with timber or hay or stubble. You can build anything on Christ.

Now there is something very relevant here. To the individual Christian: you can't start to be a Christian without Jesus. He is the one who you built your faith on in the beginning. But you can build a pretty rough Christian life on him. You can build a weak, shaky Christian life on him. What you build, God holds you responsible for. And I speak to churches too. This is very relevant in a day of ecumenical dialogue. People say, "Since every church is built on Christ, why don't we all get together?" The answer is: because of what has been built up on him. It is still impossible to get the churches together, not because we all have the same base (which we have – every church must be based on Christ or it would not be a church), but it is what we have put up above that makes it so difficult to get together. It is what we have added, some of which has been worthy and some of which has not been worthy. Until we learn to scrap all that has been added that Christ did not want in the building, we cannot have one church. We never will.

So Paul knew that what tests a building is fire. I am always amazed what fire can do to a building, or even to a ship that is made from steel from end to end. I was walking through the main street in lovely Interlaken and looked at what had been one of the large hotels, where I had stayed many years earlier. The former hotel was just a shell. At first sight it wasn't apparent, but when you looked closer through the holes that used to be windows, you could see there was nothing inside. Now the whole building was still there. There were still pillars holding up the front entrance, but every bit of timber had gone from inside. The roofs had caved in, the floors had gone and the doors had gone. Fire had only left certain things. According to Paul, what we have built on Christ will one day be set on fire by the judgment of God, and our work may not survive. I can think of nothing more terrible than to have laboured for the Lord for years and see your work go up in smoke on that day. A church secretary who was once a colleague was an aircraft designer and he spent seven years designing what would have been Britain's biggest helicopter. He gave all his experience to this. Then one day the Government axed the whole project and the first he heard about it was on a television newscast. His work of seven years had gone. The thing is only a museum piece now. It was a terrible blow to him.

I remember meeting my sister-in-law at a London Airport when she fled out of Angola. She had been there for most of her adult life with her husband. They had been building up the church in Angola. I don't mean putting up buildings, though they had done that. But thousands of Angolans had become Christians and had been baptised in the Lord and almost overnight they saw that obliterated by the Portuguese Army. They saw all their people disappear – some of them killed, some of them running for their lives into the jungle, and the entire work collapsed and there was nothing left.

They got out and they arrived at the airport, and I will never forget the look on her face. Her eyes were staring. All the work of years was just gone. According to this chapter Christian service will one day go through the test of fire. I find myself wondering: of all the sermons I have preached and all the people I have visited and talked to, how much will get through?

If you build well on the foundation of Christ, it will stand. There is the possibility that a Christian's work could entirely disappear. How important it is to build well. I believe that most of our denominational structure, if not all of it, will disappear on that day. I believe that our ecclesiastical hierarchies will disappear on that day. I believe that a whole lot that we have built up in the name of Christ will just go. What will survive? Everybody we have won for the Lord Jesus Christ will survive. I don't think church committee minutes will survive that fire – that will all go. But the church of Jesus Christ, made up of true believers, will stand like precious gold and silver in the sight of God.

This leads to another of Paul's pictures. What are we building for? I don't mean the bricks and mortar, I mean believers. What are we building a church *for*? Some people seem to regard it as a club for the religious! Some people regard it more in the light of a social service, and feel that the church is a failure unless it is deeply involved in social service as its main and primary function in the world. What is the church being built up for? The church is being built up as somewhere for God to live on earth. That is why we are building it up. In the days of the Old Testament God lived in a tent first of all, and if you wanted to meet him that is where you had to go. Then the tent gave way to a Temple and if you wanted to meet God you went to the Temple. That is where God lived on earth. Where does God live on earth today? He lives in the fellowship of believers, and the very best place you can go if you want to meet him is to a church of believers, built up on Jesus.

"Don't you know that you are God's temple?" Don't you know that this is God's address – the believers in your town or village – and that is where God lives? Therefore if anyone wants to meet God, the best place they can go is to the fellowship of believers. That is where he lives. Therefore realise that now we are not thinking of God's destruction of our building, we are thinking of man's destruction of his. Don't you know that to destroy the fellowship of believers is to touch God's holy temple? It is sacrilege. Every word of criticism I say about a fellow believer that breaks fellowship is destroying God's temple. Don't you know that you are inviting God to destroy you if you do that? This is taking the picture even further.

If we are God's temple – and you can destroy it by being a spiritual baby, destroy it by being jealous and selfish and fighting and talking about human ministers instead of the Lord – how is this overcome? Why are we doing it? We are doing it because we behave as ordinary people, and Christians must not behave as ordinary men and women. But we are not "mere men", we are spiritual men and we ought not to be doing it. Why do we succumb to this pressure? We do it because we want to be clever. We want to be thought wise, we want to be thought somebody, so Paul finishes up by saying: "Corinthians, I beg of you, grow up by becoming fools" – stop trying to be so clever. If you want to be wise in the eyes of the world, OK, but become a fool, please, I beg you. Humble yourself. Look ridiculous. Don't mind if others regard you as a fool. Climb off that pedestal. Climb off that pride. Climb out of this boasting and become a fool. I will tell you this: you become a sensible fool because you gain two things when you become a "fool for Christ". You gain wisdom. The world will not say so, but God will. The world will say: "Ridiculous, you're silly" but God will say: "Here's my wisdom." And the other thing you become is wealthy. You don't need to boast about any minister of Christ because all of them belong to you. You have got the lot. It is not a case of "I belong to Paul" or "I belong to Apollos" – Paul and Apollos belong to me! They are only your servants because they are God's servants. So when you talk about ministers, they all belong to you if they are in Christ. So why boast about one or the other? Why compare them when they are all yours? Here Paul takes off! Every now and again he gets so excited that his grammar runs away with him. He is saying: Listen, Paul is yours, Apollos is yours, Cephas is yours, the world is yours, life is yours, death is yours, the present is yours, the future is yours – the lot! You are millionaires. So stop boasting about a little thing and boast about the lot. Stop saying "I've got this minister" and say: "They are all servants of mine, for Christ's sake."

Just remember that the other side of the coin is this: in Christ, everything belongs to me, but everything in me belongs to Christ. Those two must be held together. And everything in Christ belongs to God. That is where you fix your eyes.

We started the chapter with spiritual babies boasting about this and that minister. How silly! We finish with the thought that everything is ours in Christ, and everything in me is Christ's and Christ is God's. Isn't it great to be so rich? We did it by becoming "fools" and we became millionaires.

DOWN BUT NOT OUT
Read 1 Corinthians 4

A. LORD COMMENDS (1–5)
1. TRUSTWORTHY STEWARDS
2. TRUE STANDARDS

B. LIFE CONTRASTS (6–13)
1. HAUGHTY ATTITUDES
2. HUMILIATED APOSTLES

C. LOVE CORRECTS (14–21)
1. FATHERLY DISCIPLINE
2. FILIAL DUTY

What is the appropriate attitude to the ministers of Christ? The world tends to have too low a view of the Christian ministry and the church tends to have too high a view of the Christian ministry. This is the burden of 1 Corinthians 4.

I often cringe when a dog-collar appears on television. In so many programmes clergymen are presented either as buffoons or villains. One of the disadvantages of wearing a dog-collar today is that you cannot escape from this caricature which the mass media has fostered. The world has too low a view of Christian ministers. But Paul is writing to a church, and his concern is that the church can have too high a view of Christian ministers. "I planted, Apollos watered, but God gives the growth." That puts people into perspective, so that he who plants and he who waters are nothing, and God is over all. You can have too high a view of ministers by bandying about the names of servants of Christ as if they

63

were party leaders, those whom you follow.

I visited a youth centre in Birmingham, and there was one thing that spoiled it for me. As you came in from the street there was a large mural on the wall. It was cleverly designed and it included a huge plaque with the names of "The great ministers we have had here". There they were, former ministers, some famous, blazoned in the foyer. I looked for one name and I couldn't find it: the name "Jesus". As you went down the corridor there were large oil paintings in gilt frames of all the great men who had ministered at that church. I believe this kind of thing is the reason why Birmingham became a desert. Because when you are so proud of your buildings and your men then you have signed your death warrant as a fellowship.

Jesus said "I will build my church" and it is important that you never explain things in terms of human personality where God is blessing. It is God who must have all the glory. As soon as you stick up portraits of past ministers, and put plaques and human names on stones, you are robbing God of his glory – and he is a jealous God. I know that we have human affection for each other, and we ought to. Let's hold that in our hearts. We don't need to stick that on a tablet. Let us give glory to God and to Jesus Christ alone.

So the world tends to have too low a view of the minister of Christ and the church tends to have too high a view. It usually puts the minister six feet above criticism. In the first five verses of this chapter, Paul is teaching that it doesn't matter what anybody thinks of the minister, including himself. What matters is that the Lord does the commending, and we don't know whether the Lord will commend anyone until the day when all secrets are revealed. Then, and only then, can it be said, "Well done, good and faithful servant." We must therefore not try to do the Lord's work for him. We must not make a premature judgement on God's servants.

We must not say anything before the great day. We must leave God to decide whether a man has done a good job for him or not.

What then is the position of a minister of Christ? The answer is that he is a servant and a steward. And if you get the two meanings and flavours of these two words you will never get the wrong attitude to a minister.

First of all he is a *servant*. That is a pretty rough word in the Greek language, literally meaning "lower rower". I wonder whether that conveys anything to you at all. What is a servant? He is a lower rower. If ever you have seen pictures of Roman ships you will know that they were three hundred man power. Sticking out of the sides, in two or three decks of holes along the hull, were long oars. If you could see inside the hull you would see rows of people on each oar, pulling away, and a man at the top saying "In – out; in – out", and that is how they went around the Mediterranean. The worst slaves of all were "lower rowers". They didn't have the alliteration in the Latin that I have put in English but that will fix the phrase in your mind. If you were a lower rower you were the bottom. You were just helping to pull the thing along in response to the pilot up top saying "In – out", and Paul says, "this is how you should regard us" – as a "lower rower" of Christ, just helping to pull the boat along by direction from the pilot.

Quite frankly, if you made a voyage in a boat in Roman days you would never give a thought to the lower rower. You would never bother. You wouldn't even go down and have a look. You would walk the decks, you would go to your cabin, but you wouldn't bother about the little chap tugging away at his oar down below.

That is the first thing that puts ministers in perspective. Now let us just take the word "servant". He is a servant or a slave, but he is not a servant of the church members. He is not a slave of the church members, he is a servant of Christ. Technically, as a church pastor, my National Insurance designation was "self-employed", which is a delightful expression. It means (and I will come to this shortly) that I was not under very strict supervision from anyone else. I didn't have a foreman breathing down my neck. But the pastor is a servant of Christ. I am to do what he tells me to do – not what the church tells me but what he tells me. I am a lower rower, to help the church move along, and I take my "in – out" as a servant of Christ, from upstairs. That is the most dignified position anyone could wish for. To be a lower rower for Jesus the pilot is a tremendous privilege.

Then we come on to another approach to this. Not only is it true to say "We are servants of Christ", we are also "stewards of the mysteries of God". Now a steward is someone who is not supervised but will one day have to render an account for what he has done. It is equivalent to an estate manager or a trustee. It means someone who has been entrusted with something in the absence of the owner, and one day the owner will come back and say: "What have you done with what I entrusted you with? What have you done with my property?"

The minister of Christ is a steward, a manager who isn't under supervision. I have to decide what I do most days with most of my time. Not under close supervision, but knowing that one day Jesus will say: "How did you use your time? How did you behave as a steward, a manager of the mysteries I entrusted to you?"

The word "mystery" is interesting and it means two things. It means a secret, and it means a secret that can now be shared. A "mystery" is something which is hidden in God's mind that nobody could ever have discovered, but it also means he has now told us about it, and we can now tell anybody. I heard of two ladies talking, and one said to the other "You will have to listen very carefully to what I am going to say now. I have promised never to repeat it – so I can only tell you once." Now that is exactly what a mystery is – a secret piece of knowledge that can be passed on. In fact, we are stewards of the mysteries – things that nobody knew, things that man could never have discovered with all his science, with all his brains. God has told us his secret – the secret of heaven. It is the secret of a new universe, the secret of salvation, and he wants us to keep this secret and to pass it on.

The mysteries of God are secrets which must be kept and given away, and a good steward will do both. Alas, it is possible to keep the mysteries of God in such a way that you don't give them away, and you are not a good steward. It is also possible to give them away and fail to keep them. Let me be very frank here and tell you how you lose them. A steward must keep the property intact. If the owner comes back and says, "Well, I lost that, but here's something much newer and much better and I've got this in its place," he is a bad steward. The mystery I have to keep is the old, old story of Jesus and his love – it is the theology that never changes, the way of salvation that never alters, and I must keep that. It is no use my saying to God: "God, I scrapped the old story. I've got a new theology. I've got a new gospel. I've got a twenty-first century religion which is much better than the old one." God will say: "Why did you not steward my mysteries? Why didn't you hang on to the old gospel that is the only one that you can give away and keep?" He wants his gospel kept intact. We are told in the Bible that our job is to pass on to others a pattern of sound words, passing that on to faithful men who will keep the gospel intact and pass it on to the next generation. They in turn will keep it intact and pass it on. Stewards must keep it and pass it on intact to others, and that is my job as a preacher. Therefore I must never introduce new theology, I must never introduce new ideas, I must never scrap the old ones. I must keep intact the truth and deliver it to the next generation intact. Would to God that every minister of Christ was a faithful steward, keeping the gospel intact and passing it on to others in exactly the same form that he received it. This is a trustworthy steward and if I start changing my gospel and introducing new ideas and preaching them, then I have failed as a steward. You see it doesn't matter what you think about it – whether you would be thrilled and excited or disappointed or disgusted with what I did doesn't matter. My job is to pass it on intact. You may achieve a certain kind of popularity by preaching a new gospel. The world loves something new. That doesn't matter.

Paul now goes on to consider how you judge a good minister. The answer is that you can't. Not one person is capable of saying who is a good minister and who isn't. Paul says: "What you of Corinth think of me is of little importance" – because he knows that they couldn't judge truly. He says, "What the world thinks of me, I take of little importance – no human court can judge whether I am a good steward" and then he goes on to say, "I will not even judge myself" – because I am not a good judge myself of whether I am a good minister.

I know what that means. Let me share with you the inner life of a minister. There are times when a minister has had a good time. He has "got his wings" as they say in the profession, if you don't mind me putting it that way. He might then think: "I'm a good minister", but he is a bad judge. And there are times when he gets very discouraged and depressed and he wants to get out of the ministry and for two pins would do so, and unless God had called him he wouldn't stay in it, but he is a bad judge, so a minister has to say: "I don't care what the church thinks of me as a minister, I don't care what the world thinks of me, I don't

care what I think of me, I will seek to keep the gospel intact
and pass it on, and I'll wait to find out whether God will say
"Well done!" Here are two secret things. Firstly, the things
you did that nobody else knew about. That is a searching
test, especially for those who have to be in the public eye.
God judges the things you do that nobody knows about, the
things done in secret, the private things, the quiet things,
the unknown things. Secondly, the motives, the purposes,
of the heart. *Why* did you do it? Only God can sort out your
motives. If you try to sort them out yourself you finish in
a terrible state. If you say "Why did I really do that?" (that
good thing) – was it really to help somebody, was it because
I got a kick out of doing good for them, was it because I felt
guilty because I have got so many blessings and they have
so few? Why did I do it? If you try to dig around in your
motives you will be thoroughly confused.

But one day the Lord, and only he can do this, will say:
"I know the secret things you have done, and I know the
secret motives that lay behind what you did, and I will do
the commending." Paul now says that this applies not only
to ministers but to every member. It is not just ministers who
must not judge whether they are good or not, or be judged by
others as to whether they are good or not. Every member's
service will one day be judged on the two things: the secret
things you did, and the secret motives behind them. Then and
only then will God say, "Well done." May God give us grace
so to labour on earth that in that day he says "Well done",
and let us not make premature judgments before then. Let
us not say that a man has done well or badly until the Day
comes and the Lord says what is the real truth.

At this point Paul becomes very personal and very loving
and he talks to the brethren. They are boasting; they are proud
and complacent. They are a church that says: "We're great,
we're getting on well, we've had a great line of ministers,

we've got big congregations, we've got life." They were proud of it, and Paul must deal with that pride. You must learn to live according to the scripture and not according to ministers. You must learn to say not "Mr so-and-so says" but "the Bible says...." For the steward's job is to say: "Get stuck into the Bible. Get into this. Don't accept what I say because I say it, accept what I say because the Bible says it" – and then you won't be proud in the wrong way.

Here Paul gets rather sarcastic. The Bible, of course, is not proud and boastful about men because it paints them in their true colours: Noah's drunkenness, Abraham's deceitfulness, David's lust, Peter's cowardice. They are not put on a pedestal. They are men with faults. It is Jesus who is exalted in the Bible. So Paul says, "What are you so puffed up about?" – and he asks them three questions. If ever Christians get proud of their church, here are the questions. Who saw anything different in you? Is the world proud of you? Do the people outside say you are unique? The answer is probably: "No, they think you are very ordinary." Have you got anything that you didn't receive as a free gift? Do you know, you can only boast about things that you have earned or deserved – but have you got anything at all that you can boast about that is yours? Have you got money? God gave it to you. Have you got gifts and talents? God gave them to you. Have you got energy? God gave it to you. Have you got love in your heart? God gave it to you. Then what do you have that you didn't receive? The thing that keeps a church from being proud is just to remember this: what have you that you didn't receive? We are beggars in God's kingdom and a beggar doesn't boast. Why boast about gifts? Paul is saying: you are behaving like millionaires! You are behaving like kings in palaces. You are rich. You've got everything. I wish you had and then we could share it! Paul is biting here, and a minister of Christ sometimes has to be scathing to make his point. "You think you've got everything. I wish you had – then you could give a bit to me." That is how Paul talks. Then he says: "Really, you are boasting about Paul and Apollos and Cephas. Take a look at us and see if there is anything to boast about. We are like tramps."

Now he paints a picture, and I would like to paint a picture for you. I remember going to the Forum in the middle of Rome. I hope that one day you may see that place or a picture of it – history written into stone. There at the top of the Forum is Titus's Arch – rather like Marble Arch, only much bigger. Leading up to it is a great Roman road, the main road into Rome. When I walked up that road I pictured the scenes of what was called "The Triumph". When a Roman general had defeated a barbarian army he would march up through this archway riding his horse – the people would cheer and the soldiers would march – a great victory! The general came ahead with triumph. Then at the very end of the procession would be a miserable little bunch of poor people in chains, captives who were going to be thrown to the beasts. People would jeer and laugh and mock. There would be the enemy general and he would be naked and in chains and be pulled along to his death, exhibited as a public spectacle. That is how the Romans used to celebrate victory. I am glad that we have grown out of that a bit. Paul is saying: the apostles whom you boast about are treated in the world like the people at the end of the procession, heading for death – a spectacle; humiliated. Look at us, we are ill-clad, we are homeless, we are buffeted, we can only scratch a living with our own hands to survive at all, and you are proud of us. You are boasting of us. You are boasting about vagabonds in the eyes of the world. You have got too high a view of the ministry. Then let me show you the low view the world has of us to fetch you down a peg or two. Then he goes on to say: And how do you think we react to this? When we are persecuted, we endure it. When they spit on us, we pray for them. When reviled, we bless. The Corinthians, in their pride, would have spat back. The Greeks were so proud that they said: "If anyone insults you, insult him worse. If anyone hits you, hit him back. If anybody degrades you, degrade him. That is manliness. That is courage." Paul says: the world would regard us highly if we hit back. But look at us. We let them walk all over us. We let them spit at us. We don't hit back. We bless them. We try to conciliate them. We allow them to treat us as roughly as this.

Now Paul is saying: you shouldn't be boasting about those whom the world derides. It looks silly. It will make you look silly if you go on boasting about people whom the world despises, so let's get rid of this once and for all. If you boast about a minister, you are in danger of falling into this trap. You will take someone along to hear him and they will go out saying, "Well, I don't think anything of him" and be disappointed. It serves you right. If you boast about someone to the world, don't be surprised if the world comes and says, "I don't share your pride."

Paul says, "We bring up the rear." We are a spectacle. The world looks down at us. Okay, we are fools for Christ's sake. We are clowns for Christ's sake. Who cares? Oh Corinthians, stop being proud. He says: I don't want to make you ashamed of us; I want to admonish you; I don't want you to get to the opposite extreme where you are thoroughly ashamed of the ministers of Christ. Neither be proud nor ashamed, just treat us as servants and stewards.

Let us go further. There are times when a minister of Christ has to admonish the family of Christ and to bring them down in their pride and to puncture the puffed up pride that can come: "our church"; "our denomination", and sometimes a minister has to say it is wrong to talk like that.

Paul is writing within a family discipline to his spiritual

babies. They may have many guides to tell them how to live the Christian life, but he was the one through whom they came to know Christ. He was a father to them and he felt it. If he didn't love them he wouldn't admonish them.

As a boy I used to envy the child who lived next door to me. His parents were modern. They didn't believe in punishment. They were "enlightened". They really believed that when their boy painted the cat with green paint it was self-expression. It was something good that was coming out. What a life that boy had, whereas if I broke a pane of glass there was a very painful sequel to the event. I don't envy that boy now. I thank God for a father who loved enough to admonish. You don't love people unless you are prepared to admonish them.

"Let your love be genuine. Hate what is evil and hold fast to what is good." Genuine love does both. It hates the evil in a person as well as loving the good. It doesn't shut its eyes to the evil and say, "Let's just look at the good and draw that out." Real love says: "That's wrong, but this is right." Paul teaches the Corinthian believers: I love you as a father; I am being sarcastic because I love you; I am being ironically bitter and scathing because I love you; I am telling you, because I love you, that you are strutting around like millionaires and kings in your church – and I don't want to make you ashamed of me; I want you to be admonished.

His affection is so deep that he can't overlook their faults. So he moves on and points out that a child's first interest is to imitate dad. One of the most profound things that the New Testament says about learning the Christian life is about learning to imitate. This may sound extraordinary to you, but the best way you can learn to grow as a Christian is to imitate mature Christians. I don't mean a kind of false substitute that is just parroting what they do. But learn to imitate. Those who love reading the biographies of great

Christians tend to do just this. They learn to imitate, and Paul can say: "I am your spiritual father. Imitate me." That takes some saying, doesn't it? Most of us fathers have to say do what I say, not do what I do.

Paul warns those who think that the kingdom of God is all talk that it isn't – it is power. The kingdom of God is not what you say, it is what you do. The real demonstration that God is on the throne and has sovereignty is what he does through you, not what you say about him. You may talk until you are blue in the face about God being on the throne, but unless people see power – his power in your life – then it is talk, it is vanity, it is empty.

Finally, why is it important to have the right attitude to the minister of Christ? Because that will determine his attitude to you. The final question of the chapter is this: Do you want me to be tough or tender with you? Do you want me to come with a rod or with gentleness? Do you want me to come in a harsh spirit or do you want me to come gently?

Somebody once said to me that a church gets the minister it deserves. There is enough truth in that cliché to listen to it. The attitude to the minister determines the attitude of the minister to the family. Paul is urging the people to get rid of a view of him that is too high so that he doesn't have to come in a hard spirit to them. They should regard him as a servant and as a steward of the mysteries of Christ and of God, and then he can come to them gently, lovingly and tenderly and, as a father with children, help them to walk.

Sometimes, alas, a minister, hating himself for doing it, has to come to his people with a rod and say: "You really must behave." How he loves to come in a very different mood and say: "I have come to help you to be the family of God. I have come just to help to row the boat along and move the church toward heaven. Will you regard me in that way and let me tenderly deal with you as children?"

This is a very personal chapter. It is not an easy one for a pastor to teach on because it is so personal, but ask God that your relationship to your pastor, and his attitude to you should be all that the Lord desires. You and he can both talk about the Lord Jesus – for he is the person that you want your community to hear about.

SCANDAL

Read 1 Corinthians 5

A. PUBLIC SCANDAL (1–5)
 1. DREADFUL TRUTH
 2. DRASTIC TREATMENT
   a. Removed from church
   b. Delivered to Satan

B. PERSONAL SINCERITY (6–8)
 1. PERMEATING LEAVEN
 2. PASCHAL LAMB

C. PARTICULAR SEPARATION (9–13)
 1. WORLDLY SINNERS
 2. WAYWARD SAINTS

This is a stark and rather sordid chapter and it has a very important message for us today. From time to time, I come across the idea that in the days of the New Testament the church was perfect and it has gone wrong ever since – that somehow there was a "golden age" of the church way back in the beginning and that for maybe thirty or forty years it was just what it ought to be, and all the divisions and all the things they are sad and sorry about are later additions. But, you know, they are not.

The New Testament gives us a very honest picture of the church of Christ. We are told here that the New Testament church was far from perfect. From the very beginning they had problems with people, with their beliefs and with their behaviour. To me it is the most amazing example of God's almighty power that in spite of all the scandals that have rocked the Christian fellowship for two thousand years,

Christ is still able to go on using the church for his glory. Isn't that marvellous? It would have packed up long ago if it had been a human society and this kind of thing had happened within it.

We have a particularly sordid case here. We are told about it quite plainly in the Bible so we are never tempted to put our faith in the church. If you put your faith in the church it is misplaced and sooner or later you will discover that there are spiritual babies and carnal Christians and saints with feet of clay, but if your faith is firmly rooted and grounded in Christ, then not only is it not shaken – for you never discover anything disappointing in him – but also you find that you know how to deal with things that are wrong within the fellowship of Christ's church. And Paul tells the Corinthians how to cope with what had become a public scandal in town and was being talked about by people outside.

Now in the Greek world there was no such thing as chastity. They took their pleasure when they wanted it, where they wanted it and how they wanted it. It is not surprising that the people who came out of that background did not always find themselves entirely free of it. But here Paul faces the dreadful truth that a man inside the church is living worse than people outside the church, and that can happen. I suppose it is due to the fact that our wonderful truth of forgiveness can lead to moral carelessness. It is true that because we know God covers sin we can begin to sit loose to it. This man was living in an incestuous relationship with his father's wife – presumably his stepmother. That situation is not unknown even today. I came across an identically parallel case within a church some decades ago. Now this is a thing that even pagans would say was wrong. It is interesting that you can study the history of ethics (which is the study of human behaviour, and what society has thought right and wrong) and see that although there have been societies that have said cannibalism was alright, and murder was alright and adultery was alright, there has never been a human society that has said incest was right. So the entire pagan world says that here is something that is wrong. The scandal was rocking Corinth. Corinth, with all its sin, said that what was wrong was happening in the church. The report reached Paul's ears and Paul said: Are you feeling the right thing about this, and are you doing the right thing about it? When scandal comes to a Christian fellowship, and it comes quite regularly, the first thing is: Do you *feel* right about it? The right thing to feel is *mourning*.

Paul says: You are not mourning over this; you are not weeping over it. You see, the contrast is that the world outside will be glad – they can now point their fingers at the church and say "There you are! Look!" And their tongues will get going. The Christian reaction of emotion is to *weep*. The word used means to feel bereaved. What is it to feel bereaved? It is to feel that someone has gone out of your life, out of your family, and when a Christian falls into sin, other Christians should feel that they have lost a member of the family. We have been bereaved. We must mourn. We weep about it. That is what to *feel*.

The second thing is what to *do* about it. The answer is: dissociate the church from what is so clearly, in pagan eyes, wrong. Remove the church from the situation by removing the person from the church. It is drastic treatment. It is like saying to a child: "If you cannot behave, go up into your bedroom." It is saying: "Don't stay here in this company while you behave like this." This must be done in love, it must be done in tenderness, but it needs to be done.

Now you notice that not only does Paul say, "Remove him from the church," but, "Deliver him to Satan." Now that would seem an incredible thing to say and to do. Yet what he is saying is this: Put him where he belongs; let Satan destroy his body, because that is all he can do. Let Satan destroy his body, because just as there are physical effects of spiritual sin, there can be spiritual effects from physical disaster. Sometimes physical disaster can bring a man to his senses. "Deliver him to Satan in order that his spirit may be saved." Now that is drastic treatment. Someone has said that Christians are like apples in a basket. That is quite a nice picture. Do you feel like an apple? Picture a basket full of rosy apples. One rotten one will soon damage all the rest. If you have ever set apples out in your attic or garage you will know exactly what that picture means.

This is a judgment, a strong sentence but the danger was that the whole witness of that church would crumble and its impact disappear. This one rotten apple in among them is dangerous. If Paul were using a picture today, he would say: "He is a cancerous growth that must be cut out." Now this is strong meat and strong language, yet we must pray that God will give us grace that if ever this proves necessary we may have the love to do it.

Paul goes on to paint a picture that is not familiar to us, but which is familiar to every Jew. It is a picture of the Passover. When I was a little boy we lived about five doors away from a Jewish family, and I am afraid we used to make fun, and especially about one time of year we used to hang around and we used to look for brown stains on the gate and on the door, and then we used to make comments about it. Every year that Jewish family took a lamb and killed it, and they caught its blood in a basin, and they came out and they painted their doorposts with it. We knew the Passover was going on.

Have you ever shared in a Jewish Passover? It is a most moving experience. You are doing something that goes back thousands of years. This is what they do first. They light a candle and they go around the house with it, looking in every cupboard, every shelf, every corner, every darkened place behind the curtains, under the furniture. Do you know what they are looking for? Bits of old bread. It goes way back to the beginning when God said, "Tonight I am going to get you out of slavery. Tonight I am going to set you free. Tonight you are going home" – and they got all excited. God said: "I'll get you out at the cost of death. Nothing less than death will get you out of this country. I have tried everything else but the Egyptians won't let you go. Nothing less than the death of firstborn sons will get you out. And tonight I am going to kill every firstborn son in Egypt, and then they will let you go. But I don't want to kill yours. I am prepared to accept, on behalf of your family, the blood of a lamb." So they got their lambs, they killed them and they did what that neighbour of mine did every year, they painted the doorposts so that when God came down the street with the angel, the angel would say, "That door has blood on it. We must pass over that household."

Then God said: "I want you to make new food for the journey. I want it to have no connection whatever with what you have lived on here. I want you to have a break in your food." This is the meaning of unleavened bread. They didn't have yeast in the same form as we have it. Whenever they baked, the housewife would take a little bit of bread and she would put it aside to ferment, to go stale and then to putrefy, and she would keep that. It was the leaven. It was a bit of old bread. And when she had her next baking, she took just a little bit of this old bread and put it in the fresh dough and it permeated the whole lump of dough. It putrefied the dough. It caused it to rise and the gas bubbles raised the bread. Then she would put a little piece of that aside. In this way, the food always had a little bit of old food in it. But God said, "When you get out of slavery, a clean break with the past, don't eat anything you used to feed on. Start new with new food. And every year I want you to do this as a reminder that when God calls you out of slavery into freedom it involves a break with all that you have fed on up till now. It involves new food, clean food. Nothing must be brought into your diet from the past. It must be a new start."

Hanging in our sitting room is a plate. It is a Passover plate and it has got little sections for the bitter herbs, the lettuce and all the other things that they ate. When I look at that plate I think of them all standing with their overcoats and walking sticks, and eating a bit of new bread and setting off on the journey.

In a sense, things are wrong in a church. We ought to stand with coats on and sticks in our hands. We are pilgrims. We are going forward. We are heading for heaven. We have come out of this slavery to self that we were in and we are heading for glory. And God says: Make a clean break with the kind of thing you fed your life on. Cut out the kind of food you had in the past. Cut out the leaven and start fresh with new food. Feed your life on new things.

Now it is all picture language. Thousands of years ago, God was giving the Jews a picture which becomes meaningful for us – and Paul is now saying to the Corinthians: "Stop boasting about your broad-mindedness. Stop boasting about your tolerance, that you are able to cope with this man, and allow it to happen. Don't you know that a little bit of the 'food of the past', a little leaven, will ultimately spread through the whole lump of dough? Don't you know that this could wreck the fellowship? Then cut it out." And he says, "Don't you know that there has been a Lamb who has died and whose blood was the cost of getting you out of this?" Christ, our Passover Lamb, has been sacrificed. Don't you know that Jesus died on a cross not just to forgive you for your sins but to get rid of them, not just to go on giving you a blank cheque that you could go and fill in whenever you do wrong, but that you might live free from these things. He died for sins that he might take away sins.

Therefore, says Paul, the Christian life is one long Passover. It is a festival to be celebrated. It is a happy life. Every day you get up in the morning and you think, "Great, it's a Festival today. I'm celebrating today. What am I celebrating? My freedom! My freedom from the past. My freedom in Christ. How do you celebrate it? You celebrate it by getting rid of the leaven – of malice and evil." Notice he adds "malice" here, to the evil which he has already mentioned in the chapter – malice, gossip, jealousy, talking behind each other's backs. That is a little bit of the old grub (I am tempted to use a double meaning for that) that is going to eat its way into the new. That is a bit of the old leaven that will spread through the new dough. You can't afford to mix it. Don't eat it. If you have enjoyed eating it then stop eating it and eat bread, unleavened bread – bread of sincerity and truth.

"Sincerity" is an interesting word. In the ancient world, they decorated their gardens with marble statues. I am sure you have seen pictures of Greek palaces and gardens. If you could afford it, the status symbol was not a swimming pool, it was a statue, a Greek statue. And there were shops that sold statues. You bought one of these and stuck it in your garden. Of course there were old statues that had stood out in someone else's garden for a long time, and the weather had aged them badly and the softer veins had been etched out with the wind and the rain, and there were cracks. I am afraid there were sharp dealers in those days just as there are today and they used to fill up the cracks with white wax to smooth them over – bodging, we would say. Then they would sell the statues as new. This was the second hand car dealer of the day who was just putting a quick respray on the top, only it was wax. There were those genuine statue dealers who suffered from the bad market and the lower prices, so they used to put up a notice "Our statues are without wax" – only of course they were in Latin. The Latin for "without wax" is *sine cere*. Without wax – they are good right through. That is where we got our word "sincerity". It is the opposite of the word "hypocrisy".

"Let's celebrate the festival with the unleavened bread of 'good-right-through-ness and truth'" – which means being honest with yourself, with other people, with God.

Now this is how to celebrate the Christian life. You have been set free. Christ says: "My blood has covered you. The judgment of God is passing over you because of my blood, you are free. Get your coat on. Get out. You are on your way to glory. Start the pilgrimage. You are on the pilgrim's progress now. But get rid of the old leaven of malice and evil and eat the unleavened bread of sincerity and truth and march on your way."

It is a Passover. And what the Jew celebrates once a year, the Christian celebrates every day. Now we are told to go round our own house and see that the leaven is put out of it. We are told also that it is not our job to go round other people's houses. I am going to say something very important now. Paul refers to an earlier letter which we no longer have, but in which he said: Christians, don't mix socially with sinners. And they misunderstood this and they thought that meant any sinner, which means, virtually, you couldn't mix with anybody. You couldn't go to the office tomorrow morning, you couldn't go to the shop, you couldn't go to school. You have to mix with sinners in the world.

Paul now corrects this. He meant: "Don't associate with sinning saints." Sometimes that is the only way you can tell them they are doing wrong. We are told in the Bible that there is a strategy to deal with each other. When a saint sins, step number one, go and tell him alone – just the two of you.

If he doesn't put it right, take two or three others and tell him. If he still doesn't, tell it to the church, and if he still doesn't listen, let him be to you as an outsider. Those are Jesus' words. And that is the strategy. Sometimes it may be necessary for you to take number four and not even to have a meal with a Christian brother. That is pretty drastic again.

But Paul is saying this: it is not my job as a Christian to judge people outside the church. It is not your job to tell them they are sinners. It is your job to preach the gospel to them. Now this has relevance to today because I think Christians today are in great danger of getting caught up onto a bandwagon of protest against a permissive society. I do hope you think twice before you jump on this bandwagon and before you begin to protest, and I do hope you will pause and consider.

There are those who are not Christians at all who are protesting about this and who are telling people, "We judge you." Paul teaches us here that there is enough for us to be going on with within the Christian fellowship not to do this. What right have I to judge those outside? Is it not those inside you are to judge? It is a profound lesson – the danger of judging those outside is Pharisaism. The danger of going round telling the world they are all wrong is the danger of self-righteousness which is not sincere – and it becomes a whited sepulchre. Let us therefore start with the household of God. The Feast of the Passover was for the people of God. The Egyptians were not told to go round getting the leaven out of their houses. They were one day going to face the judgment of God. But the people of God were told to celebrate the Festival. That is where we must begin.

What is the message of this chapter? It is a message which comes to me and to you, and it is like the cutting knife of the surgeon, and the Word of God is sharper than any two-edged sword. The message is this: There can be no compromise whatever between salvation and sin. Christ did not die in order that you could go on sinning. Christ did not die in order that you could go on eating what you ate before. God did not bring you out of Egypt in order that you could carry a bag of food from Egypt to go on eating. Later in the account of the Exodus, the people of Israel came to Moses and said to him: "We don't like this manna that God is giving us each day. It is boring. Why can't we have some of the garlic and leeks and onions we used to have in Egypt?"

There are times when you start your pilgrimage to heaven, when the diet of the Christian, compared with the excitements of the world, seems a bit boring – rather the same each day. But it is the only safeguard for the Christian as he travels through this barren land on his way to glory. There is going to be a feast there, and then of course there will be everything you could ever ask for to satisfy, to eat and drink. But we are pilgrims now. We have left Egypt behind and there is no mixture. Christ doesn't come into a life and say, "You can keep everything else and add me to the rest." He says, "If you have me, you must leave things behind. You must keep the Feast with unleavened bread."

I remember hearing an evangelist who, when he came to the point of making his appeal said: "Don't leave your seats unless you are prepared to leave your favourite sins on your seats." I understood what he was saying. Christ would say: Don't come to me if you want to hang on to everything else. Don't come to me if you want to go on eating that food. Don't come to me if you want to go on enjoying Egypt, but come to me and I will set you free not only from the boredom, not only from the fears, not only from your loneliness, not only from your problems, but above all, I want to set you free from your sins.

SUITS AND SINS
Read 1 Corinthians 6

A. SUITS AGAINST A BROTHER (1–11)
1. YOUR POSITION DEMEANED (1–6)
  a. World
  b. Angels
2. YOUR PROFESSION DEFEATED (7–8)
  a. To go to law at all
  b. To win the case
3. YOUR PAST DESIRED (9–11)

B. SINS AGAINST THE BODY (12–20)
1. GOD'S PURPOSE DEFEATED (12–14)
2. CHRIST'S PARTS DEGRADED (15–17)
3. SPIRIT'S PRESENCE DEFILED (18–20)

We have thought of a picture of the church as a lifeboat, which may look very fine in its own building, nicely polished and sitting there on its chocks, but a lifeboat has got to be in the sea to do its job – and the church may look very nice in its own building, all neatly ordered and sitting there, but it does have to be out in the world to do its job. It is dangerous when the sea gets into the lifeboat. Then it cannot do its job. This is the double problem of every church – how to get the church into the world without the world getting into the church; how to get the lifeboat into the sea without the sea getting into the lifeboat.

In this letter to the Corinthians, we see again and again that the sea had got into the lifeboat. The kind of thinking that went on in the city of Corinth was going on in the church. The kind of thing they did outside was going on inside. And the sea was flooding into the lifeboat. This would mean that sooner or later the Corinthian church could not save souls. Therefore the apostle Paul is trying to "bail out the lifeboat". He is trying to get hold of the sea that has got in and put it out over the side. Chapter 6 covers two ways in which the Christians were behaving like the Corinthians – people inside the church doing just the same as people outside.

The first is rather extraordinary. It is not something we do today very frequently so it may seem a bit strange to us. They were going to law with each other. Frankly, the cost of doing so today keeps most of us out of the law courts, if we can possibly avoid getting into all that. But for the Greek world it was very different and we have to understand something of the picture behind this church and behind that city if we are going to realise why the Christians were doing it. It was the public entertainment. If you wanted a good morning's entertainment you went along to the law courts. People could go along and listen to litigation and hear lawyers arguing. Fascinating! Who's going to win? Television has discovered that law courts are good entertainment, and a legal case still keeps you gripped till the end. They had the real thing. Everybody went to law in ancient Greece. If you wanted to get your own back on your neighbour, you just simply started litigation – great fun and you could really get the chance of doing your neighbour down and putting him in his place. Fancy letting his hedge grow over my garden. You could really deal with him. And so you went to law. You could choose a private arbiter who was a third party acceptable to both sides, but that wasn't much fun. You usually went to a jury. And the minimum number for a jury was 201. So it was already quite an entertainment and you could be sure of a crowd because you had got the jury! That was the minimum. The next size jury that you could ask for was 401. And there are known cases on record in Greek history of 6,000 people sitting on the jury. There was only one qualification for sitting on the jury. You had to be sixty years of age. So you can imagine the jury of all these sixty year-olds sitting together and then the case coming up and everybody turning up, all the relatives and friends, taking sides, sitting on opposite sides of the court and glaring at each other. Great fun!

The tragedy is that the Christians had got caught up in this. So when two church members fell out they said, "Right, to the courts!" and they simply did what everybody else in Corinth did. They said, "We'll have a case and we'll show you you're wrong", and you had the awful spectacle of Christians parading their differences before the public. This is the point at which this begins to be relevant to us. We may not go to law courts, but we can be guilty of the same thing because every time we talk about a difference among Christians and talk about it outside the church and tell others what has happened to others in the church, we are doing exactly as the Corinthians did here.

Paul comes down heavily upon them and is saying: "How dare you take differences between Christians to people outside the church?" It is an incredible boldness for a person to do such a thing, and he gives three profound reasons why Christians should never take their differences outside their own fellowship, which does nothing but damage. Even to another church you do damage, but particularly if you take it to your neighbours and the world outside. The reasons Paul gives are so heavy that, after you have read them, you will feel battered. I did. Here is the first: Don't you know that you are going to judge the world? How dare you take your case to a judge, knowing that one day he will have to bring his case to you! Can you imagine sitting in a law court when a judge has finally pronounced sentence, and he has told the man standing there in the dock before him that such and such is my verdict. Can you imagine him then saying, "Now that I have helped you, I've got a bit of a problem. Could you help me?" It is ridiculous, isn't it? You would say, "What kind of a judge is this, that he can't manage his own problems, that he has got to ask the chap in the dock how to manage his own affairs?" It is as ludicrous for a Christian to place his problems in the hands of someone who will one day stand before him!

The remarkable truth in the Bible is that not only is God going to judge the world, he has appointed a man by whom he will judge the world – Jesus Christ – and Jesus has appointed men by whom he will judge the world: the saints; Christians. One day you will sit on the bench with Jesus, and all men will stand before you. So what an astonishing thing for you to stand before them. It is just demeaning, degrading for a Christian, even to stand in that position. Not only will men one day be judged by Christians, all angels will too. The very highest order of intelligent beings in the universe under God will one day stand before the bench of Christ and his saints. If you then are going to judge the world, isn't it criminal to admit to the world that you can't sort out your own problems? It is ludicrous.

The second thing is that you have lost your case even before you have gone to court. Your whole profession of being a Christian has been defeated. Even if you win the case, you have been defeated. Somebody once gave me a very wise word which I am afraid I have not always remembered, but I know what he meant and I am sure it was very good advice. He said, "Remember, David, you can win an argument and lose the man." You can also win a case and yet lose something even more precious. Paul is saying that even going to law against a brother, regardless of whether you win or lose, you have lost your case. You have lost because you have told the world that we are incapable of sorting out our problems. Every time someone gossips about Christian differences outside the fellowship, they are telling the whole world that we Christians are incapable of sorting out our own problems. We are preaching the gospel of reconciliation and the gospel of forgiveness – and then we go and do that. It is just contradictory. We have lost even if we win.

It is still very difficult to get a completely fair judgment in a legal case. That is not a criticism of the legal profession which takes such endless time to try to discover the truth. But let me give you an illustration of what I mean. Until recently the divorce laws meant that when two people came out of a divorce case, one was labelled innocent and the other was labelled guilty. One had won the case and the other had lost it. But I have hardly ever come across a divorce in which there was a completely innocent party and a completely guilty one. Usually, if a marriage breaks down, both are to blame to a degree. Now in the same way a legal verdict that says "You are right and he is wrong" does not always do justice to the situation, and particularly in ancient Greece where the standard of justice was not nearly as high as it might have been. It was tending to be swayed by the eloquence of the advocates. The Greeks thought so much about eloquence that a really eloquent advocate could sway the thing. Paul says that even if you win it will probably lead you to defraud someone. You will probably get more than you deserve if you win the case and so you will get a reputation of someone who is greedy, someone who defrauds, someone who tries to get the "pound of flesh". You have lost every way, so Paul says here is the second reason.

The third reason (and a profound one) is that you are taking your life and putting it in the hands of the kind of people you used to be, and that is dangerous. You are dabbling in your past again.

Now here we have a remarkable list, a catalogue of sins which is quite clearly characteristic of the jurists of ancient Corinth. Paul (in v. 1) says, "You dare to go to law before the unrighteous instead of the saints", and now he goes on in v. 9 to tell them what he means by the unrighteous:

Those who are in a wrong relationship to God and worship idols;

Those who are in a wrong relationship to others, thieves and robbers;

Those who are in a wrong relationship to themselves, who are drunkards and homosexuals.

Believe it or not, this was the typical life in Corinth in those days, and the jury was therefore made up of people like this. You Christians, with your higher standards, are going to people with these low standards to tell you who is in the right. And when I gossip to my neighbours about things inside the church, I am going to people with far lower standards and asking them to say I was right, and this is just not on. You are dabbling in your past. You are going back to behaviour that you had before. Before, it mattered to you what people thought about you and you went to their standards, but now you are up here, you have different standards. Don't go to people with lower standards to tell you that you are in the right. They will tell you. They may be happy to tell you and say: "Terrible, did they do that to you? Oh you did the right thing. You give them one back." They will say this, and you have come down to their standards and you accept their verdict because that is the kind of person you used to be, and which they still are.

This is why Christians should never go to those outside the fellowship to settle their differences. If you do, you are in danger of going down to your past standards and letting their worldly judgement decide whether you were right or wrong.

Now we come to one of the most wonderful verses in this

chapter: v. 11. I am going to dwell on this because it is the gospel in a nutshell: "... and such were some of you." In other words, this is the kind of people you used to be. You used to go to them for help. You used to be just like them. But underline in your Bible the word *were*. Such *were* some of you. The good news of Christianity is in the word "were". You were. Not now!

Of course there are those respectable churches which would hate people who were like this to come into their fellowship. But in the New Testament days you couldn't claim that your father, your grandfather or your great-grandfather was a Baptist. You couldn't claim to have been brought up decently and respectably in a Christian home. There were no Christian grandparents at that time. This was a new church, and everybody in it had been like this. They had been living roughly before. (Note again that the Bible says "such were some of you"!) They had been caught up in this immorality, greed, idolatry, perversion and all the rest of it.

You know, sometimes a church made up of people who have had that background is a church with more love in it, and more sense of God's grace in it, and more sense of God's forgiveness in it. Because you know what you were. One of the snags of being brought up in a Christian home is that you get the respectability without the sense of gratitude for forgiveness and reconciliation. "Such were some of you" – you know what it is like to live like that.

But now – what has happened to you? You have been *washed*. This is probably a reference to baptism. But there is something deeper than that. You are clean now. You have been sanctified, which means you have been taken out of all that. You have been set apart for God. You have been made a different kind of person. You have been cut off from that. You have been justified. You idolaters and immoral people are right with God and you have heard God the Judge say,

"Case dismissed. Acquitted. Justified. In my sight this person is innocent."

Paul is saying: "I beg of you. Don't go back and get involved with those kind of people again. Don't ask them to declare you right when God has justified you. God says you are in the right. Why do you need man's verdict? Why do you need them to tell you – "I did right; please put me in the right." You don't need to now. You have been justified by God. That is all you need."

Of course, we so long to be justified in man's sight, don't we? "He, wishing to justify himself...." We want everybody to think we are good and right. But Paul is saying that God says you are in the right and that is enough. You don't need any human verdict on top of that. "Such were some of you" – but not now; you have left it all behind. Now you behave differently.

Paul says: when you've got a grievance against a Christian brother, make for a wise saint in the fellowship. Both go to a mature Christian and say, "You settle the case." Have you ever heard of a Jew initiating litigation against a Jew? You never will. I am sure they have many occasions to want to. But you will never hear of a Jew taking a case against a Jew – not if they are a religious Jew, a practising Jew. It is a fundamental principle never to display their differences before the Gentiles. It should be the same among Christians. Christians should settle their differences, guided by mature saints within the fellowship, and be restored in love. Let us therefore not even go to the court of human opinion with our grievances. Let us make up our minds that we will never gossip about differences among Christians outside the fellowship. How much anxiety and heartache would have been saved if we had just done this all through the history of the church.

That is the first part of the chapter. Now we come to

something quite different. Paul seems to jump from the question of litigation to the question of free love and sex outside marriage. It seems such a jump at first. Why does he jump from this to that? What is the connection? There are two simple links between what he has been writing and what he is now going to teach.

Firstly, he has said that if you go to law you do so before the immoral, and if you start taking what they say is right as right, sooner or later you will find yourself drifting back into their kind of ways and you will find yourself taking their standards for yourself. So that is how it flows on. And of course, to the ancient city of Corinth sexual liberty was licence. I want you to imagine a pretty horrifying thing. Let me try to make it real. I used to live in a city called Guildford where there is a cathedral on a hill. Imagine that cathedral was the Temple of Aphrodite, the goddess of love. Then you would be living in Corinth. In that temple were literally hundreds of prostitutes, both male and female. That was considered normal. The done thing for everybody going to church on Sunday was to go and have sex up at the cathedral. Now this is pretty shattering even to imagine. But that is the kind of situation in which Corinth was. And if you went up to the cathedral of Aphrodite you would meet all the judges, you would meet all the jurymen, you would meet all the businessmen and the tradesmen, everybody was there on Sunday and it was a social occasion. They were all at it. It was in that atmosphere that Paul was trying to help this little church to grow.

As someone has said: "The early church was like a cluster of chaste snowdrops growing on a foul rubbish heap." But it was difficult just to encourage the growth. Paul was teaching that if you start going to these judges to give you the standards of right and wrong, you will find yourself up at that temple before long. If you accept their morals you will soon find yourself immoral.

Secondly, Paul is saying that those who are so keen to apply the law to others are usually not very keen to apply it to themselves. Those who are so keen to throw the book at everybody else usually say, "All things are lawful for me." I am alright. You can't touch me. I can do anything.

Now let me mention here a problem that the early Christians had to a great degree, the problem of avoiding two extremes in Christian living: legalism and licence. We are still with that problem. When I become a Christian, I become finished with the law. I am set free from the law. I am not under the law any more. I am under grace. Paul says: Never go back under it, whether by circumcision or by anything else. Never get back under a set of rules. The Christian life is not a set of rules. You have been redeemed from that kind of living. But then the Christian, who is under liberty, so easily slips over into licence and says, "Fine, if I am not under the law, I can do what I like. If I am not under a set of rules, I am free. All things are lawful to me." We have to get this balance right.

Consider the kind of thing that happens when legalism takes over. You begin to get rules for Sunday observance. That is legalism. And alas, there is a lot of it about. You begin to get rules for each other in Christian fellowship. And the fellowship makes rules that don't apply to the Christian in liberty. So you become bound and it kills a fellowship. Legalism – the letter of the law. That does not mean a Christian can do anything he likes, that he is free from the law, that the law can't touch him. Paul says, "all things are lawful to me" as a Christian, but there are two qualifications to that statement. Firstly, all things are not helpful. You are free to do anything as a Christian, but some things will not help you. Therefore you don't do them. Now this is an important principle to grasp. When you become a Christian, you are not given a long list of rules. You are free now. But you are not free to do things that don't help you. That is a very important principle because it means that people make their own rules and they will vary from one person to another. What one person finds unhelpful, another Christian may not. Therefore it ill behoves us to start making rules for everybody. We will make mistakes. Some things are not helpful to me that you may be able to handle perfectly alright. Some things are not helpful to you which are alright for me. The principle is liberty: all things are lawful except the things that are unhelpful.

Secondly, not everything is controllable. The Christian may be free to do something but if he can't control it and if he is going to become a slave to it, then he mustn't do it. Drinking alcohol is a very good example of this second one. There are those who would like to make a law for every Christian on this, but the Bible doesn't. The Bible leaves this an open question. But I am quite sure that for some brethren in Christ, touching alcohol is neither helpful nor controllable and they must therefore not do it. We are also told in scripture that those who love such people and have to mix with them freely should keep off it too – for their sakes, not because it is a law. There is no law for total abstinence anywhere in the Bible. But it will be on my conscience if a weaker brother is led into something he can't control.

This is the way you approach Christian liberty. Yes, all things are lawful for me. I am not under laws. I am free now in Christ, but not free to do anything I like. I am free to do the things that are helpful, free to do the things that are good, free to do the things God wants me to do. Paul is going to apply this to certain things of the body, and the key word in this section to the end of the chapter is mentioned eight times – that word "body".

Many decades ago, I was in an audience of teachers who

were shown an explicit sex education film which at that time was rejected both by the teachers and the education authorities. The main thrust of the film was that sex is simply a physical instinct and passion which must be satisfied. It is like the stomach and food. It is seen as being unfortunate that you might start a baby by having it, so take precautions – but it is just there and it is a normal part of single or married life just to satisfy the desire. Now this is how the Corinthians used to talk, and say: "That's all it is. When your stomach feels hungry, you give it food; when your body wants sex, you give it love – and that is all." Paul is going to tackle this at a very deep level. He is not just going to hold up his hands in holy horror, he is going to give Christians a totally new outlook on the body because in the last analysis that is what will cure immorality. It is a false view of the body that leads to a false behaviour and therefore it is no use just protesting about the behaviour, you have got to go down deep and say there is a wrong attitude to the body.

I need to underline what the Greeks thought about the body. They thought of a man as made up of an envelope with something inside it, and they called the envelope or container the body, and they said the real man is somewhere inside the body, and the real man is called "the soul" and therefore the body is quite incidental to a man, it is not really part of him. The real man is the "soul" inside. They believed that at death, the "container" is smashed, finished, and the soul set free from the body is at last free for real life. That is what they believed. They thought of it as a glass with water in – the glass being your body and the water being your soul – and if you went to the seashore and poured the water into the ocean and smashed the glass on the rocks, that is a perfect picture of death. The glass is finished, the soul is "lost" in the great ocean of life and it is set free from the body. That is Greek thinking. The tragedy is that the education of this country has been based on Greek thinking for centuries and you would be amazed how many people inside the church think that death means the end of the body – and the soul floating on – and that the real man is a soul, not a body.

Hebrews and Christians have never thought this way. To the Hebrew and the Christian you are looking at my "soul" now. It doesn't say that I have a soul – I *am* a soul. A living body *is* a soul. Therefore when the message goes out "SOS" ("save our souls") you mean a living body: save my living body. Have you got the picture? A soul in the Bible is a living body and that is why animals are described in Genesis chapter 1 as living souls. The same phrase as is used of a man in Genesis chapter 2 – and he became a living soul. He became what the animals were: a living body.

This is a completely different notion. To the Greeks the idea of salvation meant to be saved *out* of the body. But to the Christians it means to save my body. Quite different. Jesus died to save your body because that *is* your soul. He died for the redemption of your body because that *is* your soul. And heaven is a place he is preparing for *bodies* and I believe in the resurrection of the body. It is a totally different thing.

The Christian creeds have never said "I believe in the immortality of the soul" and we don't believe that. The Christian says: when this mortal soul puts on an immortal body then shall the grave be swallowed up in victory and death loses its sting – then these words come true. So God's wish is to get your body. That is what Jesus died for. That is what he wanted when he made you. The body was not made for immorality but for the Lord. Your body was not made simply for the indulgence of its appetites but for the Lord. This body I use to speak, these hands, these lips, my mouth, is a body made for the Lord and he wants it permanently with him. When this old body lies in the grave, God is going to reach down his almighty hand, and he who raised up Jesus is going to raise me up with a body. That is the gospel: the redemption of the body.

This means that you regard the body quite differently. When the Greeks said that the body doesn't matter – that the soul is all-important – it led to two extraordinary extremes of attitude. On the one hand, it led to an extreme asceticism which says, "escape from the body even in this life – cut out all the body's desires, get right out of the body if you can." It is astonishing how this is creeping back in – in Zen Buddhism and all sorts of things. Pummel the body; sit on a bed of nails; yoga – get rid of the body, get out of it. That is one extreme. The other extreme (more common in Corinth) was: If I am just a soul and my body doesn't matter, I can do what I like with my body and it won't affect my soul. That is a false way of talking. The Greeks said: It doesn't matter. Your soul is pure, your body – you can have sex freely just as you can have food freely. It doesn't matter. It won't affect your soul. Paul comes in and says: Don't you know that when God made the body, he didn't make it for sex, he made it for the Lord, and only sex that is in the Lord is valid. There is a place for sex in the Lord, but it is "in the Lord" not outside him.

You see, when I became a Christian I became one spirit joined to Jesus. I "married" Jesus. Our two spirits became one. But since my body and my spirit are so linked together, my body became linked with Jesus. Therefore I am not free to do with my body what I like because it is now his body. My hands are now his hands. My face is now his face. My members are his members. My organs are now his organs. Therefore (and here we come to pretty direct talking), how can I take my members which are his and join them to a prostitute? That is actually making Jesus go to a prostitute – because it is his body. Do you see the thinking? That makes you shudder. It makes you tremble when you realise what you could do with Jesus. Let us go a little further than that.

Paul teaches that the sex act is unique among all human acts, in that when two bodies come together in intercourse, they are no longer two bodies doing something, they are one body doing something. That is what makes sex so different. Two people can go out and get drunk together, but they are still two bodies. Two people can go out and be gluttons together but they are still two bodies. Two people can go out and have a fight together, but they are still two bodies. Two people who go out and have sex are "one body" and you notice that even a man visiting a prostitute is regarded in God's sight as the "two becoming one". And Genesis 2:24 applies.

How then can I possibly take the body of Christ, for that is what my body is having become one with him in spirit, and make one body with someone else? It can't be done.

Apply this to Christian marriage. How could I, a Christian, take my body, which is part of Christ, and marry an unbeliever and join Christ to an unbeliever? You just can't do it. Such a mixed marriage becomes impossible.

Someone may say, "I have just become a Christian since I got married and now I am married to an unbeliever – what do I do?" Later on we shall study 1 Corinthians 7 which deals with that issue. Let us move on still further. Having given two very sound reasons why I cannot have free sex even though it seems to be just a bodily function to many, Paul makes it clear:

1. God's purpose is spoiled. He made the body for the Lord.
2. Christ's parts are degraded. It is his body, not mine.
3. The Spirit's presence is defiled.

Many commentators have argued as to what Paul meant by "every other sin which a man commits is outside the body", and they say: "That's not true, if you get drunk you are doing something to your body" – but, just a moment, what Paul is saying is that in considering the sex act, being unique in making two bodies one, which no other act does, you can see that you can commit every other sin and you can still have your own body, but in sex you have given your body to someone else. You have lost something which you can never have back. Not just your innocence, or your virginity. You have lost something you can never have back again. It has gone. You can no longer offer someone all of you. This is the biggest argument I know for virginity before marriage, so that you can offer your loved one all of you when you come and they can have all of you. To become one flesh with someone else has been to lose your body. It is no longer your own. You have lost it. In Christ, to give your bodies to one another is a lovely thing, because you haven't lost it at all. It is still part of Christ and everything is yours in Christ, so you haven't lost it. But outside of Christ, you have.

Now Paul says the final thing. Don't you realise that you should look at your body in the mirror and say: "I am looking at a shrine; I am looking at a temple; I am looking at the place where God's Spirit dwells on earth. His Spirit dwells within me."

It has been said that in the Old Testament God had a temple for his people but in the New Testament he has his people for a temple. He lives in bodies – my body and your body. Therefore if I do anything that he disapproves of, I am defiling a shrine. It is an act of sacrilege. It is a defiling of God's holy dwelling on earth. Not only is it a consecrated dwelling, it is a costly dwelling. If you are building a shrine for God, you put everything you have got into it. It would be an expensive building. You would want gold leaf. You would want the best cedar. Paul finishes up by saying: "Don't you realise how expensive your temple was – not to make, but to buy?" It was the precious blood of Jesus. Jesus died not only to redeem our souls but to buy our bodies. We are not our own. I can't say, "I can do what I like with my body" – it is not my body, it is his. He bought it. Therefore, "glorify God" – not with your soul, but in your body.

I have to live my life here in a body. I have to use this body for everything I do. The purpose of my body is that it should be for the Lord, the parts of Christ and the temple of the Holy Spirit, the whole Trinity of the godhead taking my body for his glory. That is the conception. If you get to this plane of thinking, then quite frankly you can see what is wrong with any form of sin.

SEX AND CELIBACY

Read 1 Corinthians 7

A. MARRIED (1–24)
 1. CONJUGAL SEX (1–7)
 2. CONTROLLED SELF (8–9)
 3. CONSENTING SEPARATION (10–16)
 4. CALLED STATE (17–24)

B. SINGLE (25–40)
 1. BOUND (25–31)
 2. BURDENED (32–35)
 3. BETROTHED (36–38)
 4. BEREAVED (39–40)

Anybody reading Paul's first letter to the Corinthians can see that there is a break between chapters 6 and 7. He begins chapter 7 by saying: "With reference to your letter..." which means that having dealt with certain other things which he has chosen to talk about, he is now going to talk about the things they want to talk about. He has received a letter from them full of questions.

By way of introduction, to get the theme it will help to see where these questions and the answers came from. But even though Paul is switching from his subject to theirs, there is a connection. In chapter 6 he is dealing with sex outside marriage. It is only right and logical that he should go straight on to deal in chapter 7 with sex inside marriage, for that is the other side of the coin. There is yet another connection. We saw that to take your body, which is part of the body of Christ, and join it to the body of a prostitute, is in fact to cause Christ to join that woman – which is an incredible thing to do – and in the same way, to take your

105

body which is part of the body of Christ and to join it to a person who is not a Christian is also to do much the same thing, and that comes up in chapter 7. We are dealing with the Christian teaching on these things.

Now first of all let us look at where the questions came from. They came from a city in ancient Greece and we have seen that they had a low view of the body, and therefore a low view of marriage. They thought of the body as no part of the real "me". On that view you can do one of two things with your body. You can either get away from it in this life by practising extreme abstinence from all the desires of the body, denying the body its food, its sex and everything else, or, since it doesn't matter what happens to the body, you can go to the other extreme of indulgence in which you give the body everything it wants. Here we have two extreme attitudes to the body, neither of which is the Christian one. The Christian says: God made the body and my body is not a temporary part of me. It is going to be raised from the dead. My body is part of God's plan. In heaven I will have my body. God hasn't finished with my body. He died to buy my body. He died to save it. My body has been bought at a price. My body is going to be redeemed. My body is all part of God's plan for me. That is a totally different way of looking at it – and it leads to a high view of marriage. If you have a high view of the body as the temple of the Holy Spirit you will have a high view of marriage.

Paul has clearly been asked questions about marriage from the point of view of abstinence. People have written and asked him, people outside the church are saying that the higher state of life is to be free from sex altogether, to be celibate, to live without marriage, that you shouldn't need it, that the body doesn't need it, and you should live abstaining from all these things.

Is this true? Do Christians think like this? Is the celibate state the higher moral state? Is a person going to be more spiritual if they remain unmarried? That is the kind of question that would spring out of Greek society which considered the state of being single as a higher state than being married. Today we have reversed this and the rule seems to be: get married if you possibly can. There is something odd about you if you don't. We are therefore living in a situation which is exactly reversed from the biblical one, so therefore we have to adjust our thinking as we read this chapter.

That was the kind of question they were asking. So much so that they asked: When a person becomes a Christian, shouldn't they divorce their partner and get out of marriage, into this higher state with no sex? If you had attended a discussion group at the church in Corinth, they would have debated whether you should get married; whether if you were married you should get divorced; what happens when someone becomes a Christian and their husband or wife isn't a Christian – this kind of question – and they still go on today.

Let us turn from the questions to where the answers came from. Paul is giving the answers, and we want to ask what experience had he of these things – and what authority had he for saying them? Because before we read his words, we need to settle these two issues.

The first thing we ought to say is that it was highly probable Paul had been married. All the indications are that way. It is never stated in so many words, but there are two very strong facts that indicate it: first, Paul had trained as a rabbi, and you had to be married to be a rabbi; second, Paul was a member of the Sanhedrin, and you could not be a member of that body unless you were married. Whether Paul had lost his wife through death, or whether as I suspect is more likely, she had actually left him when he became a Christian and went out as a missionary (and there are some indirect indications in his letters that this may well be so), certainly by the time he got to Corinth he did not have a wife. He said in 1 Corinthians 9, "Don't I have the right to have a wife with me on my travels like the other apostles do?" – but I don't. So it looks as if Paul, contrary to what many women today have thought – that he was a confirmed bachelor and that his views were all explained by that – was not, and that he had in fact known the married state, but he was certainly now in virtually a single state for one reason or another. He was free now from that bond, and he speaks out of that experience.

Secondly, by what authority does he speak? It is interesting in this chapter, again and again he says something like "I'm giving you my judgement and I don't have a command from the Lord"; "I say to you, not the Lord...." Now why did he say this in this chapter? On one point, he says "I give you a word from the Lord, not from me", but on all the others he says, "It's from me, and not the Lord." What does he mean? Is it that what he is saying here is purely human opinion and you can take it or leave it, according to what you think? No. When he says "I have a command from the Lord" he means, "I can quote something that was said by Jesus when he was on earth"; "I can actually give you a direct quotation from his teaching. For the rest, I am speaking guided by the Spirit of wisdom" – for he finishes the chapter, "I think I have the Spirit of God" – in other words, you take this not as a direct word from Jesus that he said, but as something that the Spirit of Jesus has guided me to say. It is now part of the Word of God for us, so we can't just say, "That's only Paul's opinion and I don't agree with him." We have to take it as the wisdom of a Spirit-filled man of God giving his attention to a question which Jesus never dealt with specifically in his teaching.

This is how we are going to have to deal with a lot of questions today. There are laws being passed in England about divorce and abortion and all sorts of other things which are never dealt with in the Bible. How are we going to find out God's will? The answer is: through the wisdom of Spirit-filled people. That is how Christ will speak today. So that it has the authority of the Spirit of Christ if it doesn't have a direct word from the words of Jesus.

Having said that, we split the chapter into two. The first twenty-four verses are not exclusively but mainly for married people, and the second half of the chapter is mainly for single people. Let me sum up the whole chapter by saying one or two things. Paul agrees with the Corinthians that celibacy is a good thing. Let us affirm that first. It is a good thing for a man to remain single. But then he immediately goes on to say (and this is equally important) that that doesn't mean marriage is a bad thing. The trouble is that in this discussion, people will ask which is right and which is wrong. Which is a higher moral state? Which is a lower moral state? That is a question you shouldn't ask. Both are good and both are gifts of God.

Marriage is a gift of God – and how you need God's grace to build up a lovely marriage. Singleness is a gift of God and how you need the grace of God to build up a happy single life. Both are good. To say that celibacy is good is not to say that marriage is bad. To make quite sure that they get the point, Paul says again and again in this chapter that marriage is not sin – because the Corinthians were tempted to think celibacy was good. Marriage is good.

Paul is also going to say in this chapter that celibacy is better. That word does not mean "morally higher". It means "there are advantages", and I will give you the reasons for his preference as we go through the chapter. Personally I think they are very sound reasons of which we have got to take note. So much so, that when I as a married person read this chapter I can see that I must work harder than a single person to keep my devotion to the Lord right. That is the message of this chapter to me as a married person.

Now he realised quite definitely that, in a sex-ridden society like Corinth, to remain single was a terrible strain. Wherever you went in Corinth you were confronted with sex. So Paul recognised that it would almost be a superhuman thing to keep yourself under control. Indeed, he said it would be. It would be a gift of God to do so in this society. Therefore he says that the normal pattern in a sex-ridden society is bound to be marriage. Let every man have his own wife and let every wife have her own husband – to reduce the strain of a society like this on Christian men and women.

That may seem to you a very low view of marriage, but Paul had a very high view of marriage. That comes out in Ephesians 5. If you read that chapter, you see it supplements all this. But it is a very good reason for marriage. It is only one reason for it. There are many more. Paul says: I am not commanding you to be married. This is a concession, not a command. I am not telling every Christian they must rush out and get married. I am saying that in this kind of society this is to be the normal pattern unless God gives you the special gift to be able to control yourself.

Certainly Paul was not against sex. He was the result of it, and his teaching in other epistles balances out the whole picture. Now he lays down four simple principles, and I wish I could write these large. The first principle: some of the Greeks were advocating celibacy within marriage and Paul comes down very strongly with a most modern view – and a remarkable view, considering what some have said about Paul's view of women. Here are two things in which Paul is absolutely abreast of the best modern view about marriage. Firstly, physical relations are essential to a healthy marriage. They must not be denied. It is part of marriage. If it breaks down there, other troubles are going to follow. What

110

a very enlightened view, and Paul was enlightened by the Spirit in saying it. Consider that this was said two thousand years ago. The woman has equal rights with the man. That again was revolutionary in the ancient world. But it was the Spirit of God's teaching. So he says that when you marry, the husband's body no longer belongs to him – the wife has a right to his body whenever she desires. Likewise, in reverse, the wife's body is no longer hers and the husband has the right to it. How I wish that had been widely taught and known. For even within Christian marriages it can happen that normal rights of marriage are denied for all sorts of reasons.

Paul says, "Wife, if you deny your husband, you are exposing him to Satan, you are doing even more" – and he uses a strong word: "you are defrauding; you are cheating on something you promised to give."

In the Anglican marriage service, when the ring is put on, these words are said: "With my body I thee worship" – and to worship means strictly to be entirely at someone else's disposal. Now that is a simple, real, down-to-earth principle.

Paul says the only circumstances in which this should cease is where by mutual agreement, not by one deciding, but by mutual agreement and for a season only, for the purposes of prayer together, this before God – then he says, come together, lest Satan get hold of you. Now that is the first principle. The second principle is the principle of the controlled self. He says that the basic aim and object is to be able to control yourself. If you can do that outside marriage, fine. If you can't, then marriage is to help you, not to complete indulgence, but to self-control. This balances off the previous paragraph. Self-control outside marriage; self-control inside marriage is the object of the whole exercise.

It is here that Paul gives the first reason for remaining celibate if you can. He goes on to say, "It is better to marry than to burn." One remembers the temptations of St. Anthony in the desert, and many another Christian hermit who ran away from degraded Roman society, thinking they would get away from temptation into some monastery, and finding that you don't. So he says that if you cannot exercise self-control outside marriage, then exercise it inside, but the principle of self-control applies.

Thirdly, there is the principle of consenting separation. Should Christians ever separate? Should a Christian who is married to an unbeliever ever separate? Let us tackle this briefly. For two Christians married, the rule is absolutely simple. Here Paul can quote Christ: no divorce. Which is why, when you are married in a church you say "until death us do part". God hates divorce, and Christ said no separation. But Paul recognises that even if that is the general rule, there are some situations in which a husband and wife are in such a state with each other that they may have to separate. If they do, Paul makes it quite clear that separation is very much the second best. So in some extreme circumstances a Christian man and his wife may separate – but if they do, let it be made quite clear that the separation does not allow remarriage.

What about a Christian and an unbeliever? You see, here the Christian has defrauded the unbeliever, in a sense. Say a man marries a girl whom he loves and admires, and she loves and admires him, and then two years later the girl starts going to church and then becomes a Christian. Now he never married a Christian. He would never have chosen to. He didn't intend to. And suddenly he finds himself locked up in the same house as a fanatical believer. Poor chap, don't you feel sorry for him? He didn't choose this. He didn't want to be married to a religious person, and Paul very wisely recognises that in that situation the decision as to whether to keep the marriage together or to break it up must rest with the unbeliever, not the believer. The believer doesn't break up the marriage. The believer says to the unbeliever: "I am a Christian now. I realise this can spoil life for you – that you didn't marry a Christian, that you wouldn't have done. If you consent to stay and you will have me, fine, I love you and I want to stay with you, but if you want to leave I won't keep you, you can go" – and Paul says the reason why the Christian should say this is for the sake of peace. You see, there is something horribly offensive about a Christian living in a house that is fighting all the time.

But you notice it is for the sake of peace, not for the sake of purity. There is no reason for leaving for the sake of purity, because the unbelieving husband is consecrated through the wife. A Christian must never say to an unbelieving partner: "You are an unbeliever; you are an outsider; you are unclean – I separate from you", because God recognises a marriage, whether it took place in a register office or wherever. It is holy matrimony. You don't have to go to a church to engage in holy matrimony. Any matrimony in God's sight is holy. It is not a thing that is unclean. Therefore the unbelieving husband is clean, not to be separated from her, because he is in holy matrimony with a Christian.

So if the unbeliever wants to go, let them go, for the sake of peace, but if they want to stay, you are not compromised in any way at all, being married to an unbeliever. If you were compromised, your children would be unclean. Paul says that is a dreadful thought.

Now the fourth principle, that of the "called" state. This principle states that wherever God called you, whatever state you were in, whatever job you were in, whatever relationship you were in, whatever circumstances you were in, stay there. That is where God wants you. Why do you think he called you? Because he wanted someone there for his name. If he called you in a marriage, stay in the marriage. God wanted a Christian in it. If he called you in an office, stay in that office. God wanted someone in that office.

One of the awful effects of being converted is that you feel life is so new that you want to get rid of everything old. You want to drop everything and rush off as a missionary. You want to change everything. You want to get out of your present job. "Can't be a Christian with this boss. I want to be a Christian now. Can't possibly be a Christian in this office. I know – I'll advertise, or answer for a post in a Christian firm" – and it always sounds so marvellous to go and work with a lot of Christians. Don't you believe it! You may have some unpleasant shocks. If God calls you in that place and state, stay there. He called you in that marriage – stay in it.

This is a fundamental principle. Young people often come to me soon after they become a Christian and they say: "I'm seeking God's will for my life. I don't know what my vocation is. I don't know what he wants me to be." The answer is: He wants you to be right where you are, until he makes it crystal clear that he wants you somewhere else. You don't start fishing around straight away for another kind of life. God says: you be a Christian there; why do you think I called you there? Unless he says something to the contrary, God has assigned everybody the place where he called them. That is where he wants you to be.

If he called you while you were in a family, stay in that family, unless the unbeliever wants to go. God called you right there.

This applies to slavery and to all sorts of things. To me, one of the most amazing demonstrations of this was when Jesus, at the age of twelve, which was the age of adult consent in those days, said, "I want to be in my Father's business now." The Father had called him. He knew that God was his Father, and that his life was going to be to do the Father's work. Do you know what the next verse says? "He went back to Nazareth with them and was obedient to them." Isn't that amazing? And for another eighteen years after he knew he must be in his Father's business, he stayed there in Nazareth as a carpenter. If Jesus could do it, so can we.

We move on to the second half of the chapter – to the single people. Remember that, in Matthew 19, Jesus talks about being single, and he mentions three sorts of single people. There are those who are single by birth – there is some congenital problem that prevents them ever getting married. Then there are those who are single because society has made them single. They have had no choice. Then there are those who are single because they have chosen to be – for the sake of the kingdom. The word Paul uses is actually "eunuch", but that is what he means. It is with those who are voluntarily making the choice that Paul is concerned in the second part of the chapter. He is saying celibacy is a good thing – marriage is not a bad thing, but celibacy is better. Now why?

First of all, he talks about those who are bound in marriage. It is interesting that he uses the word "bound". Because you are bound to do certain things, you are bound to a certain situation, and he says, "In view of the impending distress, I advise all the single people to stay single, but I also say that the married people must stay married." What does he mean by that? No change. He says: "You single people, don't get married; you married people, don't try to be single – in view of the impending distress." It is quite clear that Paul, who had the gift of prophecy, knew that within a very few years a great storm was going to blow up in the Roman Empire, and it did just a few years after this letter was written – a storm in which men and women would be hauled before the courts and thrown to the lions, and in a time of such distress you can face it far better if you are single. Why? Someone has said that "children sweeten labour but they make misfortune bitter." You can face anything yourself, but to see your children suffer is not easy and to see your wife suffer is not easy. A single person can face martyrdom much more easily than a married person. When a storm is brewing and there is coming a time of physical persecution, then it is very good advice to say let the single remain single and the married stay married. That is the right advice in that situation.

Let me tell you a true story. Many centuries ago a Christian mother had just given birth to a baby. Just after she gave birth she was arrested as a Christian and she was flung into jail. And she was told, "Deny Christ and we will set you free." She refused, but what did they do then? They took her little baby and they put the baby in the next cell where she could hear it crying for her milk, and they said, "You can go and feed your baby as soon as you deny Christ." You see it was one thing for that mother to say, "I'm a Christian; I can't deny Christ", but her life was not the only one at stake. That mother did not deny Christ, even though her baby died of starvation in the next cell. But how would you like to be in that situation? Paul could see persecution coming within just a few years. So his advice that celibacy was better needs to be seen against that background.

I visited a little village in another country (I am not going to tell you where) and I had a lovely time in a little place of worship, packed to the doors. I didn't understand their language. That didn't matter. We loved each other and we praised God. But afterwards, through an interpreter, I was talking to these simple, poor people. I asked, "What is it like being a Christian here?" They said, "Our children are not allowed to go to the village school because we worship God. They are growing up illiterate because we, their parents, can't read or write. They will never be able to get a good job. They will be scavengers for the rest of their lives." Now I ask you: how many parents where you live would be prepared to stay true to Christ if it meant that their children wouldn't get an education?

Do you see what Paul is saying? When the world is going to persecute the church in a particularly horrible attack, then stay single if you possibly can. If you are married you have got to stay within that loyalty, but try to uproot your attachments to the things of the world when trouble is coming. Buy things as if you were not buying. Be married, yet live as if you can do without your wife. Go about your affairs in the world as though you were not in it. Try to cultivate a detachment so that if you lose your wife, if you lose your home, if you lose your job, you can still survive. Terribly important advice this. I thank God that it is advice I don't need to give you today, but there may well come a day – and there certainly is coming a day over the whole world – a day of great tribulation when this will happen, and in that day this scripture will come to life again. Stay single because you can face the battle better on your own than with family ties.

Moving on from that kind of bond, there is something that applies to all married people everywhere that you need to remember. Someone who is married has cares, anxieties and concerns that a single person does not have, and this can divide your loyalty from the Lord. A single person is in a position to give all their devotion to the Lord quite simply. It doesn't mean they do automatically. A single person can be selfish as well. But a married person has got the family and their spouse to consider. This applied even to my own ministry. My children when young had a swear word, which was "meeting!" When they wanted to be really cross they said "meeting!" We stopped using the word ourselves because it got so tedious for them. "Where's daddy tonight?" "Oh, he's at a meeting." So we had to adjust our family life.

This applies not just to the ministry, it applies to you.

You can be out at meetings all week. A single person can do that quite happily, but a married person may suffer in a marriage and their children may suffer, and Paul is taking the simple fact that when you get married you are taking on responsibilities – and it can distract you from the Lord unless you are careful and prayerful.

I have noticed that when a couple get engaged it is lovely to see them fall in love, but it is so sad when you see them slipping out of Christian service, getting so involved with each other that they no longer do for the Lord all that they used to do, and they are now so wrapped up in each other that the Lord sees little of them. It happens. Then they get married in church but for the next few years they are busy making an ideal home exhibition – decorating, gardening and doing all the rest, and then the children have come along.

Paul is uttering a warning. Celibacy is better because it is less easy to be distracted from a single-minded devotion to the Lord. That is the object of it all. God wants all of us. He wants single-minded devotion, and a married person will have an effort to give that because of their divided loyalty. That is the reason that applies whether persecution is on or not. And it is a reason why to be celibate is easier.

Now vv. 36–38 describe an unusual situation which the commentators find very difficult to understand and so do I in a sense. The most surprising advice in the chapter, but again I think in the light of the impending distress and the shortness of a normal life that is rapidly disappearing, it is good advice: if you are engaged, betrothed, the same applies. If you can stay single, do so. If you can stay good friends, do so. Again, this is against the background of a society that is going to break down, that is passing away – and we need to remember that, because it is not offering general advice about platonic friendships. But he is saying again that the distractions of single life are fewer than for the married.

Finally in vv. 39–40 we have reached the end of the chapter. He deals with those who have been bereaved, and he says that when your partner dies you are free to marry whom you wish. There is no biblical reason whatsoever against re-marriage after death, but again, true to type, Paul is saying: I think you could be happier if you remain single and give yourself to the Lord's work. I thank God for widows who do this. It presupposes a deep love for the Lord, and if it is not there, they can't just step into this. But widows can do so much in giving their whole devotion to God's family when they are left alone.

There has been a lot of debate on these issues through the ages. Looking at the Roman Catholic position, about a thousand years ago priests were ordered by the Pope to be celibate. The early popes and priests were married, but later ones were celibate. The reason for that was very simple in the beginning, in case you don't know. It was because priests were handing on their parishes to their own sons as an inheritance and the sons were not proving to be very good priests, so the Pope stopped that practice, forbade the priests to marry and therefore he could then put the priests into the parish. That is why that started, not for any other reason.

Alas, now we have got to the position where the celibate state is considered very much higher than the other which has somehow given the idea that sin is spelt "sex" and if you ask the priest about the confessions he gets there is a preoccupation with that, and I think that the celibacy of the priesthood has fostered this idea that there is something dirty about sex all the time. But Protestants have gone to the opposite extreme and accepted the world's view that marriage is the best of all and hard luck if you are single. Now I don't think that is putting it too strongly. Whereas Paul, I think, gives the right balance.

RELATIONSHIPS
Read 1 Corinthians 8

A. CONCEITED BEARING (1–3)
1. KNOWLEDGE PUFFS UP – SELF
2. LOVE BUILDS UP – OTHERS

B. CONVINCED BELIEF (7–8)
1. MANY GODS, MANY LORDS
2. ONE GOD, ONE LORD

C. CONSIDERATE BEHAVIOUR (9–13)
1. YOUR LIBERTY ABUSED
2. THEIR CONSCIENCE WOUNDED

At first sight this chapter seems utterly remote from my daily life. For one thing, I haven't had any personal experience of idols. In ancient Greece they had statues and altars at every street corner. There are legacies of old superstitions which go back to the idolatry that used to exist in England. If you have any truck at all with these superstitions you are just going back to the ancient idolatry from which your great-great-grandfathers were rescued by the preaching of the Christian gospel. There is, incidentally, a very sound physical reason for not walking under ladders. But you can soon tell if you are superstitious. If you are superstitious you will worry about it after you have got through safely. Whereas the sound reason will just make you look up before you go through. It is astonishing how many people are so superstitious: wearing "charms" is coming back, and some people foolishly or ignorantly hope that by "touching wood" they will keep better this week.

Idols are ugly things carved out of stone, metal and wood – in the Greek and Roman world there they were and people wouldn't dream of going past them. They would bow. They would offer an animal in sacrifice. They took notice of the gods, and the problem was there were so many of them. Life is terribly complicated and confusing when there are lots of gods around. You are never quite sure if you prayed to the right one that morning.

It is a complicated, insecure, fearful life that you live when you are in what is called a polytheistic (many gods) society. So you have one for Monday, one for Tuesday, one for the garden, one for the kitchen, one for your health, one for the children, one for grandma, and it goes on like this. It really is an appalling situation. But when you have been in the grip of superstition, when you have been in the grip of gods, when you have been in the grip of pagan practices it is not something to laugh at. It is deadly serious. But most of us in this country have been brought up in what is called a monotheistic culture. We might have asked each other, "Do you believe in God?" A Hindu would say straight away, "Which one?" But in the past it was assumed that you either believe in one God, or none at all, or that you were an agnostic – in the "don't know" group.

Pagan idolatry permeated every meal they had. Thank God when someone's Christianity permeates even every meal they have. That is one of the reasons for saying grace – that your religion might not be locked up in Sundays and in Holy Communion as the only sacred meal, but that your faith might go into every part of your life. The pagans let their religion and their life intermingle and so there were real problems for the early Christians in relation to social etiquette.

Let me try to paint the picture. When you sacrificed an

animal – say a sheep – to one of your favourite gods in Greece, you only let the god have a little bit of the carcass, and the bits you didn't want usually, and then you proudly carried home the rest of it. That was for you. That is what would appear on your table. Then, when you began your meal, you would thank the god or gods for letting you have this bit of the carcass, even though the god had no choice. Furthermore, if your civic body or your tradesman's guild held a dinner it was always held at a temple, and the meat was brought from the altar to the table. It was all mixed up with the gods. Therein rose the problem. How could a Christian who had finished with idolatry have a meal with pagans, knowing that the meat had been associated with such practices? It may seem a strange problem to you, but if you have been involved in something unholy like that then you don't want to have anything more to do with it. Once you have been set free from it, there is a kind of revulsion in touching anything to do with it again. Let me give you one or two illustrations of practical experiences today in which a material object has to me had unpleasant associations that have made me hesitate to have anything to do with it.

Once I had to go to Norway at very short notice and I needed some Norwegian money. So I went to a particular place in Newcastle-upon-Tyne and asked if they could get me some Norwegian currency and the man behind the counter said, "I'm sorry, I can't get it for you quickly." Then he said, "Hold on a moment. Just stay there," and a blonde woman came up to the counter and put a pile of Norwegian notes on it. The clerk said, "Here you are, you're saved – by that woman who has just gone out. She's a one, she is, she works the Quayside down here. She really gets it out of those Norwegian sailors. Here's your money." Somehow I had a moment of revulsion and thought I would much rather wait a few days and get some money another way. Yet if you knew what the money in your church collection plate had done, you might have the same feeling.

Let me come a little more directly to something nearer idolatry. I remember a lady coming to see me in church some years ago and she said, "I want to show you something." She pulled out of her pocket an intricately worked brooch. She said, "Here, hold it", and as soon as I took hold of it I knew that it was part of a pagan religion, that in fact it had been used to contact evil spirits. Don't ask me how I knew, but I knew. So it turned out to be. Somehow the very associations of what was just a piece of metal to me had a repulsive effect. I didn't want to handle it. I gave it straight back to her. I said, "I know what that has been used for." And it had.

This was the problem. When a Christian was invited by the pagan neighbours, the pagan used to say grace and prayed to and thanked their deity, then would ask, "How much meat would you like?" and the Christians had a funny feeling: that is idolatrous meat. The Corinthian church was completely divided over this question. They had argued about it and there were two groups: the "stricts" and the "liberals". The strict Christian said, "No compromise. You must never eat meat offered to idols. If you do that, you are dabbling in things that you don't understand. You are compromising. You must cut it right out." Those were the "stricts". But the liberals on the other hand talked like this: "We have further knowledge. We know that these idols are just blocks of wood. They can't do anything to you or anyone else." So an "enlightened" Christian had a knowledge of these things and was able to take it and just laugh at it. In other words, it didn't affect them at all. So they wrote to Paul and asked, "Which of us is right?" They wouldn't have asked him if they hadn't been arguing about it. So the question was posed: Should we keep right off these things because of their associations, or with our superior enlightenment may we freely eat the meat without being spiritually affected at all?"

Paul wrote back and said, "You are both wrong" – typical Paul – and he told them both where they were wrong and, as he told them, he laid down a guide for Christian behaviour which is as relevant today as ever it was. This will help you to sort out problems of Sunday observance, problems of entertainment, problems of drinking alcohol – all these problems of personal behaviour, many of which are tied up with social behaviour, and the way people around you conduct themselves. Let us look at what he says.

The first thing he talks about is in vv. 1–3, and incidentally I can't help noticing that all his remarks are addressed to the liberal group, not the "strict" group. He goes for those who say they have got knowledge and are enlightened and are educated and have a grown-up attitude to these things. He says: first of all I don't like your attitudes. There is one problem with being enlightened. You may be absolutely right in theory, but in practice you are wrong in attitude, because if you say you have superior knowledge it is not easy to deny yourself the pleasure of feeling superior, of saying, "These poor people who can't handle these things; these poor Christians who get all these quibbles and can't do this and can't do that – they are narrow-minded. We are broad-minded Christians. We are mature. We are enlightened. We can eat this meat and it doesn't affect us. Look!"

Paul says that knowledge puffs up, but love builds up, and there is a whole world of meaning in those two attitudes. The thing that must govern Christian behaviour is not knowledge but love. That is the important thing. You may have thought this through. You may have thought it through to the extent where you can do it quite happily and it doesn't affect you at all. But that is not what should decide whether you do it or not. What is the contrast between puffing up and building up? First of all, puffing up is quick but building up is slow.

There are some structures which can simply be inflated with an air pump, and that is fast, unlike the construction of a solid building. Secondly, what is puffed up will not last, whereas what is built up will last. Thirdly, what is puffed up is hollow, and what is built up is solid. The man who has puffed himself up with pride and superior knowledge is hollow, but the man who is built up in love is solid. The fourth difference: a man who is puffed up is concerned with himself, a man who builds up is concerned with other people. If you really love then you want to build others up. If you are proud you puff yourself up.

So Paul is teaching that you may be utterly correct in logic, you may be free, you may not be touched by eating meat offered to idols, but that is not the crucial question. That is only likely to make you proud of being mature and modern and free and enlightened so you can handle these things. Love goes back to where the weaker brother is, and seeks to build him up too.

The next thing Paul says in verses 4–6 is that conceited bearing is out. So that is the first thing that is said to the liberals. You are a bit too proud of being mature. That's out. Secondly, he says convinced belief is part of the question and he then goes to the belief that is most important. "We know that no idol is real. It's just a block of wood." As Isaiah said, laughing at the pagans, "There's a dear old man. He chops the log in half and he burns one half on the fire and makes a god with the other half and says, 'Help me, help me.'" It is ridiculous. We know that. We know that there is no god but God. That there is only one God and only one way to God – Jesus.

It is more and more difficult to believe that in these days. More and more difficult because we are now living in a more relativist day when people say, "All religions are right, as long as you are sincere; everybody is right; we are all worshipping the same God; we're all heading for the same sea, like rivers finding their way through the fields." But there is only one God and only one way to God, and that is what we believe. We are convinced of this. No other god is real. Allah is not real. Buddha is not real. There is no God but the Father of our Lord Jesus Christ. We come *from* God. We are made *for* God. There is only one Jesus, one Lord *through* whom this all happened. Notice the little words: from; for; through. That is our convinced belief. Nothing will be able to shake us from this. But even that knowledge doesn't decide the issue. Let us now come to the real point: conceited bearing is out. Convinced belief must be there but it is not a deciding factor. The real factor is this: considered behaviour towards other people.

Truth by itself is not enough to tell me what to do in a given situation. Unless I am on a desert island by myself I am not free to say: "This doesn't harm me, so I can do it". Now this is very important. A Christian is not free to do something that does him no harm. I am part of a church. And I am part of a fellowship where there are other Christians to whom this would do harm, whose consciences are not as strong or enlightened or as mature as mine may be. What we are saying is that truth and love must together decide what I do. It is not enough to say: "There is only one God and idols are unreal." Truth says that idols don't exist. Love says: "To my brother, idols do exist, and I must condition my behaviour by my brother rather than by me."

It is so easy in the Christian life to go for truth or love by themselves. I thought of a lovely little cliché: Love without truth softens into sentimentality; truth without love hardens into superiority. So I must ask not just what the truth is about this situation but what the love is about it too. What is the truth about it to others whom I love? It is quite clear that when I begin to think like that, my behaviour will certainly be more narrow than it would have been if I had simply said, "I can do it because it does not harm me." All the way down the line the Christian may have to live a much narrower, stricter life than he would if he were on his own, for the sake of other people.

Let me be quite specific: If there is an alcoholic connected with a Christian fellowship, nobody else in that fellowship is free to touch drink when meeting him or her – not because they can't handle it, and not because the Bible forbids drinking (it doesn't), but because the Bible forbids you to behave in a way that harms a weaker brother. And my liberty is going to be abused if I say I am free to do anything that does not harm me.

Paul now comes to the matter of food. He says that our diet has no connection with our devotions. Whether you eat meat offered to idols or not does not affect God. Food never commended anybody to God. Secondly, it doesn't affect you. You are no worse off if you don't eat it. You are no better off if you do.

Therefore the question remains: "Does it affect others?" My decision in this matter won't affect God one way or the other. It clearly won't affect me. I will be neither better nor worse. But it may affect somebody else, and that is the important principle. My liberty is a liberty to be free not to do a thing, if it will help my brother.

The kind of freedom people are clamouring for today is this: "I want to be free to do whatever I think is right and harmless to me." But real love says: "I am free not to do it." Let me tell you again that I am a total abstainer. I am free to be. Isn't that terrific to be free to be a total abstainer? Quite free – for the sake of others for whom it would be dangerous, to see my example.

Many people get into trouble through the example of others. In ordinary social events, I beg you if you are arranging a reception, allow the guests to be free not to drink. It is important. Otherwise, you are saying, "My freedom means that I am bound to do it. I have got to do it because I am free." That is not freedom.

Let us go a little further. We consider then how our behaviour is going to affect another. Here is a silly little illustration. Have you ever had a ride on a "Ghost Train"? I remember going as a boy from school to the biggest fair in the North of England in Newcastle, and I remember going on the Ghost Train. You sit in these little engines, a couple of you, and you go through a clacking door, and then there are shrieking noises and things sort of touch your face and the ghosts light up as you go around and you come out with your heart just going a little more quickly and you are glad to see daylight again. Now of course I was old enough when I went round to have a typical schoolboy's attitude. "Well, that was a string banging from the ceiling; and that's just fluorescent paint." In fact it didn't scare me one bit. But if I had taken a little child in there I could have given that child nightmares. It would be folly to take a small child in. If I had a little brother, I could have said, "Oh, but it's nothing to be frightened about. It's just a string hanging down and loudspeakers blaring. It doesn't harm anyone. Come on." But I should think, "It may harm this little child."

You may go to see a horror film and say, "Look at all the red paint being splashed around." But someone else is going to be hurt. Now Paul says that what we can do to a weaker brother is to damage his conscience, and he here lays down the principle that the conscience is a very real thing that God has placed within each of us, as God's own direct telephone communication with my will to let me know when I am on the straight and narrow and when I am going to either side.

During the early days of the war, they used to bring our bombers in to land on the old SPA system. They used to send out a radio beam in line with the runway, and as long as you were travelling in line with that beam everything was quiet in your headphones, but if you veered off to the right or the left there was a noise and you could get back on beam, and so you found your way home to land at the airfield.

In the same way, God has graciously given us this little thing inside us, a receiving set, a conscience which keeps quiet as long as we are in line with the destiny that we have, but as soon as we get off it there is a noise, there is discord, disharmony, guilt, shame and fear.

Here is the principle Paul lays down. Never over-ride your conscience with someone else's example. This is moral suicide. It is to defile the conscience and destroy it. If I go ahead and use my freedom and say, "Well, it doesn't harm me," a weaker brother may allow my example to over-ride his conscience and the thing that would cause him to feel uneasy and guilty and ashamed he would do because I did it. Therefore I am responsible in God's sight for wounding his conscience and making him shift from his conscience's guide to mine. And the one thing we must not do is to be each other's conscience. It is so easy to do this. But the New Testament again and again says that your conscience is for you, and someone else's is for him. Your conscience, if it is freer than his, must not wound his, otherwise you are going to teach this man to become a dog on a string and you are not going to let him develop his own conscience.

The Bible freely admits that a man's conscience is conditioned by his past. It says here that a man who has dabbled in idols will be conditioned by that in his conscience. He will be uneasy about eating a joint that has been offered to an idol. Therefore you become a vegetarian. That is what love would dictate.

So never stifle conscience. Let me give you an illustration. It is as if there is a big ship being steered under its own power with a rudder, and a pilot at the helm, and you come chugging up with your tug and you say, "It's alright. Just follow me. Throw the rope in, tie up, leave the wheel, leave the rudder. I'll pull you to port" – and so the ship is no longer under its own helm, it is simply being pulled along by the tug. Then the storm comes and there is no-one at the helm to guide the ship. For the pilot had left the wheel – no longer needed. The ship is at the mercy of the elements. That is the kind of little picture to tell you what would happen to a brother whose conscience you stifled by your example, so that he became simply pulled along by you. No pilot at the helm. Paul teaches what you would do if you did that. Firstly, you would undo the work of the Cross. Why did Jesus die? To give people a clear conscience – that they might appeal to God for a clear conscience. And here is someone for whom Jesus shed his blood to give him a clear conscience and your example has given him a guilty one. You have undone the work of the Cross in a brother for whom Christ died, and therefore, secondly, you have sinned against Christ. So in doing something that does me no harm, in doing something that is not a sin to me at all, I have sinned against Christ in my brother. No wonder Paul finishes up by saying this: I will be a vegetarian all my life rather than do that. I would rather live a narrow life giving up meat, than have someone say to me one day: "Well, I saw you do it so I thought it must be alright and I felt guilty afterwards." So that in a sense you gear Christian behaviour to the weaker Christian who has not yet matured.

Let me try and sum all this up. At the end of the book of Judges is a very sad text. The very last sentence after chaos, after idolatry, after immorality, after break-up of families, after murder, all kinds of horrible things: "Every man did what was right in his own eyes." That is the reason for the chaos. What a word that needs to be said in our own age when people proudly boast, "I did it my way"; "I did my thing." "I will decide what is right for me and let you decide what is right for you, and let us each do what is right for ourselves." Let every man do what is right in his own eyes and that is chaos. That doesn't build up, it puffs up.

What is the alternative then? What guides our behaviour? Two things should be considered whenever I am facing a moral issue: my own maturity and my brother's immaturity.

First of all, my own maturity. Have I really grown up? Am I really able to do this? There are three stages through which a Christian passes: excess; abstinence; moderation.

Before you are a Christian, you usually go to excess. When you become a Christian, Christ usually calls you to abstinence. When you mature, you can live in moderation. I will give you two practical illustrations. There was a dear lady in our former church called Miss Clark, a lovely simple, down-to-earth Christian soul, and one night I said, "Would you get up in church and give your testimony?" She said, "Yes, I will" and she got up, bless her, and in her testimony she said "I used to worship idols." You looked at this dear old lady and wondered what sort of idol she had. She continued: "My idols were babies. I was a nanny and I worshipped babies. They were my life. I idolised them. I gave my whole self to them. Then I became a Christian and the Lord took me away from being a nanny, and for four or five years I had no babies to look after at all." That was the abstinence period. She said, "I was converted in the Salvation Army, and I knew the Lord had to get me away from babies to get me to himself – and the Salvation Army asked me to take over an Army Home for orphans and the Lord gave me a whole house full of babies." Wasn't that lovely?

Let me give you another illustration of a young man who came to the Lord and told me that a football was his idol. He used to worship a little round thing! He gave himself to it.

Everything was given to it. Until things came to crisis. The big match was to be on Good Friday. He suddenly realised. Christ spoke to him through that and said, "Is it the football or me?" For some years that boy gave up football completely. Who dare say he was wrong? I think he was right. He gave his love wholly to the Lord. I saw him some time later and he said, "I am playing for Hastings next Thursday evening." I replied, "Good for you, Ken. You've come through to the third stage now." He said, "It won't be my god any more. Now I can pray about the football match and I can go into it."

Do you see the three stages? There is the stage where you gave yourself excessively to things and were bound up in them. Then the stage where you became a Christian and had to cut them right out so that you might have a honeymoon with the Lord and give yourself wholly to him; and then the stage when he lets you go back and with moderation fit it into place.

The first question when I am asking, "Should I do this or should I not?" is this: am I mature enough to do it or is this going back to my past? Am I going back to excess? It could be television. You could be a slave to television. If you are, then the best thing is to get rid of the set until you have reached the third stage and you can have it again. Excess, abstinence and then moderation.

Now comes the second issue: I must consider not only my own maturity – whether I can handle this properly – but I must consider my brother's immaturity. If he is still in the abstinence stage and I see his life and he sees my life, then I have no choice as a Christian but to do the abstinence with him. I must get alongside him as a stronger person goes back to help the weaker along, rather than leaving him floundering behind me because I kicked him out. I have no right whatever as a Christian to do something which is harmless to me if it is harmful to him. The world will tell you that you are narrow and it is so easy to want to impress the world with the fact that as a Christian you are broad-minded and mature and you can handle all these things properly, but God looks at your brother, your fellow-Christian. He says: Go back and help him. Cut it out for his sake.

Let us go back to v. 11 – the Cross. Every problem at Corinth, Paul puts in the shadow of the Cross, and when he does, it looks so different. When they are arguing amongst themselves and saying, "I like this minister best," and, "I like that minister best," Paul says, "Was this minister crucified for you?" Get back to the Cross. Where people say, "We have knowledge; it doesn't harm us; we can eat these things; we are enlightened, mature, grown-up Christians," Paul says: "Get back to the Cross." What do you find at the Cross? Do you find that Jesus said, "I am free to live"? No, you find that Jesus said, "I am free to lay down my life. I am free to give up my life."

Talk of "I'm mature" and "I can handle this" and "I'm free to do it and let the church members say what they think" shrivels up at the foot of the Cross and you begin to realise that truth is not what decides behaviour but truth and love, and therefore your consideration is for the weaker brother.

PAUL'S MINISTRY

Read 1 Corinthians 9

A. HIS MOTIVES: no self-interest (1–18)
 1. RIGHT
 2. RENUNCIATION
 3. REWARD

B. HIS METHODS: no self-righteousness (19–22)
 1. SERVICE
 2. SYMPATHY
 3. SHARING

C. HIS MORALS: no self-indulgence (23–27)
 1. DETERMINATION
 2. DISCIPLINE
 3. DREAD

Paul talks a lot about himself in this chapter, though he said he would only preach "Jesus Christ and him crucified". Also he speaks of preaching as a job. Why? There are many surprising things here and he says, "I'm not going to let anyone stop me boasting."

Paul now gives an example from his own life. His position was that of one of Christ's apostles. They decided the doctrine of the church, they began the church; the apostles' teaching is continued to this day. An apostle has seen Jesus with his eyes – after the resurrection. Paul had authority, rights and position. His proof is what happened when he came to preach to them. God honoured his apostleship. That gave him a right to have finance from them, based on a principle that runs right through life, that labour deserves a living. Therefore an apostle has a right to a living wage for himself and his family from the church. We can't have people opting out. Soldiers, market gardeners and others are paid and apostles were in spiritual service. God thinks of all who work – that is a principle which runs right through. If I work to give you spiritual food, is it too much to expect you to give me physical food for myself and my family? Paul observes that those who work in the temple get their meals from the offerings brought there. Jesus said that the labourer is worthy of his hire.

Nevertheless Paul says that he has renounced that right. Simon Peter didn't and nor did all the other apostles. Paul was the only one – and he did not imply that the other apostles were inferior. It is always open to someone to live without pay, but that doesn't make them more spiritual or more Christian. It is simply that God has called them to live in a different way. He may call one to be a pastor on a salary and another to be a pastor without one.

Paul says, "I am not asking for money from you. I don't want it." Since he had renounced the right, he felt free to talk about it, and he supports Simon Peter for supporting a wife. Incidentally, Paul hadn't a family, which meant he was free to renounce his right.

There were two reasons. Firstly, there was no obstacle to the gospel. In Greece, lecturers spoke, then took an offering. With that background, he renounced the right to avoid misconception. Billy Graham, when he came to Britain, never took any money here. He took a normal salary of a minister in the USA, but not more.

Secondly, renouncing this right gave Paul pride in his work. "I would rather die than have you take my pride away." Is this right? I believe every Christian should have pride in his work. How? By voluntarily doing extra that is not expected – beyond what is needed.

Preaching is not a voluntary thing. I can't boast about

preaching. God told me to do it. If I didn't preach, God would curse me. "Woe is me...." Why am I in it? I couldn't stay out of it. I have to do it. Think of what you need not do – that is the area at which your pride in your work will count.

What is the reward? It is to have no reward! It is a joy to do something for nothing – but also I am able to leave people with the right impression, namely that God's grace is free. It is a tragedy that so often the church gives the impression that we are always wanting to get something from someone. (Christian Aid – "calling back for the envelope"?) "Come to our cake sale ... our church fete – we want to see your purse too." It is one of the reasons I decided early on in a church where I ministered never to take the fees for weddings or funerals. I wanted them to feel I was there to serve and to give. Go out giving – serve them free of charge. Paul said it with his life as well as his lips: I am here to give, not to get. He is quite frank about this, and "it is more blessed to give than to receive."

The reverse of all this is that Paul actually became more free because he had renounced his rights! How? No-one is his boss. No man has a claim on his life. Jesus taught this: the more you renounce your rights, the more free you are. The less claim anybody has on you. Now this is the opposite of the world's thinking, which is: protest, claim your rights, march for your rights. Paul is saying: "I am self-employed. I am nobody's servant. I will not let anyone hire me. Therefore I have made everybody my boss." Let us think this through. "I am nobody's servant. Therefore I became everybody's slave." At the beck and call of everybody. Most think of freedom as freedom from others for self. Paul is teaching that real freedom is *from* self, *for* others. Nothing could be a greater contrast than between the world's idea of freedom and Christ's. Freedom to become a slave, to become everybody's slave. Elsewhere, the advice is that if you are a slave and can buy your freedom, get it. Now Paul is saying he is a free man, so he is becoming a slave. How? By letting other people decide his manner of living – by changing his life according to the company he is in. We are now on thin ice. Real freedom is to be free to be what other people are. Why? In order to *win* them. You must get alongside first. You are free to behave as they behave, except in sin.

He then illustrates how he does this. A slave has to fit in with the way of life of others, to behave as the people in the house behave, to do what the people want him to do. And we are called to be everybody's slave. It is the most difficult thing in the world for a Christian to do.

With the Jews, I observe the Sabbath, I eat kosher meat, I do all that they do. I want to win them for Christ. When I am with the Gentiles, I ignore the Sabbath, I ignore kosher meat, I will eat anything. I get alongside them.

Now let me speak to my own heart and yours. We Christians are bad at social life with people who are not Christians. We much prefer social life among ourselves where everything is just as we have been brought up with and we can behave the same. Paul is saying that if you are going to win people you will have to get out of that rut. You must learn to love freely and socially in situations where you don't feel at home, where you don't feel at ease. Learn to be adaptable to win people for Christ.

I was an RAF chaplain, having gone into that from a sheltered minister's life. I remember having to go to cocktail parties, which I loathed, but I got alongside some of the officers. I also remember a Flight Sergeant (a Christian) drilling me up and down, giving me orders to help me as I was sloppy on the parade ground. He came along one night, we drew the curtains, and he drilled me! We had to reverse roles. Why? He was saluting me one day, marching me up and down the next! The answer was that we were trying to get alongside people that we might win them. Funnily enough, on parade, though I was a Squadron Leader I saluted a Warrant Officer! I won more friends that way!

What is Paul saying? I am ready to adjust my behaviour. I won't sin for anybody but I will go as far as I can without sinning. I will change my way of life, my social habits, if I can get through to people. May God grant us this adaptability. A Pharisee would say, "I thank you that I am different. I don't go to these things. I don't mix." They said of Jesus he was a glutton and a winebibber. Paul teaches us to renounce our rights to be different. Be free to be like others. Again, it is the opposite of the world's view. Paul tells us that real freedom is freedom to conform and get alongside people and win them for Christ. Why? To share in the blessings of the gospel. It is an incentive. The ploughman ploughs in the hope of sharing in the crop and the preacher preaches in the hope of sharing the blessing of people coming to Christ.

He changes the picture now from the world of employment and slavery to the world of sport. The Isthmian games was second only to the Olympic games. Look at an athlete who deliberately limits his liberty for the sake of a prize. Entering a race doesn't give you a prize. All the Christians running the Christian race won't get prizes. Only those who run well. Those who win the game. As soon as you become a Christian you are "in the race". Run as though you are determined to obtain the prize. We are not in Alice's Wonderland where everybody wins and everybody gets the prize. We are running in a race that is not competitive but in which there is a prize only for those who make it – who run well. It is the prize of the honour of being recognised by Christ as a good runner.

In the Greek games they would train for a year before a race. During that year the discipline was such that they cut out not only bad and harmful practices but good things.

You can't win a race unless you are prepared to cut out good things as well as bad – unless you are prepared to watch others having their food and refuse yours. The discipline of an athlete in training must be continuous and complete. It is no use having a week off to indulge. He would undo months of training. The discipline must be over every area of his life. He must cut out all that holds him back, even good things, denying himself things that others have a right to, if he is going to win the race. Paul says: limit your liberty as an athlete who is cutting out even good things in order to get a prize. It is tough. It is hard. Paul says: I do it. It is no good playing at it. Shadow boxing is no use. Literally, your body is a good servant but a bad master. He says: "I punch my body". It is the body he has to deal with. It is the body's desires so often that cause the old fight between the pillow and prayer, the blanket and the Bible. It is the body that needs to be pummelled and here he comes to his one great fear: "... lest I be disqualified from running".

I remember one of my most embarrassing moments when I was about ten. It was a race in which all the form had to compete in a school Sports Day, and it was a long race. The Lord never blessed me as a runner. He blessed me with flat feet and while I can catch a bus as well as anybody on a short sprint, on the long hard grind I am no good at all. I was one of the smallest in the class. They passed me on the second time around. The P.E. teacher finally patted me and said, "I think it would be best if you went and sat down and watched the others." In front of all the parents and staff I had to go and sit down! Most humiliating.

A Christian will limit his liberty, stop thinking of his own rights and, for the sake of others, deny himself the things he has every right to have.

A challenging missionary book is: *Have we no right?* – to a home of our own, to have chosen furniture, to have children at a good school, to stay in our own country and choose where we live? Have we no right? The answer is no. The Christian has no rights at all.

Paul is teaching them: I am an apostle. Have I not seen the Lord Jesus? Yet if you study my motives there is no self-interest in them. If you study my method there is no self-righteousness, being different from other people. If you study my morals, there is no self-indulgence, and if I can forgo my rights, then so can you at Corinth.

DIET AND GENDER
Read 1 Corinthians 10:1–11:16

A. FOOD AND DRINK (10:1–33)
 1. HISTORIC CALAMITY (1–5)
   a. Protection – cloud and sea
   b. Provision – food and drink
 2. HUMAN CONDITION (6–13)
   a. Paganism – idolatry and immorality
   b. Pettiness – dubious and discontent
 3. HOLY COMMUNION (14–22)
   a. Participation – body and blood
   b. Partnership – idols and demons
 4. HEALTHY CONTACTS (23–33)
   a. Principle – feast and fast
   b. Practice – stumbling and salvation

B. MALE AND FEMALE (11:1-16)
 1. FEMININE: glory of man
   a. Long hair
   b. Covered head
 2. MASCULINE
   a. Short hair
   b. Uncovered head

There are some misunderstandings about Christianity that are very difficult to remove. One is that eternal life comes as a reward for doing good. Many say, "I have never done anyone any harm; I've tried to do my best" – and it reveals that they have never understood that eternal life is a free gift. A man can be saved on his deathbed after a lifetime of selfishness and sin and he can get to heaven because God in his mercy loves to give everlasting life, quite free, to anybody who believes in Jesus. In our pride, we would rather work our passage to heaven – a bit like George Bernard Shaw who said, "Forgiveness is a beggar's refuge. I don't want anybody paying for my sins. I'll pay for my own."

Another misunderstanding is this: that once you have been given eternal life, it doesn't matter how you live. Now some start well, but don't finish well. They begin and then something goes wrong. Paul illustrates it from the Old Testament. When a Christian reads about the Jews, he finds Christ in it all. Paul goes back to the Exodus, how two and a half million people escaped from chains. It is the biggest escape there has ever been in history. They were out of slavery, even though their masters were after their blood. They had no money, no army, no weapons. They didn't even fight. They got trapped, surrounded by the mountains, the Egyptians, the desert and the sea. God then showed them what he could do! He used water. Water in the atmosphere formed a thick cloud. It enveloped them and hid them. They got through the Red Sea. It was Moses whose faith led them forward. Can you see envelopes in the cloud and the sea – God's water? They were going through what we would call a baptism. They were being baptised into Moses, the leader of God's choice.

That was one problem behind them. Now came the problem of survival. The Sinai desert is a dreadful place to live in. In modern times the Egyptian army were trapped there and within three days they were dying of hunger and thirst. God gave the Hebrews tons of bread six days a week and twice as much on the day before the Sabbath. It amounts to thousands of tons, to feed those people for forty years. There was a big problem of water. There were a few springs, some of them bitter and they cannot be touched. God gave them water from dry rock wherever they went. Moses touched a rock and there was water until they got the feeling that this Rock was following them.

Paul is teaching: I want you to see in this a person who has been baptised and is having bread and wine at the Lord's table, and that God baptised them into Moses and fed and watered them through Moses to keep them going. All experienced this and it all came from Jesus Christ, the Rock, the provider.

With most of them God was not pleased. Most failed to reach the land of promise. Classic understatement of the Bible. Only two got in. The trail was marked by grave mounds all the way – in one place, 23,000 graves. They had set out with great hopes. Chains were off. They were free, yet all but two finished buried in the desert. They never knew the blessings God had for them. Why? Because they were not pleased with him. There was discontent – grumbling, complaining. They had left bondage (and security, and an interesting diet and life) and they had monotony, scenery, food, sky.

How many Christians *start* to believe? Where are they now? Buried in some wilderness? Why? The wilderness is a miserable place. Meet a Christian who grumbles – they are in the wilderness. A Christian doesn't grumble if he is through to the land of God's promises. The grumbling is so deadly. This historic calamity is a human condition, a common thing. Take the warning from it. What displeased God? Why from such high hopes did they become such miserable people? There were three reasons, of which two belonged to the country they had left: idolatry and immorality. Why did they make an idol – the golden calf? They wanted a god they could see, they didn't like God as he was – they saw him as too holy, too narrow. They wanted to make a god they could like. Thirdly, they couldn't hurry God. It is a common weakness of human nature that we can't wait. Weeks to dictate Ten Commandments! One of the besetting sins of this age is wanting everything right now. Jesus told the

145

apostles to wait for Pentecost. Those who wait for the Lord renew their strength. They could push a golden calf along quite quickly. Sexual undertones fitted in with their desire, wanting to make god in their own image. They succeeded. Having been baptised into Moses, they said, "We don't want him. We'll have Aaron and a new god."

The second thing followed quickly. If you get a wrong idea of God, you get a wrong idea of life. If you start switching about his character with your own images, you will start switching about your behaviour: orgies, all kinds of nameless things. God was cross with them. Baptised, fed, watered, and now they chose someone else.

They also wanted proof from God that he was still with them. They wanted to put God to the test, push him to the brink to see how far they could go with him. "You shall not tempt the Lord your God." God never tempts you. Don't you tempt him. Don't put God on the spot. It was unbelief.

Fourthly – plain grumbling. Their diet wasn't as spicy as when they were slaves. This dry, white flaky stuff, wasn't very tasty. There are Christians who find the Bible less interesting than the spicy novels they used to read. There is a going back in imagination to Egypt.

I believe very few things spoil the Lord's work as much as grumbling. We would be horrified at blatant sins in our midst, but what about grumbling about things not to our liking? The more people have, the more they grumble. Those who have a simple way of life are more content. This atmosphere is around us and penetrates our Christian life so that if something isn't exactly to our taste, then we grumble. It is damaging to the cause of God. God was as angry with grumbling as he was with idolatry, as angry with complaining as he was with immorality. God's perspective! What can stop you getting into the land of promise? Any one of these things can bring your pilgrimage to a dead stop.

Now comes one of the loveliest promises in the Bible. When we think about temptation to idolatry, immorality, scepticism or grumbling, firstly, never think that you are above temptation. Let him who thinks he stands take heed, lest he fall. You will not be safe until someone pronounces over you: "Dust to dust, ashes to ashes...." The devil can get you until your last breath. No temptation will ever come to me that other people haven't faced. Secondly, never believe that you must go under it. Why not? God in his mercy will never let you be pushed too far. He does not promise to remove temptation. It is a shattering thing when as a Christian you have your first real temptation. You thought you were finished with sin and temptation. God will allow it. He wants you to grow up. It is part of the race for which discipline is needed. He wants you to get that prize. So he won't let you be tempted above what you can bear. He will always provide for you a way of escape. That is a vivid word. It implies you are trapped in a deep valley and the army of Satan is at the end of it. The "way of escape" is a Greek word that means a hidden mountain path up over the peaks that will get you up over the valley. It means a tough climb but it means a way out. Whatever temptation, whatever moral difficulty you are in, bear in mind that God has a way out for you. All those Hebrews had a way out. If only they had looked for it and said, "God, we are trapped. Show us how to get out" – but they didn't and they fell.

Paul goes straight on to talk about the Lord's Supper. Why? Because you can't mix this act of eating and drinking with the kind of thing they were doing in the wilderness. They were eating supernatural food and drink and they were grumbling, complaining, making idols, being immoral. You can't eat God's food and drink God's drink and play about with this.

Paul nearly always brings you to the Cross to answer your

problems. Was Paul crucified for you? Don't you know you were bought with a price? Don't you know he is a brother for whom Christ died? It is all about the Cross. At the Lord's table we think about a body that is broken and blood that was shed. This is the point at which the Cross enters your life. Look at the Cross and say, "How can I mix that with these other things?"

A minister said, "I was handling a piece of white bread and I noticed my fingers were all brown (through smoking). It struck me my body is a temple of the Holy Spirit and I can't get it clean now." So he stopped smoking.

How can you take the food and drink that God supplies and go back to Egypt in your imagination? Just as the Israelites were eating that bread and drinking that water, when you eat that bread and drink that wine you are in touch with Jesus.

There are two extreme attitudes to the Lord's Supper. You find in the Catholic churches the view that at some point in the service suddenly the bread and wine is changed. You find in Baptist churches that these are merely symbols, that it is just a memorial, that we are only remembering through a symbol something that happened long ago. Listen! That bread which we break, is it not a participation in the body of Christ? – something much deeper than a memorial.

It is not magical and it is not a memorial. It is something in between. It is very real, and as that bread touches your lips, Christ touches you. It is a participation. That cup of blessing which we bless, is it not a participation in the blood of Christ? You will be in contact with the body and blood of Christ when you take this bread and wine.

As the Jews were in contact with Christ in the wilderness, how then can we touch these other things at the same time? Dabble with idols and take this? Paul says, "I know that idols are nothing. They are just lumps of wood and stone. But behind the idols are evil spirits, demons, and if you take a meal in the presence of demons, you participate with them."

Children sometimes dabble with things (like ouija boards) that could bring them through to demons. Did you think that horoscopes are just a bit of fun? Behind them are evil spirits seeking to get a grip on you. You cannot take the bread and wine and then read your horoscope tomorrow. You can't play around with spiritism and take that bread and wine. It is idolatry.

Next, consider immorality. Two things were happening. Firstly, they were having sexual relations outside marriage. We know that is wrong, but what made God angry about it was not just that it was happening outside marriage but it was happening with people who didn't belong to the people of God. For a Christian to marry a non-Christian is fornication. It is to take the body of Christ and join the body of Christ to someone he is not married to. I cannot take that food and drink unless I belong wholly to Christ. To take bread and wine together means that you can never marry someone who is outside of Christ. God loves you, and his love is so strong that he is a jealous God. Jealousy is a good thing – to love your husband/wife enough to be jealous about them. It is not a consuming passion that destroys and hurts, but goes with the love that says, "You are mine and I will not share you with anyone else. You are mine and I am jealous for your love." Shall we provoke the Lord to jealousy?

If I am baptised into Jesus, if I feed on the bread and wine, then God says: You are mine, and you stay with me until I get you to the Promised Land. It may be tough here, monotonous or dry, but ahead is a land of milk and honey – glory. Leave Egypt, don't even think about it. Walk with me. I don't want to be jealous for you because my jealousy might harm you. My jealousy is stronger than you.

As the Hebrews were baptised in the cloud and the sea, and Moses gave them food and drink from God, you and

I are baptised into Jesus and he gives us supernatural food and drink from God. We are to come to the Lord's Supper determined that God will have all of us and that we will never share ourselves with anyone else but him.

We move on to the passage 10:19 – 11:16. I suppose that "freedom" is the most abused word today, so when a preacher says that when you become a Christian you are free, that will be misunderstood straight away. There will always be those who think that once you become a Christian you can do anything you like. Nothing could be further from the truth. The real truth is this: at last we are free to love God and to do anything *he* likes. That is great freedom. I am also free to love my neighbour, and therefore what I do will not be what I like but will always be conditioned by my love for God and my love for my neighbour. I am in a world full of people, and what I do affects them.

In this passage a new dimension enters into Paul's treatment of Christian liberty. Not only should you bear in mind the human beings all around you, but you should remember that we are also surrounded by spiritual beings. What I do has an effect on them, and what they do has an effect on me. This is a dimension of life many don't realise exists. The first man in space, Yuri Gagarin, landed back on earth. The reporters asked him, "What was it like?" He said, "I didn't see any angels up there," and they all laughed. But the angels saw Yuri Gagarin! Our behaviour is not only conditioned by the fact that other people are watching us, but there are spirits also who are witnesses of our lives.

There are two sorts of spirits in this universe, highly intelligent beings who are witnesses to your life. There are good spirits, generally referred to in the Bible by the word "angel", and there are evil spirits, generally referred to in the Bible by the word "demon". Demons and angels are to be taken very seriously. Because we are surrounded by them as well as by human beings, there are certain things a Christian is not free to do. Discussing whether women should wear hats when they go to church, Paul says, "because of angels" – because of the spiritual beings around – which puts the whole thing in a different perspective. So you are not choosing a hat to be seen by the choir, but choosing something because the angels are present when you worship. Yes, they do watch what goes on every Sunday. There is joy in heaven over one sinner who repents. So you can give the angels a great thrill if one person comes to Christ. The demons are watching too – for every opportunity they can find to get into your heart and confuse your faith, and destroy the good things that God has put in your life.

We start by considering the demons. Because this world is inhabited by evil spirits as well as human beings, there are certain things we have to watch. In the ancient Greek world was this matter of "meat offered to idols". You couldn't buy meat that hadn't been used in a pagan worship and used as part of a carcass offered to some pagan god. This raised real problems. Many of the social events of the day were held in the pagan temple and the meat was brought straight from the altar to the temple. What did you do? How did a Christian behave socially? We face this in other forms every day.

Paul teaches the Corinthian believers to distinguish between a sacred and a secular situation. I mean by that, one that is directly religious in a pagan way and one that is indirectly connected, and which is more a social occasion. If it is a directly spiritual occasion, then the Christian must have nothing to do with it at all.

Here are three of the things that a Christian cannot dabble in if he is going to stay with Christ. First, a Christian cannot mix in other religions. These are directly spiritual situations, and if a Christian tries to go and worship Christ and then worships "Allah" or goes along to a Buddhist shrine, then he will sooner or later arouse the jealousy of God. We cannot mix the religions. We must say this more and more clearly. Already the ecumenical urge has spread beyond the borders of Christianity and is establishing links with other religions, because, as the Bible predicts, there is a movement of Satan to bring all religions under one religious umbrella and call it a "world faith" (e.g. World Congress of Faiths, where Buddhists, Hindus, Christians and Jews all meet to see how much they have in common). No Christian can take the cup of the Lord and dabble in other religions. Secondly, no Christian can mix his faith with superstition. I hope you never say "touch wood", or get caught up in silly fears about "black cats" and "salt" and "Fridays" and "thirteen" and "broken mirrors", etc. Thirdly, the Christian cannot meddle or dabble in the occult and play around with white magic or black magic or spiritism or any such thing. Why? Because there are demons. I have already mentioned ouija boards. Playing around with getting in touch with spirits "on the other side".

A Christian cannot mix. Although there is nothing in a ouija board to be frightened of, and other religions are empty (because "Allah" does not exist, and the other gods do not exist, they are not real) and though it does not matter whether you throw salt over your shoulder or not or whether you read your horoscope, the real truth is that behind these nonentities, behind these "nothings" are demons who would give anything to get through to you. If you dabble and mix, then the demons will take you and sooner or later something will happen that will so grip you that you will become curious and you will want more and more. It will not satisfy.

I once gave a lecture on "spiritism". I knew as soon as I entered the room there was evil present and I discovered afterwards there were two ladies who were mediums who had come along. A spirit medium in Edinburgh reported to someone that I had given that lecture and the spirits had told her that something was going wrong. You see, there is nothing in these things but behind them are evil spirits.

A Christian must never dabble in spiritually pagan situations. God is jealous. He won't share you with the demons, and his jealousy can be terribly strong.

Now we come to the social contact. I once went to a home on a hot summer's day when I knew they had had a spiritist's seance. They offered me a glass of orange squash and I took it. As I did so, I had the thought: I wonder if they used this glass last night on the table? Then I remembered how Paul taught: "Don't raise questions like that. Don't fuss." This is not a direct seance. You are not involved in a pagan ritual. This is something that may have been used for that, but you are entirely free to take the glass and drink the squash. It will do you no harm. Therefore we are not to raise questions about social contact. We are to leave that alone. Paul teaches that when you go to someone's house for dinner, don't ask where the crockery has been. Don't ask what it has been used for. Just take everything set before you and take it thankfully from God, because everything in the world belongs to God. That meat on the table (wherever it has been before) started with God and you can take it with thankfulness from him. Even if it has passed through a heathen temple on the way to the table, it started from God. So take it and say "grace" over it and take it thankfully.

But suppose, says Paul, the person who gives it to you says, "That is idol meat". Let me give you a modern illustration. Suppose you came to me with a gift for the church building fund and said, "I just won that in a lottery", you have raised the question of an issue of conscience. Paul would say: if the person who offers it to you raises it as an issue, don't touch it. This may sound a bit illogical to you, but the principle is consistent. If someone offers me a cheque simply as a gift, I will take it simply as a gift, in good faith. But if it is offered to me as having come from a source that is a contradiction to the principles of love to God and love of neighbour then I cannot take it. Why? For his conscience's sake, that he might never be able to say: "They took the money, knowing where it was from – fancy accepting that!" Say, "I don't want it" – that he might be enlightened and know that you stand for certain things.

So don't you raise the questions, but if they raise the questions, take the stand. You can apply that right through the problems of social contact. In other words, the main concern in all your contacts should be that God is thought well of, that God gets the glory, and you should adapt yourself according to that basic principle.

Therefore, whatever you have, say thank you for it. God put everything in the world for you to enjoy, and even if it has been misused and abused you can enjoy it, but if it is given to you as something that has been abused, then don't touch it.

Chapter 11 brings us to deep waters. Paul here claims the authority of an apostle. He says, "You imitate me, because I imitate Jesus" – not, "You imitate Jesus". Sometimes it is difficult for us to imagine what Christ would do in a certain circumstance. Look at the life of a man of God in those circumstances, and see how the Lord led him. Guidance can frequently come this way. Paul, having spoken of Christian liberty in such large terms, begins to be so pernickety about what people have on their heads in church. It looks almost a contradiction to say that in Christ we are free and suddenly to lay down the laws for what you wear. Surely Paul, you are more concerned about the state of the heart! God doesn't look at the outward appearance. His concern is with the heart, not with how we are dressed in church, but how we feel and whether our hearts love him. Paul is going to say that the angels look at our appearance, that it is important to them.

There have been numerous attempts to explain this chapter away and get rid of the rather uncomfortable teaching here. I have seen four attempts. Some suggest it is Paul's attitude to women again. If he had been happily married he wouldn't have dared to talk like this. (But Peter did, and he was happily married.) Paul did not have a neurotic attitude to the opposite sex. Paul had a very high view of women. It is Paul who said that in Christ there is neither male nor female, and that marriage is a mystery that will enable you to understand the love between Jesus and his church. Secondly, some have said that this is Paul's Jewish prejudice, that even today women sit in a gallery and the men sit on the main floor. But when Jews worship, the men always cover their heads. You go to a synagogue. You must take a hat with you if you are a man. Paul is here saying the exact opposite to what he was brought up to say as a Jew. So you cannot say it is a Jewish idea. Thirdly, some suggest that Paul just said this because of Corinth, a seaport city of loose morals, where women went around with their hair hanging down, and he was doing this for reasons of respectability in Corinth. But Paul says, "We have no other practice in all the churches", so it was universal. Fourth, some maintain that this was due to the Roman empire and the Greek culture, that it was necessary to show respect and reverence in this way, and that not to wear a head covering was irreverent. But all the Roman ladies and the Greek ladies used to go to the pagan temples without hats, and they didn't count it irreverent.

So this is a unique Christian teaching. It only arose with Christ. It was not only unique to Christians, it was universal among them. Therefore we must think again. For what reason does Paul go into these details about hair-do and headgear, when Christians worship? The reason he gives is nothing to do with Greek society, with Roman society, with morals then or at any other time, nor with Jewish background or his attitude to women. It is all summed up in v. 3 which is the real nub of the argument. If you have an argument about hats or hair-dos you are straining at gnats and swallowing the camel. The camel in this case is a fundamental principle, and if you don't accept this verse there is no point in going any further with the discussion. There is no point in even talking about what to wear in church, unless the verse is accepted as God's pattern for society for all time. Paul is laying down a basic principle that applies anywhere, everywhere, at all times and in all places: God never meant the human race to live in a democracy; he made men and women to live in a kingdom ruled over by himself. In every kingdom there is an order of control and this is the order: God is the head of Christ; Christ is the head of every man – so every man is to be subordinate to Christ. A man is the head of woman so women are to be subordinate to men. That is the big thing – not the bit about hair and hats. Do you believe that that is God's order for running society? If you do you will have no difficulty with the rest, but if you don't then you will have difficulty with God's ordained pattern.

This pattern "God, Christ, man, woman" is God's pattern for the family. It is God's pattern for the church. It is God's pattern for the whole of society. If we are in a society that is unhappy, or in a church that is unhappy, or if we are in a family that is unhappy, one of the first questions to ask is: Are we ordering our family according to the pattern of God? This implies no inferiority. Christ obeyed God the Father. Does that mean he was inferior? Never! He is God but he said, "I do nothing but what the Father tells me to do; I say nothing but what the Father gives me; not my will, but yours be done" – a beautiful relationship in which Christ didn't become inferior. He didn't become a slave except to serve all men. But God the Father told Christ what to do and he did it. Can anyone say that the pattern of relationship between Jesus Christ and God the Father is a bad one?

Yet now the Bible teaches that relationship is to be the same relationship between every man and Christ. Every man is to have the same relationship to Christ as Christ had to the Father – to let Christ tell him everything to do and everything to say and everywhere to go; to do nothing of his own will, but to do everything that Christ wills. That is the pattern for men. No man has the right or authority to talk about his authority over the woman until he is under the authority of Christ. It is offensive when man becomes a little dictator in his own home, or in the church or society, and is not under the direct command of Christ.

But now the third step. The relationship between Christ and God is to be the relationship between man and Christ and between the woman and the man – in social contact, in the church, in society, in the home. Does that mean the woman is inferior? No, of course not. There is a partnership between man and woman that is a beautifully balanced one in the scripture. Here it is. Woman came out of man originally and now every man has to come out of a woman which makes them dependent on each other. Neither can say: "I can live as if the other sex didn't exist." You can't. That doesn't mean that all live within the marriage relationship, but you cannot live socially without the opposite sex. We complement each other; we are partners; we help each other, but the relationship between us is to be characterised by the same submission of Christ to the Father, of man to Christ and woman to man. Therefore if a woman wants to know how to behave towards her man let her study the life of Christ and she will see the perfect pattern.

This cuts right across the world's idea of the relationship between the sexes. We live in a day when the Women's Liberation Movement is asking for things that are utterly contrary to 1 Corinthians 11. My question must therefore be: Who is going to decide how Christians behave? Universal suffrage outside or the Word of God inside? Do we let our minds become conformed to this world or transformed by the will of God which is perfect and good and right?

This means that Christians are going to behave differently from everybody else in the world and they will be criticised and commented on for doing so, but the church is to be in the world a little example, a picture of what God intended society and every family to be like.

We can apply this to men and women. When a woman becomes a Christian she doesn't cease to be a woman. Now that needs to be underlined. I know that in Christ there is neither male nor female, bond nor free, Jew nor Greek, for we are all one in Christ Jesus. But I know that when my wife and I married, because we are both Christians it doesn't mean that I can have children! She had our children. She is still a woman. If you start trying to behave as if when you became a Christian you lost your sex and you are no longer male or female, that is ridiculous. When God created mankind, he said: I am going to make man male and female. And when he redeems us he is re-creating the order that he intended at the beginning – the perfect relationship between the two.

How do you express outwardly your subordination to another? The answer is: a woman will do it by putting a hat on; a man will do it by taking his hat off. It is one of the differences. What would you think of a man who came to preach or lead worship wearing a trilby? Paul starts with the man, you notice. What do you do in the presence of someone whom you are to obey? Taking off your hat used to be the most natural thing to do in the presence of someone who is above you. That is why men leave their hats outside when they go to worship. It is an outward and visible sign of acknowledging the Lord's authority.

Now we come to the critical point. Paul says that if a woman takes part in the worship in prayer or prophecy (prayer – speaking to God on behalf of the congregation; prophecy – giving a word to the congregation on behalf of God), then let her do so with an open visible acknowledgement that she is not exerting authority over men. Let her make it quite clear to everybody else that she has no wish to usurp another's position.

Notice here that Paul allows for the possibility of women leading in worship in prayer and prophecy. It has always seemed strange to me that the groups of Christians who most insist on ladies wearing hats, insist on them keeping quiet in the services, which seems to me most illogical, but I would say, at the very least, a woman should show visibly when she leads in worship, either speaking to God for men, or speaking to men from God, that she is not exercising an authority over the men present. It is simply acknowledging that she has still her place in God's pattern for society.

Long hair, says Paul, is a prize for a woman. It is a disgrace to be shaven or shorn. During the Second World War, what happened to French women who collaborated with the German occupiers? Their heads were shaved – and it is a disgrace to take a woman's hair off. Paul takes this very deep natural instinct and he is saying: can't you see that nature says it? Nature gives a woman pride in a good head of hair. We are not going to argue about relative lengths. Nothing is laid down in the Bible about inches. I would say that the simple principle is that women's hair ought to be longer than men's. You can take that where you like.

The other side of the coin is that men's hair should be shorter than ladies. This is as nature intended. What would you think of a wedding in church when the bride came in without anything on her head and the husband in a top hat? It is not just social custom. Paul is saying that there is a deep instinct of nature here. You have got to suppress it deliberately if you don't observe it, because it is there naturally. The people who go against it have had to decide to go against it. There is something in them that has said: "I defy this convention."

Why "because of the angels"? In the pattern for society we have missed out one step. God, Christ, angels, men, women. The angels are above human beings in God's pattern for society. But there are angels who wish to usurp their position. Many have already done so. They did not want to be told what to do by God. Therefore they rebelled. And I take this phrase to mean that if women on earth deliberately flout the authority of God through men they are giving a shocking example to the angels to do the same. Angels can be influenced by our insubordination. Indeed we know already from the very beginning that woman, given to man to be his partner and help, was the one whom the evil angel went for. He said, "You decide to do this. Don't ask your husband. You do it and lead him along." That was the very first case of a hen-pecked husband, and I am afraid its results were disastrous.

Now the men. If the ladies were spoken to in some verses the men must be spoken to in others. What happens in a society without God? We see it happening in society around us. Let me be quite direct. A society with God in control is a society in which the men are masculine and the women are feminine, complementing each other. As soon as God goes from a society and his wrath takes the brakes off, first of all clothes and fashions go unisex and men and women begin to wear the same clothes. Unisex obliterates the difference. Clothes obliterate the change. The next step is: a change of clothes. Men begin to dress effeminately and wear embroidered blouses and necklaces and beads and carry handbags, and women begin to wear leather and boots and to look aggressive. They have changed over. This is a deliberate defiance of God's order. The point that Paul takes up here is the length of men's hair. It is at this point that you can reverse God's order and make yourself look effeminate by wearing hair longer than the ladies in your society, just as ladies can do the opposite.

What he is saying to the men is this: How long was Jesus' hair? Every Jew kept his hair cut, and relative to the ladies it was shorter than theirs. That is the important thing in society. You take your cue from the length that there is in society and men keep it shorter, ladies keep it longer if they are going to keep God's pattern. Jesus had cut hair. It was only certain people in the scripture who didn't cut their hair. John the Baptist was one. Samson was another. Jesus was not. He looked a man. He looked masculine. That is why Paul takes this up. It is unnatural and degrading for a man to have the hairstyle of a woman.

That doesn't mean we have to be dreadfully old-fashioned and odd, but it does mean that Christians have to achieve a very delicate balance here. Not being so "way-out" that people dismiss them as cranks, but giving an example to society of accepting what Paul taught in 1 Corinthians 11:3.

The devil is trying to smash God's pattern for society in every link in that chain. He tried to break it between Christ and God the Father and he used all the power of hell in the temptations to try to stop Christ obeying his Father, saying: Why don't you have the kingdoms; why don't you do this ... throw yourself off the pinnacle.... He was trying to break Christ's obedience to the Father. Jesus replied: There is only one God, and him only I am going to serve. So Satan, having tried to break the chain up there, is now trying to break it down here. The first thing he tries to do is break women's subordination to men – try to make them feel that they are inferior if they allow men to lead them. But I was thrilled to hear of a lady who was not married and was asked recently why she had never married. She said, "Because I have never met a man who could master me." That is tremendous when you think it through. She had learned something very deep about human relations. The devil loves the Women's Liberation Movement, on the march, fighting for what they call their rights. It is turning society upside down. But let me say this about men: the link that the devil has most succeeded in breaking is the one between every man and Christ. When you break that middle link, the others fall. The chain of God's command breaks, and society gets away from God. The tragedy is that men who no longer put themselves under Christ lack the authority to lead their womenfolk. And I go into house after house where the woman is the spiritual leader, the man tags along with her and he has abdicated his authority in God's sight because he is not wholly given to Christ. And the woman expresses herself the more strongly and the man – well, he is just not the leader under Christ.

The happiest homes, the families that are most integrated, are where the husband is under the authority of Christ and then the wife respects her husband and loves him and she has no hesitation about saying: "to love, honour and obey". Who wouldn't obey a man who does everything Christ tells him? This, then, is the pattern. Men, I beg you in the name of the man Jesus, accept his authority and exercise yours as a result. Be the leader, as God called you to be. Take the responsibility. Every husband should be a better and a stronger Christian than his wife, that he might lead her closer to the Lord and Saviour to whom he belongs.

That is his pattern and the devil just loves to see the wife a stronger Christian taking the lead, because he knows it is not fitting and it is not the right order. I am sorry if I have offended you, but I do want you to face v. 3. God is the head of Christ. Christ is the head of every man. Man is the head of woman. When we get back to that in our homes, churches and society I believe we will see peace and joy and love and all that God wants us to have.

HOLY COMMUNION
Read 1 Corinthians 11:17–34

A. SELFISH ABUSE (17–22)
1. DIVISIONS IN THE FELLOWSHIP
2. DRUNKENNESS AT THE FEAST

B. SACRED AUTHORITY (23–26)
1. DECLARATION OF THE COVENANT
2. DEMONSTRATION OF THE CROSS

C. SENSITIVE APPROACH (27–32)
1. DISCERNMENT OF THE BODY
2. DISCIPLINE OF THE BROTHERHOOD

Certain activities are essential to a healthy Christian life. Praying is one, Bible reading, regular churchgoing to worship, and taking the Lord's Supper are others, yet none of these things does you good automatically. Indeed, they could do you more harm than good. These things can do you spiritual damage. It is not whether or when but how and why you do them that matters.

You could come to the Lord's Supper in such a way that you are in a poorer state afterwards than you were before you came. Then it would be better for you not to have come. Paul deals with this subject here – he is telling them not just to do it but how to do it in a worthy manner, lest by doing it unworthily they do damage to themselves and to the church of Christ. Here is a shattering revelation of what went on at Corinth: at the Lord's Supper, people were drinking as much wine as possible (and it was clearly alcoholic for they were getting drunk at the Lord's own table).

But are there other ways of coming to his table that are just as bad? In vv. 17–22 Paul deals with the selfish abuse of this act, the kind of attitude that has me going to the Lord's table purely for what *I* can get. They were concerned with their own benefits rather than the fellowship of other people. If you come simply to have communion with God regardless of the others, then it would be better for you to take a little bread and wine at home and not go to church at all. We come not only to have communion with Christ but communion with Christians. This is an essential element. If you miss that, then you have failed to discern the body.

First, there is not a denomination in this country today that observes the Lord's table as the Lord intended it to be observed. We shall discover something delightful when we do, but in what way? The simple truth is that the breaking of bread and the drinking of wine is intended to be part of a normal full meal. The Lord's Supper should be a supper, and in fact the Greek word translated is nearer to our expression "evening dinner". It means the main meal, the big meal of the day after work to which you settle down, digesting the food at leisure afterwards. God grant that some day we may have the faith and the courage to step out of the tradition of centuries and say that we are going to do it as they did it in the Bible days.

It is obvious that when our Lord sat down in the Upper Room at the table, they sat down to a full meal, not just bread and wine. He gave them the broken bread at the beginning of the meal and after supper he gave them the wine. So you have the bread distributed, then a full meal, then the wine distributed.

That combined perfectly the spiritual and the social, and these must be kept together. Some churches have emphasised the social at the expense of the spiritual, and others the spiritual at the expense of the social. We have elevated the spiritual to be a purely religious rite. So people who have never had a meal together come and take bread and wine together. He intended them to take bread and wine together after they had eaten a meal together. Socially as well as spiritually they were one fellowship in him. It was a meal.

This was a common practice in those days, even outside the church. Most clubs, societies and guilds had what they called "fellowship meals". Every member simply brought some food and it was all pooled. To sandwich our social life with the spiritual dimension of the shadow of the cross gives the balance. Otherwise you could have communion with people you do not know, people with whom you have no fellowship.

The breaking of bread became increasingly a religious act or rite, and not as it was intended to be. It was meant to be deeply spiritual, but the kind of spirituality that invades the meal table. In scripture, the Lord's table is a table for a meal. Because it was a meal, it was more open to abuse. One could say that at least we avoid this dreadful abuse by not making it a meal, but we lose something very important in the Christian life by changing its character.

The abuses were these. Firstly, there were divisions. They developed little cliques, sitting at different tables. It would be catastrophic if, after doing it a few times, you noticed that all the people kept to little groups. Then Paul writes something and I do not know what it means: "I hear there are divisions among you, and I partly believe it for there must be factions among you in order that those who are genuine may be recognised" (see v. 19). It almost seems to be saying it is necessary to have divisions so that you can see what is true. I don't see why factions are necessary, but I do know that the false highlights the true. The "clique" makes it more obvious what true fellowship is. The false, the counterfeit always helps you to see the real more clearly. In a church with cliques that also means there are those who are genuine and loving everybody, and the contrast becomes obvious.

It was no longer "the Lord's table" but "Mr So-and-so's table" and "Mrs So-and-so's table" – a deadly thing. If you only mix with a few in the church, then I beg you to consider the word of the Lord here.

Another abuse was that they were grabbing all the food. That can be a real issue when we have meals together. It is possible for church people to rival one another in better and better refreshments. That is why there was a rule in the house groups of one particular church I knew of: one thing only to drink and one thing to eat. I know from bitter experience how in Lancashire we had a house group which began with a cup of tea, then something was added, then something else and then it became hot-pie supper, and it ended with a magnificent four or five course meal and no house group. It developed with each person trying to do better than the last. Paul said that some of the people were coming early and getting all the food and all the wine and making pigs of themselves. Paul is so sensible. Stay at home if that is how you are going to behave! They were humiliating those who had nothing to bring. Then and now, some could bring more food than others. Those who brought more were eating it as soon as they got there and not sharing, so others came and sat at an empty table, only receiving the bread and wine when it was handed round.

Paul points out that this is an abuse. When you come together, don't humiliate those who have nothing. Don't lay on such refreshments that those who cannot lay on that kind of food are embarrassed and wouldn't feel they could invite you to their house. Keep refreshments simple at church so that no-one says, "I could never invite someone to my house after that." To share together, consider one another.

Paul is saying: because of these abuses it is no longer the Lord's Supper, it is your supper. You have turned it from being his meal, at which he is the host, into being your meal. You are just out for what you get and this brings no glory to him.

There is a spiritual form of this selfishness. We have talked about the physical in which you are concerned about your stomach. But you can do this in the same way with your soul. If a much larger number start attending the Lord's Supper, I fear there may be some thinking, if not saying, "This is spoiling the atmosphere for me. It was nicer when there were fewer people. It wasn't so much rush to get the bread round and it was quieter and more reverent." But remember that everybody who attends is part of the body of Christ.

Why did the early church have the Lord's Supper? Was it simply an idea they picked up from the societies, clubs and trade guilds around? No – the reason is because the Lord Jesus commanded it. Paul said, "I pass on to you what I have received from the Lord himself...." Christ told us to have meals together; "... and day by day attending the temple together and breaking bread in their homes, they partook of food with glad and generous hearts." Scholars have argued as to whether breaking bread refers to the Lord's Supper or to an ordinary meal. No wonder they argue because the answer is: both. They broke bread in their homes and partook of food with thankfulness of heart – both together – because the Lord commanded it.

Verses 23–25 are the first known words of Jesus that were ever written down by anyone. Paul wrote this letter long before Mark wrote his Gospel, long before Matthew and Luke wrote their Gospels, and therefore we have here the very first account of the Lord's Supper ever to be committed to writing. Where did Paul get it from? Paul was not at the Last Supper. He tells us that he got it direct from the Lord.

No-one had told Paul what had happened that night. How did Paul write it down? The Lord told him what he did the night he was betrayed. We have here a direct revelation from Christ about the Lord's Supper. That was straight from heaven to Paul, not even through those who were at the last supper.

It is quite clear it was at a meal and meant to be at a meal. Have you noticed the words "as often as you drink it" – what do you think that means? Do this – "as often as you do it". Does that make sense if it just means "drink that little cup of wine as often as you drink that little cup of wine"? What he is saying is: whenever you have wine on the table, do this; whenever you have bread, do this. Whenever as a church you have a meal: do this. Which almost implies that whenever we sit down to refreshments in the church we should include bread and wine. Whenever you are together as a fellowship, sharing a meal, remember I am in the midst of you – do it till I come. I am taking this through to its logical conclusion. As often as you eat together as a church...! That would be revolutionary. We would be the first church in the world to do it, yet that is what he is saying here.

The first word that strikes me is – "The Lord Jesus on the night when he was betrayed...." Why that phrase? Was it just to date it as the night before he died? No. He is saying it was when men began to do their worst to him that he began to do this for them. It was when one of their own number was going to sell him for money that Jesus gave this lovely symbol. This should encourage anyone who feels that they are too bad to take the bread and the wine. Remember that even Judas was given the bread and the wine. It was the night in which Jesus was betrayed, when all the forces of evil were building up, when even his own follower was going to be caught up in the maelstrom of Satan's dreadful attack – that Jesus said: take this ... to remember me. It was in an atmosphere of human sin that this was given. One of the things we are not told in 1 Corinthians 11 is that you have to be perfect before you can take it. Let us get rid of that idea.

There is a lovely story of a woman who, when the minister held out the bread to her, said, "I cannot take it. I'm a sinner", and the minister said, "Take it woman, it's for sinners." This is the right way to approach the Lord's Supper. Jesus didn't say, "Let us wait until Judas has gone." He didn't say: "Because of all the dreadful things you are going to do to me ... You are all going to run away. I'm not giving you this." He said: "I know it all ... but take it", and that puts the setting right. You are going to let Christ down and so am I. Yet he holds out the bread and wine to us.

Talking of the bread, he says: "This – my body, for you." Two words in our English Bible that Jesus didn't say are: "is" and "broken". Normally we say: "This is my body which is broken for you". He said: "This. My Body. For you" – almost telegraphic, missing out words. It was so direct.

It is quite obvious that they would never think that the bread had miraculously changed into his physical body, because his physical body was still holding the bread. But what they would guess from the way he put this was that whenever they took the bread later, they would have contact with his body. They would receive it from his hand.

This I believe to be the real truth about the bread we break. It is not miraculously changed into his physical body, but as you take the bread you are taking bread that has been his body, in contact with his body, that will be to you the communion of his body, a real relationship with his body, not just a symbol but a sacrament in the deepest sense of that word. Consider those two words "for you". When you take the bread, just say to yourself "for me". He says: "to remember me". Who would forget Jesus? How could we possibly forget? It is not just to remember Jesus. You don't need such a reminder. You are among his people. You are in his body. You need reminding of his pain – for you. I remember when I went home for my mother's funeral and her body was lying in our house. I thought: "That was the body whose pain brought me into the world." You can forget your mother's pain at your birth. You can be so taken up with your mother's love, with her present relationship with you, that you forget what she went through to bring you into the world.

This is why Jesus gave us broken bread and poured wine: you won't forget Jesus, but you could in the joy of your present relationship with him, in the joy of all he is doing for you now, forget the pain that he went through to bring you to the miracle of the new birth, and you could leave the cross behind. Jesus wants you to remember all your life what he went through to bring life to you. Recall the cross. Stand under its shadow. Take your stand beneath the cross of Jesus and then you will never cease to be grateful and give thanks. Jesus took the bread... and gave thanks. We take the bread and we can say: "Thank you Lord for the pain you went through. Thank you for reminding me."

Now he comes to the wine. Only there is a gap between the bread and the wine. He doesn't go straight on. In between there is a meal, a supper, and they talked together around the table. Then "after supper...." After supper he starts again, and takes the cup they have all been using for their common drink and says, "Drink ... This is the blood of the new covenant". That word "covenant" is a lovely word. It means a relationship between two parties, that has freely been entered into by one of those parties, promising to give something to the other. That is all. A marriage is called covenant. When we put the ring on, it is a token of the vow and covenant now made between the man and woman, freely entered into. No-one made them get married. Covenants made in the Bible were sealed in blood. The old covenant made with the Jews in the desert of Sinai was sealed in blood and the blood of bulls and goats was sprinkled on the people. So serious a covenant was it, and freely entered into, God said, "I will give you a land flowing with milk and honey." They broke that covenant. They kept breaking it, saying: "We don't want your blessings; we don't want you, God" – and so through Jeremiah God said he would make a new covenant in which he would forgive sins and remember sins no more; a covenant in which he would write his laws on their hearts, not on tablets of stone. Jesus, the night before he died, said, "This is my blood of the new covenant" – and it was sealed in his blood. So we are given the wine to remember that the lovely messianic covenant that we now stand in by the grace of Christ, was sealed within his blood and it is as serious as that.

Whenever you "do this" you are "preaching to the eye". There are two ways of preaching: you can preach to the ear, which is what I mostly do. But I preach to the eyes when I take a piece of bread and break it. "You demonstrate", says Paul – you show forth, you make visible the death of Christ with something people can look at. I remember a lad in the RAF after one communion service in a tent out in the desert. He took the bread in his hands. He said to me afterwards: "Padre, when I looked at that bread, I suddenly got the thought: 'That piece of bread is as real as the body of Christ, and the body of Christ was as real as that piece of bread.'" Every time you eat the bread and drink from the cup, you make visible, you *demonstrate* the death of Christ. How long will this demonstration be necessary? The answer is: until he comes. This lovely feast is a forward as well as a backward reference. We are not merely going back two thousand years, we are going forward – I don't know how many years, months or whatever. But we are looking forward to the day when we don't need a visible illustration of Christ's death, when he welcomes us, then we will see in his hands the mark of the nails, the mark of the broken body and the shed blood.

Paul then comes right down to earth and says that if you are going to do this properly, worthily, then some self-examination is necessary beforehand. When I read this I thought it was remarkable that he misses out most of what we would think is necessary. He doesn't say you have to have it on a white cloth or silver plate or in special crockery. We think that is necessary. He doesn't say you must surround this act with a great deal of dignity and ritual and liturgy. In fact there was very little liturgy and ritual attached to this. Simply a prayer, and then it was passed round. Nothing more. We think we have to go through a whole service and say "Thank you" and "sorry" and "please" and all the rest of it before we can worthily approach. He didn't say that you have to have a long service beforehand or fast before you have this, although many Christians have come to the conclusion that you must do without breakfast before communion. He didn't say that. Above all, he didn't say you have to be perfect before you come. What did he say? There is only one thing needed if you are going to take part worthily and it is that you *discern the body*. But that is not straightforward. Which body? Christ has two bodies. Which one is referred to here? There is the body which he has in heaven – his resurrected, glorified body which he took to heaven; the body that still has the nail prints. Is that what is meant? If that is so, then as you look at this bread and drink this wine do you see the body with the nail prints?

But there is another meaning to the expression "the body of Christ". He still has a body on earth. It is made up of your hands and your feet and your mouth – it is made up of the body of Christians. And the whole context of the divisions of the church of Corinth and their not waiting for one another, and their being greedy before one another and humiliating one another seems to me to point very clearly to an emphasis on this second meaning. When you take the bread and wine, do you see in the other people eating and drinking with you the body of Christ?

I think the answer is that both meanings apply, for they merge into one another. Therefore the two questions you need to ask before partaking are: "Do I discern the body of Christ in what is eaten; and do I discern the body of Christ in those who eat it?"

But now comes a very serious word. If you do not ask that question and you eat and drink this bread and wine without discerning the body, then your body will be damaged. Your body – not your soul. You could actually become physically weak, physically ill, and die physically as the result of abusing the Lord's Supper. If you fail to see the Lord's body, then he damages your body, for the Lord Jesus not only heals the sick, he can make the body sick. It is his way of chastising and disciplining, not because he wants to condemn, but because he loves. "Whom the Lord loves, he chastises" – and therefore he could chastise us at the Lord's table itself if we profaned the body and blood and came and just said, "I want what I can get out of this; I don't care about the others eating and drinking with me; I just want a blessing for me." That would be profaning what is sacred and desecrating it.

Paul said if you want to be selfish, then stay at home. If you want a good time for yourself, then you can have it at home before you come, but when you come together it is the Lord's Supper, and we are his family and we are the guests, not the hosts. It is not our table. It is not our communion, it is not our supper – it is his. And it is a holy privilege to be there.

We come to discern the body and to rejoice in the

covenants sealed in blood whereby his life is ours forever and ever.

SUPERNATURAL GIFTS

Read 1 Corinthians 12

A. THEIR ORIGIN (1–13)
1. ULTIMATE (1–11)
  a. Validity (1–3)
      i. Demonic insult
      ii. Divine inspiration
  b. Variety (4–11)
      i. Same God behind them all
      ii. Different gifts bestowed on each
2. IMMEDIATE (12–13)
  a. One body of Christ
  b. One baptism in Spirit

B. THEIR OPERATION (14–31)
1. WRONG ATTITUDE (14–26)
  a. Inferiority – isolation (14–20)
  b. Superiority – insolence (21–26)
2. RIGHT APPRECIATION (27–31)
  a. Divine appointment (27–28)
  b. Human activity (29–31)

Chapters 12, 13 and 14 all deal with the subject of spiritual gifts. They are a sandwich but we often lick the jam out of chapter 13 and leave the bread of chapters 12 and 14. It all belongs together to be eaten whole, as part of the word of God about these gifts.

Firstly, God loves giving presents to people. That is his nature. He loves to give. All he wants from us is a receptive hand. All he asks of us is that we receive what he gives. Now there are many, many gifts that he has given, but we are going to deal with *spiritual* gifts. These are in contrast to what I would call natural gifts.

Natural gifts he gave you before you were converted.

Long before you became a Christian you had natural gifts. They varied. Some have a gift in music, some of making things with their hands, some have a gift of administration and organisation, some have a gift of finance. I am always amazed at people who can add up figures correctly! But you had natural gifts and thank God that when you became a Christian he could take these natural gifts and use them.

But we are not talking about that kind of gift at all. We are talking about gifts that are only given to God's people. They don't appear anywhere else in the world, and they don't even appear among all God's people, because not all God's people are willing to receive them. But those who have an open hand for these gifts find out that God can do wonderful things. They remain his gifts. They never become ours. We can never say, "I have the gift of...." You can only say, "He has given the gift of...." They remain his gifts right to the end.

These spiritual gifts can be counterfeited. They can be substituted, and there are both human and Satanic counterfeits to all the gifts that God can give. It is as if the devil himself says, "I can give you something just the same", and you take it and you discover it is not the same, that it has a horrible sting in the tail, that it leaves a nasty taste in the mouth, that it gives you a hangover, but at first sight it looked just the same. This is the devil's own approach. That is why the prodigal son thought he had better go to the far country. He thought he could have fun there, and he went off, tried to live it up and he found out it was a dead-end, and that sooner or later there is an awful famine in the far country and you get hungry and you finish up like an animal. Then he came home to his father's house and within five minutes there was music and dancing and a feast laid on. There was all the joy and all the happiness and all the celebration that he had gone to the far country to seek, and it was waiting at home all the time.

It is because of the devil's counterfeit. He can offer his counterfeit love and it is not love. He can offer his counterfeit joy and it is not joy. He can offer counterfeit peace and it is not peace. And he can duplicate any gift of God.

It is for this reason that the first thing you need to do when spiritual gifts are being exercised is to test their validity, to examine them to see if they really are gifts from God or from someone else. The gifts of God are sent down from heaven. The things of Satan and men are worked up and there is this big difference between something that is sent down and something that is worked up.

Christians need to be informed as well as inspired. They need heat and light together. You not only need to feel inspired in the service, you need to be instructed also, that heart and mind might work together, testing everything to make sure what we have got is from God. That is why Paul said: I don't want you to be uninformed. I want you to be inspired but I want you to be informed so that you will be able to test inspired and moving experiences.

He now appeals to their pagan past. He is saying, "You now know that those little idols you worshipped are dumb! They never open their mouths. They can't speak. They can't communicate and yet you were moved! You had real experiences when you worshipped pagan idols." And I have seen pagans worshipping and realised they were having a real experience – as a person practising Zen Buddhism or some other form of meditation or as a person taking dope or drugs. They are having a real experience, they are moved, but when they come out of the trip they find it is not real.

The test is not whether you have been moved. That is no way to test a service of worship or any other thing. You may be excited. You may be all worked up. That is no test whatsoever of the validity of spiritual gifts.

So Paul is teaching these Corinthians: you know that you

could get all worked up in your pagan days, and yet you now know that the idols couldn't do a thing; there was no reality there, and yet you were moved. So he begs them to test all their religious experience. How? Not whether you were moved but where you were moved *to*. Not that you were moved to open your mouth and say something, but what you said when you opened your mouth. Paul goes on to say this very simple thing: you can always test a spiritual gift by what people are led to say and think and do about Jesus. If they were moved to their depths and deep emotional experiences but didn't think more highly of Jesus as a result, it wasn't of God. You can forget it. You could have all the experiences the devil can offer you. You might take drugs every day and have a wonderful trip, but if you don't think more highly of Jesus, it is not real, it is not of God.

Paul mentions two possibilities of inspired utterances or speech when people are carried away and say things perhaps without realising what they are saying, and he says: "No man can say 'Jesus be cursed'." Now who would say that? Pagans said it, of course, but then pagans wouldn't be in church. The Jews said it because anybody crucified was under the curse of God. They said it – but they would not be in that service. Who would have said this thing? I am afraid it is only too possible when people *are* being moved of the Spirit for the devil to get right in and inspire things that are just the opposite of glorifying to Jesus. I was told of a group in England who had an orgy in which they killed a young boy and covered him with blood and spoke in tongues and were using the name of Jesus while they did it. That is the devil's own work. The devil is not afraid to use the word "Jesus". Any "Jesus" movement and any movement that uses the name "Jesus" must still be tested, because Paul said "No man can say 'Jesus be cursed'" but you notice that they were saying "Jesus". A young man who committed dreadful cultic murders in Hollywood called himself "Jesus". They don't mind using the name. The word "Jesus" is not only being used by the people who love him, but also by others. How do you tell? It is what you say about Jesus that is the objective test. And anybody who disparages Jesus in any way is not speaking of God. I say with shame that at our Baptist assembly some years ago a speaker got up and said things that disparaged Jesus. I am thankful that there was such an immediate response, a protest about such a thing being allowed. Somebody disparaging Jesus publicly is not of God, and you know it straight away.

What *is* of God? When people say spontaneously – not because they have been told or taught to say it, but when they can pour out "Jesus is Lord!" then you know that is of God. Those whom the Spirit has touched call Jesus "Lord". You talk to somebody about Jesus and they say, after a bit, "The Lord" and you know straight away. The Lord is wonderful and you know they are believers. Those who disparage Jesus in any way, who give limitations to him that he didn't have, who say he was a "child of his times", and who say he was *only* a great human – this is not of God.

What do we mean, those of us who say "Jesus is Lord"? We mean two things by the word "Lord" – his *authority* and his *deity*.

The authority is this: that Jesus is my *boss*. That is what the word "Lord" means. A slave in the ancient world said of his master, "That is my lord, my boss." Therefore it is not just the confession of the lips, it is the commitment of the life. "Jesus is Lord" – and the word "lord" in the ancient world meant someone who has authority and it also meant someone who has deity. Someone who is my God. Someone who has absolute right to me because he is my God.

They called the Roman Emperor "Lord". They said "Caesar is lord" as they raised the arm in front of his statue, a thing that the Christians would never say and they were thrown to the lions as a result.

This is the big test as to whether it is a spiritual gift or not. If it is exalting Jesus, then it is of God. If it is degrading or debasing or criticising our Lord Jesus, it is not a spiritual gift. It is either of men or of the devil.

So we have changed from dumb idols that cannot help, to a living Lord who can. I heard about a man who died in Paris after a lifetime of sin, crying out "God will forgive me, that is his trade." I read that he worshipped the Venus-de-Milo. That was his god, the goddess of love. He would go and visit the Louvre and bow before that statue, and when he was dying he managed to make a last pilgrimage to the statue, dragged himself there and lay before it on the floor, and while the tourists went round the Louvre, he cried to Venus to help him in his last hour of need. These words came into his mind: I have no arms. I cannot reach you. He had been so moved by that beautiful statue all his life, but it was dumb. He had been moved all right. But the experience was unreal. Dumb idols! It did nothing for him when he came to die. And someone has said that the best test of a man's religion is: will it help him when he dies? We have turned to the living Lord. Jesus is Lord.

Now we turn from the validity of these gifts to the variety of them. There is no doubt about it that as soon as you discuss spiritual gifts you will find a great variety of opinion even among the Lord's people. The Corinthians had written to Paul and asked him for his opinion about spiritual gifts. Remember again that when we speak of spiritual gifts we are not speaking about natural gifts that have been dedicated to the Lord, we are speaking of gifts that only appear among believers, that are supernatural rather than natural, and are given direct by God to someone who never had them before, and they are all gifts enabling a person to do something that otherwise they could never have done – to say something that normally only God can say, or to do something that normally only God can do. Speaking, for example, in languages that God knows but no man knows, or performing miracles such as God performs.

These spiritual gifts raise a whole host of questions. For example, how do you get them? How are they given? Secondly, are we quite sure that we want them? From my own experience, the majority of Christians in this country do not want spiritual gifts and would be terribly upset and disturbed if they were given. Yet there they are being offered to us in the Bible by God. Thirdly, who gets these gifts? Do we expect that the minister will get most of them? Or who will get them in a church? That is a very relevant question. The fourth question, and the one I want to deal with now, is this. If God, as it is stated, gives gifts to all sorts of people in a congregation, won't this lead to a disorganised, divided, chaotic church?

"Wouldn't it be terrible," says someone, "if we came to church and we didn't know who was going to preach that morning, who was going to do this, who was going to do that – if we just all got together and anybody could do anything." It would be thoroughly disorganised. And I am afraid nowadays we tend to play for safety. We say we will get one man we can trust and we will put everything in his hands and then there isn't going to be chaos – he can manage the lot, which is a very unscriptural position and a long way from the New Testament church. But some people say, "I much prefer worship when it is in the hands of one person who is prepared and who is in charge and who controls everything, rather than this kind of open worship where anybody can do anything."

Let us look at this whole question. Does it mean dis-organisation? Does it mean that if anybody can have any gift and anybody can do anything at any time, that you are going to finish up in complete confusion? Paul addresses this very question.

Corinth, as a church, we are told in chapter 1, had every spiritual gift. Paul said to them: "I give thanks to God that you are not lacking in any spiritual gift." But one of the results in Corinth was chaos, division, confusion, rivalry, jealousy. So people read through this letter to the Corinthians and say we don't want the gifts here because we don't want that kind of chaos here. We would rather do without. We would rather have peace and quiet and order, even if it is the order of a cemetery. We would rather do without these lively, disturbing elements. We like a nice, ordered service in the hands of one man.

The real answer that Paul gives to this is not to avoid the confusion of Corinth by doing without the gifts but to realise that the church is not an organisation but an organism. Let me explain that. The church is not a business. If it were, then it would be better to have one man in charge – a boss. You don't get very far in business by committees. Every business discovers this, that if you want to get organised you had better form committees of one, and you really get things organised and done well. But if you put a large group in charge, the larger the group the less things will get done, and if you make everybody equally responsible you will finish in chaos. But the church is not an organisation and it is not a business. While that is no excuse for doing things in a haphazard way, we must beware of ever letting the church be treated as an organisation. All kinds of committees have sat and considered church organisation, but the church is not an organisation and that is why none of their reports brings the kingdom. I was in a denomination that was highly organised, far better organised than the Baptists have ever been, and it disturbs me to find that Baptists envy that denomination their organisation and wish for more and more committees, better headquarters and bigger powers at the top. But the simple fact is that that denomination is reporting greater losses in numbers than the Baptists, with all its organisation. The church is an organism, not an organisation, and an organism is a living thing. It carries its own life within it. It isn't something that is contrived. It isn't a machine. It is a living, growing organism. You see this in plants. Every part of a plant is different from every other part. If somebody were organising a plant they would have it all nicely mechanical, every leaf the same shape so that you could mass produce them, but God gave to plants an organic life and therefore there is an interesting variety. I often used to walk around our garden before a service and I find that to look at God's work keeps me right. There it is. God's work is as varied as a congregation. Looking around the people they looked just like my garden! All nice flowers in rows but every one different from the others – and the variety and yet the unity is there. Have you noticed that in nature you can almost put anything together and it always fits. The colours you can put together in flowers! But you couldn't do that with your clothes. There is a wonderful unity and variety in it all that really speaks of beauty.

You see this not only in nature but you see it supremely in the organism that we call our body. Of the millions of cells in my body, there aren't two the same. There aren't two parts of my body the same. I have two kidneys but one is a different size to the other, I am told. My heart has two parts to it but one is bigger than the other. I have got a right and a left hand that are nearly the same, yet when I look closely they are different. I am an amazing example of an organic growth, of a life that has infinite variety in it with all the parts doing different things, and yet I am co-ordinated, I am one body, I can act perfectly well as one body even though every part of my body is doing a different thing from every other part.

Paul uses this notion of the body. He actually uses the word "body" nineteen times in the rest of this chapter. He teaches that if you want the answer to the disorganised, chaotic church fellowship, it is to look at your own physical body and then say that is a picture of what the church is and ought to be. This is more than an illustration. God, who created your body, created the church. He is the Creator and the Redeemer and just as he made your body – which is fearfully and wonderfully made – intricately working your parts in secret before the world had any glance at you, as he made this body full of variety to work together in harmony, he made the church and he wants to give different functions to different people, that it might work together in harmony.

He does not want to give all the gifts to one man and he never does. The tragedy is that every church looking for a new minister is looking for someone with all the gifts, and alas, always discovers to their cost that they have called a man without all the gifts and they say, "Well, he's very good at this but he's not so good at that," or, "He's very good at the other but this is a bit of a gap." Some men have one gift and some another, and if you will treat one man as the body of Christ then you will be disappointed. But God's will is to distribute all the functions and then to have them co-operate so that there is no lack of co-ordination or care between members of the body.

Now this is a physical world, and to live in it I need a body. I cannot do things for others without my body. Imagine that I had sent a message to my congregation one Sunday morning that was read out by the church secretary: "Mr Pawson sends his love and will be with you in spirit this morning." I couldn't preach. I couldn't use a gift of teaching – because I need my body. Therefore if Jesus is going to do anything in the world at all he has got to have a body to do it. That may sound pretty obvious but it says in the Bible that when the Son of God came to the earth to do God's will, this is what he said: "A body you have prepared for me ... I come to do your will." Those are his words, quoted in Hebrews chapter 10 which is itself quoting from Psalm 40:6. You can't do the will of God without a body – not in this world. So Jesus came to earth and he had a body to do the Father's will, but that body he took back after resurrection and ascension to heaven, and Jesus no longer has that body on earth. How is he going to do his work now? The answer is that he has got another body. The amazing truth is that the believers together on earth constitute the body which has many members and yet is one. He is saying we actually are a body, all together. Our bodies are part of his body now, and are to behave as one body, each part contributing to the whole and every part functioning normally.

Now we can go to the first real question: how do the gifts appear? Is it just God's whim? Does he just say, "I'd like to give gifts to that church?" Is God arbitrarily saying, "I give them when I like to whom I like?" No. There are conditions. If you are ever going to know spiritual gifts there are two fundamental conditions. One is in v. 12 and one is in v. 13. Verse 12 tells us that we will not have gifts unless we are in the body of Christ. How do you get into the body? You get into the body as soon as you have real contact with Christ – as soon as you believe in him you are *in* him. When you become a Christian you have entered his body and you are now a part of it. But, sadly, that does not mean that you act as such.

Ezekiel had a vision of a great valley full of dry bones littering the floor of the valley. And as he watched and prophesied over them the bones came together and linked up to become skeletons and they became bodies, and there were complete bodies lying where there had just been bones:

separate pieces – complete bodies. They didn't move; they didn't talk; they didn't walk. They didn't do a thing. Then God said, "Son of man, speak to them again." There is something more needed – a second thing. They have come together, they are related to each other, they are bodies but they have no breath, they have no life. So: prophesy. And the wind of God blew and the bodies stood up on their feet, a mighty army.

Now here we touch the diagnosis in the Bible of why there are not more gifts visible in the church today – as there were in the days of the New Testament. Why are there not? The answer is: we are in the body but we lack the breath. We are joined to one another. When we came to be in Christ we became part of his body, we were linked up and the bones linked up and we became a body but we are lying there, doing nothing, or sitting there, doing nothing. What is it that makes a body stand on its feet like a mighty army? It is when the breath of God blows, when the wind of God comes, or as v. 13 puts it, when you are baptised in the Holy Spirit.

Now let us go back to the early church. When did the disciples become the body of Christ? There is no doubt that they were connected to Christ for three years and they were connected to each other for three years for they lived together and had things together and ate things together and walked together and talked together. They studied their scriptures together. They prayed together. They did all that together. I would have said they were the body of Christ, wouldn't you? They were together in Christ and yet Jesus said, "Wait...." Wait until you are baptised in Holy Spirit and then you will get on your feet like a mighty army. You are already mine. You are already clean through the word I have spoken to you. You have already been with me and yet there is something missing.

Now we come to v. 13 which tells not only that the early

apostles needed this but that this is the introduction to spiritual gifts for Christians of all time. It is not just enough to be in the body, because it is patently obvious that most of the Christians in England who are in the body do not have spiritual gifts. It is when the breath blows through the body and when, as Paul says here, you are baptised in one Spirit that the body gets on its feet and begins to operate. Then the gifts appear and they begin to be used in a fellowship.

This verse 13 has caused so much controversy. You wouldn't guess that there were such problems over it but it has been bandied about and I believe the trouble is that both the translators of our Bibles and the commentators on it have suffered from one terrific handicap in translating this verse and explaining it: that they do not know what it is to be baptised in the Spirit. The result is that while they have got scholarship, natural dedicated gifts of translation, they have missed the meaning of this verse, so let me go through it very carefully indeed.

When I read it I change a word back to what Paul originally said. It is a tragedy when people change words in the Word of God. Every word matters. Every word was chosen by the Spirit. The word that I change is "by", which I replace with "in" because Paul said "in", not "by". If it was "by" then this would be the only case in the whole of the Bible where the Holy Spirit is said to baptise someone, but he never does. He is not the baptist. He is not the baptiser. John was the baptist in water and Jesus is the baptist in Spirit. And John said, "I baptise you in water. He will baptise you in Holy Spirit". The phrase here is "baptised in Spirit" (and for those who know a little Greek, it is the Greek verb *baptizein*, which means "baptise", "plunge" or dip') and then it is the little preposition *en* which means "in" and then it is the word *pneumati*, from which we get the word "pneumatic". *Baptizein en pneumati* – "baptised in Spirit" is the exact same phrase that John the Baptist used and which Jesus used. It is the same phrase here. John said, "I will plunge you in water. He will plunge you in Holy Spirit." Jesus said, "You will be plunged in Holy Spirit not many days hence." Pentecost came. And here is Paul saying to the Corinthians, "You were plunged in Spirit too."

Now this same phrase must mean the same thing all the way through. It means to have a pentecostal experience yourself, to be plunged in Spirit as they were on the day of Pentecost in Acts 2, to be baptised in Holy Spirit, to be immersed in Spirit and to be made to drink of Spirit. Then and only then do you find the spiritual gifts appearing, and if people ask why it is that for so long Christians have managed and lived without spiritual gifts, I will tell you. It is because for so long people have not said, "You need to be baptised in Holy Spirit" – and that is why the gifts are not to be found in a lot of churches.

Those who are in the body but not baptised in Spirit do not exercise spiritual gifts. They don't appear. That is why this scripture was written for our learning. Now let us go a little further. The tense of the two verbs (I am sorry for being so technical but it is very important) – the verb "baptised" and "made to drink" are a peculiar Greek tense called the aorist, which means something that definitely happens once. Not something that goes on but something that happens once. You were all plunged once in the Spirit. You were all made to drink once. The verb is not "to go on drinking". You were made to drink once. And it always refers to a definite, discernible event which is quite clear and everybody therefore knows whether they have been plunged into Spirit and made to drink of Spirit or not. If you haven't known this then you need to seek it if ever you are to exercise spiritual gifts. So it is referring to a "once for all" event, as we have noted before, of being baptised in one

Spirit, made to drink of one Spirit, being plunged into one Spirit – as a definite experience which is discernible, can be dated, clear, conscious, something that you can look back to. Paul is saying: You look back to that. You were plunged and made to drink once. Do you remember it? That is what made you part of the body. That is what gave you gifts. That is what made the body stand on its feet and live and become a mutual, ministering body.

Now we go even further. You notice that the words used are pretty liquid – watery words. "Plunged" – an external word for being plunged into something so that it is all outside you. And "drink" – an internal word so that you are filling up inside. It is a total experience, outside and inside. It is to be plunged into the Spirit so that the Spirit is all round you, and to drink of the Spirit so the Spirit is in you. So it is an external and an internal experience, and those who have been baptised in the Spirit will tell you that it is a total experience. You feel that you are totally surrounded outside by the Spirit and totally filled inside by the Spirit. That is what this verse is talking about. Jesus himself always used liquid terms of the Spirit. Think of what he said to the woman at the well.

The unity of which he is speaking here is the unity that prevents the disorganised church. It is a body that has one breath. Do you know that every part of my body that I use has the same life flowing through it? I am breathing when I give talks, and that breath is taking oxygen in, and the oxygen is going to every part of my body. The breath is making every part of my body act in a co-ordinated way. It is all acting together so that my hands can be "saying" things as well as my face and my mouth – it is all acting as one body because there is one breath that is the secret of its life. If I were to stop breathing when preaching, all the rest would pack up and you would still have a body on a platform and that is all you would have and you would have no life, no gifts and no teaching and no helpfulness. You might have an organisation but the organism would have gone.

Now I move on to the second section, which we can deal with more briefly, though it is longer. Having seen the unity of the human body and the unity of the body of Christ, Paul now draws attention to the variety of the human body and the variety of the body of Christ.

Undoubtedly problems are raised because there is a variety of gifts. Some are more spectacular and sensational than others. Some are more public and therefore more praised than others. Some are more obviously necessary than others. But now there is one peculiar feature about the body of Christ that there isn't in my human body. The peculiar feature about the body of Christ is that each organ has a mind of its own. It ought not to have but it does, and therein lies the problem.

Paul now has an extraordinary picture. He says: supposing this hand starts talking. A hand won't talk! But anyway he says: "Now supposing this hand starts talking to the foot or the foot to the hand." The body of Christ can do this but my human body can't. But in the body of Christ each member can talk to the other members and each member can think about the other members, and therein lies the problem in church life. If the church were the same kind of a body as this physical body we would have harmony in the church, all the time, automatically. It is because members can think and talk – every member – that you get disharmony. How do you get this? Well, first of all, some people develop an inferiority complex. Some people develop a superiority complex. Both wreck the harmony of the church. Let's look at the inferiority first. A person who has no great gift, a person who has no gifts that are obvious or as marvellous as somebody else's is awfully tempted to begin to say, "I don't belong. I am not needed." Not every man is a preacher, for example, and the public ministry of a large church is in the public eye – alas,

I wish it were not so but it has to be. But it is easy for a man to say, "Because I am not preaching I am not needed in the church. I don't belong. I don't have a function."

Paul gives us this picture: supposing the feet should say to the hands, "I am not as useful as you." It is interesting that both hands and feet have nails. There is a similarity between them. They have separate things at the ends – fingers and toes. And it is interesting that the feet talk to the hands and not to the eyes, for example. They are rather alike and yet so different. My toes are useless as far as I am concerned. I know people who have had frostbite and they can walk. They can manage without them. The little toe is about the most useless part of the body, it seems. What is it there for? Whereas, the hands! What can the hand do? It can not only hold a hammer and sword, it can not only hold food. The hand can be most expressive. It can shake hands. It can caress the head of a crying little child. The hand can soothe. The hand can do so much. If the foot could say to the hand, "I don't have as many gifts as you, I don't feel I belong, I don't feel I am needed or wanted," it would be disastrous for the body. Likewise, imagine an ear being able to say the same thing to the eye. The ear hears and it is to hang your spectacles on, and that is about all. But the eye! That can do so much more. In addition to seeing, the eye expresses so much – your joy, your sorrow. It is part of your communication.

A kind of inferiority complex is very common in Christian fellowship. People with only one talent tend to bury it because there are people with ten or five. And people who don't have a public position and who say, "the church hasn't called me to be a deacon", for example, feel they are not needed and say that kind of thing which is quite false. They say, "I would be better off in a smaller church because then I would stand a much better chance of being a deacon." But a larger church has more need of gifts, more need of help, more need of everybody saying, "I am not going to be a passenger. I am going to be a member of the crew. I am going to contribute my little gift. I would rather be a doorkeeper in the house of the Lord than dwell in the tents of wickedness. I would rather give out hymn books to the glory of God than say 'I have nothing to do. I am not needed or wanted'." Let us get rid of the inferiority complex. You don't need to think like that. Paul says three things to someone who feels inferior in gifts.

Firstly, you can't leave the body. If the ear says, "I am not as good as the eye", does that make it any less a part of a body? No. If the foot says to the hand, "the hand can do more than I can", does that make the foot any less a part of the body? The simple fact is that if you are a Christian, you are in the body and you can't say, "I don't belong and I am not needed." You are. What is wrongly happening is that you haven't asked what your function is. I heard of one preacher who preached on "You are the body of Christ" and he said, "Some of you are like the appendix. We don't know you are there until you give us trouble." I don't know what the appendix is for, there isn't a single member of the body of Christ who is not needed. He has a job for every member.

Secondly, Paul is saying that we can't all be the same. "If the whole body were the eye, where would the body be?" Not everyone can be a preacher or a deacon. But everyone has a job.

Thirdly, we learn that if you feel inferior, if you feel you haven't a gift, you are grumbling at the way God has arranged things. God gives this gift and that gift and you are grumbling at his arrangements if he hasn't given you a more prominent one.

What about the eye saying to the hand "I am very superior. I don't need you." This is the opposite. Some church members are tempted to say "they don't need me" but others are tempted to say "I don't need them". But where would the eye be without the hand? It is true that it is the eye that tells the hand what to do, so that if I pick up a book it would be my eye that has directed my hand. Ah, but the eye needed the hand. I can't just stare at that book and see it hop into my hands. I need the hand. Each needs the other and when we look at the body we discover that those parts of the body which people don't see and which need more protection than others are the very parts that God has given greater honour to.

The most obvious example would be the organs of reproduction with which we carry the power of life, to pass it on. Those organs are hidden from others, and should be. We treat them with care and with modesty. We buy clothes for those parts where we don't for our hands. And that is a very important lesson that Paul has from the physical body. Sometimes, in the body of Christ, it is the unseen, quiet people who don't have a public job who may have the greater powers of reproduction. In almost every church where I have been pastor I have found that there have been some quiet people in the church who just get on with winning others for Christ. They never get in the pulpit. They are never noticed. Only in heaven will their work fully be realised by the body of Christ. They just get on with it, quietly and they are modest about it.

Those with the more prominent, public and spectacular gifts should care all the more for those who have the quiet, humble gifts. In fact in any church, even if one man or a few men may be prominent and may get the praise for the church, it would be quite impossible for any of those public gifts to be exercised unless there were other quiet things being done that made it all worthwhile. This is the body where we all belong to each other, and it is those hidden, quiet ministries, those little secret things that are done to build up the body that God invests with greater honour.

I find this very encouraging and beautiful. So close is the care for the body in reality that literally, if one part suffers they all do. If one is honoured they all rejoice. Have you ever noticed that you never say, "My tooth has a dreadful ache"? You always say, "I have a toothache." You don't say, "My stomach has a dreadful pain." You say, "I have a stomach ache." You don't say, "My foot really is in trouble." You say, "I am crippled." You notice that when it is one body that is how you talk because that is reality. You can't divorce a toothache from every other part of the body and just say, "Well, there is my tooth" – like the man who used to sleep with his feet out of the bottom of the bed because he couldn't stand those cold feet in bed with him! You can't live like that. It is part of the body and you can't say, "That part of the body suffering is nothing to do with me." Therefore when you are truly one body, baptised in the Spirit, ministering together, then you are bound together so closely that if one member is out of sorts and going wrong, every other one says, "I feel this." If one member is used of God, you don't say, "I am jealous of that. Fancy God giving that gift to that other member." You say, "That gift has been given to our body" – *our* gift.

I thank God for the modern interest in spiritual gifts, which is sweeping right through the world and that is great, and I think it is going to bring revival if we accept it properly. One of the dangers, though, is that far too many people are seeking things for *themselves*, saying: I want this; I want a gift; I want that. How about praying that the body may have all the gifts? How about asking God to give all those nine gifts in 1 Corinthians 12 to our body, whoever they come to? Let us pray for that. Wouldn't that be lovely? I am not concerned to have all the gifts. I am concerned that the body should have them all. I don't care which members are given the gift of healing or the gift of miracles or the gift of speaking in unknown languages, as long as we get these gifts. We want all that God has for us but we don't mind who has them. It is the body that we are concerned about. One body, so that nobody feels inferior because they haven't got gifts and nobody feels superior because they have, but together we are one body acting in a co-ordinated, caring way.

Finally, let me come to vv. 27 – 31. Paul keeps in beautiful balance the corporate and the individual, the body and the members. You can exalt the body and lose sight of the individuals or you can exalt the individual and lose sight of the body, and either destroys fellowship (fellowship – our individual members acting like a body), and Paul keeps them both together. To the church can be said: "You are the body of Christ"; and individually you are members of it.

Now we come to the question: in practice, does it mean that anybody does anything any week? Does it mean that you should arrive at church next Sunday and the preacher should leave the pulpit and say, "Anybody come into this pulpit this morning and teach"? No! God appoints and God orders the church and he has a way of giving one gift regularly to this person, and another gift regularly to that person, so that the gift becomes a ministry and an office. Therefore God appoints certain people to be apostles, teachers, prophets, healers, miracle workers. God develops a gift into a ministry and the person who receives the gift should always ask, "Lord, are you wanting me to develop this gift into a ministry?"

The first stage is that God gives the gift. The second stage is when that gift is developed and is given regularly to that person. The third stage is when the church recognises the office of that gift and says, "You are a prophet", "You are a teacher", "You are a healer", and will expect those people to minister regularly in that gift. Now that is how God orders the church. It isn't a "free-for-all". It isn't a chaotic, disorganised state in which anybody does anything any week. Every time where spiritual gifts are given, the Holy Spirit develops certain people into a particular ministry and I can only say that God has told me to develop the gift of teaching and to exercise it and use it for the body of Christ. But how I long to see others developing these other gifts which I don't think God will necessarily give me, but the body needs them and I look forward to the day when more have developed these gifts.

If this is so, do you realise that the church can never elect a man to office in the church? How could you say, "Let's get together and have a ballot next Thursday at the church meeting to decide who we will have to be the healer in our church"? You couldn't do it. No more can you decide who will be a teacher. Nor can you decide who will work miracles. Therefore the idea of churches having elections to choose whom they want to be in a particular office is ludicrous. An organisation can do that but an organism can't. All you can do is recognise certain gifts that God has given regularly to a man. If a church decides to have elders it can take some time to select those whom God has already appointed by giving the gifts. You can't say, "We like so-and-so, we'd like him to be an elder." You can only say, "God has given the gift of wisdom to this man and he exercises it, and he is to be an elder." So these gifts are given by God. God appoints teachers, prophets, apostles and we can do nothing about it except recognise (or, regrettably, refuse) but we can't appoint. We can only recognise these gifts.

Therefore, looking at the human activity, in practice only some in the church will exercise each ministry. That is the order of it. The hand doesn't do what the foot does. The eye doesn't do what the ear does. And therefore you will never get the state where all the people in the church are prophets, where all the people in the church are healers, or where all the people in the church speak in unknown languages in the meeting. You will never get this. God arranges the body to be an organism.

You notice that God will give these gifts to more than one. Paul never says, "God has set in the church an apostle, a prophet, a teacher, a healer." He says teachers, apostles, prophets – always plural but never them all. So Paul asks: Do all do this? Do all do that? Do all speak with tongues? Do all heal? No, but God has given the ministries to some within the fellowship.

There are two things to mention as we conclude this section. First of all, we are allowed and exhorted in the New Testament to covet. The tenth commandment does not apply to one thing. "Thou shalt not covet thy neighbour's ox, ass, wife nor anything that is his" is still true. But there is one thing a Christian can covet. Covet the higher gifts. Long for the day when you will have gifts to minister. Why don't you have an ambition to be an elder? To be a teacher? Earnestly desire these things. A man who has a desire to be an elder desires a good thing. There is a place for ambition in the body of Christ. Have ambition, that you may have gifts and there is a more excellent way even than gifts.

Finally what I have said about this in chapter 12 was true of the Corinthian church. Whatever else they were not, they were a live body. What is true of them is not true of many churches. They were all baptised in one Spirit. Therefore they did not lack any spiritual gift. If we are not all baptised in one Spirit, we lack the spiritual gifts. But I thank God that there is a growing number of believers who are being baptised in the Holy Spirit. It is absolutely vital that when the gifts come they be exercised in love.

GIFTS WITHOUT LOVE
Read 1 Corinthians 13

A. LOVE ESSENTIAL – gifts trivial (1–3)
1. TO EMOTIONALISM
2. TO INTELLECTUALISM
3. TO ACTIVISM
4. TO HUMANITARIANISM
5. TO ASCETICISM

B. LOVE EFFECTUAL – gifts treacherous (4–7)
1. SUCCESS
2. STRIFE
3. SCANDAL

C. LOVE ETERNAL – gifts transient (8–13)
1. SUPERIOR TO GIFTS
2. SUPREME AMONG GRACES

Someone has said that this chapter (including the last verse of chapter 12 and the first verse of chapter 14) is the greatest, strongest, deepest thing that Paul ever wrote. Certainly it is a chapter that has become a great favourite of many. People are interested in love. They want to write poetry about it, they want to sing songs about it. This chapter becomes poetic.

Therefore, we tend to tread very delicately. It almost seems as if when a preacher takes this chapter it is like taking a flower and pulling a petal off and saying, "That's a petal," and pulling a stamen out and saying, "That's a stamen," and when you're finished the flower lies crushed and broken. Many preachers have read this chapter in the pulpit, not so many have preached on it. Indeed, any preacher feels he's treading on holy ground. But therein lies a danger. The danger is that the beauty of this chapter blinds you to its utter practicality and we must tackle the chapter and take it to pieces so that we might put it together in love and this I am going to do.

What is the subject? You might say, "Don't be silly, it's love." But in fact the subject of this chapter is not love, the subject is spiritual gifts. I have already mentioned that chapters 12–14 are not three separate items, they are one section of the letter, which Paul began by saying, "Now concerning spiritual gifts brethren...." He continues on the same subject to the last verse of chapter fourteen.

This is the jam in a sandwich which we must eat whole. The sweetness of this chapter is needed for the bread of the other two. Spiritual gifts compared with love are bread compared with jam. But you would get sick if you just ate nothing but jam for your tea, and you would get bored if you had nothing but bread. God, in his wisdom, wants us to have spiritual gifts and love. So often the alternative is put to us as if we must choose between the two. Which would you rather have, love or gifts? The answer is love every time, but why do you present me with the alternative when God wants me to have the whole sandwich and have a real meal? I include v. 31 of chapter twelve because there Paul says, "Covet the best gifts." A Christian is allowed to covet spiritual gifts, but not material possessions. Earnestly desire the higher gifts. I want your ambition to go even further than that. It must include that, but it must go beyond that. There is something even beyond the gifts that we are to aim at and seek.

I want you to notice that love is not a gift. It is not listed in the New Testament among the gifts. Not once in these pages is it said that love is a gift of God to us. The gifts we have looked at we know: prophecy, knowledge, unknown languages, miracles, healings, and so on. No mention of love in that list. For love is in a quite different category:

"Earnestly desire the higher gifts, and then I'll show you something even more excellent than gifts" – something that goes beyond gifts, something that is more than a gift, something that is the very nature of God himself.

So let us move on to the more excellent way. The gifts by themselves are trivial, almost valueless. Indeed Paul would say, "worth nothing". That doesn't mean that gifts are of no use at all. Only by themselves are they trivial. Without love, they are nothing.

With love, they are tremendous (vv. 4–7). They carry awful dangers and temptations with them if they are without love, but with love these temptations are overcome and the gifts are beautiful.

Likewise, gifts by themselves are transient. But with love the gifts can produce something that is eternal. So every time, Paul devalues gifts by themselves, but he values very highly indeed gifts with love. I would emphasise again and again that Paul is *not* saying in chapter 13 that to have love is far better than to have the gifts – so you just have love. He is saying: earnestly desire the gifts, then add something more to them and you have got the lot. You have got all that God wants for you.

I give you a little illustration, which I have pinched from somebody else. Supposing a man is dying of thirst in the desert and a search party full of love and compassion for this man goes out to get him, and they find him and he says, "Water, water, give me water," and they say, "Well we don't believe in giving anything, we just want to love you. We've come to tell you that we have compassion for you. We love you so much." He needs a gift. Oh, he needed the love that would go and give it to him, but he needed the gift.

To say that we just need love and we don't need these gifts is silly because there will be situations in which you can't help a person however much you love them unless you have got a gift for them. You can sympathise with a sick person and you can say, "Oh my love really sympathises, I have compassion for you," but when Jesus had compassion on a sick person he gave them a gift of health. How much better you could help a sick person if you could say, "Love has sent me here with a spiritual gift of health for you."

So let's never put the gifts on one pan of the balance and love on the other and say, "Well, love is obviously far better so I'm going for that." Gifts by themselves, yes, are useless, but Paul is not saying, "Therefore, leave them behind and just love," he's saying: Add to the gifts love; press on from the higher gifts to the more excellent way of gifts and add the love. That is why he begins by saying, "Gifts without love – valueless." In fact, he says, "nothing". Being very humble he doesn't say, "If you have these gifts and lack love..." he says, "If I do...."

The only way to read this chapter is to read it for yourself. Don't read it for other people. Don't be like the lady who thanked the minister for his sermon and said, "Thank you so much for that sermon. Everything you said applied to someone I know." Don't be like that. Don't say, "That sermon went over my head because I was hoping it would hit the man in the pew behind." But let this come right through to: "Lord, is it I?" That's what they said at the Last Supper and that is what we should say.

The first thing is that Paul in v. 2 says: "It doesn't matter what gifts I receive, without love they are useless." Then in v. 3 he says, "No matter what gifts I give, without love they are useless." Whether you receive a gift or give it, unless there is love in the receiving and love in the giving – nothing. Now he mentions four gifts: tongues, prophecy, knowledge and faith. He is saying that you can have all these gifts in a superlative degree – they are spiritual gifts; you could know all the languages of earth and heaven, and that would be at least six thousand. There are six thousand on earth, and I don't know how many there are in glory – it implies that the angels have different languages among them, I don't know, "but, I may speak in the languages of men or of angels, the whole lot," and, he says, "I'm nothing but a big noise. I'm nothing but an instrument that can only play one note and make one sound," because both a cymbal and a gong can each only make one note, one sound—sounding brass. If I blow a single note on a brass instrument, what good has that done you?

"Even if you had the gift of tongues of heaven and earth," is quite a statement. "Supposing I had all knowledge" – that would be amazing. Supposing I knew all the secrets, the mysteries of God! Supposing I had years ago said to a hill near my church building, "Jump into the English Channel," and the congregation looked out of their bedroom windows the next day and saw that it was as flat as Lincolnshire! Supposing I had faith to do that. You notice what Paul says: "I am nothing." He doesn't say, "I do nothing." You would have done a lot. You would have made a big noise and you would have shifted a mountain but you would not *be* anything. In the last analysis it is not what I have, or even what I do, but what I *am* that God is interested in. So you can make a big noise, you can throw your weight about and throw your faith about, you can declare mysteries, you can even be a prophet, and Paul says you may be no better than when you started. You may still be nothing. The question to ask therefore is not, "What gifts do I possess?" or, "How big a noise am I?" or, "What do other people think of my faith?" the question is: "What am I?" Love is something that you *are*. You are a loving person. You can have a big noise from just a couple of bits of metal knocked together, but you can't have love without a person. Love doesn't exist outside people. Noise does, but love doesn't.

The second thing that Paul says here is in v. 3: I may receive all these gifts and without love I am nothing; I may give all these things away and without love I gain nothing. Normally, if you give in love you gain a great blessing. "It is more blessed to give than to receive," said Paul, quoting the Lord Jesus. Therefore if you give in love, you will find it is a real blessing to do so. But if you give without love you gain nothing. Now he doesn't say that *they* gain nothing, he says, "*I* gain nothing." You are no better off. What he is saying in all this is that no matter what you receive, no matter what you give, you are no better and you are no better off, and that is the important thing that you should be concerned about: that you should be a better person.

Now he talks of renouncing two very big things: all your property and then your life. The Greek word translated "give away all I have" does not mean to sign a cheque for your total bank balance and send it to a needy place. It says literally, "To give away all I have in little morsels." In other words, to go to that situation of need and say, "Here's a little bit for you, and here's a little bit for you" – and to go on giving it out in bits until everything you have is gone. Now, surely, that would be a wonderful act of love? No! It could be a grand gesture, it could be done for display. It could be done for many different motives, and it could all be done without love. That is why we have a proverb in English: "as cold as charity". That proverb has killed the Authorized Version translation which says, "If I give away all I have and have not charity..." and we can't say that now because charity without love has killed the word "charity". It has become a cold Dickensian word that we shrink from. Even the word "love" has its difficulties now.

Not only to give away all your property, but even to go to the extent of burning your body. In Athens, not far from Corinth, there was a statue to an Indian philosopher who was so dedicated to an ideal that one day he set himself on fire and burned himself to death. He did it for an ideal, he did not do it for love. Everybody knew of that monument and knew of the Indian who burned himself to death as the grand gesture – a thing that we might have considered incredible but it has been common news over the last few years of people going into a public place and committing suicide for an ideal. However, you could do that without love. You can go to the stake for some people you love and you can be hating someone else as you do it. Or you can even do it without any love in your heart at all and you gain nothing. You have thrown a life away for nothing.

So the first thing is that gifts are trivial by themselves, because love is absolutely essential not only to what you receive but to what you give. When you put something in the collection plate for some situation of need, I hope it comes with your love because without that you gain nothing. The needy gain something, but you miss the blessing because it was a loveless gift.

Let us turn to the second thing. Again by themselves there are real dangers, treacherous snares and temptations, when gifts come without love. This is true even of natural gifts. We talk about people with an artistic temperament, or the musical temperament, or all sorts of other temperaments. We say sometimes, "He was a genius but impossible to live with, you know." Even with natural gifts, it is possible to have great gifts and lack love so that people can't get on with you. It is, alas, even more true with spiritual gifts. Here we have the clear teaching that even if you are baptised in the Spirit and exercising gifts of the Spirit you may still be a very awkward person to get on with. It does not automatically follow that being baptised and filled with the Spirit and exercising gifts will make you a loving person, because love is not a gift of the Spirit. It is a fruit and that comes in a very different way from gifts.

Someone said to me that they were filled with the Spirit. Quoting the words of another, they added: "I do not feel any better than anybody else, but I do feel better equipped." That is perfectly expressed. Whether love develops does not follow from whether you are filled with the Spirit, but whether you go on walking in the Spirit afterwards. That is very important. This is why you may be puzzled when you meet someone who undoubtedly has spiritual gifts, and you say, "They're not a very nice person to know. I would have thought surely if they get these wonderful experiences and gifts that they would be saints, but they're not." No, they're not! The sanctity comes from seeking after love, which must be sought separately from spiritual gifts. Make love your aim and earnestly desire the gifts. The two ambitions don't automatically come with each other. So you can have a man who has the love of the Holy Spirit without the gifts, and you can have a man who has the gifts without the love.

Regrettably, people with spiritual gifts can hurt others. I can list from Paul eleven ways in which someone with gifts can hurt his fellow Christians. They are mostly negatives. First of all, someone with spiritual gifts can get very impatient. They may say, "Oh, why won't the church have more gifts," and "Why won't the church open up more quickly," and, "Why can't I exercise my gifts?" He gets exasperated. Invariably he becomes so impatient because the church is not going all the way straightaway as quickly as he has seen the truth, and his exasperation leads him to go out of the church to a fellowship where he thinks he can have greater freedom.

England became littered with little groups of Spirit-filled Christians who got impatient with their own churches. That is a tragedy. Love is patient. You may have gifts, but love says, "I am prepared to wait until the fellowship of which

I am part is ready for them. I am prepared to wait until the Spirit has moved others how he has moved me. I am prepared to be patient." Now let me say that it is no virtue of mine because by nature and temperament I am impatient. It is only that the Lord has had to teach me the hard way. But I would be prepared to wait five or ten years before gifts appeared in a church if they came in a healthy way and if they came in God's way and in God's time. I would love to see them this Sunday, but I am prepared to wait, and we ought to be.

A second way in which those with gifts can be hurtful to others is to be unkind, to ride roughshod over the others. In Cumberland there is a little chapel which is full of memorial tablets to members who have died. The walls are covered with them. There are some very big ones with whole essays written about the dear people – you know, telling us that they were Sunday School superintendents, and this, that and the other. But there is one little memorial tablet in the middle, and it has the name of the village schoolmaster on it. Underneath his name there are just three words: "Kind and good" – a lovely epitaph. I have met plenty of kind people who aren't very good and I have met plenty of good people who aren't very kind, but those two things go together as beautiful partners. Love is kind.

Thirdly, it is very easy for a person with spiritual gifts to get jealous. Your gift may be a very simple gift, one of the lower gifts. For example, tongues is put pretty well down the list as a lower gift. Teaching is put higher than tongues; prophecy is put higher than tongues. It may be that somebody with a simple gift is a bit jealous of those who have greater gifts. Or it may be that somebody who has a higher gift is jealous because somebody else also is given that gift, and their monopoly is broken. It is possible for envy and jealousy to come in when gifts come in.

Fourthly: boastful. You can have the gifts of the Spirit and brag about it and say, "I can speak in tongues you know," and you have spoiled the gift. You have boasted about it. You are showing off. You can be arrogant. The word literally means: to be blown up, to be puffed up, to have an inflated idea of your own importance. Later Paul says, "Love is not easily pricked." Of course, if you are blown up you are easily pricked. The quickest way to be deflated is to inflate yourself. Somebody is going to make one little remark that will just deflate you. Or maybe an angel will make the remark. I wonder whether you know this little poem: "Once in a saintly passion I cried with desperate grief; 'O Lord, my heart is black with guile and of sinners I am chief'. Then stooped my guardian angel and whispered from behind, 'Vanity my little man, you're nothing of the kind.'" Sometimes you can blow yourself up, even saying, "I'm chief of sinners," and somebody comes along and pricks you.

Jay Denham Brash , that lovely Methodist minister whose life story was called by his biographer *Love and Life*, one day was castigating his own soul for all his sins, and he said to his wife, "I'm a hound of hell." Later she brought his supper in on a tray and she said, "Here's your supper, hound of hell." She just brought him down – pricked him. Yes, you can even inflate yourself spiritually. You can have spiritual gifts and blow yourself up out of all proportion and you're easily pricked.

Next: rudeness. That means lack of courtesy. Here is a simple example. When two or three people want to exercise gifts at the same time and interrupt each other, that is just plain rudeness. Paul would say: one at a time, wait for each other. Let courtesy be characteristic of your worship. Courtesy is love in little things.

Next, you can be domineering. Love does not insist on its own way. Love does not dominate the situation, become aggressive and say, "This is how it's got to be done." You can easily do that and want to run everything.

Love is not irritable, and that means touchy. Oh, I wish we could get rid of touchiness among Christians – people being easily upset. What anxiety it brings! What nervous energy is swallowed up over people who have been upset. "Have you heard so and so's upset?" How much of our energy is swallowed up when this happens and no longer available to go out and love. Love is not easily touchy. You can have all the spiritual gifts and be very touchy about it.

Love is not resentful. The word means to write down in a ledger something that you intend not to forget. I am unhappy when I hear somebody talking about a conversation they had a year, two years, five years previously. They say, "He said to me, and I said to him, and then he said to me...." They have got it all written down in their memory and they can turn it up. They are nursing their wrath to keep it alive. Do you know in certain South Sea Islands they hang mementos of their enemies above their tables when they eat, so that they can look up and hate their enemies while they eat – constantly have a reminder of someone who has done them an injury? But, you know, you can hang things up in your memory too. You don't need to hang them up on the ceiling to do this. Love doesn't keep accounts of evil.

Love is not spiteful, it doesn't rejoice when others go wrong. Let me be quite practical. Some people have talked to me about those who have received spiritual gifts and then slipped morally. That can happen. Almost with glee, "There that's what happens to Pentecostalism." Love never rejoices when things go wrong. It doesn't do that sort of thing. It can work the other way too. Someone can say, "There, that's what happens when someone hasn't got the gift." Ah, but it can happen to any. Whether they have been filled or not, let him that stands take heed lest he fall.

Finally, those who can't be happy about what is right—let

me again be quite practical. Early in the twentieth century it was the Pentecostal denomination that brought back onto the Christian scene spiritual gifts. You could hardly find them in any other church at the time and they brought this contribution to the total Christian scene of things that had been neglected for years – as others have brought other contributions, as I believe Baptists and others have helped to keep alive a biblical view of baptism. However, what happened in the mid-twentieth century was that spiritual gifts appeared in almost every denomination. They appeared among the Baptists, among the Anglicans. They have appeared among the Roman Catholics, and one of the most exciting movements is the Catholic Renewal Movement around the world. I know people who have been given spiritual gifts in the Roman church and I meet with them.

But I read an article in a paper by a Pentecostalist who couldn't feel happy about the gifts appearing among the Roman Catholics. Now this is where you get either a narrow outlook or a loving outlook that says, "That's real, that's of God, I recognise it gladly." It doesn't mean that the Roman Catholics haven't a lot yet to learn from the scripture – so have we. Wherever the right thing appears, love rejoices with the truth – with what is real and what is true!

Well now, this is love. You see love doesn't hurt people; it holds on to them. Love hangs on. It doesn't say, "Oh, I'm fed up with this fellowship, they're just going too slowly for me, I'm off." Love holds on. Love bears all things, believes all things, hopes all things, always looking for the better. Even if the worst happens, it endures all things. Love says, "You may think I'm cranky because I exercise these gifts – I can put up with that. You may insult me and say I'm crazy, I can put up with that and I can go on loving you." Love holds, it doesn't hurt.

Have you noticed that in this entire chapter there is no

definition of love? There isn't in the whole Bible. I don't know of a *definition* of love. I only know of *descriptions* of love. You notice that these descriptions are not in terms of what you *feel* but how you *behave*. Love is very practical. It is not so much your feelings for another person as the facts of what happens when they insult you, and what happens when they criticise you, and what happens when they get a better gift than you – then you can see love in action.

When you read verses 4–7 you can cross out the word "love" and you can put in "Jesus" and it fits beautifully. "Jesus is patient and kind. Jesus is not jealous or boastful. Jesus is not arrogant or rude." Now try putting your own name and see how far you can get. Quietly take the chapter and say, ".... is patient and kind." Just put your own name and see how far you can read without feeling very uncomfortable.

Finally, gifts are transient. Love endures because it is itself enduring; it never collapses. That is the Greek word: "It never collapses." It is a word used of flowers. What happens to flowers? They will collapse in a few days. Paul says that love never collapses. It is used of a man on a long journey who gets to the point where he literally drops from tiredness; he collapses. Love never collapses. You can punch it. You can hit it. You can insult it. You can degrade it. You can do anything you like to it, but it doesn't collapse. Jesus' love never collapsed. "Having loved his own, he loved them to the end." They spat on him, they laughed at him. They said, "Look at him!" He said, "Father, forgive them for they know not what they do." Love never collapses.

We shall advance beyond the gifts. We are going to leave them behind some day. Prophecy will cease. Tongues, they shall be done away with; knowledge – that will cease. Every spiritual gift we have been looking at will one day be obsolete, finished, done for – but not love. Such gifts will be done away with for the simple reason that the spiritual gifts are sent by God into an imperfect world, to imperfect people, with imperfect knowledge. They are there to help us in our imperfection. But when the perfect comes there will be no need for gifts. When I am made perfect as I am going to be, and you are going to be, and when I am living in a perfect world, and it's going to be a perfect world, I won't need any of the spiritual gifts.

Paul uses illustrations: a man and a mirror. I think back to the days when I was a child. You behave like a child and one of the things that you do is play with toys. When you grow up, what do you do? I hope you put away those toys. Some men still play with model railways but never mind! You put them away. When a boy in the Roman Empire came of age he went proudly down the main street with his dad wearing the *toga virilis*, the robe of a man. They walked hand in hand down the main street, and the boy carried his toys: the ball, the bat, and the rest. He went to the temple of the gods and he left his toys there. He put away childish things – that is what the phrase refers to.

Toys are needed, they are good. They develop a child. You buy toys for your child to help them to develop. One day my daughter was talking to me – I was standing in her bedroom, and we were looking at the doll's house. She said, "I think I'll give it away. I've got too big for it now." But it was a grand toy for her. She learned in her little mind to arrange a home, to arrange furniture, put little bits of carpet in. I hoped she would one day have the privilege of doing it for real, but as a child she was learning through a toy.

Paul is teaching us that the gifts are like toys – we need them to learn. We are spiritual children. But one day we are going to grow up. One day we shall reach the full maturity of Jesus Christ. When you reach that maturity, and his knowledge, and his wisdom, you won't need the toys any more. You will put them away. But beware of misquoting this chapter. We don't put them away until the perfect has come. Therefore we do still need them as they needed them in the New Testament days; we are still children.

The other illustration is a mirror. Corinth was famous for its mirrors. They were made of polished copper. A sheet of metal was polished very highly, but of course they didn't have glass and other substances that we now use, so their mirrors were not like the ones we have today. People couldn't see terribly clearly in them. Paul is saying that now we see everything in a kind of mirror. We see God reflected in the Bible – but we don't see him so clearly that we know everything about him.

Then Paul makes the most remarkable statement of this chapter. One day, we will know as much about God as God knows about us. We won't then need the gift of teaching. I will be out of that job in heaven. I will have another job in heaven. I don't know what it will be yet, but I won't be teaching. I won't be preaching. I won't have a Bible in my hand. I won't even need a Bible then. No one will teach anyone else – we shall all know. So we will go beyond these things. To think that one day I will understand the Trinity! I keep getting questions about that from our little minds that can't understand three persons in one God. People say, "How can you explain the Trinity?" You'll understand it all one day. Just be content to believe that it is true until you get there.

Even though the gifts go, one thing abides and that thing is called: faith, hope, love, because the verb "abide" is in the singular in the Greek and it means these three things are one thing. "Now abides faith, hope, love." That is how it ought to be translated. Love stands up above the others for two reasons. First of all, it is the end and not the means. Faith and hope are the means. Secondly, it is the only one of the three that is the nature of God. We do not say, "God is faith" and we do not say "God is hope" but we do say "God is love".

The thirteenth verse of the thirteenth chapter – whenever you are tempted to be superstitious about the figure thirteen, just say, "1 Corinthians 13:13" and my faith is in God and my hope is in God. It is a lovely verse to live with.

It might be nice to end this exposition there, saying, "Fine, let us allow the last word to be love." But I am going to bring you down to earth with a bump. Paul will not leave you with love. He will not say, "Love is all you need." He will not leave you just with the impression that we have left the gifts way behind, and that love is all we are going to have now. No, we are still in this life. The perfect has not come; we are still children. So back to where we were. "Make love your aim and earnestly desire the spiritual gifts." Right back down to our toys, to the things we need to grow up, to help each other, to learn. In chapter fourteen he tells us how to cope with gifts in the assembly of believers.

GIFTS WITH LOVE
Read 1 Corinthians 14

A. TONGUES AND PROPHECY CONTRASTED (1–25)
1. SPEECH: GOD AND MEN (1–5)
2. SOUND: SPIRIT AND MIND (6–19)
3. SIGN: BELIEVER AND UNBELIEVER (20–25)

B. TONGUES AND PROPHECY CONTROLLED (26–40)
1. SELF: SPEECH AND SILENCE (26–33a)
2. SEX: MEN AND WOMEN (33b–36)
3. SCRIPTURE: LIBERTY AND RESTRAINT (37–40)

As you read this chapter, do include again in your reading the last verse of chapter 13.

There is an awful sense of anti-climax when some people read this chapter. Many feel this is really coming from the sublime to the ridiculous to come right from love and then to come down to a discussion of a thing like tongues. I want to tell you that I believe chapter 14 is the climax not chapter 13. For chapters 12–14 are all one section about spiritual gifts. I would give them these chapter headings: chapter 12 — gifts; chapter 13 — gifts without love; chapter 14 — gifts with love. The real climax is not to live a life of love, but to live a life in which you use the gifts in love — that is the more excellent way. Paul is not saying, "I've spoken about the gifts and the better way is to love rather than exercise gifts." The more excellent way is love *plus* gifts. Gifts without love are futile but love without gifts is frustrated.

Chapter 14 is to bring us right down from the mountaintop of noble visions of love to the valley where it has all got

217

to be worked out into your ordinary, everyday church life, where love, this mountaintop thing, must be exercised in helpfulness to others. Just as on the Mount of Transfiguration Peter, James, and John saw the glory of the Lord, and they had to come down to a valley where there was a boy in desperate need of help, and work it all out there. So 1 Corinthians 14 is the climax. In a sense it is more exciting than chapter 13 because it gears it right down to earth.

There are two gifts mentioned here and discussed all the way through the chapter. One gift is tongues (or unknown languages) and the other gift is prophecy – and they are both gifts of speech in which the Lord miraculously provides words for someone to say. So they are very similar. In both cases, somebody opens their mouth and starts talking, and in both cases God gives the words. The words do not come from the speaker's mind but from God's mind. The one big difference between the two, and it is a huge difference, is that tongues are words given in a language not known to the speaker or the hearer, whereas prophecy is in a language known to the speaker and the hearer. But apart from that single difference, the gifts are identical in that they are miracles of speech.

I would like to shoot the translators (metaphorically!) for putting the English word "tongues" in. The Greek word means "languages". If that word is used it saves an awful lot of this funny feeling that the gift of tongues is a kind of babbling in which you move your tongue round and round and just make the funniest sounds you can. We don't talk of a speaker of a foreign language using a "tongue". We usually say "language" – that is the word and it is the word here. So I would like to go through chapter 14 and cross out the word "tongue" every time and just put the word "language" in, and then people would not get all hot and bothered about it and think it is something peculiar. You know what language is. You have a language already. Maybe you have got two or three languages, so you understand.

There is no real difference between having two or three languages and having six thousand languages. God has them all and he can listen to prayer in any language on earth or any language of angels too. So God is a great linguist. Don't ever get the wrong impression that God is English and has to translate every other prayer into his own language (or even Welsh, and sometimes the Welsh say it is the language of heaven; they are thoroughly mistaken—it may well be Hebrew for all I know).

This gift of languages is overvalued by some and undervalued by others. It is usually overvalued by those who have the gift and undervalued by those who haven't. Those who have the gift tend to get over-excited about it and are tempted to show off that they can speak languages that they have never learned – and to use it too freely. So freely that it becomes not very helpful to other people. It is for that reason that to those who have got the gift and overvalue it Paul says, "I would rather speak five words that people understood than ten thousand that they didn't," and I share his sentiments there. I would rather teach five words in a language you understand than, say, ten thousand in a tongue, which I believe God could enable me to do. Actually I prefer ten thousand that you can understand.

Paul is showing those who haven't got the gift that they undervalue it, and for those who haven't got the gift of unknown languages, who tend to say, "Well I don't want that; I can do without it," Paul affirms two very positive things. First, he says, "I thank God that I speak in tongues more than you all." If Paul thanked God he did, don't you ever thank God that you don't! Second, Paul says, "I want you all to speak in tongues". I share that sentiment also. I would to God that every church member spoke in tongues (but not in church) – because you would edify yourself if you did and you would be a better and stronger Christian. So here are the two balancing statements and the Bible keeps you right on course. Don't overvalue it (especially in church), but don't undervalue it. See this as a gift of God, a good gift, and as something he wants to give you.

We turn to the other gift – prophecy. Paul is saying: "I want you to have this even more." It is a greater, higher gift. It is the gift of being able to open your mouth and let God fill it with a message for someone else without any preparation, without any sermon notes, without any study beforehand so that it is not your mind at all, but just being willing to be God's mouthpiece and let him speak through you. I suppose that this is one of the greatest difficulties that we have – unwillingness to let God use our mouths. "Oh, count me in on making cups of tea. Oh yes I'll do this, that, and the other, and if you want a nail knocked in I'll come and knock it in, but don't ever ask me to come and speak!"

I was thrilled to meet a lady in her late seventies who was at one of our former churches. Throughout the seven years I was there she would say, "Now I'll make tea for you but don't ever ask me to do anything public. Don't ever ask me to speak, I couldn't do it." But it was a very different story when I met her again. She came up to me and said, "Isn't it wonderful – I can pray in a prayer meeting now. I'm taking part now." She said, "It's glorious. I never knew that the Spirit could enable you to do this." There she was in the latter part of her life, and she discovered that the Holy Spirit can enable you to be a mouthpiece of God. She was full of it. She was so excited. Gone was the reluctance, gone the self-consciousness, gone all the hesitation, and instead an overflowing willingness to be used of God to speak – now that is prophecy.

Let us look at the contrast between the two. Paul is looking at both gifts and he weighs them up and there is no doubt which of these two he prefers in church: it is prophecy. He gives three reasons, looking at tongues and prophecy first in terms of speech, then in terms of sound, and finally in terms of signs. For in fact, noise is always one of those three things or all three together. Look first at these two gifts as speech. Both are gifts of speech and words have only one use. Words are to communicate a thought from one mind to another mind – that's all. They are means of communication. I use them – it is my trade if you like, my profession. I could not do what God has told me to do unless I could use words. I don't believe in worship in complete silence, nor does the Bible. The Bible states that when you come together to worship you should each come ready to use words – a hymn, a lesson, a revelation, a tongue, an interpretation, all this is words. He will also say there are times you should be silent, but essentially worship is expressed in word: your words, my words, sung words, spoken words, but it is expressed in words.

The first question about these two gifts of speech is: to whom are the words addressed? The answer is very simple. When I speak in a tongue, I talk to God and he understands what I am saying because he knows all the languages there are. If God did not understand my tongue then there would be no point whatever in praying in a tongue. But he does understand, which is the point of praying in tongues. He understands and you are talking, communicating with God. Your spirit and his Spirit are in communion as you do so. Prophecy, on the other hand, is addressed to people. If tongues is a believer speaking to God then prophecy is God speaking to us – and is addressed therefore to people in a language they understand.

This puts these two gifts in completely different categories. In church, there is no doubt that prophecy is the gift that is needed: in private, tongues are needed; in public, prophecy is needed. Furthermore, we ask who benefits from these gifts. Well, when a tongue is used, the person who speaks is edified. It is funny, you know that until somebody has a gift of tongues they can't see any use in it at all. They say, "Well of all the silly things I've heard of, this is it" – until they are given the gift. Then they say, "This is one of the most edifying and useful and constructive [the word 'edifying' and the word 'constructive' are the same word] – building up."

But prophecy edifies another. If I speak in a tongue in church it would help me but no-one else. It would build me up, not those who are listening. Whereas if I prophesy in church, it wouldn't help me but it would help others who are listening. That is the difference. So which is better, for a gift to help one person or many? The answer is: it is always better to help a lot than one. It is always better to help others than help yourself. Therefore, in church prophecy is the better gift. But there is an important "unless" in v. 5, because if we stop there, then frankly, you would say that tongues have no place whatever in church and ought never to be used in fellowship. *Unless* to the gift of another language is added the gift of interpretation. Then tongue plus interpretation equals prophecy in benefit. Prophecy is only greater than a tongue if the tongue is not interpreted. But this lovely gift of interpretation is given so that everybody may benefit from the words that have been used. Then it becomes a blessing. All this is building up to a simple pattern of how to use gifts in public. Never come to public worship for your own enjoyment. Come for the edification of the church and the glorification of God. Then you will never be tempted to do anything for your own private enjoyment. You will stop and say, "Will this help other people?" If the answer is "yes" you will go ahead and do it.

The second principle in contrasting these two things

looks at the two not just as speech but as sound. I don't know if you realise how much we use sound in worship. Perhaps most of our services are occupied with sound. We have quiet moments but, true to the New Testament, most of our service is noise. Now Paul emphasises strongly that tongues by themselves are simply noise, and that noise by itself is of no value. I remember going to a Pentecostal prayer meeting once with a fellow Baptist minister and we sat there and as we came out, my companion who has a lovely sense of humour, said, "Well if noise is power we're in for a good time tonight," and I knew just what he meant. There was an awful lot of noise in that meeting. But noise is not necessarily power. It is only noise with meaning that has power in fellowship.

Paul gives three illustrations of the absolute necessity of meaning in the noise. First of all he says, "Take a musical instrument, a flute, or a harp." Now a musical instrument makes a noise. I can make a noise with a brass instrument but that would mean absolutely nothing to any hearer. There would be no lasting edification or benefit from it. Incidentally, music is no help in a service unless it has meaning for the people listening. Words are of no help to you unless they mean something to you.

I constantly have to ask myself: what words can I use that will mean something to those who are listening? If I use words that are way out of the experience and vocabulary of listeners, it is a waste of time. The sermon has been a little interval in which they shut off. Likewise, an organ voluntary that is simply noise that has no meaning for you becomes nothing more than a little interval in which you relax and do nothing. The music has got to have meaning if it is to do anything at all. That meaning can be in words that accompany the music or the meaning can be an association of the music.

Too much modern music has no meaning – quite deliberately. It is expressing the belief that life is meaningless. I think of Schoenberg's music. I think of computerised music. It is meaningless and therefore valueless. There is a Christian comment on modern music (as on modern art) which conveys no meaning, no message. The artists and musicians are saying there is no meaning. Let them say that but Christians won't touch music that has no meaning and they won't touch art that has no message. Music must say something meaningful. It must be recognisable and associated with the right thoughts and feelings.

Paul mentions a bugle. Every army used to have a bugler and I think they still do sometimes. The bugler gets up in the morning, he plays, reveille sounds through the camp and people get up. Now if the bugler made just a noise with the bugle they would stay in bed. If the bugler just before the battle was asked to play the charge and he just played noise, nobody would go charging forward. This is the same message. If there isn't meaning in the noise, there is no recognition and no response. So you can have a very noisy service, the music can blast away and people can sing their heads off, but if there is no meaning then there is no recognition and no response.

There will be no relationship either. Now Paul illustrates this from language. Let me do so as well. Each language means something, but only to those who know it. Bible translators work at translating the Word of God. They say: "There's meaning in those languages even if they are not written down – we must discover the meaning and then we can communicate; then there can be a relationship." Paul is teaching us that if you are talking to someone who can only speak a different language from you then you remain foreigners to each other. There is no real relationship because you can't talk and share. We need to know each other's language to have real fellowship. I know that you can sense that you are meeting a brother or sister in the Lord even if you don't speak their language, but there is a very strict limit on the relationship until you can talk together and understand one another. So from all these illustrations from music, from the army, from language: Paul is teaching us: if there is no meaning – no use; no meaning – no recognition; no meaning – no response; no meaning – no relationship. It would be tragic if you ever came to church and you went out with no recognition, no response and no relationship as a result. Now the second thing Paul is saying here is that if you are going to have meaning then your mind must be involved. I have got to use my mind if I am going to convey meaning to my hearers. Do you see that? Meaning involves mind.

I remember going to a Bible school in the Swiss Alps. On top of that alp we took the children to their morning service, but alas, it was all in German. Thankfully, they told us to sit in the back row and put some headphones on and our children were thrilled to sit with these headphones on and some dear lady, who we met afterwards, came out of the service, went into a little room behind, and denied herself the joy of worship so that she could concentrate mentally the whole time on translating the service into English for us. We could listen to the prayer through the service and take part meaningfully because she was prepared to use her mind. She had lost a great deal by doing that but we gained.

I remember asking someone who did deaf and dumb sign language while I preached how much he got out of a sermon while he was interpreting and he said, "Very little – you go too fast for one thing, but I have to concentrate so much on the translation and think how to put it across to them that I get very little out of the sermon." But he was prepared to use his mind to help someone else to get meaning. I can say that when I am preaching I think my hearers get far more out of the sermon than I do. I get it beforehand as I spend the hours studying the Word, but when actually preaching I am trying to use my mind so I get less. If you are in church you use your mind to convey meaning, mental effort is required.

When you pray in a tongue, your mind is not used. Your mind is unfruitful. It's not operating. Your spirit is operating and communing with God's Spirit. There is no mental effort whatever in speaking in a tongue. It requires no IQ – it is a spiritual exercise. There are two kinds of prayer: praying with the mind, in which you think what to say; praying with the spirit, in which you don't think what to say. There are two sorts of church music: singing with the mind, in which you have trained and you are thinking how to present the music and the words; and singing in the Spirit, which requires no mental effort whatever, no training, no conductor, no accompaniment.

Paul wants to develop both: praying with the mind and praying with the Spirit. When I go to church I am going to use my mind. I am going to keep my spiritual singing and praying for my devotions. Do you see what a bearing this has on church? Some people think that all prayer in church ought to be unpremeditated, unprepared, unread, that it ought to be off the cuff and immediately inspired and then it's real prayer. Paul would say that if you are really going to help people in prayer then the best prayer will involve mental effort – thinking about it. I can only say that I am often immensely helped by a prayer that reveals careful thought and preparation beforehand – by somebody who has thought about it, who has made the effort to think what will help these people to pray, and isn't just saying, "I'm going to get up and let the Lord provide." Preaching and teaching also involve this mental effort to get the meaning from mind to mind.

So Paul thanks God he speaks in tongues more than

others but in a meeting would rather speak five words to help others than ten thousand in an unknown language. The reason is that I may be giving thanks to God superbly in a tongue but nobody can say "'Amen." What does "amen" mean? It means, "truly, certainly, agreed – that's it, Lord". How can you say "amen" if you didn't understand what was said? Never say "amen" unless you understood the prayer. It becomes a hollow, empty word, but if you understood the prayer and you believed it and it is yours, then say "Amen."

Now we turn to unknown languages as a sign. Paul's teaching here means: grow up in mind; morally remain a child, mentally be an adult. That is the opposite of what I find in the world today. Morally people want to be adult and mentally they remain children, but in fact you should keep the innocence of childhood in the moral realm and you should leave behind the ignorance of childhood in the mental realm. Morally stay as innocent as a little child, mentally grow up; use your mind and explore the greatest unexplored territory in the world under your hat – this mind God has given you to love with.

How do we do that? Paul is going to stretch the mind now, and he teaches us that tongues and prophecy are signs. What is a sign? It is something which points beyond itself and assures you that there is something else waiting to be discovered. Every sign does that. A sign on the road points to something else that really exists. Even a danger sign points to a real danger.

Tongues and prophecy are both signs pointing people to God. They both convince people that he is real; that he exists. But here comes an important difference: tongues convince the unbeliever that God exists; prophecy convinces the believer that God exists. Therefore, the kind of point or proof that the church needs is prophecy, not tongues. Straight away, the Corinthians are going to say, "Ah, but outsiders and unbelievers come into our service, therefore wouldn't it be great if we all had tongues and the unbelievers are convinced?" Paul would say: no, they would say you are mad. I remember being present at a most unfortunate meeting in the Royal Albert Hall when three or four thousand people went off in tongues. I saw the official who was in charge of the amplification in his booth, measuring the distance to the nearest door. You could see he thought he was in among the most crazy lot of people.

Unknown languages do convince an unbeliever but not when people just go haywire with them – that is not edifying to anybody, believer or unbeliever. But where you have got a group of Christians who are prophesying to one another in a known language, and God is speaking, do you know what happens when an unbeliever comes into that kind of assembly? He falls flat on his face and he says, "My, this is my heart, my secret sins. This is me, God must be here. How does he know all about me?" Have you ever had that experience?

Sometimes when the Word of God is going forth someone comes to me after the service and asks, "Who has been telling you all about me?" My answer is: the Holy Spirit. Nobody else knows you and me, and God can lay bare the secrets when he is speaking. When prophecy is being exercised, people say, "God must be real. He is in this place, I worship God." Isn't that what we want? We don't want to impress people that we have got gifts. We want to impress them that God has us, and that is a different kind of impression—so much then for tongues as a sign.

We move now to the control of tongues and prophecy, as distinct from the contrast between the two. We now have the earliest account of Christian worship – the earliest description of what happens when Christians get together to praise God. It is interesting that Paul begins with the word "brethren". There are some Christians today calling themselves Christian brethren, who claim that they are reproducing the worship of the early church. They are to a degree, in that they do tend to allow more participation than other Christian groups, and that is scriptural. But I don't know many brethren assemblies where all the things listed in v. 26 are freely contributed: unknown language, interpretation, revelation and song. If you are going to have participation then you need the gifts too. You need everything that God has for you so that each may come ready to contribute anything and there are no limits or barriers to what goes on other than scriptural limits. Paul has room in open worship for tongues and prophecy – any open shared worship that will not allow these two things is not biblical – and other gifts too. But, and this is the important thing, all the gifts must be under strict control. If they are not, then it is better not to have open worship. The control is threefold: control by self, control by sex, and control by scripture.

Of these three elements in the control of gifts, take first of all *self-control*. Paul lays down very simple rules: if the gift of unknown languages is going to be used, then only two or three at the very most in one service, and then one at a time. How many meetings I have been to where that rule was not observed. Furthermore, if there is not known to be someone present with the gift of interpretation, then no tongues. You see, different people have different ministries and one person (or two or three usually in a fellowship) develops the ministry of interpretation. If they are not there that Sunday morning, one should hesitate to use a tongue – that is what is being said here.

If I go and speak in a foreign country where English is not understood, it would be madness for me to go if there was no one to interpret. What a sheer waste of time and money! So my first question is: who is going to interpret?

Likewise if you feel you have got a ministry of tongues for the fellowship, then look around – is there a ministry of interpretation there? If not, keep your mouth shut. Likewise the gift of prophecy – only two or three in one service, only one at a time, and let each prophecy be weighed and thought through and discussed and prayed into before you move on to the next. Let all things be done in a constructive way. Otherwise keep quiet. If one of the regular prophets is speaking and someone who is not a regular prophet is given a prophecy, let the prophet sit down and keep quiet and let the other person stand up. These are just sensible rules, but do you notice they all imply self-control? You see, if somebody speaks in a tongue and says to me after a service, "I couldn't help it. I just had to," I reply, "That is not of the Spirit, it is of the flesh." There is no teaching in scripture to say that God suddenly rushes on us, impels us to do a thing, whoever is talking, and that they just have to come out with it. No, you can keep silent, for the spirit of the prophet is under the control of the prophet – *not* the control of God, the control of the prophet. Every gift of the Spirit is under the complete control of the one with the gift. Let there be no mistake, there is no helplessness here, no being rushed or forced into something. You can keep quiet even with a gift of tongues or prophecy. Self-control is the fruit of the Spirit. Why? Because God does not make a disordered, chaotic noise; he does not like confusion; God is a God of harmony and peace. Therefore, he doesn't want things that upset worship, but things that make it more beautiful and more worthy and more acceptable in his sight.

The second word of control mentioned here is a word about sex, about men and women. I must tread very carefully here because I want to be true to scripture. I am not worried about offending feelings. I think that these words have been misused. When gifts are being exercised, it is necessary for women to remember their place. Now let us go a little further into this. The atmosphere of course is freer, it is more emotional. I have been in assemblies where they told me that among the greatest difficulties with open worship were the difficulties of women who could not be controlled. It is a pity if that spoils it for the others.

But having said that, there are those who go to the opposite extreme and forbid women to take part at all, which would be a contradiction of 1 Corinthians 11:5 where Paul talks about women praying and prophesying. So what does this mean here? Quite simply, Paul bases it on the universal principle in all Christian churches that God's pattern of society is: Christ is subordinate to the Father; man is subordinate to Christ and woman is subordinate to man. We must not depart from the pattern in either New Testament or Old Testament days because that is the pattern in both. The Corinthians had stepped out of that pattern. Paul said: do you think the word of God began with you? Do you think you are the only ones who have got the truth? When everyone else recognises this pattern, you should too. But what does he mean?

Philip's four daughters were prophetesses; they prophesied. I believe that women should be free to pray. We notice that they were told to wear hats if they did, but it's madness as I have said, to tell them to wear hats and then tell them not to pray. Paul says, "When they pray let them put a hat on." But he says when they pray or when they prophesy. Now what does he mean? Quite simply this: insubordination is whenever I set my mind over against the mind of my leader. That is the only situation in which there is insubordination. When I hear a woman say about her husband, "I gave him a piece of my mind," that worries me. I remember the reply of one well-known minister to a remark like that. He said, "Are you sure you could afford such a generous offering?" But nevertheless, it is setting her mind against his.

Now in what situations could a woman be doing that in church? Situation number one: by getting up in church and teaching. So Paul said quite clearly: no woman teaches in the churches of Christ. This is not just Corinth – all the churches. Secondly, in the discussion of how to apply God's Word, whether it has come through the scripture or through a prophecy, the men should then weigh it up and decide how it applies to the fellowship. Paul is saying that it is shameful, even embarrassing if a woman gets up and tells the men what to do about the prophecy.

So what Paul is saying I think is this: a woman is free to pray, for that is addressing God. She is not exercising authority. A woman is free to prophesy because that is not her mind operating, it is the mind of God speaking through her mouth. But when it comes to teaching or discussing the application of God's Word or telling the fellowship what to do about what has been said, then let the women keep silent and discuss it at home with their husbands. That seems to me so sensible. Alas the tragedy is that some husbands are not even capable of giving their wife spiritual truth at home. But the ideal is that a husband should be fit to be his wife's teacher and explain to her the Word of God and build her up in the faith that way.

Paul I think already senses antagonism to what he said. Believe me, he didn't just have opposition in modern times. He sensed it already and so he says, "Look what I am writing to you, I Paul, it's not human advice. It's the command of the Lord. If anybody claims special revelation that can contradict what I've said, don't acknowledge him. He's not a true prophet." Here comes the biggest test of all prophecy and all unknown languages: does it contradict the apostles' writings or not? Scripture is the final control. If a man gets up and says something, and declares, "I'm a prophet and God says this," and it contradicts anything the apostles said, don't listen. He is not a true prophet because the Holy Spirit never contradicts himself. The Holy Spirit caused the apostles to write what they did.

If anybody says, "I don't agree with Paul," never let him into your pulpit. He is not acknowledging the Spirit's inspiration of scripture. If you disagree with Paul on something then you are disagreeing not with Paul but with the command of the Lord, and that is very serious. Can I put it this way: when the Spirit gives gifts today he has also given a book of instructions as to how to use them. You can't say, "The Spirit has told me to use the gift ignoring the book of instructions." I have been in some churches where they knew the Bible back to front but there wasn't the power of the Spirit. I have known others where the Spirit was present but oh, how they needed the book of instructions to keep it on course and balanced.

Let scripture put the restraint on and let scripture give the liberty. Here are the limits. The limits of restraint: don't forbid speaking in tongues – and desire prophecy; and the limits of liberty – don't lose decorum and order. These are the limits, and within those limits let us be ready for anything. It may be that most of this chapter is not relevant to your local church, until the gifts appear among you. But God will give gifts, and then we need the book of instructions to keep them right.

Let us summarise this teaching. When you come to church your concern should be to be constructive to the fellow believer and convicting to the unbeliever present. If you are going to do that, then worship must be intelligible, the music and the language must be full of meaning to those who have come, not just to those who are speaking and playing. Secondly, worship must be balanced. There mustn't be too much of one gift. Thirdly, worship must be orderly, one by one, not chaotic. Fourthly, worship must be shared so that it comes from all of us and each contributes. Fifthly, worship must be real, so that the outsider goes away saying, "God is really there."

RESURRECTION
Read 1 Corinthians 15

A. THE MESSAGE (1–11)
 1. ITS CONTENT
   a. His death
   b. His resurrection
 2. ITS CONFIRMATION
   a. O.T. prophets
   b. N.T. apostles

B. THE MOCKERY (12–19)
 1. NO SALVATION
 2. NO SURVIVAL

C. THE MEANING (20–28)
 1. RACE OF IMMORTAL MEN
 2. REIGN OF INFINITE GOD

D. THE MORALITY (29–34)
 1. PAGAN RITES
 2. PAULINE RISKS
 3. POPULAR REVELLING

E. THE MANNER (35–44)
 1. SOWING – physical
 2. REAPING – spiritual

F. THE MAN (45–50)
 1. EARTHLY ADAM
 2. HEAVENLY CHRIST

G. THE MOMENT (51–57)
 1. SUDDEN TRANSFORMATION
 2. SURE TRIUMPH

H. THE MOTIVE (58)
 1. IMMOVABLE
 2. INDUSTRIOUS

There is the story in the Bible (see Esther) of a certain king who suffered from insomnia. As he lay awake one night unable to sleep, he read through his old diaries. He read one written twenty years earlier and he suddenly saw his own account of how a man in his kingdom had saved his life. To his horror he realised he had forgotten all about it and never rewarded that man – a moral to us that we need the constant reminder of the most important things. You can forget the biggest things in your Christian life and Paul begins this chapter by saying, "I want to remind you of some of the biggest things – that you believed right at the beginning. So now to the fundamentals – the most important things you believed. In this chapter Paul has changed from talking about Christian *behaviour* to Christian *belief*.

Consider this question: do you begin to be a Christian by behaving in a certain way or by believing in a certain way? Most people seem to think that you start with behaving and they will say they try to do good and that they don't do anyone harm, so of course they are a Christian!

But you began to be a Christian, if you are one, not by trying to behave like one, because you can't, but by believing. It is what you believe that starts you on the Christian road, not how you behave. Paul takes them right back to the beginning, and reminds them of the first things they believed. When you get away from those first things, you suffer.

The gospel – the good news of Christ – can go on saving you provided you stay with it, but if you get away from it, it loses its power. A man who came to know Christ years ago by believing the good news of Christ, can so drift away from it that no longer does it go on saving him. Paul says that the gospel saves you now if you hold on to it. (Unless you didn't even believe it properly in the first place.)

The glorious thing is that the gospel can not only save me in the great Day when we all stand before God, it can save me today from all kinds of things. The power of the gospel goes on saving you from all kinds of things in your life that you wish you could be free from – provided you stay with the first fundamental beliefs. If you lose those you are finished – the gospel can become something you just hear on a Sunday.

Now what was this gospel? Paul says: "I only gave you what I received." You never invent good news. It is something you can receive and pass on and then others can pass it on to someone else. If it were not true, it would not be news, it would only be fiction. Broadcast news is not the news unless it is fact. Other programmes can share opinions. Of the gospel you can only say, "I have heard it. Here it is. I've been told this. I tell you...."

Assuming that you are addressing someone who knows nothing about Christianity, what could you say it is all about? Is it a way of life (an ethic)? Is it a code of behaviour? No, that wouldn't be very good news. If I told you to go out and never to do a wrong thing again, would that be good news? On the contrary it is bad news because you know perfectly well you will never do it. Is Christianity an ecclesiastical institution? Is it an organisation – a kind of religious club? Is it the church? What good news is there in telling you about the church? Is Christianity a religion? Thank God that it isn't. If you are religious that doesn't make you a Christian and if you are a Christian that means you are finished with religion. It is not a religion because none of the religions of the world could be put in the category of "good news". Every way of life that is taught among men, religious institutions, religions themselves are "do-it-yourself" jobs, telling you what you have got to do, but I have got the gospel to preach and therefore I have got to say, "It is not what you've got to do, it is what Christ can do for you." That is good news. And "what he has done for you" – that is great news.

I have heard that he has died on a cross for you. I have heard that he burst the gates of hell and he is alive today. That is good news! It is not something you have got to do. It is something he has done for you. It is great news that I pass on.

I don't mind people calling me a "fundamentalist" because it means I stick with what is fundamental and I don't change my gospel, with all the fashions of philosophy and theology. I preach what has been preached for two thousand years in exactly the same way. First of all: Christianity is about a person, not about a system or an organisation, or a religion. "I delivered to you what I received that Christ ...." and it is tremendous to be able to talk to people about a *person* and not try and get them into a system, or make them part of the establishment but to say, "You need Jesus and he can help you."

Secondly, we are told that the good news is centred in a particular period in the life of that person Jesus. Not in his birth – the Christmas story is not a fundamental of the gospel, which is why people can get so excited about Christmas without becoming Christians. It is not fundamental. Nor is the first thirty years of his life fundamental to the good news. Nor is the next three years fundamental to the Christian good news. The gospel of Christ centres in a period just three days long. That is all. And it covers three events: his death, his burial and his resurrection.

If you grasp those three days in the existence of that person Jesus, you have got the gospel. This is fundamental – not all that Jesus said and did, not all his miracles and not all his parables. I will tell you what is fundamental: he died, he was buried and he was raised. That is Christianity. And if you have never really grasped those three things, however much you think of Jesus, however much you have admired him and respected him, you are not yet a Christian.

Notice that those three things are all things done to his body. It was his body that died, it was his body that was buried and it was his body that was raised. And Christianity is concerned with bodies. Archbishop Temple called Christianity the most materialist religion of all religions in the world. I would only quarrel with the word "religion" there. But what he meant was that Christianity is concerned with bodies.

At the heart of Christian worship we take a loaf of bread and we break it to remember the body of Jesus and what happened to his body. In his own body he bore our sins on the tree. We are not talking about ghostly, vague, spiritual things. We are talking about a body which died at the age of thirty-three after cruel torture, that was buried in a tomb (as men thought, forever) and then was raised.

Two of these three things are true of everybody else. I will die, my body will be buried in one form or another, whether as ashes or a corpse. The good news is that death and burial was not the end of Jesus' body. He was raised to life. We have an empty tomb. Christ – died, buried, raised. That is the good news. Three events within three days in the life of one Man have changed the world. That is the great news of the gospel.

Not only are we told that Christianity is about a person, about a three-day period in his life, we are told the purpose of it all: he died for our sins. Why is this good news? Is it because he can deliver us from our fears? He can. From our doubts? He can do that. From our illnesses? He can do that. From our complexes? Yes, he can do that. But Christ died primarily to get rid of our sins. Not our vices – the things we do against ourselves; not our crimes (which we do against others), but our sins which we do against God – and that is the most serious.

What is preventing you from enjoying the life that God intended you to have? Is it that you haven't enough money? No. Being tied to a person you wished you could be free from? No. What is holding you away from real life? Sins! And Christ died and was buried and was raised for our sins. It was all for that.

Finally, we are told of the proof of these events. When people ask me "Can you prove the truth of Christianity?" the answer is yes – if you are prepared to accept the kind of proof that you would accept for any other event of history. For the evidence for the proof of the events of which I have spoken – his death, his burial, his resurrection – the evidence is as strong as for any event in the life of any man in the history of the human race. Not only that, but all the historical evidence for the events for Julius Caesar's life or anyone else's life were written up after the event by those who witnessed them and you weigh up the evidence of the witnesses and say, "Are there enough people who saw it happen?" These three events in the records about Jesus are unique in this: they were written up *before* as well as after. He died and was buried and raised according to the scriptures and they had been written centuries earlier. And then we have the written record of apostles afterwards, to confirm that they had proof afterwards. You have got double evidence for these events. All other events of history have only single evidence – records written up afterwards. God in his mercy has given to men double proof that these events have happened. He wrote them up, before through prophets and afterwards through apostles.

The Bible is in two parts. One part was written by prophets before Jesus – the Old Testament – and the other part was written afterwards by apostles – the New Testament.

There is the historical evidence that one day Jesus died and that night he was buried, and three days later he was raised. Think of Psalm 22, written many centuries before it happened. "They have pierced my hands and my feet and for my garments they cast lots." It was written when nobody was put to death on a cross and the piercing of hands and feet was unknown, yet there in detail is a description of what was going to happen.

Isaiah 53 was written seven hundred years before Jesus died. "He was wounded for our transgressions, bruised for our iniquities. They made his grave with the wicked and with the rich in his death." A rich man's grave, yet near to the place where criminals were thrown.

What about the evidence afterwards? Paul says that Jesus appeared to Peter – the greatest untold story in the Bible because we don't know where it was or when. He appeared to twelve men, none of whom were expecting him. All of them were convinced. I remember hearing a preacher talk about those twelve and saying "there was a tax man among them and a tax man is not usually given to hallucinations – he saw him." There was an underground fighter. They are tough men (not given to fanciful thinking) and he saw him.

There was a time when five hundred people at once saw him – and were convinced. And he appeared to James, his own brother who was antagonistic and didn't believe in him but later became the leader of the church. What happened to that man? He saw Jesus. Then Jesus appeared to all the apostles. Paul had fought Christianity hard because he couldn't believe it. Jesus was dead and buried. And then one day he was travelling along a road, and a voice said "Saul, Saul, why are you kicking against the goads?" Paul said "Who are you, Lord?" and he said "I am Jesus".

If I could produce some five hundred first-hand witnesses in a law court today, no jury in the world would doubt my evidence. Most of those five hundred were still alive. Paul could introduce others to them. It is amazing that the world will accept far less evidence for other history and will not accept the evidence for the facts of Jesus' death, burial and resurrection. What an array of testimony of witnesses! Paul says "I was like someone born far too late". He didn't even walk with Jesus for those three years, yet somehow Jesus pulled Paul into being his apostle, his witness of the resurrection. The apostle tried to make up for it. He worked harder than any of them to tell others the good news. And it was all of the Lord's kindness and grace that he did.

So here is the first point. The heart of Christianity is in the death, burial and resurrection of the body of Jesus. As a result of what was witnessed to by prophets centuries before and by apostles afterwards, there is all the evidence you could possibly ask for to prove that these things happened. With all this, you have got the proof of Christianity, the truth of what we do.

Secondly, the Corinthians doubted it. They doubted it because the philosophers said that dead people don't rise. Let me make it clear that the Corinthians and the Greeks believed that it might be possible for a soul or a spirit to float on in some vague existence in the future, but as to the idea of the resurrection of your body, they said no. They were troubled with modern doubts. They were troubled with the supernatural miracle of a body coming back to life. They were prepared to believe in survival but not resurrection.

I find Christians today who believe in survival after death but not resurrection. Resurrection is something that happens to your body. Survival is something that people believe happens to your soul. The difference between, for example, spiritualism and Christianity is that spiritists believe in life after death in the sense that you can float on as a spirit, but they will not believe in the resurrection of the body. They say that the resurrection accounts in the Bible are not true.

Jesus said, when he came back from the dead, "Handle

me". They knew that he had flesh and bones, and that spirits don't have that. "Give me some of the fish to eat" – he made a bonfire and cooked breakfast. Spirits don't do that. He had a real body and he was raised in the body.

The Corinthians were having difficulties with this belief. So do many people today. The editor of one of the best-known Christian presses in England wrote: "The bones of Jesus lie rotting somewhere in Palestine but that does not affect our Christian faith" – but of course it would! If the bones of Jesus lie rotting in Palestine, if his body did not rise, then frankly we really would be wasting our time. So many things follow. If you can't believe that a body can come back from death, and that we can't rise from the grave with a body, then Christ has not been raised from the dead and the whole of Christianity collapses. My preaching is a waste of time if bodies don't rise. Your faith is empty, futile, hollow if bodies don't rise. Even more, you are calling the apostles liars – Simon Peter, Paul, James, John. Here are two other appalling thoughts. Firstly, if Christ's body did not rise again, then you are still in your sins. You have got all your temper and all your gossip and malice and envy hanging round your neck like a millstone and you will go on living with that forever and ever. You are still in your sins, deluded if you think they have gone. If Christ's body didn't get out of that tomb, then you are still in the grip of your sins and you will never be free of them.

The other frightful possibility would be this: Christians who die you would never see again. If Christ's body didn't get out of that tomb you will never shake hands with someone you knew, never see the face of those whom you loved.

So Paul says: "If Christ's body is still in the tomb, you are of all men most pitiable, because you have got more to lose!" Christ makes this life so sweet, but to think that death ended it would be dreadful. It would end it all. How miserable we would be. Our personal relationships in Christ become so sweet that we can't bear the thought of breaking them. Yet if only in this life we have hope in Christ, we are to be pitied.

I love God's "buts" – have you ever noticed how often God comes in with a great "But..."? – *but* stop thinking like that. In Ephesians 2 we read: "We were dead in trespasses and sins, but God in his mercy...." and there is a miserable list of what would follow if Jesus' body didn't rise from the dead – in fact, Jesus *was* raised.

When Jesus died, it was on the Passover, and in the Old Testament law it said that on the third day of the Passover you must bring the first little bit of your harvest to God. It was called "the first fruits" – and you offer it to him. That little first-fruit is the beginning of a great harvest. It was their harvest festival. We tend to have a harvest festival after everything is "safely gathered in" – they had theirs before. They brought their firstfruits to God – not when they had got everything but beforehand.

It was on that very day when the Jews were bringing their first bit of the harvest that Jesus rose from the dead, the firstfruits of them that are asleep. Notice that from then on Christians talk of death as "falling asleep". The phrase "falling asleep" means that you expect to wake up in the morning! "Passed away" would be very different. But a Christian need no more fear death than going to sleep at night. That is what it is like to die. It is just like going to sleep at night with the knowledge that you wake up in the morning.

Why do we have this new attitude to death? Because Jesus has been raised from the dead, the firstfruits of them that have fallen asleep. He went to sleep, he woke up and he is alive now and for evermore. This is what begins to follow. Paul now declares the future to them. He says the resurrection is only the beginning. He says it is the beginning of two things. The first is that it is the beginning of the raising of all Christians.

One of the meanings of baptism is this: it is looking to the future, to a day when we will be physically buried, and it is saying as certainly as we are lifted out of the water: Jesus will lift us out of the grave. It is a resurrection rite. It is a looking forward to waking up in the morning and seeing each other again.

It was one man's act of disobedience that brought death into the world. Death was never intended for the human race. It is an unnatural thing. It is not a natural event. Let the scientists say what they like – death is not natural for people. It is a penalty, not a process. It is something that came in through a man's disobedience. Adam disobeyed and therefore led the human race into funerals. It was introduced to the human race and we have got to die as a result, so through one man's obedience, life has come! And, "as all in Adam die, all in Christ shall be made alive" – but in the right order. Christ first, and then when he comes again, we shall rise. The word used here for his second coming is the word used in the ancient world of a royal visit. What an air of expectancy there is for a royal visit! Signs go up. Children with flags and flowers strain to see the first glimpse of the royal car, a motorcade comes past, police cars; excitement rises – and then the royal visitor comes. That is how it will be.

We can begin to see even now the signs that he is getting near. You can see the unfolding of history. You know that we are much nearer to our Lord's return to earth than we were. What is going to happen when he returns? There will be a lot of empty graves in a lot of cemeteries! Those people will have gone. They will be waiting for him.

The dead in Christ shall rise first. You don't need to worry about death any more. Think of "falling asleep" – lying back and going to sleep, that is easy, knowing that you will be there at the Royal Visit. "Then at his coming, those who belong to Christ" – all of that is involved in the resurrection of Jesus' body. I will get out of the grave and see him and meet him.

What else is involved? Not only will his followers be raised, but his foes will be destroyed. Every enemy of man will be destroyed. Christ is going to reign until every enemy is under his feet, and the last enemy to be destroyed is death. The world's most powerful people must one day meet the last enemy, called death.

But Jesus is one day going to send "death" to hell. Does that make sense to you? In the Book of Revelation it says that death and Satan are cast into the lake of fire. One day, death will die. One day, death will be destroyed and buried. And when the last enemy is destroyed, then Christ, having defeated all the enemies of God and the enemies of man, will say: "Now, Lord, here it is back again."

Why did Jesus come to die and be buried and raised? He came to get back everything for God. There is much in the world that doesn't belong to God at the moment. There are many ungodly things happening which all can see, but the ultimate object of the whole thing is that "God may be all in all". That everything may belong to God and God be everything to everyone.

Jesus came to get it all back, to rescue it, to make the kingdoms of this world his own kingdom, that he might one day subject it all to God the Father again, and even Jesus himself, not as a slave but as a Son, will submit to the Father, that one day God may be all in all. Nothing will be there that doesn't belong to God. No-one may be living who doesn't belong to God – and no part of the universe that does not reflect God's glory. That, then, is the great vision of this chapter.

A baptism service reflects the fundamentals of the gospel: dead, buried, raised. The person being baptised is being buried with Christ in the present, and raised with Christ. They go through their baptism not like him but with him. They are raised, burying the old life with all that was wrong and being raised to new life.

We move on to vv. 29–34. One of the most common objections made to our faith is that Christians are so heavenly minded that they are no earthly use, that we are too busy thinking about the next world to be concerned about this one. It was this that lay behind the criticism made by Charles Kingsley, the author of *Tom and the Water Babies*, the Anglican clergyman who was distressed by his congregation who would come and sing hymns heartily on Sunday but seemed absolutely blind to such social injustice as the treatment of the chimney-sweep boys. It was he who said, "Religion has become the opiate of the people" – a phrase that Karl Marx later took up, and I am afraid Marx is wrongly credited with the original phrase. In other words, it is alleged by its opponents that religion is escapism. It is running away into heaven from all the problems of earth; supposedly, Christians are simply closing their minds to all the problems in this life and are just looking forward to the next, and they are simply escaping.

There is an element of truth in this criticism of which we must take notice. If ever we do use religion this way, then it is not the religion of Jesus Christ. If ever we get so wrapped up in heaven that earth becomes a matter of indifference then we have got out of balance and we are certainly not following Jesus. But, having affirmed that, there is an element of truth in this criticism – there is an awful error.

In fact, how you behave in this life depends on what you believe about the next. What you think about the future is going to affect what you do tomorrow. What we discuss about the resurrection today will affect how you behave tomorrow morning. What you think about the next world profoundly changes your behaviour in this.

Broadly speaking, there are three sorts of belief about the next world.

There is the belief that no part of the individual survives death; that, when you die, other people's memories of you will last on, the work you have done may last on, your children may survive you, but you die. Every part of you is finished. That is one idea about the future, a very common one, and a growing one in Britain today.

Secondly, there is the belief that only a part of you survives. Now this is what the ancient Greeks believed and this is what many modern people believe too – that after death your body is finished with, a whole lot of you goes back to rot in the dust and that is the end of it, but some part of you (we could call it "the soul" or something else) goes floating on into the future. When you ask people who believe this, "What kind of life is it going to be?" it is thought to be a very partial sort of life. It doesn't have about it the wholeness of this life. There isn't the attraction of this life about it because it is vague, shadowy – only a bit of it floating on, and that is the bit I am not sure exists. I know that I am a body, but where is this thing called "soul"? This second view is certainly not the Christian view.

The third view is that life after death can be the life of a whole person – body and spirit. The life will be complete. Therefore the Christian creeds from the beginning have never said "I believe in the immortality of the soul", they have said "I believe in the resurrection of the body". In other words, all of me is going to survive. I am going to be a complete being in life after death.

This is what Paul is concerned about in chapter 15. It is all about bodies. Remember that our gospel is rooted in three facts: the death, burial and resurrection of Jesus, and all those three things happened to his body. We are not so much concerned with what happens to the spirit of Jesus, it is what happens to his body that is good news. His body died. His body was buried. His body was raised. Therefore Christianity is concerned with saving people's bodies – ultimately saving them completely, setting them free from disease, death and weariness forever, and that is good news. That is a life which is really worth looking forward to. I wouldn't look forward to floating around as a soul, just like that. I want to be in a body as I am now, so that I can see you, and you can see me and I can shake hands with you – that is life that I know! If I had to choose between life with a body and life without a body, I would choose life with a body every time. Of course, I want to be complete and whole, a real human being.

Now this is the heart of the Christian gospel: that because Jesus came out of the grave with a body and said 'Handle me and see. I am no ghost. I have flesh and bones, come and touch me, give me some of your supper to eat...' We can also promise in the name of Jesus to people that after death you can have a new body, you can be a complete person all over again. Now that is good news.

Paul is going to illustrate the difference that is going to be made to life here by believing in that – in three different ways. The first is a very strange way and it takes a bit of understanding. The second is better known to us, but not by all of us, and the third illustration he uses is from ordinary everyday experience.

The first illustration is something I have never seen, or know very little or nothing about, and which many Christians have known nothing about, but which Paul and the Corinthians clearly knew about. You notice he talks about "they", then "I", then "you". He draws an illustration from a group of people whom he doesn't define, but he describes as "they". Then he draws an illustration from his own life.

"They" were a group of people who were doing something rather unusual. A lot of ink has been spilled by the scholars over v. 29. Forty different explanations may be found in the commentaries! I don't think I can sort it out if they have argued for almost two thousand years as to what it means. There is a double difficulty. Firstly, what does v. 29 actually refer to? Secondly, how does it fit in to the rest of the New Testament? That is why scholars are so divided and discuss it so deeply. Some of the explanations of this phrase: "baptise for the dead" are these:

1. Some say it means baptise *over* the dead and imagine people were getting baptised on top of someone's grave.

2. Some think it means to be baptised *for the sake of* the dead – a Christian has died and they loved you and prayed for you and wanted you to be an all-out Christian and for their sake you are getting baptised.

3. That to be baptised for the dead is to be prepared for death, and to be baptised just before you die.

4. That as Christians are dying and the ranks of the church are emptying, so new converts are coming to be baptised in their place.

5. That Christians are being baptised for the dead, meaning: a Saviour who has died.

But all these are evasions of the simple meaning of the words! I have to tell you that the simple meaning of the phrase is: a proxy baptism. It means being a substitute in the waters of baptism for someone who has already died. We cannot get round that simple meaning. But it is an extraordinary idea – that somebody should get baptised for someone who is already dead.

Now who are "they" who are doing this thing? Quite clearly it is not Paul doing it, though he did not baptise many people anyway. But if it was Paul he would have said "we". Nor is it all the Corinthian Christians. He would have said "you". It is some group of people – known to him and known to the Corinthians – who were doing it.

It is just possible that it was being done by pagans in Corinth. Pagans knew baptism as a religious ceremony. They went through pagan baptism. They washed somebody all over. They immersed them in water. It may be that Paul is using pagans to make Christians embarrassed. Jesus did this when he held up an unjust steward who showed more sense than many Christians. The children of darkness are often wiser in their generation than the children of light.

But I cannot avoid the implication of this verse: that in fact, some Christians had done this. The reason they had done it, I imagine, would be this: that somebody had been converted, had repented and believed, but before they could be baptised they had died, and therefore the Christians left behind, knowing that the person who had died had intended to be baptised, carried on, as it were, in their place, in much the same way as you get a posthumous award of (say) the Victoria Cross and you see a soldier's wife and family going to Buckingham Palace to receive what he should have had.

It was a practice that was obviously open to terrible abuse. Fortunately there are only a few traces of it in the early church and it died out very quickly. Paul is not approving it. He would never have done it, I am quite sure. But what he is saying is this: "You know people have done this. Why have they done it? If there is no resurrection of the dead, there is no point in doing a thing like that." Why not? Because they are doing it in order that the person who has died may stand before God as a baptised person, but baptism is something you do to your body, and if there is no resurrection of the body, then why do this? There would be no point whatever.

Paul is therefore not approving of this. He is simply drawing an illustration from what some people have been doing: that there is no point in doing certain things if there is no resurrection of the body.

Now see v. 30. The second illustration he uses to show how belief in the resurrection affects how you behave in this life is a more common one, though not universal among Christians, and it is one that we will understand. It is something that Paul goes through. So it changes from "they" to "I". And we do understand Paul. He argues like this: every day of my life I face the possibility of losing it. Now we don't live like that. I know that when I drive – even to a church service – the chance of being killed on the roads is high, but it is not a direct threat, not so direct that I have to prepare for it in my morning prayer. Paul is telling us that every day, when he got up in the morning, he faced the possibility that it was his last day. How would you behave if you believed that? It would have a profound effect on your life. This also comes out in his 2 Corinthians – we commend ourselves in every way, through great endurance and afflictions, hardships, calamities, beatings, imprisonments, tumults, labour, watchings, hunger....

Do you face that every day? Read on some pages and he says, "I have far greater labours, far more imprisonments, with countless beatings and often near death, five times I have received at the hands of the Jews the forty lashes less one." We know from records that it usually killed a man or drove him insane. Three times he had been beaten with rods, and that often left a gibbering maniac. Once he was stoned. Three times he had been shipwrecked – a night and day adrift at sea. On frequent journeys, in dangers from rivers, from robbers, from his own people, from Gentiles; danger in the city, in the country, at sea, from false brethren, in toil and hardships, through many a sleepless night, in hunger and thirst, often without food, in cold and exposure. To cap it all, there was his anxiety about the churches.

Do you live that kind of life? No. Do I? No. But some

of our brethren do. In some countries Christians are facing death, imprisonment, loss of family, and facing it all every day. When you face it every day, you begin to ask "Is it worth it? What is the point? Living as recklessly as this, risking the most precious possession of life – life itself." Paul may seem to sound selfish here, and you may be asking why he thinks of what he will gain. What do I gain if I have to fight with wild beasts? – either referring to the arena, or to men who would tear him limb from limb. But it is not selfish. Paul is saying: God has given me life. If I lose it I don't get it back again. There is only one life to live in this world. Therefore one should not recklessly throw it away. It is a most precious, valuable thing and to throw a valuable thing away is folly. Young men, to get on a motor bike and go tearing around at a hundred miles an hour with no thought for the life God has given you is folly. Older men: to go around making more and more money and building up your business until you are riddled with ulcers is folly. And to throw away the life God has given you is folly unless there is point and gain.

Paul is saying: If there were no resurrection of the body, and this was the only body I had, then I would be utterly foolish to risk it so recklessly and throw it away and face death every day. How am I able to face death every day? Why am I able to face these dangers? Because I believe in the resurrection of the body. I have everything to gain by death. Nothing to lose. I long to depart and to be with Christ for it is far better!

You see, if you don't believe in the resurrection of the body in the next world, you hang on to the body in this world. It is bound to affect your behaviour. Self-preservation becomes the important thing. It is possible even in Christian circles to talk as if a person being rescued from death is the most marvellous thing that could have happened! It isn't.

It could be a very sad thing, to bring someone back from the brink of the grave. That is how Paul would have talked.

But if you don't believe in the resurrection of the body, you want to hang on to this one as long as you can. You wouldn't risk it recklessly. So there is a balance here. The Christian has received from God "life" for this body. On the one hand he must not recklessly throw it away for nothing. Paul ran the risk for the gospel, not for nothing. He wasn't being a fool. On the other hand, the Christian doesn't hold on to the body so that personal safety becomes the main thing.

I remember talking to a young lady who went out as a missionary to Eritrea. I knew that the country through which she would travel was infested by bandits who for a handbag would murder. I said, "How do you feel to travel like that? Are you afraid to die?" and she said something amazing. She said "I died ten years ago." A few months later that girl was murdered for her handbag. She ran the risk and she knew it, to take the gospel to an area where the gospel had not been. It was because she believed in the resurrection of the body and because she died daily that she could face such peril. In other words, if we really believe in the resurrection of the body, it affects our attitude to danger in this life most profoundly. We do not recklessly throw our life away but for the sake of the gospel, we "present our bodies a living sacrifice".

The third illustration that Paul uses is one that will mean something to all of us. It will make sense because you meet it every day. The first and the second illustrations are unusual activities. I have never come across being baptised for the dead except among the Mormons. As I say, it is terribly open to abuse. I have not myself faced the kind of dangers that Paul faced, though I have met people who did.

But the third thing I meet every day and it is this attitude: if I am not certain of the next life, then I will enjoy this one as much as I can. If I do not believe in another body, then I will indulge this one now. This is the attitude we find all around us. Paul quotes a proverb: "Let us eat, drink and be merry, for tomorrow we die." That proverb occurs in every culture known to humanity! It is normal human wisdom. You find it among the ancient Egyptians. Euripides tells us they said this. You find it among the Greeks. You find it among the Jews, for this proverb comes at the beginning of Isaiah, when the Babylonians besieged Jerusalem and they knew that their days were numbered and that there was no hope. Awful lust broke out among the Jews in Jerusalem. They said, "We are going to die tomorrow. Marriage can go, everything can go. Let us just enjoy ourselves. Our time is limited."

When you no longer believe in the next life, you are bound to say it is wise to get as much as possible out of this one. Notice that Paul says that if the dead are not raised, then it is wise, right, sensible to "eat, drink and be merry". That is logical. If there is nothing beyond this world, let us enjoy it as much as we can now! Let us indulge ourselves. Who cares? Who cares about the sanctity of marriage, or property, or life or anything else? Let us enjoy ourselves and get away with it.

Of course in our day we are living under the threat of limited time on earth. The threat of the atom bomb and the mushroom-shaped shadow of 1945 began this rot. People felt their days were numbered. An opinion poll in the second half of the twentieth century revealed that over half the teenagers in the sixth forms of Surrey believed they would not live to the age of forty. That is how they expressed themselves. And that is not just the atom bomb. There are now greater threats to mankind than nuclear weapons, including the biological time-bomb, the threat of pollution. We now know that this earth is more like a space-ship, with limited supplies of air, food and power and water.

No wonder that with that background, when people feel their days are numbered, they are saying, "Let us eat, drink and be merry ... let us squeeze every ounce of enjoyment we can, and when we have exhausted all legitimate pleasures, let us go for perverted pleasures, let us get everything we can, anything we can enjoy!" Can't you see why permissiveness in society has come? Can you not see why the threat of limited time has said to people "eat, drink and be merry" – it is the only sensible thing to do; get the house you want, the garden, the cars, all you want. Take it if you want it. And Paul says: If there is no resurrection of the dead, then let us all do that. That is why people behave as they do. They do not believe in anything real beyond the grave. They say: I am only going to have one body, so I will give it everything it wants, I am going to indulge every pleasure, passion, desire, lust that it has. That is the world in which we live.

Paul is saying: Don't be deceived. Don't be fooled. Don't let the world kid you that this is the only chance of enjoying anything you will ever have. Then he quotes another proverb that you will find in the Bible and you will also find this in other cultures: bad company ruins good morals. In other words, just being with people of the wrong outlook has a contaminating, infectious, corrupting influence on your own attitudes if you are not careful. Even as Christians, there is a risk we might adopt this same outlook so that we never consider the next life.

Even Christians have fallen for this. They have been fooled. They have been so bogged down in this world and the needs of this world, that while in England the money pours in for feeding the hungry, money for saving souls overseas is going down. We have been fooled by bad company.

Notice that the opposite is true. Good company builds good morals. If bad company inevitably has an effect on you subconsciously, good company has the opposite effect. And to be among those who are looking forward to glory is to be balanced and kept on an even keel. So Paul is saying that what you need is not godless company but godly convictions!

Christians should know that we are passing through. Sojourners in a land of promise on our way to glory, we are not to behave as if we are here forever.

So Paul says: "Sober up". That is the literal word. Stop enjoying everything. Have you noticed how many advertisements tell you to drink as much as possible now, to enjoy it now? Everything you can enjoy now. Paul calls us to wake up. Come out of this bemused state. The world is bemused with this life. Wake up and "sin no more" – those words were said to a girl by Jesus, a girl who had been caught up in bad company, enjoying herself in the wrong way. Do a bit of straight thinking. Think about the future resurrection. How does the present look now? It looks very different.

Paul is pointing out that the real trouble is this: the world has no knowledge of God. The Greek word he uses means *agnostic* – it doesn't know. I suppose ours is the generation of the "don't knows". Ask a typical person in the street: do you know if there is life after death? "There may be – I don't know." Paul says this agnosticism has crept even into the church. It has in our day too. But a Christian is one who *knows* he has passed from death to life. A Christian is one who *knows* that after death there awaits a new body; and because of that he has knowledge of the future that God has planned – "...what eye has not seen, what ear has not heard, what the imagination of man has never conceived...." The Christian says "I know what God has prepared for those who love him." This knowledge wakes the believer, straightens him out and gives him a different attitude to this world.

Again we recall that there will come a day when we must all stand before the judgment seat of Christ, to be judged by him for the things done in the body. "Therefore I beseech you by the mercies of God that you present your bodies a living sacrifice, wholly acceptable to God, which is your reasonable service."

We come to the final section of this tremendous chapter on resurrection. We now look forward to the day when we are going to have new bodies which will never feel too hot, never too cold, too tired or too old. The Christian belief is that the mortal soul must put on an immortal body, to know real life. So, far from being an immortal soul locked in a mortal body, the Christian thinks quite the other way round, that this mortal soul must put on an immortal body and then, and only then, is death swallowed up in victory. For the thing that death does to me is to rob me of my body. Death is something that happens to my body. Therefore death will not be swallowed up in victory until I get a body again, until body and spirit are reunited and I am a whole person again. Then, and only then, can we say "O death, where is your sting?" Death beaten at last – body and soul together again, as it were; the whole man recovered.

That is why, for example, the Bible doesn't just talk about "going to heaven". That is a common phrase often used in church, but you don't find it used so much in the Bible. The Bible talks about "a new heaven and a new earth". It is so thoroughly real. Just as it talks about a life beyond the grave that has a body, it talks about a life beyond the grave in a new earth.

So we are not just looking forward to "going to heaven", we are looking forward to going to earth – a new earth – with a new body. I mention all this because I am astonished how much pagan belief about the afterlife you find even among Christians. That somehow the body stays here in the grave and the soul goes wandering along to heaven.

Let us believe in the whole gospel, the good news, that there is to be a new heaven and a new earth, that I am to be saved not only spirit and soul, but body too. How one groans, waiting for this new body. How we would love to be off and have that new life.

Now there are many questions raised by this. Some people feel it is like Alice in Wonderland trying to believe six impossible things before breakfast! They say: "You don't honestly believe that from a little heap of decomposed rubbish, God can make a new body?" People ask: "Have you ever seen inside a coffin after some months? Could you still believe in the resurrection of the body if you did?" And what about all those who have been cremated, or those who were blown to smithereens by bombs, those who were in Hiroshima and Nagasaki and there was nothing left of them but a burnt shadow on the doorstep where they had been sitting. Do you think God can make a new body out of that? How? What are the mechanics of it? What is the method that God will use? Paul deals with such people. He says you are a fool if you ask such questions. But I am fool enough to answer them, so here is the answer.

First of all, go into your back garden. There is an analogy in your own garden that will help you to understand this. There is a miracle of re-birth that you witness every day. You see it so often that maybe it has never struck you, yet it is so like the resurrection of the body. What do you do in your garden or in your field? You take a seed and you bury it in the soil. When you do that, the thought in your mind is this: even though that seed is going to die and go back to dust, you have sown it confidently, expecting that from the ground there blossoms life, that there are going to come flowers and plants, that from that dead seed there is going to come new life and ultimately new bodies, just like the one you planted. I could illustrate it clearly by burying a potato. Is there anything that looks more dead than a potato? There it is, just a dirty lump, and you take that and you bury it carefully and make a little mound, just like a grave, over it. Why do you do that? Some months later you will dig that ground again and you come across a little husk, if you can find it, a little dead rotting husk, but you will also find something else - some new bodies, some new potatoes. That is why you did it all. Now here is an amazing thing. Put a body, we will call it a potato, or a seed, or what have you, and bury it in the soil, and lo and behold, new life springs up. And a new body comes. If that happens every day in your back garden, why may it not happen in the cemetery also? That is how Paul is arguing. It is a miracle that it happens at all in your garden, especially when you look at the little seeds that you put in, and you see what comes from them. It is a miracle. And God gives life. Unless God was at work in your garden that would not happen, and what you buried would simply disappear.

Incidentally, people have sometimes asked me whether it is Christian to be cremated. I think it is at points like this where your Christian faith shows. I have told my wife that I want to be buried and not cremated. I will explain why. First of all, I have no doubt whatever that God is able to raise up the new body from dust or ashes or anything else. Otherwise what would happen to the poor old Christian martyrs who were burned alive at the stake? It doesn't matter to God whether you are cremated or buried. He is able to raise you up. But I think it does matter a bit to the bereaved. The psychological impression made on people is different as between burial and cremation. Of course, those with strong Christian convictions are not affected either way because they take their ideas from God and not from psychological impressions, but those present at a funeral do get psychological impressions, and the difference of the impression is this: what you put on the fire you never expect to see again; what you bury in the earth you do expect to see again. You are planting it. It is for that reason that in the Roman Empire, though most people got cremated, the Christians always got buried. As our Lord was buried. They wanted to be "planted". It is marvellous to stand at an open grave, after one has laid to rest the remains of a loved one and hear those words: "In sure and certain hope of the resurrection to eternal life, whereby the mighty working power of the Lord is able to fashion anew this body and make it like unto his glorious body."

It is all about bodies coming back. I find it more difficult to say those words at a crematorium. As I said, what you put in the soil, you plant. What you put on the fire, you tend to say, "Well, I won't see that again." In burial you are taking something and you are planting it. I know all the difficulties and hygienic problems of keeping cemeteries. I understand all that. But oh, it is so meaningful to plant a body in the earth.

Sowing and reaping – that is the first picture from nature that Paul draws. You have seen all this already in your garden. Why does it seem strange to you that planting a seed in the earth and expecting a new body to come from it is any different from planting a body in the earth and expecting a new life to come from it? In other words, our new body has some connection with our old body. As the new body, new plant has some connection with the old seed. It will not be the same body revived. It will not be the same atoms put together again, any more than the plant that came up is the same seed that you put in. There is a connection and a continuity, but a new body has come where the old has gone back to the dust.

The second illustration Paul uses is this. Go into your garden and look up. You will see that God has made different kinds of bodies for different kinds of environments. You can see this right through nature. He has made some bodies for animals that burrow in the ground, some bodies for birds that fly through the air, another kind of body for a fish that swims in water and another kind of body for a man who walks in open spaces. Look up in the sky – he has made the sun the brightest body up there, and the moon the next brightest, and the stars. The heavenly bodies and the earthly bodies all tell you that God can make any sort of body he wishes to fit any kind of environment. And since he is going to create a new heaven and a new earth, he is perfectly able to make a new body for you, to inhabit that new environment. So you just need to look at nature to believe in the resurrection of the body. And it is God who gives it this power. Paul is able to argue from nature to salvation because the same God does both. God, who is working in my garden, bringing out my dahlias, is the God who is going to work in the cemetery. The same God, Creator and Redeemer, the God who created the first universe is the God who re-creates the new one, and therefore you can argue from nature to the future.

Let us look at the second question. We have answered the first: How are the dead raised? In the same way in which it happens in nature. *With what kind of body do they come?* The manner of the resurrection. Now here let us look again at the fact that when you put a seed into the ground, it is not that seed that comes out, but another plant bearing seeds. And the body which we shall reap will be different from the body we are sowing. Look at the differences. We sow a physical body. That means literally an animal kind of body, a body which is suited to life in this world, not to any other. And because this body which we sow is tied to this world of change and decay, there are three things you can say about it.

Firstly, I speak as a dying man to dying men and women: it is a perishable body. You see it in your hair, your teeth, your skin, your bones, your muscles. You are perishing and so am I. We have certain parts of our body whose job it is to repair the wastage and that is happening all the time. But those "repair workshops" are wearing out too. We are perishing. That is the kind of body you sow – a perishing body; a worn out body.

Secondly, it is a dishonouring body. I was visiting a man in hospital. I remember talking to him and he was a strong man normally, shoulders on him like an ox, real hard worker, fit as a fiddle, and now he was struck down. There he was in the hospital, tubes in and out of him, every single thing had to be done for him. He was going through all the humiliation, having to lie like a little child in a cot. He said, "Oh Pastor, this body of our humiliation!" I knew what is meant by the phrase "we sow a body in dishonour". You might have a fine physique in your twenties. You won't have it in your eighties. This body of dishonour brings us down. It humbles us. We get embarrassed with its handicaps, and ashamed of it.

It is weak body that we sow in the cemetery. You don't think of this when you are young. There comes a time when you say, "Oh, if only I had more strength, I could do more. I've got to take an afternoon nap now. I need a few more hours sleep", and you start buying pills that offer vitality for the over-forties and you realise it is a weak body. It gets weaker. A draught of air or a drop of water can kill it. A tiny thing so small you can't see it except through the most powerful microscope can carry you right off.

It is a weak body and that is the body you sow. It is a perishable body, but there will be a body that is imperishable, which will never wear out – a body that is full of glory, a body that will always be lovely to look at, a body of which you will never be ashamed and that won't embarrass you; a body that will have all the strength you want to serve God day and night in his holy temple – twenty-four hours shift every day and no tiredness, no need to go to bed. The idea, which some people get, that heaven is a lot of armchairs with "RIP" embroidered on the headrests, utterly misses the point! We shall be serving and praising God. Won't it be lovely to do that without ever getting tired? So we sow one kind of body and reap another.

The third point Paul makes is that every physical body you get from a man. I got my physical body from my father and he got it from his father; he got it from his father, and take it right back and you come to a man called Adam. The body I got which will finish up in a grave I got from Adam. It bears the image of Adam. It came from dust and it goes back to dust. There isn't a particle of body which you can't find in the crust of the earth. I am just made of communal garden mud, and the very name "Adam" translated from the Hebrew is "mud". "Dust thou art, and unto dust thou shalt return." That is the image I bear. The image of my great, great, great, great ... grandfather Adam and the inheritance I got from him was death. He passed on to me a body that began to die the day it was born.

But now I am in Christ, and as I have had an image and an inheritance from a man on earth, I have also got an image and an inheritance coming to me from a Man from heaven. Adam came from the mud; Jesus came from glory to this world, and was made flesh, and from him I shall one day have the image of royalty, for when he appears we shall be like him, for we shall see him as he is. And one day I shall have an inheritance that I shall receive from the Man from heaven, in his kingdom.

Do you notice the order? You have to go through the body of Adam to the body of Christ. I have known Christians who became so impatient, who became so frustrated because they still had to live in a body from Adam. Yes, we have to. All Christians have got to die, unless the Lord comes again before the end of their lifetimes. Every Christian has got a body from Adam, and how conscious we are of this body from Adam, and all of us know that our birthdays are numbered.

But then! Having gone through the groaning and travailing of this body and saying "Oh I want to be free of it, I want to get rid of it" – one day we shall leave behind the image and inheritance of Adam which is death, and we shall bear the image of the second Adam, the new progenitor of the human race who is starting a new humanity of men and women who live forever.

We are told in v. 50 that this body I am using to preach and teach with nowadays is just not fit to go to heaven. I can understand that phrase. It would be horrible to go to heaven with this body. Wouldn't it be dreadful to see all the glory and then be in a sick-bed the next Thursday – to see all that heaven is, and then know you could only see it for a limited time? Seventy years, or even by reason of strength, eighty years.

This body is not fit for the kingdom. Therefore we must be changed if ever we are going to be fit for the kingdom. And we shall be changed!

Now comes the moment of resurrection, a magnificent climax, a mystery that no scientist could ever discover, that no biologist has ever mentioned, that no doctor could ever claim to be true. Here is a mystery that God has revealed. Listen, I am going to tell you a secret! We won't all die. Isn't that tremendous? There will be one generation of Christians who will never know death. Every generation hopes that it will be that one. It is my hope that I live to see the second coming of Christ. If I do, they will never need to call an undertaker for David Pawson. Isn't that terrific? Then there would be no funeral for me. That is a hope which every Christian has – that they will be among those who will not sleep. For when Christ comes again, there are two groups of people he is coming for: the quick and the dead. Those who are still alive and those who are buried. But whether I am in that lovely generation or not, I will tell you something more wonderful: we shall all be changed! Here is one for the evolutionist, who says you have got to have a long process of change to develop a new body! "In a moment, in the twinkling of an eye!" Totally against evolution – it is a creative act. God is able to bring something out of nothing in a moment. He was able to create Adam from the dust of the earth and he is able to re-create us from dust and ashes.

As quickly as it takes me to blink my eye, it will happen! And the dead and those who are still alive, all the Christians, dead and alive will be changed and we will say, "What a lovely body you've got!" and they will say, "Well, you've got one too!" Won't it be exciting?

Some people like their religion nice and quiet. They are not going to like the second coming. The noisiest verse in the Bible is 1 Thessalonians 4:16. The archangel descends with a shout and the trumpet shall sound, and the dead in Christ shall rise. Loud enough to wake the dead!

Jesus said it: "The day is coming when those who are in the graves will hear the voice of the Son of God and come forth" – and that is going to happen when God sounds his trumpet. What a noise that will be, and the noise will shake the cemeteries – you will see the graveyards emptying of all those in Christ, and you will see them in their new bodies together.

Then! Then, when these mortal natures of ours (and we are mortals, not immortals) have put on (and the word means: to put on clothes) have put on an immortal body – when we have got dressed up in our new bodies, then and only then, we can laugh at death, then and only then can we say: "You can't sting me any more. You can't pain me or hurt me any more. I've got a new body now. I am one whole man, and death cannot touch me ever again."

When Jesus came out of that tomb he rose, and he lives to die no more. Nobody will ever get Jesus back in a tomb. His new body is untouched by death. Jesus could only die once.

When I come out of the grave, I can say, "That is death conquered for ever" – and that means the whole of me is free from death. What is it that makes death such a horrible thing? That it is the end of good things? That they are lost? Well, that is horrible. There is something even more painful. That it is not the end of bad things. The sting of death, the thing that hurts most, is this: the memory that life is over and that you have broken God's laws, that you go to the grave with a dirty conscience, that you are going to face God with all the things you have done wrong. That is the real sting!

It is interesting that people don't fear death today like that because they don't believe in a God of law. They don't believe there is a judgment day. They don't believe there is a reckoning for all that we have done in the body. So they are not afraid of death.

But it is interesting: the conscious fear of death that is due to sin has given way to the unconscious phobia of death that dare not mention it! The Victorians didn't dare mention sex. Times have changed since then. The modern people of our day dare not raise the subject of death. If you raise it in polite society you have committed a social gaffe. Fancy talking about death! It has become a phobia. It has been repressed into the unconscious and there it is: a phobia.

"O death, where is thy sting?" You can look it squarely in the face now and say: "I may in the moment of death recall so many things that might not have been, so many good things that might have been and were not, so many bad things that were and shouldn't have been, and yet I face death and say 'Christ has died' and the sting of death was drawn into him at the cross." The sting has been taken away, the poisoned fang of the law removed, and I can face it without fear. Thanks be to God who gives us the victory through our Lord Jesus Christ.

When you come to the moment of your solitary journey from this life into the presence of Jesus, the sting is removed because the law and the curse of the law on disobedience has been drawn into the body of Jesus on the Cross, and it can't sting any believer who dies in the light of that Cross.

A great preacher once said, "One of the acid tests of a man's religion is whether it will help him when he comes to the moment of death and reviews his life."

Now we come down to earth with a bump. Isn't it like Paul? Paul is not one of those who has flights of fancy and remains in some dream world of spiritual meditation. He always brings us right back to the here and now. Having seen the glimpse of the future, how does this affect you now? In two ways. Firstly, it is the constant thought of the resurrection, that great moment and day when we rise from the dead, that keeps us absolutely loyal here. "Therefore be steadfast, immovable". Don't shift. There is no need to shift. With this security of the future, you have got stability in the present. It therefore follows that the less you think about the future, the more unstable you will be as a Christian. The less you think about the resurrection, the more shifty you can be in your spiritual life. Do you find you are having ups and downs? Sunday night you are up. Monday morning you are down? Do you find you are never really sure? Sometimes you feel wonderful and sometimes you say "How am I getting on spiritually?" I will tell you the cure for that. Think about the resurrection. Think about the day when you are going to have a new body, until the very thought makes you stable here.

Secondly: "... always abounding in the work of the Lord" – the labour of the Lord, Paul says, which means "to toil and sweat" which means to work hard for the Lord. Do you know what the world says about what I am doing when I preach or teach? It says: what a waste of time, what a sheer waste of energy, waste of effort, what can it achieve? I look at those who say that and think that the boot is on the other foot. Where is all your effort going? All the achievements of man will come to nothing. What is it really to get to the moon and back, when the moon is going to disappear one day? All human achievements finish in the cemetery. All the great lives finish in a coffin; even if they are embalmed in a glass-topped coffin, it is still death. But we need never feel like that! Everything we do in the Lord is of eternal value. Do you realise that every soul you win for Christ will stand with a new body in that day? Your labour is not in vain. Isn't it wonderful to be building for eternity, not just for time! There is within the human breast a longing to do something that lasts.

Do you know why people put graffiti on monuments? Go to any monument open to the public and within arms-reach you will find somebody has written "So-and-so from Blackpool was here." Why do they do it? Because they want something lasting. There is a deep instinct to have their name on a monument. There is something within us that wants to last beyond the grave. It is a perverted instinct when it comes to writing on monuments. But when the Christian is saying to someone "Come to Christ", he knows his labour is not in vain, that it will come to something eternal. That is why we are always abounding in the work of the Lord. It is this work that will last for ever! It is this work that is infinitely worthwhile. That is why we keep on.

I have one last word on this passage. I never assume that everybody in a congregation is a Christian believer. I have not mentioned what happens in the future to those who do not believe in Jesus. Do they have a future? The answer, alas, is: yes, they do. Listen to two texts from the Bible which tell you that those who don't believe in Jesus have a resurrection. In Daniel 12:2, "And those who sleep in the dust of the earth shall awake, some to everlasting life and some to shame and everlasting contempt."And in the New Testament, John's Gospel – what does Jesus say? John 5:25, "Truly, truly I say to you the hour is coming, and now is, when the dead will hear the voice of the Son of God. Do not marvel at this, for the hour is coming when all who are in the tombs will hear his voice and come forth, those who have done good, to the resurrection of life and those who have done evil to the resurrection of judgement."

Yes, we will all rise from the dead, but whether that is a wonderful day or a terrible day depends on your attitude to Jesus Christ now while you are in this body.

ODDS AND ENDS
Read 1 Corinthians 16

A. CONTRIBUTION (1–4)
 1. SACRIFICIAL
 2. SYSTEMATIC

B. VISITATION (5–12)
 1. TIMOTHY
 2. APOLLOS

C. EXHORTATION (13–14)
 1. TOUGH
 2. TENDER

D. COMMENDATION (15–18)
 1. STEPHANAS AND HOUSEHOLD
 2. FORTUNATUS AND ACHAICUS

E. SALUTATION (19–24)
 1. HEARTY
 2. HOLY

Please include the last verse of chapter 15 in your reading of this passage.

I used to find myself asking why it is that so much of the teaching in the New Testament comes in the form of letters. Why didn't Paul publish his sermons? Why did God take hold of his letters rather than his prepared utterances? He was a theologian; he must have had systematic thoughts about all these things – so why letters? I came to the conclusion it was for two reasons. Firstly, letters are always personal. Theology has got to be personal and somehow it has all got to be translated into people. Letters are the most personal form of writing – from one person to others.

Secondly, letters are always practical. They deal with real problems, real situations. When you are preparing a theological paper, and I have done a bit of that, you tend to get off into flights of fancy and you think of all the scholars and the phrases that impress scholars, and you just get miles away from real life. I remember taking part in theological seminars in Cambridge which were divorced from reality. The real life seemed far away and you were up in the ethereal areas of intellectual exchange, but letters are practical.

All these great chapters we have been thinking about were written in response to practical problems. We would never have had those lovely words about the Lord's Supper unless the Corinthians had been getting drunk at the Lord's table. We would never have had chapter 13 unless the Corinthians had been lacking love. We would not have had that glorious chapter on the resurrection unless some Corinthians had been doubting whether there was anything after death. So these letters are practical and chapter 16 is the most practical of all – it is the continuation of chapter 15, though you may not see it. Let me give you the link: chapter 15 ends: "Always abounding in the work of the Lord." Now what does that mean? In practical terms, how do you abound in the work of the Lord? Well firstly, in what you put in the collection – right down to earth like that. Secondly, in visiting the people of God, ministering to them. Thirdly, in exhorting them to stand firm in the faith. Fourthly, in introducing them to each other. Fifthly, in passing greetings. Here are five utterly simple, practical ways of abounding in the work of the Lord, and every one of the five is within the reach of every believer. So here is a lovely application of all that Paul has been saying. He is teaching them to let this kind of practical thing – these lovely ministries to the saints of God – be your abounding in the work of the Lord, knowing that none of it is wasted; your labour in the Lord is not in vain.

Now let's look at the first thing—the subject of contribution. I find two extreme attitudes among Christians towards money. There are some churches you can go to and you will think that the main thing in that church is money raising. You live from one fund-raising event to the next and it is just money, money, money. The impression is given that the main object of the church is to raise money to keep its own organisation going. I am caricaturing it so that you can see the extreme. At the other extreme I come across fellowships of Christians that think it is almost indecent ever to mention it, except to God, and that you should only talk to him about money and never talk about it sensibly to each other. So you try and hide it all and you just have the collection box in a little dark corner under the stairs, so that people who want to can slip by and put something in. Paul says, "I direct you to have a collection." It is part of the Christian life to give. Isn't money a lovely thing? It can go where you can't go and it can act as your agent, your representative. It can help someone whom otherwise you could not help. Isn't that tremendous? Money is a beautiful thing when it is in the hands of God, so we bring money into our worship and we want money to be part of our praise.

So Paul, having talked about great themes like the gifts of the Spirit and love which is the fruit of the Spirit, and the resurrection, which is the life of the Spirit, now writes concerning the collection. Is that an anticlimax? No! Incidentally, it can be good to have the collection at the end of a service, which means you let God pour out his goodness and mercy on you first, then as your loving response you can come and say, "Lord here's my gift to you in gratitude for what you have given to me this morning." So Paul, right at the end of 1 Corinthians refers to the collection. The word he uses means, literally, "an extra collection" – something over and above what you normally give, because he has a

273

special need in mind. God loves to give and he wants to give to his people everything that they need but he doesn't distribute it according to the need. Here is one of the great discoveries of the way God gives. We will say that here are two churches and they both need the same amount of money – a thousand pounds. Do you know what God invariably does? He doesn't give a thousand pounds to this church and a thousand pounds to that. He gives two thousand pounds to this church and says, "Give a thousand to that one." That is how he operates. He loves to give his gifts through some of his people to others. Therefore, he quite deliberately allows part of his Body to know prosperity and part of it to know poverty, that there might be learning to give to one another. Just as I used to give a bag of sweets to one of my children and say, "Now share that with the others." It is nice to see them giving to each other.

Therefore, in those days, God had allowed the church in Jerusalem to go through poverty. There had been a famine in Jerusalem. The lovely thing is that God told other churches about the famine before it happened, so that they were already saving up. Here is one of the uses of prophecy in God's church – to get the church ready for a future crisis that man knows nothing about. Agabus the prophet got up and prophesied: "There will be a famine in Jerusalem." So immediately the churches which were prospering began to save up and Paul was concerned about this gift.

You notice how he is saying to the Corinthians: "You prosper so let each of you save up as you prosper for those who haven't got it. Those brethren of yours in Jerusalem are poor; you are prospering." It is understandable. Jerusalem was never an industrial town. It always depended on subsidy from Jews elsewhere to keep it going economically. But Corinth was a free seaport and there was trading going on and it was affluent. So Paul says: "You save up."

Now here are some principles of Christian giving. Firstly, you save up systematically; you don't respond to an emotional appeal. Paul is saying, "I want you to have the money ready before I come. I don't want to have to come and make a big appeal to you." Moses was the same. When they needed hundreds of thousands of pounds for the tabernacle, the people, when they listened to Moses' vision, said, "We want to give," and they were pulling their purses out straightaway. Moses said, "Don't give me a penny. Don't give me anything. Go home; pray about it. If you want to come back tomorrow with a gift, then you come back." How different that is from the way the world appeals. The world will appeal to the emotions, show you a dreadful photograph, and play on your feelings. Paul doesn't do that; he points to the need: your brethren are poor; you prosper. Let everyone of you every first day of the week put a little by.

Notice that he asks them to give not when they are paid, but when they worship. According to my Bible, we give to the Lord when we receive from the Lord. Therefore the giving is not related to when we get our salary, it is related to when we worship. It is related to the day when Jesus rose from the dead; it is related to the day when God said, "Let there be light," and there was light. It is related to the day when the Holy Spirit came; it is related to the day when God has given us all the biggest things – and on that day, we give to him.

Just suppose every Sunday morning at breakfast time we had a little money box on the breakfast table, we just put a little by for our brethren in need, so that when the need came to us, we were ready with something to give, over and above what we give to the Lord for his work in the church, just something that we had saved up to help needy brethren. This is practical and beautifully loving. Being sensible about this, when the money is saved and ready, Paul would come and he wanted the Corinthians to accredit certain men they could trust with money. That is very important in Christian work – the money of the church must always be in hands of men who are trustworthy, lest it put a temptation and a snare in the way of someone.

He said, "Then we will take it." Isn't it lovely when you can send a human representative with your gift? If you are a businessman who travels the world, may I suggest that you might think of taking a gift from your church to some brethren in the countries where you go to on business? It is always so much better to receive a gift from someone's hand than in an envelope. It is so personal and so real. It is not charity – nothing is charity within a family, it is love. If you hesitate ever to receive a gift from your Christian brethren, it means you don't think of yourself as family.

If I give a gift of money to my child to go out and buy some sweets and the child says, "I don't like charity", how ridiculous that would be. Yet, you know, we are sometimes so proud that we won't even receive a gift from a fellowship fund graciously. A church should be a family, and it is not charity to share out the money that God has given to us. You notice that in the New Testament, after the Spirit filled his people, no-one said that anything was his own. They all said not just, "It's his," but, "It's ours." Therefore, you don't talk about *my* money, you say, "It's alright, this isn't my money I'm giving you – it is his money and it is our money. So we just share it out in the family." That is the way to do it.

Now, vv. 5–11, visitation. Yes, you can set a little gift aside as you prosper, in proportion to your income; if it goes up, then you can set a little more aside. There is something, secondly, that you can do for the saints of God. You can go and see them. Paul says, "I want to visit you." Not just to pick up that collection. That involves the precious commodity called time. You know, we all have different amounts of money, but we have all got the same amount of time, twenty-four hours every day for God.

It takes time to go and visit people, time to spend with them. Paul says, "I want to come and spend the winter with you. I want to spend time with you; I want to be able to give to you, not just receive from you." When I was pastor of a large church, one of the anxieties I had was that with a growing number of people to visit and look after, I was awfully afraid that my visits to people might become limited to the occasions when I wanted something from them. For example, when I wanted a new Sunday school teacher or somebody to help with a meeting, that they might see me coming up the garden path and immediately say, "I wonder what he's wanting this time? Hasn't been to see me for so long, he must be after something!"

Paul is suggesting this: why not just visit somebody just to visit them? May I again be very practical. Why don't you go and visit another Christian this afternoon? Just ring them up and say, "May I visit you? May I come to see you or would you like to come and see me?" I think it would be lovely to build up the Body of Christ. It would minister to the saints; it would be abounding in the work of the Lord. If you made up your mind, just once a week to go and visit another Christian, you would be blessed in your soul. You really would. You would find that you didn't give them so much as they gave you, but here is the ministry of mutual visitation.

The problem is: where do you visit? Where should you be? Because you can't visit everybody. Paul couldn't be in Corinth and Ephesus at the same time. So he says, "I'm under the Lord's will. I visit where he permits." You have got to ask: "Lord, who do you want me to go and see?" There are two principles that come out here. He says, "I won't be with you before the winter because the Lord has told me to visit Ephesus just now," and he gives two reasons for being in Ephesus and for staying there a bit longer.

Here is one. Ephesus is the place of opportunity. A wide door is opened. Now I'll tell you what a wide door is: sometimes you knock at a door and the person opens and says, "Yes?" I've had that and it is a narrow door. Sometimes the voice says, "Come in" and that is a wide door. There is a welcome, an opportunity to do some effective work for the Lord. There is a person who is open; there is a person who is just wanting for someone to talk to them. There are people whom the Holy Spirit has prepared for you to visit. You know, it may well be that if you went home and had your lunch and got on the phone and said to someone, "Can I come and see you this afternoon?" they might say, "I was just hoping someone would come." You find that the door is wide open before you get there.

Paul found that the Lord had opened the door before he got to Ephesus. There were people waiting to be helped, to be visited – just longing. There are so many lonely people waiting for someone else to go and visit them. They daren't go and visit themselves but they just love to have a chat. When there is a door opened, go through it. It is the first indication: a place of opportunity is the place for you to visit. A place where God is opening a door is the place for you to be.

Second, the place of battle is the place he wants you to be. I was amazed when I read this: "I'm staying in Ephesus because a wide door has been opened to me and there are many adversaries." Not "*but* there are many adversaries" – but this is the very place where the front line is. This is where the battle is; this is where people are fighting with the forces of darkness. I want to visit the place where the battle is on; I want to visit the frontline. You may know some of those who are in battling situations. The adversaries are many and people are struggling against things. Why don't you go and visit them? It is where the battle is. You could go and help them fight it.

Here are two guidelines for visiting: go where there is an open door; and go where there's a battle on and you could help them fight it. So Paul is staying right where it is tough, where he is needed because the forces of evil are strong there. Where I am needed is where evil is rampant, not where it is all nice and good and comfortable, but where there is a battle. So here is the guideline for our visitation.

Now the third ministry to other Christians – to the saints to build them up. Paul mentions here abounding in the work of the Lord – to encourage them and exhort them to be strong Christians. You don't need to be a pulpit preacher to do that. I used to get letters from my father when I was evacuated in the early part of the war, homesick and a long way from home. My mother's letters were always newsy. Father's were sermons – exhortations. It was a bit of news but it was always telling me how he hoped I was behaving and so on. I think, at times, I got a little tired of sermons and letters, but looking back I can see they had a profound influence, that there is a place for preaching to someone privately, for telling them what they ought to be doing. Oh, you've got to do it in love. You can't rebuke a person unless you're doing it in love.

So Paul slips into the letter now, in the middle of all the newsy bits – all the news of his visits and other people coming and going – and in vv. 13–14 there is an exhortation, a word that will strengthen the Christians. He says, "I want you to be two things – I want you to be tough and I want you to be tender." It is so very easy to be one or the other of these two things. You can be so tender that your religion is just pure sentiment and you will never rebuke a person. You can be so tough and hard that people don't respond. A Christian is called to be tough and tender. Secondly, stand firm in your faith. The Roman soldiers had a unique strategy for standing firm. They put their shields together in an impenetrable barrier, then they got up behind those shields and they just stood. Then they advanced when they could, but they said, "No retreats; having done all, we'll stand." Paul takes that out and says, "Put on the whole armour of God. Get that shield of faith up and stand." Of course, if you stand firm in the faith without love, you become a pretty hard person. You notice you have got to stand firm in the faith because one of the tricks in the war is propaganda. One of the worst things that is happening to the church of Jesus Christ is Satan's propaganda. He will put out any lie he can, any slander he can, any half truth he can, to undermine the morale of God's people. There is propaganda of the enemy to undermine the faith once delivered to the saints, to change your ideas about the faith. Stand firm in the faith. There is only one faith and it is the apostolic faith of the New Testament. It was once delivered to the saints and we are to contend for it, defend it, preserve it in a form of sound words and pass it on to the next generation, so that the faith may go right to the end of history intact. Stand firm in the faith. Don't let enemy propaganda destroy your morale.

Thirdly, be courageous. The thing that holds us back from so much advance in the Christian life is fear – all kinds of nameless fears. An army, if it is going to win a victory, has got to advance. If we are going to advance in the Christian life, fear has got to be done away with – fear of other people, fear of Satan, fear of all kinds of things. It is so often a little fear that is a blockage to your advancing spiritually. God calls you to something deeper and you are afraid to take the step – to step out in faith. Be courageous.

Fourthly, be strong. How do you get strong? I'm weak and we are very weak people. How do we become strong?

The answer is to stand firm in the might of God. It is not by our might, nor by our power, but by his Spirit that the Lord strengthens his soldiers. The victory will go to the strong; the stronger army will win the battle. The church has got to be strong. Now that is tough talk. It sees the church as an army, but it is not just an army. If it is just an army, it gets too tough. The church is a family and it must be tender. All these things must be done in love. We must watch as sentries, but we must watch over each other in love.

It saddens me that there are those who are standing firm in the faith today, but not in love. I must stand firm in doctrine. I dare not compromise on doctrine. I dare not deny the truth of the gospel, which means that I cannot identify with those who deny those truths. That is no excuse for not loving them. It is no excuse for getting so hard that you have no love left. It was said of one man that he loved God so much he had none left for anybody else. Of course, that is a contradiction. You can't love God and not love other people. Let all things be done in love. The church is a family. You see, you will never win the battle that God has put you in unless you love. You need to watch; you need to be brave. You need to be firm; you need to be all these things, but you also need to love. Otherwise, you lose the battle.

A wonderful ministry is seen in vv. 15–18, that of introducing Christians to each other. What a ministry it is to introduce saints who are unknown to others. Recommend Christians to one another. Paul does a lot of this in his letters. He says, "Now brethren, the first converts I ever had in Achaia, lovely people. They all lived in one house; they all came to God together. They were my first converts. They've devoted themselves to the service of the Lord. Oh, submit yourselves to them when they come. Sit under their ministry when they come. Let them help you when they come. Be open to them when they come."

Notice this: they have become servants so you submit yourselves to them. Those who are devoted to the service of others are the sort of people you can submit to. Put yourselves under the servants. It's just topsy-turvy, isn't it? But this is the way the Lord talks. Another group of people he mentions: Fortunatus and Achaicus. He said, "They're just the kind of people who refresh your spirit." Do you know that kind of person? They were able to refresh one who was lonely and homesick. So commend people to each other; talk about other Christians to each other.

Finally, we see a ministry of salutation; greetings. Christian greetings are so different from worldly greetings – or ought to be. You can tell whether a church is a worldly church by the greetings between the people. If it is a worldly church, then frankly the greetings will be the same as the world. "Nice weather. Now, who should I send Christmas cards to this year? Well, who's going to send one to me? Make a list." But Christians have a unique way of greeting. In an African tribe, there is a particular greeting between the people. One says to the other, "How are you?" That is normal enough. The reply is beautiful: "I'm fine if you are." Isn't that lovely? That should be the Christian greeting: "I'm fine if you are." Sometimes people feel: "Well he got a blessing and I didn't," but then they are no longer thinking of themselves as the body. If you are a member of the Body of Christ you say, "He got a blessing so I did. To bless him was to bless me." If any part of the Body rejoices, then every member rejoices. That is when you find out whether it is a Body, a real Body of Christ. So I am fine if you are. If you have been blessed in the Spirit, then I have been because it is my Body too. If you have received a gift from God, then I received that gift; we all did. There is this lovely corporateness that comes out in Christian greetings.

There are two adjectives applied to Christian greetings

here, which make them different from others. They are hearty and holy. A *hearty* greeting comes from an open person, an open personality. Their heart is open and their home will be open. Hearty people open up. Therefore, Aquila and Priscilla send hearty greetings from themselves and the church in their house; it was an open house because they were open people. Now I know there can be a false heartiness, sort of "Hail fellow well met." I encountered it in Lancashire. "Come on lad, we'll call a spade a spade here. Come in." But that is a worldly heartiness. It didn't go much deeper than that and I discovered that we were at the same level at the end as at the beginning. But a real heartiness comes out of the heart. You can't force it, and don't try to be hearty if your heart is not in it. That is hypocrisy and it damages the church. If you don't feel like greeting someone with a hearty greeting, don't, because that would be hypocrisy, but rather go home and get on your knees and ask, "Why didn't I want to be hearty? Why didn't I want to want to hug someone?"

Paul now mentions that if you really do love each other, you express it physically through your body. What is a kiss but a bodily thing? You can't spiritualise that away. I will tell you a rather naughty story now. When I was a student I led an evangelistic campaign in Lincoln with about five other students from the theological college. One of them was going down a street and he knocked at a door, and in the house lived a dear Pentecostal lady, who took this literally, and did hug him. So he then came and told us all about this, so we had a rota for visiting that street! But let us take it quite seriously. I am also reminded of one morning when I went into the bedroom of my two little girls. They were just waking up and little Angela was lying in the bed and I said, "Good morning, Angela." Straightaway, her two little arms came out and she just pulled my head down to hers and we hugged. You know it seems the most natural thing in the world. When a little child says, "Love me," it doesn't mean stand at the other end of the room and say, "I love you." It means something quite physical. The early Christians loved each other like this. They wanted to be arm in arm. It can be beautiful to see how Christians are more often hugging each other these days. But it is extremely important when the Lord gives you such love that you remember that it is to be holy as well as hearty. The devil is so subtle, and a kiss or a hug can have too much passion in it and become lustful, or it can have too little in it, as with Judas when he kissed Jesus, and it becomes a betrayal. There is a beautiful balance of Christian love—hearty, but holy. Up to the limit, but not beyond it.

Greet one another. You see the greetings flying backwards and forwards at the end of this letter. Christian love is expressed in greetings. You do send greetings in a letter.

We have reached the last four verses. Paul now writes his greeting in his own handwriting. If you have typed a letter to a fellow Christian on your computer you might think: maybe I ought to write just a word or two at the bottom in ink.

He writes two things and they are both about love. The first is extraordinary: he makes a negative statement about love and a positive statement about love, but this is the key word in this chapter: "love". The first statement he makes is this: If anyone has no love for the Lord, let him be accursed. What a statement! Yet he is saying it in love. I thought much about this verse and I wondered whether I could teach about it. The Lord showed me this: nothing is more damaging to the church than to have professed Christians in it who don't love Jesus. Nothing can hold back the blessing like people who have been faithful members, who have held office, who have worked hard, who have given money, who are always in their pew, but who don't love Jesus. To do it without the love of Jesus – what a terrible thing.

When we have bread and wine before us we invite all who love the Lord Jesus to receive it. It would be a terrible thing to take that if you didn't love him. So if you don't love him, just sit quietly when others take the bread and the wine, and ask him why you don't love him. How you love Jesus is as simple as this: he who has been forgiven much, loves much. Those who don't love Jesus are those who have not been forgiven by Jesus: those who thought they didn't need forgiving; those who thought of themselves as good, respectable, hardworking church members and who never realised that their sins were of hardness, of jealousy, of worry, of shyness – all kinds of things that needed forgiveness. So Paul says, "Such people are damaging to the Body of Christ." He only twice said, "Let a man be accursed." Once was concerning truth. He said, "If I, or any other preacher, or even an angel from heaven, preach any other gospel to the one that's here, let him be accursed because he's a curse to the church." Truth is one thing that must be kept and the other thing is love. "If anybody preach another gospel, let him be cursed. If any love not the Lord Jesus, let him be accursed" – what a terrible statement and yet how necessary.

How do you know if you love the Lord Jesus? Utterly simple: when you love someone, you want to see them. I remember when I fell in love with my wife. I schemed, I twisted my week's programme, I did everything I could to get to see her. You know I would walk miles. (I take the car now, I'm afraid – that's how life changes), but literally, I wanted to see her as often as possible. It is one of the dangers of courting that you can spend too much time just trying to see the one you love. Paul says, finally, "Maranatha – O Lord, come." It was a watch cry of the early church. I want to see you, Lord. I'm longing for the day when you step back into history and I'll see the nail prints. That is how you can tell when a church doesn't love Jesus: they never mention the second coming of Christ; there is no sense of anticipation.

When we take the bread and wine of Communion, remember it is only until he comes. I am longing for the day when we can do away with bread and wine, when we will see the body. We will see him and we shall be like him, for we shall see him as he is. That is how you tell love for Jesus.

Now the positive statement: Paul having pronounced a curse on those who try to be Christian without loving Jesus, writes, "The grace of the Lord Jesus be with you and my love in the Lord Jesus be with you." Fancy putting yourself into the benediction; what presumption, we might think – yet Paul has no hesitation. He can say that because his love is just the grace of the Lord Jesus coming through. So he is not being proud; he is not putting himself on a pedestal with Jesus. He is saying he can put his love in the benediction. Isn't it tremendous when you can pronounce a benediction on someone including your love, not simply saying, "The love of God be with you," but, "The love of God and my love be with you"?

INTRODUCTION
Read 2 Corinthians 1:1–11

A. PRAISE FOR COMFORT (3–7)
1. OUR SUFFERING (3–5)
2. YOUR SHARING (6–7)

B. PRAYER FOR CONQUEST (8–11)
1. OUR THOUGHTS (8–10)
2. YOUR THANKS (11)

I have a very strange message now. The Lord made clear to me that in fact we are all going to need it at some point in the future, and it is as well to be prepared. It is a message about suffering and about comfort, but you can't have the one without the other. It has been said that the Holy Spirit cannot be the comforter to the comfortable. You will never know that God is a God of comfort until you have suffered; the two things go together.

Why do I think it is going to be necessary? Most of us in this country don't suffer much for our faith, though some do. I think Christians serving in the forces suffer quite a lot for their faith. Christians in the workplace suffer a lot for their faith, and Christians who have to live in a home with those who are not Christians suffer for their faith. But there is a day coming when every Christian will suffer for their faith. You see, what is happening on a world scale is that God is preparing us for the final conflict of history. Evil is becoming more and more open, more and more bold, and the world is becoming more and more godless. At the same time, for the past half century or so, God has been doing a new thing in his church. There is conflict as Satan gets more and more of a grip on the world and Christ gets more and more of the church, and the conflict is going to come as a head-on clash. The day may not be far distant when the blessing that we are now beginning to enjoy leads us straight into the front line of the battle. Already there are many areas of the world where it is an extremely costly thing to be a Christian. In a sense one fears this and longs for it. You fear it because you don't know how you will stand up to it yourself; you long for it because if anything would make the church of Christ in this country what it ought to be, it would be persecution. If anything would purify us, it would be that. It would sort us out into whether we were going to go all the way with Christ or whether we were going to call it a day. All this comes out of this first chapter of the second letter of Paul to the Corinthians.

The opening greeting is almost identical to the greeting at the beginning of his first letter to Corinth, with just a few changes of names. The two words that Paul nearly always includes in a greeting are "grace" and "peace" – the great cause and effect in the spiritual world. Grace is the cause; peace is the effect, and it is so pathetic to see people trying to get the effect without the cause, trying to get the peace without the grace. The peace that we are all longing for is the peace that means harmony, health, wholeness – *shalom*, the Hebrew word for this, is a beautiful word.

I recall hearing in Guildford Cathedral a girl playing the viola in the Spirit – playing a tune that the Holy Spirit composed, which came from no man but direct from God. What a lovely tune it was. She called it *Shalom*, thinking that that just meant peace, and it was such a peaceful tune. But then she found out from a Jew that the word *shalom* means "health", and she discovered that this tune that God had given her and had enabled her to write down in a manuscript to play, was a tune God used to heal people. It was beautiful, and it left standing every other instrumental piece of music that has ever been played in that cathedral. It was God's music, directly written by the Holy Spirit. Why? It brought peace because it was a gift of grace. The grace gave the peace. Oh, I know there is plenty of soothing music that has been composed by many people, but this was composed by God, and the grace gave the peace so beautifully. You just felt the peace of God fill the cathedral, soothing away the pains and heartaches of life and all the problems and burdens that people carry. God was healing through a piece of music – how lovely.

"Grace to you and peace" – what does "grace" mean? Because until we ask that, we are never going to find peace. Grace means something that you don't deserve. Her Majesty the Queen has a number of mansions called "grace and favour" houses. I have seen one or two of them. She has never given me one! I gather they are for her family and that she has given to members of the Royal Family a place to live free of charge. Well, I shall never live in one of them, but I can tell you this: I do belong to a royal family. There is royal blood in me; it is the blood of Christ. This means that one day I shall live in a grace and favour residence, a place that even now is being prepared by the Lord Jesus Christ for those who love him. It is free, no rent to pay, and it is yours for ever and ever.

Now *grace* means that God, in his great love, loves to give us things that are free. He doesn't make us do a lot of good deeds for them. He doesn't make us pay for them with a great deal of money. He doesn't say, "If you do this, that and the other then you have deserved it, and I'll give it to you." He says, "It's free." As soon as you know it's yours, free, then there is peace and no longer do you try and strive for it.

Sometimes you have to search for the key word in a

passage, but here you don't. It is "comfort" – ten times: a word of comfort for every one of your fingers; a total comfort from the hand of God. Let us look at this thing called "comfort". Let me draw the distinction straight away between being comforted and being comfortable. I am afraid that what many of us want is to be comfortable. A lady once said to me, "I'd like to hear you preach a sermon on comfort." I said, "What kind of comfort do you mean?" She told me, and she was wanting to be comfortable, and that is a sermon you can never preach. "Blessed be the God and Father of our Lord Jesus Christ, the Father of mercies, the God of all comfort...." It doesn't say, "The comfortable God who makes you comfortable." I'll tell you what "comfortable" means. Comfortable means you are in no danger and no discomfort, and you don't need any help from anybody else. A comfortable person doesn't need the God of comfort. They have no need of anyone else to comfort them. That is why I stated that you will never know the God of comfort until you have suffered. That is where you discover comfort. The word itself is an amazing word, and it means not what we think of. The word "comforter" seems to speak to us of a warm vest or a hot water bottle; that is the kind of tone it conveys. Cross off the first three letters, which simply mean "with" and look at what is left: "fort". It comes from the Latin *fortis*, which means "to be brave". You can't be brave unless you are in danger. You never know if you are brave unless you are facing some peril. Therefore there is this comfort which means to make a person brave, to make them strong.

If you follow Jesus, you share the life of Jesus. If you become part of him, then his life becomes part of you. One of the outstanding features of his life was that Jesus was the greatest sufferer who ever was. His whole earthly life was a life of suffering and danger from beginning to end. As I thought through this, I saw our Lord's life, and I saw at every point: danger, peril, suffering. I saw that even after he was just born his family became refugees in the Middle East and had to go and live in Egypt. He did not have a proper home until a few years later when they were able to get back into their own country. Then I saw a boy of twelve suffering from misunderstanding parents. Let me address young people now: have you ever felt that you have parents who misunderstood you? Maybe you misunderstood them too, but they misunderstood you. Especially Christian children of parents who are not Christians – that is a very difficult situation. Jesus had a special relationship with God the Father, but Mary and Joseph didn't understand that he had to go to the temple to worship, and that he had to be engaged in his Father's business. But he was subject to them at Nazareth. If you defy your parents because of your relationship to our heavenly Father, expect trouble. It is just a little word of wisdom to young people whose parents don't understand why you must be in church on Sunday. Some see that as fanaticism! Why do you want to be engaged in your Father's business, going talking to people and going to a prayer meeting? They don't understand. Well, be subject to them. Jesus was subject to Mary and Joseph.

Think of those three years that we have got so clearly, recorded in the Gospels. Do you know that one of the things that Jesus suffered was the fact that his own brothers and sisters thought he had gone right off his rocker? One day they came to take him home and lock him up. They said, "He's beside himself." We might have said, "He's got schizophrenia; he's beside himself, he's two people. He's gone mad, he's cracked." So they came to restrain him. Did you ever have relatives who thought you were mad? You are sharing the sufferings of Christ. Don't worry, he had all that.

Isn't it lovely that later the pastor of the first church of Christ in Jerusalem was James, the Lord's brother? He came round years later because Jesus after his resurrection appeared to him and it was put right. As we look at the earthly life of Jesus, we find that everywhere he went he made enemies as well as friends. If you are going to follow Christ and stay close to him, you will make enemies as well as friends. If you thought that becoming a Christian was such a lovely thing and such a beautiful thing to you that everybody would welcome you, then I am very sorry to tell you it is not going to be so.

Jesus made it crystal clear, "They hated me; they'll hate you." He said, "I came not to bring peace but a sword to divide even families. For parent will be against child and brother against sister, for my sake." He knew all this in his own family. He suffered from people who were afraid of him. He suffered from people who talked behind his back. He suffered from people who plotted to kill him. He suffered from unpopularity. There was a time when he started one sermon with five thousand and finished with twelve in the congregation, and he said to those twelve, "Are you going to leave me too? Are you going to go?"

It is a lonely life to follow Christ. You lose friends. But you gain the greatest friend in all the world – the friend who sticks closer than a brother. But you lose friends and I dare not tell you any other. It is criminal to tell you that you will not suffer if you follow Christ. You will share his sufferings. They got more and more fierce as he got nearer to the end. He had no home of his own and there were homes in which he was not welcome. He was hungry, thirsty, tired, and he knew all that. The growing opposition was matched by a shallow response which hurt him to the quick. When the crowd said, "Hosanna! Hosanna!" he wept because he knew that it meant nothing. He knew what it was to have an apparent success and know that it would fade away in just a few days. He suffered that, too. When you are disappointed at the effects of something you have done for him, remember he had this.

Now it builds up. He had to face the fact that one of his best friends would betray him and all the others would run away and leave him alone. He had to face the indignity of being stripped and spat on. He had to face the pain of being scourged. Let me share with you a thought that someone else once shared with me which moved me so deeply. He said, "You know, in all the Old Testament, when they sacrificed a lamb, they never caused it any pain. They cut its throat, clean and quick. They killed it straightaway. They never tortured the animal before it died." But when the Lamb of God came, they didn't make it quick and clean. They flogged him within an inch of his life and then they nailed him to a block of wood. It took many hours for a man to die in that condition. Here then are the sufferings of Christ.

Finally, after having suffered more than any man for three years, a man of sorrows and acquainted with grief, he died and lost his life at the age of thirty-three, in his prime. Now Paul says, "If you're going to follow Christ, you'll share his sufferings." I don't know at what stage you are along that road I have described. Maybe you are a young person suffering because your parents don't like you getting so interested in church. I know that some of the people I have met in countries where there is persecution of Christians are away at the end of the spectrum, and they face death.

A pastor I knew had been in prison. I went up to him. He had such a lovely, happy, beaming face, like sunshine. I said to him, "I understand you've been in prison." His face creased up and the tears began to roll down. He said, "I wish not to speak." I thought, "Oh, how insensitive of me to touch that wound, just because I haven't been through it. If I had been through that, I wouldn't have been such a fool as to mention it." But you see, we haven't been through it, and I almost feel ugly talking about this because I haven't suffered for my faith. I am not far along that road.

But I believe it's coming, and we must be ready for it. Christ made no bones about it at all. He was so honest, that man, the Son of God. He said, "In the world you'll have trouble, big trouble, tribulation. You'll have that but be of good cheer – cheer up, it's all right. I'm on top of the situation. I have overcome the world." You will have trouble, and I beg you Christian, remember that when you follow Christ, you follow trouble and he calls you to a cross before he calls you to a crown.

Here is the glorious thing we are told now: it is in that situation that you discover the comfort of God. The affliction mentioned here means that affliction which you get in the service of Christ. It has nothing to do with your rheumatism. I am not belittling rheumatism, which can be a terrible, painful thing, but the word "affliction" in 2 Corinthians 1 must not be applied to other suffering. It is clearly the suffering we have in the service of Christ. It is in that kind of affliction that you find this kind of comfort. Paul goes on to describe how he was afflicted at Ephesus because he was preaching the gospel. It is only in that situation that you can claim these promises.

Why is it that Christians are afflicted more than other people? Why do we suffer when we are trying to do good, when we are trying to help people, when we are trying to bring them life and joy and peace? Why should we suffer? I will give you three good reasons. Reason number one: the world. People of the flesh, who are born of the flesh, hate people of the Spirit deep down. You are friendly with them, and then you discover the gulf. Ishmael hated Isaac because Ishmael was a child of the flesh and Isaac was a child of the Spirit. I heard a lovely saying which is so true, "There is no generation gap; there is only the regeneration gap." That is the only gap there is between people. There are those who are not regenerate and those who are—those who have been born of the flesh only and those who have been born of the Spirit too.

It is because of that gap that there is a jealousy and an envy and a hatred – as there was anti-Semitism all through the years against the chosen people of God, the Jews. There is an anti-Christian-ism that you experience. It is almost inexplicable, as anti-Semitism is. Why should people have this dislike of Jews? Why should they dislike Christians? It is because the world and God are not friends. You can't be a friend of God and a friend of the world in the deepest sense at the same time. Therefore that is the first reason.

The second reason is that there is a personal devil. There is a personal being called Satan who hates God. This world is the devil's world. Have you heard that song *He's got the whole world in his hand*? Let me quote a text to you from the New Testament: "We know that we are of God, and the whole world lies in the power of the evil one." Who has got the whole world in his hand now? Satan has. You don't need to go far to see that – just look at the news media. Therefore Satan himself is against you. You are turning his world upside-down and you are engaged in a revolution. The only real revolution that is happening today is the revolution of Jesus. The real revolutionaries are the growing army of people who are going to turn the world upside-down for Jesus, and the devil just hates that.

But there is a third reason why Christians suffer and that is God. The world will cause you to suffer, Satan causes you to suffer, God allows you to suffer. Why? Because gold is refined by fire. Good things are not harmed by fire, they are improved. It is the fire and the furnace of fire that brings the children of God out stronger in their faith in God, makes them rely on God in a way they never relied on him before. Do you know how they used to refine gold in Johannesburg in the early days of gold mining? They used to prepare a great big vat, and they got a colossal fire under it, and they put the gold ore into the vat and it would melt. Then a man with a thing like a rather shallow frying pan with a handle would skim off the scum from the top. He would go on doing that until he could see his own face perfectly in the gold, then it was ready. God says, "I will let you go through the fires, I'll let you be thrown into the furnace, I'll let you be afflicted because I'm skimming off the dross until I can see my image perfectly in you and then you are ready." This is what he is doing to Christians.

When I go to countries where Christians are persecuted I get this impression: I shouldn't be talking to you; you should be talking to me. They have asked me to go and minister to them. How can one do that? Only the Spirit could minister to them through me. But who am I to minister to them? They have been through the furnace. You can see the face of Jesus when you look at them. They have been refined by fire. So God allows you to go through it, but he doesn't allow you to go through it alone.

Remember that word "comfort". The word "fort" means "brave" but the first part of the word *com* means "beside" – to be brave beside. Now that is the secret of God's comfort. Three men were thrown into a fiery furnace. Nebuchadnezzar saw not three but four. The fourth looked like a son of the gods; there was something divine about him. They were brave *beside*.... To be comforted is not to be brave all on your own and sing and whistle in the dark, it is to be brave beside the Lord. This is how he comforts you – he is right there with you in the affliction.

At a time of renewal someone said to me, "My, you've got something on your plate now, haven't you?" I knew what they meant, but I said, "Yes." To myself I said, "Yes, but I'm going to enjoy the meal." Another person said, "Have you ever walked down a dark road and had a feeling you were getting followed, and someone was behind you and got a little afraid of something behind you? Well, Christians have goodness and mercy following them. Next time you are walking down a road on your own, just remember that you are being followed by goodness and mercy. Well, that's the Old Testament." Then he said, "In the New Testament, it's even better: signs and wonders follow you." Isn't that lovely? You need never be afraid. Goodness and mercy are following along. Signs and wonders are following.

God doesn't keep you out of affliction. He doesn't say, "I'm going to give you a comfortable life. No more danger, no more trouble, no more worry, no more crises." He never said that. Don't you ever say it to anybody else; it's a lie. No, he comforts us in all our afflictions so that we may be able to comfort those in any affliction. He stands by us in danger so we can stand by someone else in danger. Isn't that a lovely channel of courage flowing? God does give courage to his people. They don't whistle in the dark; they are in the light so they sing, and this has been behind the amazing courage people have shown.

There is a little book that used to be compulsory Sunday reading in Victorian homes. The psychologists would just tear their hair if you gave it to a child today. It's *Foxe's Book of Martyrs*, and the drawings in it are like a horror comic. It was written centuries ago, and the author tried to write in that book a brief account of Christian martyrs from Stephen up to his day. Of course, you could go on adding chapters to it for there hasn't been a period of ten years since Jesus died without people dying for Christ. People are still dying for Christ now. As you read that book, it gives you strength and courage. I read of a little teenage slave girl called Blandina who loved Jesus. She was sentenced to be roasted on red-hot iron plates unless she renounced Christ. This little girl didn't know how she would face it but she claimed the comfort of God, and she was stripped and thrown onto the plates and roasted but she praised Jesus. There have been so many martyrs.

I once said to someone, "I don't think I could ever be a martyr." They said, "You don't have to be. If you will be faithful in the little trials you have now, God will give you grace in the big trial," which means that those little niggling things that you have to face tomorrow, those little sufferings in the office, in the home – if you are faithful in those, you will become a martyr if the big trial comes.

God comforts that we may comfort. We can all share in it; it goes down the line. It springs from one person to another. Many were comforted by hearing how Pastor Wurmbrand went through terrible experiences of persecution in the twentieth century and yet how even the Communist guards turned to Christ as a result. Somehow that puts strength into your soul. God comforted him to comfort others. God stood beside him in solitary confinement that others might be encouraged by his example.

Paul uses strong language about his own experience. He says, "We were utterly, unbearably crushed and despairing of life." I don't think anybody could get much lower than that, but the root of all depression is self-pity; all normal depression has self-pity at the heart of it. You get sorry for yourself and now here is rock bottom. Utterly, unbearably crushed, despairing of life – have you ever been as low as that? Paul said that the Lord allowed them to be brought that low in Ephesus, and they felt like people walking to the gallows, the sentence of death on them – they never expected to live to see another sunrise. We don't know what that was. We know that he had a rough time, and do you know why? Because the commercial interests of Ephesus were shaken by revival. I believe that is one of the points where suffering is first going to appear in this country of ours. Commercial interests are going to be touched.

Ephesus was at the centre of a fertility cult around Artemis, Diana – people worshipped a goddess and foul things went on in that temple. You may have seen in archaeological books photographs of Diana – horrible little squat, black statues of women, and they have about forty or fifty breasts to increase the erotic appeal. There it was, and they did a great trade in this. People came from all over to Ephesus and they took part in all that worship. A mural was erected in the University of Surrey that is supposed to be secular and supposed to be non-religious, and it is a mural of fertility cults with a Buddha figure sitting in the middle. They have had permission to put it up. This is the battle that is on. You know, there was a silversmith called Demetrius who was the head of those who made the ugly little statues and they made a fortune out of them. When Paul preached, you notice he didn't march around with banners, and he didn't protest against Diana. He just got people converted. That is the best way to deal with that, and the result was that trade went right off. When men's pockets are touched, they get very angry. Paul was utterly, unbearably crushed. He felt the battle was lost, he felt he was finished, but God came in and delivered him. Do you know that God decides how far he lets you go before he delivers you? He doesn't deliver you at the beginning of affliction, he lets you go into it. Somewhere along the line, he knows when, he calls a halt to it.

He may even let you die, but don't worry, he will deliver. He is the God who raises the dead. At some point down the line, he will deliver you. Paul says that God brings you into this experience of suffering that you may rely on him. The trouble is that until you have suffered, you rely on yourself. Until you have come to a dead end, until you have come to rock bottom, you tend to rely on yourself. But when you are utterly, unbearably crushed, you look up. You have nowhere else to look at rock bottom. You look up and you say, "God, I can't stand it any more." Then God says, "I can – I can lift you up and help you to stand. I can deliver you."

One of the greatest factors in that is the prayer of people who are not suffering. There is a sharing in the perils that face God's people. If there are young people in a fellowship who are suffering because their parents don't understand their Christianity, the rest of us who have never had this should be praying for them. Paul is saying to the Corinthians, "You pray that I may go on being delivered. You pray and then you will be able to give thanks with me for the deliverance. You have had a share in it, you will be able to praise God."

Baptist pastors who were thrown into prison in Cuba were set free in answer to prayer. They had been through it for three years. Some of them had very little food. They suffered tremendously but they relied on God. People around the world prayed for their deliverance, God opened the prison door and they came out. Then they were able to comfort others and give courage to God's people. They went through the furnace and stepped out unscathed.

There is a lovely account in Acts 12 of a prayer meeting, the believers praying for one of their number in prison. There they all are, earnestly praying for the deliverance of their brother in prison and his name was Peter. As they are praying, there is a knock on the door. One of the girls goes to answer it and she recognises Peter's voice. She rushes back to the others and says that it is Peter standing at the door. They said, "You're mad!" That prayer meeting was not expecting Peter to get out of prison. What is a lock to God? Nothing! What are all the guards to God? Nothing! They were all asleep and the gates opened as Peter came out of the prison.

Yes, the Lord knows when to deliver his people. He lets

them go into suffering and he brings them out of suffering. He comforts in their suffering so that when they get out, they can comfort those who are in any affliction – any at all. Those who are suffering just a little are strengthened by those who have suffered a lot.

I have mentioned elsewhere a little prayer meeting in India that met to pray for a man who had gone into Nepal as a missionary from India. This missionary had been imprisoned after baptising seven Nepalese, and all eight people were in prison. This little group of Indians met to pray for them and they prayed, "Lord, keep them safe; deliver them." So they all prayed around the circle until they came to an older Indian lady. She said, "Lord, why did you give them the privilege of suffering for you and not us? Why can't we go to prison for you? Why can't we know your comfort in such danger?"

The atmosphere of the whole prayer meeting changed! They had been pitying the people suffering. You envy them; envy our brethren in countries where they can't meet freely. If I had taught in some churches some of the things I have taught here, I would be in prison now. Envy those who don't have this freedom. Envy those who suffer. Why? Because they know the God of all comfort.

When in this land we begin to go through it, and when commercial interests begin to suffer because of revival that is coming, and when the battle is joined and when we really are up against it, then we are going to know the God of comfort. Reading this passage is almost like talking about something we don't know anything about. Praise God, I believe one day we will, and may the God of mercies and the Father of our Lord Jesus and the God of all comfort, comfort you then.

SELF-DEFENCE
Read 2 Corinthians 1:12 – 2:17

A. SINCERITY (12–14)
 1. PERSON – no hidden motives
 2. PEN – no hidden meanings

B. STABILITY (15–22)
 1. PLANS
 2. PROMISES
        Note: Jesus – Yes and Amen

C. SENSITIVITY (23–4)
 1. PAIN
 2. PLEASURE

D. SOLIDARITY (5–11)
 1. PUNISHMENT
 2. PARDON

E. SERENITY (12–13)
 1. PEOPLE
 2. PLACE

F. SOVEREIGNTY (14–17)
 1. PERFUME
 2. PERISHING

I can't see a church calling St Paul to be its pastor today: an unmarried man of peculiar appearance, rather dogmatic in his pulpit, never staying in one church for long, often in trouble with the authorities and leaving division wherever he went. Can you imagine a call going to such a man from many congregations today? Nor can I see many church members nowadays choosing the church in Corinth as their spiritual home – a church where they got drunk at the Lord's table, where there were cliques and party splits, where immorality was openly condoned and where they were unsound on as fundamental a doctrine as the resurrection. Imagine putting such a preacher together with such a church – you are going to have fireworks, and indeed it was a very stormy relationship between Paul and the church of Corinth. That is understandable.

We just catch glimpses of it reading through what we call the first and the second letter to Corinth. Actually, just to complicate things, as we noticed earlier there were four letters and I have already given you a rough outline of Paul's dealings with the church. Remember, Paul paid three visits to Corinth and in between the visits he wrote two letters between the first and second visit, and two more letters between the second and third visit. What we call the first letter to Corinth is in fact the second one of the first couple. What we call the second letter to Corinth is the second one of the second pair. So between the two letters we have, he had paid one visit and written one letter. He refers to the middle visit as the painful one. He refers to the letter which he wrote immediately afterwards (which thankfully we have not got) as his severe letter.

Now 2 Corinthians is following up a painful visit. They had big trouble. You know how sometimes you hear this said in Christian circles, talking about another church: "Well, I believe they have trouble." Thank God for trouble in churches and I'll tell you why. Do you remember that in an earlier chapter I wrote: "I don't know what this verse means"? You go on and the Lord makes it clear. Here is the verse, "There must be factions among you in order that those that are genuine among you may be recognised." At first I am afraid I did not take it at its face value. How silly we are not to take the Bible at its face value. I now see that when things are running smoothly and everything is calm in a church and everything is going well, you find it very difficult to tell who is genuine. It is so easy to be nice, friendly, smooth, in good relationships when everything is going well, but when trouble comes you really do find out who is genuine, who is walking with the Lord and who is close to him. There must be factions in a sinful world and in a church that is bound to reflect something of that world until we get to glory.

Troubles have a way of bringing out the very best in those who are genuine and this is what is happening here. Paul had been slandered, criticised. There had been a ringleader of opposition in the church in Corinth who stood up to Paul's face and called him all sorts of things, imputing wrong motives for what he was doing and saying all sorts of unkind things. They had a scene and Paul didn't want to go back to the church and have another scene like that, but out of that came a genuine relationship. There are certain things here in this little section of the letter, which at first sight seems again just the trivia of people arguing, talking with one another. Six things come out of this letter that should characterise the relationships of true Christians.

The first is *sincerity* (see vv. 12–14). Paul is going to lay bare his heart and let us look into it and see that his boast is this: he is proud of the fact that he was straight with them, sincere with them. He didn't come to them in the kind of worldly wisdom that talks one way in the hope of getting around someone, or says something when the mind really means something else. He had gone to them in godliness – in godly sincerity and holiness. By the grace of God, he came to them with a straight message. They knew what he thought – he told them. Sincerity is one of the greatest allies of the gospel and hypocrisy is one of the greatest enemies of true Christianity. That is why Jesus, whenever he met hypocrisy, came out with some of the most strong language: whited sepulchres; you are washed on the outside and you are filthy on the inside. Hypocrisy was a thing for which Jesus reserved some of his most severe words, and sincerity thrilled him. The Greek word for hypocrisy means, quite simply, to put on a face. On the ancient Greek stage when acting a part the actors would hold a mask in front of them on a little stick. They didn't bother with any more makeup than that. Hypocrisy is to hold a mask up so that people don't know what you are really thinking behind that – a kind of "church face", and people don't have any idea what is behind that face. There was none of that with Paul. We saw that the latin root of sincerity meant "without wax" and go back to the days when you could buy a marble statue to put in your garden. Some dealers would fill it up with white wax and you would never know until the sun came out, or the weather beat on that statue and then the cracks would begin to show. It looked alright but then under stress and strain it wasn't alright. Sincerity comes straight from that word and meant good right through. Paul is saying that he is proud of the fact that when he came to them he was open; they knew what he thought. He had told them he had spoken straight to them even though it hurt, and they knew where they stood. Thank God for this deep honesty, this sincerity in which people know what each other think because what they say and what they do reflects their real self. Of course, there is a balance here. I remember a young convert coming to me once and he said, "Here, I don't think much of this Christian lot" and I said, "What's the matter?" He said, "Well, I thought we were supposed to be honest, to tell the truth now that I am converted." I said, "Yes, what's happened, Don?" He said, "Well, our next door neighbour, a lady, asked us to go in and look at her bathroom. She had just decorated it and the edge was pink and the walls were yellow; it was horrible, ghastly. She said, 'What do you think of it?'" And he had thought: Right! Now I am a Christian, I've got to be honest. "I think it's horrible." He continued, "Now she won't speak to us; things have really gone wrong." There is a brutal, blunt frankness that is not necessarily Christian. But there is much greater danger or hypocrisy in what I would call polite society. Politeness can be another name for hypocrisy. In the scriptures you are taught to be loving, to be real – and this is important. To be polite is to say, "Thank you for this lovely evening," and then get in the car and say, "What a bore." To shower compliments or flattery is so alien to real relationships. So Paul is saying: I am proud of this. Yes, I am a proud man. I'll let you know that, but my boast is this: that you knew where I stood and you knew what I believed; you knew the real me and I was sincere with you.

Not only is such sincerity necessary when you are face to face with people, it is even more so when you write to people. Because written words don't convey tone of voice and it is important that your writing should be sincere as well as your person – that there shouldn't be any hidden meanings or ambiguous phrases that leave your reader guessing what you mean. Paul is not trying to say anything subtly here – just writing what he feels and thinks.

I got a letter after I left a previous church and the writer said, "Things have been even better since you've left." I am quite sure that they meant it beautifully. Someone wrote to me after a radio broadcast: "Dear Mr. Pawson, I would have known it was you even if the announcer had not said so. Yours Sincerely." I began to wonder whether that meant he liked what I had said or not! Then I realised that it was just a simple, straightforward letter saying something, and I shouldn't read anything more into it than that. Why? Because of the ending: "Yours sincerely." Why do you put that at the end of a letter? If you write that it means that you can take everything I have said just as I say it with no hidden meanings, no hidden motives. How very important it is that when we are going through the stormy patches and having troubles – and there are troubles in every church – that we be sincere and that we tell each other what we really think, and write to each other with such sincerity.

The second thing that should characterise good relationships among Christians is *stability* or, as a modern version has it, "stick-ability". They had expected Paul to visit them and he had not turned up. That is always something that disturbs. If somebody has promised to visit you and they don't come, it can disturb. It had disturbed Corinth and they began to say horrible things about him as a result. They said: he is a yes and no man; he puts it in his diary but you really don't know if he means it. He may find something he wants to do better so he won't turn up. It will be at his convenience. This kind of instability is, of course, destructive of mutual confidence. A diary is a very important part of a Christian's equipment so that we can keep promises in relation to plans and promises we make.

Said one letter to a person, "I am sorry I cannot come owing to a subsequent engagement." Now, we may not dare to say that in a letter but sometimes we do it. This kind of instability, of course, makes people unreliable.

You will find this in the world—you go around doing some house to house visitations. "Yes, I'll come along on a Sunday" – and you will have such a disappointment with some of them; they won't be there. You will arrange to take them to a meeting and then they are not there. But you shouldn't find that among Christians. Why not? Paul defends himself now. Twice he was going to come to them. There was a very good reason why he had not done so. It was not because he was a "yes and no" man, vacillating, fickle, changing his mind. He wanted to tell them about God. How can a man who follows God and believes in Christ ever be a "yes and no" man? Why? Because Jesus is the yes man. Jesus is always yes. I went through the Gospels to see if Jesus ever said no to anyone and I could not find it. I know people sometimes wanted things from him which he refused to give them – the Jews wanted signs and Herod wanted to see a bit of conjuring – but when a needy soul came to Jesus and said, "Jesus, help" it was always yes. Every promise of God is yes in Jesus. It is a title of Jesus: he is "the yes". It is a little word but full of content. Did you mean those things you said all through the Old Testament? Jesus replies yes. God, did you mean that you would forgive my sins and never bring them up again, and remember them no more? Jesus says yes. God, did you mean that you are going to change the whole world and make a new heaven and earth like you said you would? Jesus says yes. Two little words mentioned here now are the most important words in Christian faith: *yes* and *amen*.

God says yes to us, we say amen to him. This is the certainty, the confidence; it affects our whole Christian living. Two things that it most certainly affects: our preaching and our praying. My preaching must never be "yes and no" preaching. There is an awful lot of that preaching about. "Do you believe the Bible?" "Well, yes and no." "Do you believe the account of the virgin birth?" "Well, yes and no; well, I don't believe in just the actual facts but yes, there's some truth in it." This kind of "yes and no" preaching is no use at all; it doesn't reflect God – God is yes. Therefore, preaching is confident. To some it will sound dogmatic, to some it will sound cocksure, bit it is sure. It is the "yes" – you can trust every word that God has said. Can I trust the Word of God? As I face the problems of life, does he mean it? Jesus says yes – always.

A "yes and no" prayer life is miserable and it is not

the kind of prayer life that Jesus wanted you to have – an uncertain prayer life that is hesitant. Why did Jesus say, "If you ask anything in my name you can have it"? "Yes!" You will hear loads of sermons and all the other different answers you get, but I want to preach a sermon on the answer "Yes, you can have it." We are so busy saying, "No, wait", and all the rest of it, but isn't it lovely when you get through the kind of prayer life that says, "Lord it's yes, so I can say amen."

Of course, that doesn't mean that you can ask for anything you like. It must always be in his name. I must not ask for anything that the Father didn't give to Jesus. I must not ask him to spare me from anything he didn't spare his own Son from. No, it must be in his name but when it is in his name it is in the will of God and when it is in the will of God it is yes. So I can pray confidently and I can say "amen" at the end of the prayer through Jesus. That is why we finish a prayer: "Through Jesus Christ our Lord, Amen." The word "amen" means: absolutely, certainly; truly, verily it is going to happen. It is a way of saying "thank you" for the answer to your prayer before it comes, and that takes tremendous faith.

So here God is saying "yes", we say "amen", and it doesn't stop there. Christianity is such a sure thing. Why? Because it is God who establishes us, God who stabilises us. How does he do that? By anointing us with his Spirit, by commissioning us, by giving us the seal of his Spirit, stamping his own image on us, and by giving us the earnest of the Spirit as a guarantee. Look at those words: establishing us, anointing us, sealing us. This is not "yes and no". Somebody says, "If I come to Christ, will that make me a Christian?" Yes, of course it will. "If I want to be filled with the Spirit, can I be?" Yes. If there is any blockage at all it will be on your side, not his – the promise is to you and to your children and to all who are far off, with no qualifications.

So it is always yes in Jesus and that is why we can preach

and pray with such confidence when we discover the yes. How can a man who believes all that say yes and no? How can someone who is rooted and grounded in Christ vacillate? Paul is telling them they have got it all wrong. If he didn't turn up on that visit it must have been for a very good reason indeed.

I heard of an example of this. A church had a lady coming to speak to them, quite literally a lady – Lady Lee, the wife of Sir Thomas Lee. She did not turn up. They waited and waited and she never came. Do you know where she was? She had gone into Hyde Park on a Monday afternoon to talk to a crowd of hippies about Jesus and they would not let her go. They gathered around her and kept her for fourteen hours talking about Jesus. She lost her voice after a few hours. They crowded in and said, "Go on whispering, we'll catch it." They still would not let her go. She said "I must go" and they said, "We may not meet you again, we can't let you go, we want to know more." So she told the church about what had happened and the church was thrilled. She had been talking to people who wouldn't have heard the gospel unless she had been in Hyde Park. The church understood straight away that it wasn't that she was a "yes and no person"; it wasn't because she vacillated like a worldly woman who would change her mind about wanting to go or not wanting to go, making some excuse. No, there was a fixed purpose behind the change of plans – it was a yes to God behind it all. If God wanted something else she had to say "yes, amen".

The third thing that Christians need in their dealings with each other, especially when there is trouble is *sensitivity*. Paul was often accused of being callous and harsh and indifferent, but nothing could have been further from the truth. The next few verses are filled with words of deep feelings: grief, anguish, tears, rejoicing. Paul was a man who *felt*. He had a brilliant intellect that God had given him. He could argue logically, clearly, but with the head there went a heart, and he had deep feelings for people. He could feel pain and he could feel pleasure from other people, and he felt both most keenly. Now he is saying: "It's not that I want to domineer. I don't want to Lord it over your faith. I want to work with you not over you." Nevertheless, he said, "I stayed away from you because I didn't want to cause you more pain." A Christian must be sensitive to pain, and the first question you must ask is: have I caused pain rightly or wrongly? Has it been my fault or has it been something wrong that needed to be corrected? Paul looks back over his visit with no doubts and examines his own heart. He knew he had caused them pain and that it was right to do so, and he wanted them to have joy. Real joy can't be obtained unless wrong things are put right. Joy is not there if you are condoning a wrong situation. Paul could preach, argue, convince and persuade – but he could feel. When he caused pain he felt it and knew when to stop. Which leads straight into the next thing that is needed when there is trouble: *solidarity* – meaning that when wrong has been done the fellowship should stand together. Now Paul is here referring to the ringleader of the opposition at Corinth, a man who had been rude and deliberately antagonistic. Isn't it lovely that Paul never mentions his name? Did you ever notice that? He talks about it but the name has not come down to us. When you get to heaven you will not be able to go to someone and say, "Oh, you're so and so, I've read about you. You messed up the church at Corinth, didn't you?" The name is hidden and even the nature of his opposition is hidden. Paul's message is: in hurting me, your pastor, your preacher, your leader, he hurt all of you. It was a hurt done to the Body. To criticise one is to criticise all. I thank God that you all took it like that and that you stood together and that you punished this man. There is a place for punishment in Christian fellowship and there is a biblical way of doing it.

But now Paul is saying: you have all stood together against this and you dealt with it, or the majority of you did, and that's enough.

Now he says turn right around quickly; something has happened that means you should stop the punishment straightaway. What? The man was sorry. Doesn't that apply in your family? Is it not true that the first sign of genuine sorrow is enough to change your attitude? It ought to be. If you go on after that, there is something wrong with your love. Paul knew that the man who had done such terrible things had genuine sorrow about it – so turn right around; together in your solidarity love him, forgive him, draw him back into your affection, and whoever you forgive I forgive too. I'm solid with you; we have been together in dealing with this man; we will be together in loving him back. How important this is – to stand together.

What happens otherwise? You get differences over personalities. You get factions and arguments. Solidarity in love means that a whole fellowship acts in discipline and a whole fellowship acts in pardon when that is needed. How important that is. Rather than half the church say, "I think we should punish," and the other half say, "I think we should let him off" – no, stand together. Solidarity of the Lord's people – this is a family. I will tell you what breaks down the discipline of a home: when the dad punishes and mum lets a child off, or when mum punishes and dad says, "Oh, go on with you." That is no use at all. Father and mother must have solidarity of love. When a child has done wrong they must both punish, and as soon as the child is sorry they must both say "come."

Solidarity in the fellowship deals with this kind of issue and is greatly needed. Why? Lest Satan gain the advantage. We are not ignorant of Satan. I don't know what he looks like; he doesn't look like a little black imp with horns and a forked tail. If he did, I would have no problems with him at all. He would never get past our front gate. No, I don't know what he looks like but I know what he thinks like and how he behaves. I know five things that Satan loves to see happen in a church. Firstly, he loves to see a church failing to discipline those who do wrong. He loves that, because it is no longer a family. Secondly, he loves scandal to be an occasion of gossip rather than the silent discipline that should happen. Thirdly, he loves to destroy a believer, and if a man is punished too much the devil takes him into despair and he may never pick up again. Fourthly, the devil loves to drive wedges into a fellowship – to split it if he possibly can. That is his device for reducing the power of that church. Fifthly, he loves to use discipline to make Christians hard; he loves to make them over-strict. I have seen all these things happen in a fellowship that has had to deal with difficulties of this kind. Satan is just crouching outside the door you might say, waiting to jump in. We are not ignorant of that. Therefore we are not going to become his tools in a situation.

Next, the Lord's people must have *serenity* in their relationships – peace of mind. Success in Christian work is no substitute for serenity. You may be having a great evangelistic campaign, you may be having a wildly success-ful time in Christian service, but if you don't have peace of mind then far better to leave the successful evangelism and get peace of mind. This kind of serenity comes from right relationships. It is important to get this first. Paul's message is: "When I came to Troas, I was hoping to meet Titus there to tell me how you were getting on. I'm anxious about you, I don't know how you feel. I don't know if you're cross with me. I don't know if you're thinking things through. I don't know if you're repenting. I don't know what's happening. A great door was opened to me in Troas, people wanted to hear me preach, it was great, yet I had no peace of mind. Titus was not there and I wanted to know what was happening. I needed peace of mind about people before I could do my work properly without distraction .. I had to change places, I had to go to Macedonia. I had to go and find out." We may be successful in Christian work but we must go and find out why things are happening as they are. We must find out what is happening to people for whom we are concerned. We can't just forge ahead because we are being successful. Young people, old people – whatever you are doing, go back and find out what is happening to others whom you have known before. Don't just forge ahead because a door has been opened.

Finally, in vv. 14–17, *sovereignty* or victory. Now, the Christian life is a battle and I will tell you this: your biggest battles will be inside the church and not outside it. Your biggest conflicts and struggles will be with your fellow Christians but never be content until you have got through that struggle to victory. Remember that when the Roman generals came back from a campaign at the distant borders of the empire they had a triumphal procession. I have walked down the road in the middle of the Roman forum where they used to do this. There is the arch of Titus, and one could imagine the great procession with the general in his chariot, the crowd cheering him, everybody thrilled – a great pageant of triumph. Paul says that when he went to Macedonia he met Titus, and Titus said, "The trouble is over." Titus said that the Corinthians realised they were wrong, and it was all over. The pain has gone and victory has come. Paul is saying that he has felt like a Roman general marching in. "Thanks be to God who makes our lives a constant pageant of triumph." That is the picture here, and the church in its relationships should be a constant pageant of triumph. There will be battles, serious warfare, struggles. But when you get through to victory it is a constant pageant of triumph.

When the Roman general marched in they used to light bonfires and altar fires all down the route and they used to throw incense on to get the smell of victory. The clouds of incense, the aroma, used to float around among the crowds and they smelled it so that they began to associate the very atmosphere, the smell of incense, with victory. The whole place smelled of victory. Paul is saying that when Christians come through in triumph, you can smell it. There is an atmosphere of victory, an atmosphere of triumph, and it is sweet and beautiful and people love to sniff it in the air and say: these people are on the march; they are enjoying victory in Christ.

What a lovely smell it is, but there were some people in every procession like that to whom it was a horrible smell. They were the poor conquered people in chains at the end of the procession. When they smelled the incense they smelled death, execution. When Christians are on the march, when there is victory in the air, to some people it is an offensive atmosphere. Why? They are smelling the horrible smell of death. I don't think there is any smell more horrible than death. Why is it that an atmosphere of victory in a church, an atmosphere of triumph, is so offensive to some people? Literally, their nostrils seem to dilate, it is so horrible to them. That is because it smells of the death of the sort of life they have lived. It is the end, not the beginning, for them.

So wherever we go, this will be the atmosphere we shall have around us. Some will say, "What a sweet atmosphere" and some will say, "It's horrible." Some will say, "This is life" and others will say, "It's dead because it's taking away from me all that I've had in my life." Who is sufficient for these things? You know, it is a horrible thought to me that when I get into a pulpit, some people will be nearer to the Lord and some are going to be further away; some are going to smell and say it's sweet and some are going to say it is horrible. Who is sufficient for these things? Paul says he is – because he is not a pedlar but a preacher. He is not in it for the money, ambition, vanity or power. He is in it for the gospel. He speaks as a preacher with sincerity: I mean what I say; I speak with authority – I am commissioned by God. I speak with responsibility because I speak in the presence of Christ. Only a man of sincerity, authority and responsibility is sufficient to walk in such a pattern of triumph.

TRANSFORMATION
Read 2 Corinthians 3

A. STONES TO HEARTS (1–3)
 1. HARD TO SOFT
 2. MATERIAL TO PERSONAL
 3. OUTWARD TO INWARD

B. LETTER TO SPIRIT (4–6)
 1. COMPLICATED TO SIMPLE
 2. DEMANDING TO OFFERING
 3. DEADLY TO LIVELY

C. DEATH TO LIFE (7–11)
 1. CONDEMNING TO ACQUITTING
 2. BRIGHT TO BRILLIANT
 3. FADING TO LASTING

D. VEILS TO FACES (12–18)
 1. FEARFUL TO BOLD
 2. BOUND TO FREE
 3. HIDDEN TO DISPLAYED

There is one thing I have had to do many times for other people that I have never had to ask anyone to do for me, and that is to write a reference. Many people think a minister of religion makes an ideal referee. Well, it certainly may impress to say "Minister of Religion" on the form, but really I find it a little embarrassing. I may know what people are like in church but not what they are like at home or at work. I presume that a future employer is far more interested in that than how they behave in church. I overheard an employer once say that he did not value references from ministers of religion precisely because they just wrote nice things

319

about people they only saw for one hour a week. So I have always tried to be absolutely honest. If I felt I couldn't write a reference for someone, I've asked them to go to someone else. If I have written one, I have written an honest one – warts and all. I stand to be corrected but in my years of ministry I cannot recall writing a reference for someone who didn't get the job or the position. But don't queue up for a reference because I might say to you, "I'm sorry, I can't do one for you" – and that would embarrass both of us.

Why have I never been in need of a testimonial or a reference? Because preachers write their own! That may sound conceited, but we don't write it in ink, we have to write it on people. If any church is looking for a minister, and feels that Mr So and so might be the right one, all they have to do is go and look at the people in the church where he is. They don't need any written testimonial because it is our calling to help people. That is the reference, and the only one. Our ministry is the only capital we have got to carry on the business.

Paul is talking like this here. He says, "I'm not a pedlar of God's word." I'm not a salesman. I'm not in this for what I get out of it. I'm not in it for the money; I'm not in it for the prestige or the power that it gives me to be a public speaker. I am in it because God commissioned me. When God tells you to do something, you can't say no. I am in it because I speak in the presence of Christ. I know we are sometimes more conscious of the faces of the people, but anybody who preaches the gospel is conscious that there is another face he can't see who is watching.

The Corinthians might have said, "Well, Paul, you say you have sincerity; you say you have authority, you say you have responsibility, but you don't seem to have much humility." Paul is saying, "Do I need to commend myself to you? No. Do you need to write a letter of reference for me when I move on to somewhere else? No. Our letter of recommendation is written already in the lives of those to whom we preach. That is a letter which is known and read of all men."

I could not care a brass button about what people think about me. But I am preaching Christ and I speak in the presence of Christ. His reputation in your area depends on what people read in your life. You are the letter of testimony. Your life is a living testimonial to Jesus. You are either getting him a bad name or a good name. It is the pastor's task under God, to try and help you to be a good letter and a good reference for Jesus, so that people look at your life and say, "If that's what Jesus is like, I want to have him as my Saviour."

I heard about a man who was asked if he had certain Christians working in his factory. "Oh, you mean the hallelujah lot – yes, we've got them. They're the best workers. You know, they tell me that they work for Jesus. He's the best foreman we've ever had on our payroll!" But he wasn't on the payroll. You can't have Jesus on the payroll. But that factory employer was able to look at Christians and read a letter of people who worked not with one eye on the clock and the other on a pay packet but with both eyes on Jesus – and did a good job for him.

This is the subject and Paul, having said, "You are my testimonial; you are my letter of reference," suddenly realises he has said something wonderful. Did you ever feel that? Sometimes occasionally, I go home and say, "I said something wonderful in that sermon" – and it hits me. You may have been talking about the things of God and suddenly you said something and stopped and thought, "What did I say? I think I've said something very profound." Paul realised that in saying, "You are my letter, my testimonial, my reference," he had seen the whole difference in a flash between religion and Christianity, between the highest religion he knew – Judaism, the Old Testament – and Christianity and the new covenant; between his life as a Pharisee and his life as a believer in Jesus; between Moses and Christ, between the old way of getting through to God and the new way that Christ has opened up. He saw it all. In that little remark, "You are my letter of reference, written not with ink but in hearts," he realised that the difference is between the letter and the Spirit.

Let us explore that contrast. Contrast after contrast come to me out of what Paul said here. The first great contrast is that the old religion of the Old Testament was written on stone and the new one is written on hearts. I imagine Moses on the top of Mount Sinai, chipping away. I have got some stones from the top of Mount Sinai. I look at them and I see they are granite. Moses was way up there for forty days, chipping out just ten simple, straightforward rules for living. They can't have been very big stones because he brought them down under his arms – down what is a pretty steep mountain.

That immediately shows three differences between religion and Christianity. First of all, *religion is hard; Christianity is soft*. Granite is tough – you have to chip the rules in. The difference between Moses and Jesus you sense straight away: Moses was a great but tough man. He chipped those commandments into granite and that gives you the man. When Jesus came, he didn't write a book; he didn't chip things into granite. The only time we read he ever wrote anything was with his finger in the dust and then it was soon trodden out. Why didn't Jesus write a book? Why didn't he chip some new rules into granite that everybody might read them? I'll tell you why – Jesus wanted to write on the heart. It is a softer place to write. You have to be more tender if you are going to write on people's hearts; you have to be patient with them. It may take three years, not forty days, before you have written the rules on people's hearts. But this is the change: from Moses' forty days chipping to Jesus' three years teaching, writing on human hearts. When Jesus died, he left no tablets of stone, no book. He left twelve men, eleven in the last analysis, and on their hearts he had written the message. He is still doing that today. The reason is this: there arc people to whom the Bible is a closed book – they might have one in the house but they never read it. It is written in ink. But they will be reading the letter that you write in your life that is known and read by all.

The second change I notice is this: that it is the difference between holy *things* and holy *people*. Those two tablets of stone that Moses brought down were treated as holy for ever afterwards. They were kept in a special chest in a holy place, and nobody could go near them or touch them. This is the religion of holy things: holy clothes, holy furniture, and holy this, that, and the other. We don't think like that because we live in the New Testament in which it is holy people, not holy things. In the Old Testament the holy things made people holy because the people touched them. People used to think they could be holy and healthy by touching something holy. It is just the other way around in the New Testament. Get the people holy and everything they touch becomes holy. Do you see the difference? I don't call the table where we place bread and wine a "holy table". It is just a table but we hope that holy people sit around it. If they are holy people when they go home to have Sunday lunch, the dining room table becomes a holy table and the washing up water becomes holy water. What a revolution: no longer holy things, but holy people sanctifying everything they touch; no longer Sunday being a holy day, but every day being a holy day because of holy people doing things in it. Religion has changed from being holy things, like tablets of stone that people gazed at in awe, to becoming holy people who, whatever they do, touch it with sanctifying power.

A third difference is that it is *a change from an outward religion to an inward one*. Tablets of stone are always outside us. I remember one church of which I was minister which had a sort of gothic archway behind the pulpit and there on the wall were the Ten Commandments painted in true nonconformist Victorian fashion with gothic lettering – chocolate brown against a sort of prune and custard background. You could only read them from the first pew, and there they were, *outside* people. No doubt when the sermon was boring they just read through those commandments if they could. But God wanted to write them inside people, not outside.

Jesus came to destroy outward religion. That is why he came unstuck with the Pharisees. With them it was all on the outside. They were religious, respectable, whited sepulchres. What was on the inside? Jesus said it is what is inside that makes a man dirty. They criticised him because he had a meal without washing his hands first. He said that it is the things inside a man, in his heart, that come out: dirty thoughts, lustful ambition, jealousy, pride, covetousness. What makes a man clean? Is it becoming respectable? No. Jesus came to give us a new heart. "I will put a new heart within you," was the promise given through the prophets of the Old Testament, but that promise was not fulfilled until Jesus came.

I remember a testimony of a man who was a hardened criminal in Northern Ireland, Willy Mullan, leader of a gang that used to go around armed after dark – looting, plundering. Willy Mullan came to know Christ in the middle of a field. He became the pastor of a large Baptist church in Lurgan, Northern Ireland – a wonderful man of God. When he gave his testimony he would say, "Listen, so many people tried to give me a new start in life and they all failed, but God gave me a new life to start with." Believe me, if you ever get a heart transplant from the surgeon, it is not new, it is secondhand. Only God can put a new heart within. It is the change from an outward religion that is respectable, that does the right things and says the right things, to an inward religion that is pure in heart and sees God.

Next, there is a *change from letter to Spirit*. If you are going to go the way of the Old Testament, which is the way of religion, then you will finish up with a book of rules as long as your arm; you will have to write laws and sub laws and more sub laws. You need a big library if you are going to study law and you are constantly adding to the books. It gets so complicated. Among the Jews there emerged a group of people called scribes just to write the laws. The scribes took one law, "Remember the Sabbath day to keep it holy," and they divided it into thirty-nine sub-heads. Then they divided each of the thirty-nine sub-heads into thirty-nine sub-headings. The things you couldn't do on the Sabbath! You couldn't wear a safety pin, it was work to put it through the cloth. You couldn't wear your false teeth; that was carrying a burden. This happened. You can read all these rules in the Jewish *Mishnah* and it became a burden. So many rules there were that you didn't know whether you could put a foot forward on the Sabbath, and Jesus said to people burdened down with all these little rules and regulations, "Come unto me, you that are heavy laden...." Letters kill, the Spirit gives life.

I want to see people who will make Sunday a holy day because they want to, because the spirit within them says, "What a privilege to have a day that is different from the other days, a day for God, a day when we can worship, and enjoy being with his people." That is so different from saying, "Mustn't do that, not on Sunday." It is the difference between the complicated and the simple. Why take just the

Ten Commandments? Do you know what Jesus did with the Ten Commandments? He showed that two will do: love God with all your heart and soul and mind and strength; love your neighbour as yourself. You will keep the Ten Commandments if you keep the two. It is so much simpler. If I love my neighbour, I don't kill him; I don't steal from him; I don't run off with his wife or spoil his reputation. No, if you love someone, you keep the law. So Jesus changed from the complicated to the simple. Let us change from the demanding to the offering. In the Old Testament the religion is terribly demanding.

I remember in Arabia watching the Muslims, five times a day down on their foreheads. Their religion demanded it. Off they went to Mecca, wondering if they would ever get back; some of them wouldn't. They went there on pilgrimage. They fasted during Ramadan; their religion demanded it. But Jesus came to bring a new religion that doesn't demand things from you, it offers things to you. It only demands of you what it offers because the Holy Spirit gives you all you need in Christ. What a difference between a religion that says, "Give, give, give," and the religion that talks of the gifts.

It is *a difference between the deadly and the lively*. I remember hearing a lovely story about a preacher who was speaking on the parable of the ten virgins. He elaborated on this and said, "You, young men in the gallery, where would you rather be: in the dark with the foolish ones or in the light with the wise ones?" He got no uncertain answer from the young men in the gallery! Why is it that so often goodness is off-putting? Look at the two sons in the story of the prodigal son. Which one do you like of those two sons? There was one lad who went away and lived it up. He learned his mistake the hard way. He came back home but he is a lovely lad and your heart goes out to him. He's real; he's alive. Now look at the elder brother: "I never transgressed a commandment of yours. You never gave me a fatted calf." No wonder! He wouldn't have a party anyway, that one. Why is it that there is often this impression given that religious people are the deadly people and that if you want life you must go to the others? A little girl was saying her prayers: "Lord, make all the good people nice and the nice people good" – as if they are in two separate brackets. I will tell you why. It is because some people are still under the legalistic religion of keeping the letter and it is deadly, it kills, it takes away life. But for people who have come into the fullness of the Spirit there is life, and that is what the world wants to see. We want to get from the deadly to the lively. The letter kills, but the Spirit gives life.

From death to life – let me take that a bit further. It is literally a matter of life or death whether you live in religion or Christ. Religion condemns you; it produces an agonising torture of conscience in which you know what is right, and the more you know the greater the gap you realise exists between what you are and what you ought to be. It kills; it condemns – tells you what you ought to do. You try and you can't do it. It is a condemning religion. A country squire in England used to sit in his family pew and when the vicar read the Ten Commandments, he said after each one, "Never did that; never did that, vicar." "Thou shall not steal." "Never did that, vicar," came the voice from the squire. But you can't go through the Ten Commandments and say that, not when you read them in the light of Christ – that a thought of doing something is just as bad in God's sight as the act, or the word.

So religion of law kills you. It condemns you to death because, quite literally, the law of the Old Testament, which came from God, says this: "If you don't keep all the laws of God, if you don't keep all Ten Commandments, you have broken the law and you deserve to die." God will not let you live for ever in his universe for you will spoil it. It is no good my jumping the traffic lights and then saying to the policeman who stops me, "Well I've kept within thirty miles an hour." It is no good my saying, "Well, if I've broken the seventh commandment, I've kept the fifth." To break this beautiful chain of behaviour at any point is to break the law. God's law says: If you break it then I do not let you live for ever in my universe. I cannot. Therefore, your life is limited and you must die. But Christianity doesn't begin there – Christianity begins with forgiveness. That is just what I need. Christianity begins not by condemning but by acquitting; not by saying, "Guilty," but by saying, "Justified, innocent, go out of this court; case dismissed." When you come to Jesus Christ, God says, "I will never again bring up the wrong things you have done—never." Now, that is life. Life begins with forgiveness. It was the considered opinion of a Harley Street heart specialist that 75% of the heart cases that were brought to him were due to guilt, the fear of being discovered and the tension that it sets up. But Christianity doesn't condemn; it acquits, for the blood of Jesus cleanses from all sin.

The next contrast drawn here is this: *remember that the law came from God as the gospel did*. Moses was sent by God, as Jesus was, and therefore whatever God does has something of the glory and the splendour and the light of God about it. When Moses came down with the Ten Commandments, his face was shining. But Paul is teaching that even though there was a touch of the glory of God there and it was bright, it pales into insignificance beside the brilliance of the gospel. It really does. Mind you, until they had the New Testament, until Jesus came, it was the most wonderful thing that had ever happened that God sent Moses and gave men and women rules to live by.

It was bright with God's glory—the brightest thing the Jew

knows today is the Law, but it is as when the sun comes up over the horizon and the moon pales into utter insignificance. So when the gospel dawned, the law paled; Moses fades and Jesus shines. We know that the law came through Moses, but grace and truth came through Jesus and we beheld his glory, the glory of the only-begotten Son of the Father.

There is the difference between a fading glory and a lasting glory. Do you know why Moses covered his face with a veil? Because he knew the glory was going to fade; he knew it wouldn't last. That is the Old Testament. Under the Old Testament you might meet God once in a while and you would glow for a time, but then it would fade. You would be ashamed to let people know it had gone, but in Christianity the glory of the Lord can be on your face every day. You don't need to put a veil on your face; the glory need not fade. It is there. For the glory of Jesus has not faded. Moses has had his day and gone, and the glory of Moses is gone. The Jews look back to something past. Jesus is still alive, so the glory of Jesus has not faded and therefore it doesn't fade for us. Christianity never fades; it never gets less than it was, not even in numbers. Christianity is growing today faster than it has grown in two thousand years. Thousands are rushing into the kingdom in many countries.

Now we come to the last contrast: *the difference between having to hide something with a veil or having an open face, reflecting the glory of the Lord*. It says here that the Jews still have this veil. That doesn't mean that if you went to a synagogue you would see all the Jews with veils over their faces. What does it mean? The veil is in their minds. The veil is the same as the veil of Moses. Moses put the veil on because he believed that the glory of the Law would fade. He hid from the Israelites the fact that the Law was passing, and the same veil is in their minds. They go to the synagogue every Saturday. They hear the Law being read, and they have no idea that the glory is faded. The veil is still there, so they can't see that it has gone, that it is past and that it has given way to something much better. That is the tragedy of God's chosen people. But God doesn't give them up. He has not done with Israel yet. One day the whole nation of Israel will become Christian. I have that on the authority of the Bible. I had it on the Bible's authority that one day Israel will get back to their own land. We have seen that happen. I would love to live to see the day when Jews realise that the glory of the Law has faded and Jesus has come – and the veil is removed.

When you introduce an Israeli or a Jew to Jesus, you will feel within five minutes that you are back in the kindergarten yourself. They are such normal Christians when the veil is removed and they turn to Christ and they see that he is their Messiah. I once had the privilege of leading a Jewess to Christ. As soon as she came she said, "Do you mean that Jesus is our Christ, our Messiah?" Suddenly she saw it all; she saw things I have never seen. It was all there, waiting for the key that would unlock the truth. To this day, that veil is there and they don't see that religion is fading – not just the Jewish religion but every religion. Jesus stands out as the only-begotten Son in glory.

When you do turn to the Lord and the veil is taken away and you see that it is not religion that saves you but Jesus, when you see that religion is inside you, not outside you, that it is not a matter of outward observance but of inward love – three things then happen. From being a fearful person, you become a bold person. "Seeing that we have this hope," Paul says, "we are bold." Why are real Christians such bold people? Have you noticed that they are? It is because they have got something permanent. In the Spirit, they are not afraid it is a flash in the pan; they are not afraid that it will die off later. If you go on being filled with the Spirit, it gets better and better. I have met people who have been walking in the Spirit for fifty years and they will tell you it is better now than ever it was. Even some fifty years ago, I was talking to young people in our local grammar school about how thousands of hippies in America and elsewhere were turning to the Lord Jesus. Those who had tried sex, drugs, Zen Buddhism – people tried the lot and they tried Jesus last. The reaction of the school students was sceptical: "Ah, but it's just a passing fancy, just the latest craze. It's just a fashion; it won't last." I replied then, "We'll have to wait and see." But when people find Jesus, it does last. You can be bold about Christianity. You can recommend something to a youngster and say, "When you are seventy, this will still meet your need." You can say to anybody, "This doesn't fade. No, this is real."

If you go on with Jesus, where the Spirit of the Lord is, you have liberty. Next, *it is the change from being bound to being free.* So much religion is bound; it is in set forms. It is in what I would call "rut-ualism. It is in a rut, and the only difference between a rut and a grave is the depth. Well now, how do you get free religion? Where the Spirit of the Lord is, there is liberty – there should be freedom to do anything the Lord wants to do. It is good to be free to love God, to be free to worship, to be free to say no to wrong things; that is a wonderful freedom that not many people enjoy.

We are not meant to jump out of religion into nothingness, we are meant to jump forward – from religion into Christ, into the Spirit of the Lord, and there is liberty.

Then, when you have found this liberty, when you are full of the Spirit of the Lord, there is no need to hide anything. Display it; let it show: "unveiled face" – let it come out; let people see because you have found the real thing at last. No longer are you ashamed or afraid to mention that you go to church, that you are "religious" (in the right meaning of that word). Even though you are still in a minority, now you don't mind people seeing.

What a change that is from a religion which you want to keep sort of private to a religion that you don't mind showing to people. "We all, with unveiled faces..." – now there is a verb here that the scholars are divided about; they don't know what word to translate it with. It either means "gazing" or "reflecting". I am going to cut the knot and say that I think it means both. I see a double truth here. With an unveiled face, gazing into the face of God, you reflect. Do you know you get like the people you gaze at? Have you ever noticed that husband and wife get to look like each other? Oh, I'm sorry for my wife therefore, but do you notice that the same expression begins to occur on their faces? Do you notice that adopted children often look like their adoptive parents? You get like the people you gaze at, and this is the secret of real religion.

How do you get like Jesus? Is it by trying so hard, by saying, "Jesus said I've got to do this and I've got to do that, so I'm going to make an effort to do it now." You don't get like Jesus that way. You get like him and share his glory by gazing at him until you reflect. Then people will look at us and say, "That's what Jesus looks like." Believers are being changed, little by little, one degree of glory into another, until the day comes when actually our eyes will look on the face of Jesus. For he is coming back to earth as he said he would. Then we shall be like him for we shall see him as he is.

It is often the case that a person has to come to religion before coming to Christ – to face the demands of God's law before appreciating the offer of God's love. They must realise how far they have fallen short of God's glory before they can reflect it in their lives. The first Christians to discover the Spirit were Jews who had been under the law. Paul said, "I was a Pharisee. As touching the law, blameless; you couldn't fault my life anywhere, but it was so dead that when I found Christ, all my religion was rubbish, to be thrown into the dustbin" (see Philippians 3).

The Holy Spirit was given to people on the Day of Pentecost – but what was the Day of Pentecost? Why were there two and a half million Jews in Jerusalem on that day? What were they celebrating? What do Jews celebrate today on the Day of Pentecost? It is the date on which God gave the Ten Commandments. Isn't that striking? It was when the Jews gathered in Jerusalem to remember that God gave the Law, written on stone. On that very day, the fire fell and the Spirit was given. People were filled with the Holy Spirit and a new religion was born that was not a religion but a life. It was the life of Jesus.

What sort of religion do you have? It is either like a rowing boat or a sailing boat. Both are hard work, but you go much faster and further when you sail. Why? Because the wind is blowing. In a rowing boat it is all your effort – you won't make heaven that way before the last trumpet sounds; it will blow and you will still be rowing. But those who have got their sails up and know the wind of the Spirit and this exuberance and this life that carries you along – you have still got to work hard, yes, any sailor will tell you that – but you have the thrill of knowing that it is the Spirit himself taking you there. The Spirit is the Lord, and the Lord is the Spirit. This is how Jesus steps right into your life today and becomes real – by filling you with his Spirit.

PREACHING
Read 2 Corinthians 4

A. STATING TRUTH (1–6)
 1. UNALTERED WORD
  a. Adding
  b. Subtracting
  c. Changing
 2. UNBELIEVING WORLD
  a. Gods of this world
  b. Father of Jesus Christ

B. SUFFERING TROUBLE (7–12)
 1. HUMAN VESSEL
 2. HEAVENLY VICTORY

C. SPREADING TRIBUTE (13–15)
 1. THOUGHTFUL PREACHING
 2. THANKFUL PRAISE

D. SHAKING TRIALS (16–18)
 1. RENEWAL
 2. REWARD
 3. RELIANCE

The first person to whom I confided the deep feeling that God wanted me to be a minister of the gospel said this to me very bluntly, "David, don't go into the ministry if you can possibly stay out of it." I know now why he said that and what he meant. There are few callings that are more frustrating and more discouraging than the ministry of the gospel, which is why every preacher and every Christian worker has to discover the secret of how not to lose heart. This passage begins "we do not lose heart" and that is repeated later in the same chapter.

To lose heart in such a calling is a terrible thing. There have been few professions that have seen such a widespread loss of morale and a drift from its ranks as the Christian ministry. There has been such a crisis in the ministry that books have been published about it. What happened? Why did so many lose heart?

Many who carry on no longer have the impassioned desire to go on ministering the Word of God to other people. There has been a decline of confidence in preaching as a method of communication. How can a man go on preaching sermon after sermon if he feels deep down in his heart that it is futile and that it does no good? This then is the background to what we are going to consider, because it is no new problem, it has been there from the very beginning.

There are three discouragements in particular that I want to mention which Paul, laying bare his own heart as a minister of the gospel, says he has had to come to terms with. Number one: the problem of *indifference*. That is when you have prepared, when you have prayed, when you have preached your heart out, some will be completely untouched, unconvinced, unmoved, unchanged.

We have to come to terms with the fact that you can preach until you are blue in the face things that mean so much to you, things that you believe to be the truth from heaven itself, and somebody sits there like a dummy and goes away without having received any of it. I suppose a wife feels the same if she has spent hours preparing a beautiful meal, putting all her skill into it, and then somebody comes in and looks at it and says, "I'm not hungry," and pushes it aside. It is something you have got to come to terms with.

The second discouragement that Paul mentions here is *hostility*. This is rather different from indifference and a little harder to bear. To preach the truth of God disturbs people; it upsets and even angers them. Therefore, hostility is built up and nobody likes hostility unless they have a kind of perverted, masochistic desire deep down in their hearts. But sooner or later everybody who preaches the truth, the whole truth, and nothing but the truth will cut across other people, and hostility is set up.

The third discouragement Paul mentions here is the discouragement of those who treat preaching with *contempt*, with scepticism. There are those who say, "What a silly waste of time and energy and everything else"; those who say, "Sermons do no good at all. If you really want to help men you ought to be out of the pulpit and into something else." It was this kind of scepticism that caused Nicholas Stacey to leave the pulpit and go and sit at a desk in the Oxfam office, feeling that in this way he was helping to meet the needs of people in a much more practical and useful way.

Paul had faced all these three, and even though they had all come to him with tremendous force, he says, "We do not lose heart." We're still in it and we go on in it. None of these things can break us – and he is going to tell us why in this chapter. Forgive me if this seems a chapter for the ministry, but if you are a Christian you are in the ministry. You are a minister of the gospel as much as I am. You may not do it from the pulpit but you are called to do it wherever you are. You will meet the same three discouragements that will tend to make you give up. I want to help you to discover why we do not lose heart – why you need not lose heart.

The first thing is to discover that you have this ministry by the mercy of God; that you are not in the job to do someone else a favour – you are receiving a favour to be in the ministry. It is a holy privilege, utterly undeserved. I don't think, if they had known everything about me, my former church would have chosen me for their minister, but I know this: God knows everything about me yet he did choose me. It is his mercy. I don't deserve to be preaching the gospel;

you don't deserve to tell anybody else the gospel. What a holy privilege! It is by the mercy of God that you are in it at all. If you are in it to do someone else a favour, then of course you could leave it at the drop of a hat.

If you are in Christian service because you think you are conferring favours on others, then I beg you to go back to God and say to him, "God, it's your mercy that I'm in this job, that I'm in any Christian service at all, that I can give out hymn books at the door, that I can sing in the choir, that I can help to keep the house of prayer clean, that I'm a deacon, that I'm a Sunday School teacher. It is the mercy of God. You mean that I can have that privilege? You mean that I could do it? Thank you Lord." Do you know, that's the first step? It gives you a new standpoint, a new perspective. You are not in it for the sake of others, you are in it because God in his great mercy said, "You can do this for me."

Having this ministry by the mercy of God, we do not lose heart, but that doesn't mean we don't face the other discouragements. That doesn't mean that we don't have to come to terms with the problems of preaching the gospel today, of telling people the truth, and there are problems. First this matter of *indifference*. It is horrible to be met with sheer indifference when you feel that you have got the only real truth there is – and let me say straightaway that no preacher wants to give the impression that he has the truth, but he does want to give the impression that the truth has him, and that what he is saying he believes to be the absolute truth. They are burning convictions, otherwise they wouldn't be said so emphatically and so forcefully. Then imagine being met by someone who says, "I don't see anything in it." You might bring a friend along to church, and afterwards the friend says, "Well, I don't know what you see in it all. I didn't get anything," and you feel so flat and you wonder what was wrong. This is the matter of indifference.

When you come up against indifference, when people are not interested in the truth, when they are not moved by it, when they don't open their minds to it, the big temptation is to tamper with God's Word. When people won't listen to a straight gospel message, when they are not interested in straight Bible study, it is a frightful temptation to start messing up God's word to try to please them, and Paul had faced this temptation. How do you manipulate it? Well, you add to it, or you subtract from it, or you twist its meaning. All the time what you are doing is turning God's Word into man's word, because man's word is interesting and you feel you can improve on God's Word and make it more interesting by gearing it to the thoughts and philosophies of men. So you are still standing with a Bible in your hand but what you are preaching is not God's Word, you have tampered with it. You are avoiding certain passages; you have skipped certain truths. You take other things because they please. You are playing to the gallery. A man who does that should get out of the ministry straight away. There comes a point in your ministry where you have got to renounce that kind of thing and say, "For me, whether men are indifferent or interested, I will just simply state the truth as plainly and directly as I can."

One of my heroes was a man called Thomas Cook, one time Principal of Cliff College. In his early days he was an orator. He could hold the people riveted by feeding them with what they already thought. He used great quotations from famous people. He put it all together in brilliant oratory and he could move the mind and the heart. Then one day he said to God, "Why don't you bless people through my ministry? I can hold a large congregation but why is nobody getting changed? Why is nobody getting converted?"

God said to him, "Because you are tampering with my Word. You're twisting it to please the gallery." Cook stood on the high level bridge that crosses the River Tyne in my home town of Newcastle-upon-Tyne, and he says in his diary that he threw his reputation as a preacher into that river. He said, "Lord, from now on I'll just state the truth – whether people are interested or not, I'll just preach your Word." That is when Thomas Cook's ministry began, because then for the very first time he preached and people were converted.

I renounced tampering with God's Word even if people aren't interested, even if they say, "Oh that's old hat, he just preaches the Bible." I refuse to tamper with God's Word. No twisting it, no adding to it, no subtracting from it. God's Word is what matters – not my words, not your words, but God's Word. But the fact remains that even though you refuse to tamper with it, and you have given the truth of God unvarnished, making a simple statement (and if you want to know what preaching is, Paul says, "It's manifesting the truth, letting the truth be seen") there are still those who will just sit and listen with blank faces and blank minds and won't go away with anything. That is hard.

Why? I have felt like saying, "Sometimes a preacher feels like a salesman selling colour television to the blind." According to Paul the real problem is that you are trying to show the light to people who are blind. It's not that they're being wilfully obtuse, that they are being obstinate in their minds. It is not that they won't see, they can't see. It seems so clear to you. It is light; it shines so clear that you wonder how ever you missed it. Yet, somebody else can't see it. It is not physical blindness it's mental blindness. Their mind literally cannot see the light so it doesn't dawn on them what you are talking about. They are living in perpetual midnight. Oh, they are intelligent people. They may have a high IQ but it is locked behind a veil of blindness and that is the real problem.

In other words, as Paul says, there is the god of this

world and the God and Father of our Lord Jesus. Everybody belongs to one or the other. People are either in the grip of the god of this world, or else they are seeing the light of the glory of God in the face of Jesus.

Behind all the chaos, suffering and heartache of the world in which we live, there is the god of this world who is behind it all, manipulating, controlling, seeing that people just cannot live together without fighting, seeing that even in family life, a family becomes a bickering, irritable group of people who hate the sight of each other. The whole world lies in the power of the evil one. I fear that if I call him Satan or the devil you will treat him too lightly, so let us use the phrase here: "the god of this world". He has got supernatural power and he has millions in his grip, and the reason that you and I cannot get the light of God's truth across to people is that the god of this world has blinded their minds – they can't see. In a sense, you can't blame them for that. You argue and you talk and you seek to persuade, but they can't see because they are blind.

It is like describing a sunset to a man who has never been able to see. It's a terrible position to be in. The god of this world has done it because he doesn't want to lose his kingdom. He doesn't want to lose a single soul. But I will tell you this: before the sun goes down tonight he will have lost thousands. People will have been translated from the kingdom of darkness, the kingdom of Satan, into Christ's kingdom. It is happening right now. People are walking from darkness into light.

What is it that the devil doesn't want you to see? He doesn't want you to see the divine; he only wants you to see the human. He allows people to see Jesus but not the Lord Jesus Christ. He allows people to see Jesus as a human being but no more. He doesn't want them to see that Jesus is the likeness of God the Father. So you find that people of this world acknowledge that Jesus was a great man, a person who lived two thousand years ago. They see that. Who couldn't? The evidence is there. They can see Jesus, but they can't see the likeness of God. They can't see the glory of God shining in the face of Jesus. They can't look at Jesus and say, "My Lord and my God" – they are blind to that.

When they listen to a preacher they can't see Jesus speaking in the preacher. They can only see a preacher doing his thing and so Paul says, "Look, we preach not ourselves, we preach Christ Jesus as Lord." Can you see that? Or when you hear biblical preaching do you just see a human being getting up and using the advantage of a pulpit six feet above criticism to air his own opinions and views dogmatically? The devil says, "I don't want you to see Jesus as Lord. You can see him as a human being, keep everything human, stay down here and then you won't see the truth."

Paul says that you can tell if someone is on their way to hell. When a man said to me that he got nothing out of my sermon, do you know what my reaction was? "You've just told me as plainly as you could that you're on your way to hell." It is a sign that they are lost. They may be awfully nice people. They may be courteous and kind and love their children. They may be all this, but if they cannot come to God's Word and see anything in it, they are perishing.

Somebody may say, "Well, they can't help that." Yes they could. According to this scripture, the god of this world only blinds the minds of those who *disbelieve*. At some point in their life, someone who sees nothing in the Word of God has said, "I don't believe." He has heard the truth; he has heard at some point something from God. Everybody has heard that, whether through their conscience, or through Creation, or through some contact with Christians. Everybody has heard some word of truth from God and at some point they have said, "I don't believe it. I reject it. My mind says, 'No.'"

The result of disbelieving is that you put yourself in Satan's hands to blind you to the truth, and from then on you will only see the human side of Christianity: you can see no divine glory in it, just a human club of religious people; just a man getting up and using the gift of the gab – just a lot of people living at a human level.

Is it hopeless? No! I believe in the God who said, "Let light shine out of darkness" – who looked at a dark world, darkness over the face of the deep, and he looked at that physical world that was so dark and said, "Let there be light" – and there was light. That same God can shine in a man's heart; that same Creator is the Redeemer. The God who looked at a dark physical world can now look at a dark moral and spiritual world and say, "Let there be light."

The Son of Righteousness rose with healing in his wings. A person's moral and spiritual blindness can be removed and that is why we preach. It is the God who said, "Let light shine out of darkness" who has shone in our hearts to give the light of the knowledge of the glory of God in the face of Jesus. We have seen the light. It has dawned on us who Jesus is, and we now know what God is like, and we now see his glory.

Literally, God can give eyes to the blind. Do you remember when Jesus preached the first sermon we have got recorded from his lips, in his own home town of Nazareth? He said, "Listen, the Spirit of the Lord is upon me. He's anointed me" – to do what? "To give sight to the blind and to preach the good news, the acceptable year of the Lord." This is what we are here to do: to open blind eyes. Even if a thousand people remain blind and go away saying, "I got nothing at all out of that," one person may go away and say, "I see. It's dawned on me. Jesus is the Lord. Jesus Christ is the Lord – the likeness of God." That is how it came to Paul. Paul was a man with high intelligence, religious zeal, but spiritually he was so blind that he attacked every Christian he could lay his hands on, pursuing them. He became a missionary for antichrist. He left his own country to go to another country to put the Christians in prison. Oh, what moral and spiritual darkness he was in. But on the Damascus road, when the noon sun was directly overhead, there were no shadows, it was so bright, even the sun paled and he saw the light of the glory of God in the face of Jesus. He was then physically blind for three days, but he was spiritually in the light. He had seen the light. That is how it came to him – on that black mind, and so dark was it that he couldn't see any good in Christians at all – and now he was in the light. He is just describing what happened to him. It was the same God who caused light to shine at the beginning of the universe who had shone in Paul's own heart, and he became a preacher of the gospel.

That is how we face the first discouragement, and therefore we in turn become lights. Jesus said, "I am the light of the world," and then he said to his disciples, "You are the light of the world" – the only title he ever passed on to them. He shone – this was the light coming into the world, and the darkness could not overcome it. You know, a little candle is stronger than all the darkness in the world. This little light of mine, I'm going to let it shine. That is what you are called to do. Though we are in a dark world in which people are blind to God and can't see Christ, you go around with the light of the gospel, and the darkness can't put it out. One day you will have the joy, if you haven't had it already, of seeing the light dawn in another person's face. Have you ever seen that happen – somebody's face light up? "Is that true? Is this what God is like? Is this what God will do for me?" The God who said, "Let light shine out of darkness" has taken a poor soul in darkness and shone in their heart.

Let us look at the second discouragement. So far we

have been thinking about indifference, the blindness of people's minds, now let us think about *hostility*. People do get disturbed, angry and upset when you preach the whole Word of God. As long as you stick to the bits they accept and approve then it is alright, but sooner or later if you go through the whole Word of God something is going to hit. You see, Paul in preaching the gospel doesn't appeal to men's minds or their hearts. He says, "I commend the truth to every man's *conscience*." Entertainment just goes for the mind or the heart, but preaching goes for the will. It is after a person's conscience.

Sooner or later, if you preach the truth, somebody's conscience begins to trouble them – it is not very pleasant. One preacher described it to me like this: he saw people sitting on drawing pins. Well, I think you know what that means. "It's hard for you to kick against the goads, Saul" – and something begins to happen. That is a good sign. Hostility is much better than indifference. I remember going to speak at a youth club and about thirty young people were there. I spoke and then invited questions. For the most part, twenty-eight of them were just sitting there chewing gum and quite indifferent, but two were so hostile and they attacked what I said with tears in their eyes.

I came home and my wife asked, "How did you get on?" I said, "Well, I think there's hope for two of them." Sure enough, within six months those two were baptised. We got letters from them both regularly and they were both going on with the Lord, working for him and winning others. Hostility is a good sign, but not very nice at the time. I am afraid it is because vested interests are being touched, ways of life are being challenged, things that have been done before are being questioned and conscience is beginning to be active.

Paul says that we have this treasure of this light in earthen vessels. I am reminded of a historic earthen vessel I saw – a

345

little clay lamp. It had a Jewish branch candlestick engraved on the top and two holes to put the oil in, and a wick. It was the little lamp that was not to be put under a bushel but was put on a lampstand in an eastern house in those days. It was very fragile and had I dropped it, it would have broken. Just a blow with a hammer and it would have cracked – it was very vulnerable. Paul is saying that we are vulnerable. We are earthen vessels, just pots of clay. We have got this lovely light to shine, but it is just in a clay pot and that's all I am – an old clay pot, and therefore very vulnerable, rather fragile. A preacher has feelings as a congregation has feelings. A preacher can be hurt as a congregation can be hurt. We are vulnerable, like those fragile little vessels holding a light – easily smashed. You can find bits of smashed earthen vessels all over the Middle East. Paul is saying here that he is easily smashed too, and when hostility comes and when he is attacked for preaching the whole truth he is weak.

Look at the things he says can happen to a preacher. "I can be afflicted, perplexed, persecuted, struck down" – nobody enjoys that. Feeling black and blue, feeling buffeted, feeling tossed around, feeling just as if you are in the middle of a circle of schoolboy bullies who are all having a go at you, or if you have met a gang of thugs who are just having a go. Yes, you can feel like that too. Paul felt it very clearly indeed. He is saying that he experiences in this clay pot of his the dying of Jesus. The word he uses is "dying" not "death". He is thinking of Jesus as a human being so he uses the word "Jesus" not the word "Christ" or "Lord" here. He is thinking of Jesus as a human being on the Cross. Now the Cross did not kill very quickly; it was one of the slowest kinds of death there has ever been. It sometimes took as long as six days for a man to die on a cross. It wore him down with pain, with weariness, ultimately with suffocation trying to breathe – a horrible death. Paul's words mean: sometimes I feel I'm going through the dying of Jesus; this gradual killing, this wearing down, this buffeting, this constant strain which wears you down. That was how he felt as an earthen pot, just a little lump of clay holding the light of the knowledge of the glory of Christ.

But he is not complaining and he is not losing heart. Oh yes, he feels it is a slow death to preach the Word. He feels it is killing him; he feels it is wearing him down. He can see this: If I share the dying of Jesus then I share the rising of Jesus; if I share this gradual killing experience, my life can be a series of resurrections; the life of Jesus can be seen in me as well as the dying. We come back up again. We do not lose heart. In a series of amazing contrasts he describes what it is like to know the dying and rising of Jesus every day. You can't know the rising unless you know the dying. You can't know the resurrection unless you know the Cross. There is no crown without a Cross.

He says he is under pressure from all sides, yet never trapped. What a picture! I am hemmed in and under pressure from all sides but there is always a way out: the way up. So you can't bring the pressure to bear so much that you have got me trapped. The second contrast he makes is this: I am often perplexed and puzzled, at my wits end to know what the problem is, what to do next, but I am never ultimately at a loss for a solution to the problem. Jesus knew this perplexity – in his dying he cried out, "Why have you forsaken me?" Jesus knew what it was to ask "Why", and every preacher knows what it is to be so perplexed that he says, "Why, Lord, did you let this happen?" But he is never at the point where he is saying there is no solution. There always is.

Thirdly, there is this contrast: I am pursued by men but I am never abandoned by God. God doesn't run away and leave me. People may run after my skin but God doesn't run away from me. I am pursued but not abandoned. That is the dying and the rising.

Finally: knocked down but not knocked out. There is a motto for the Christian worker: I may be knocked down but I'm never knocked out; I'll be back up in the ring again – you may have me on the canvas once, twice, more times, but I shall be back up in the fight. The dying of Jesus leads to the rising.

If you experience the gradual killing of Christian service, you will also experience the constant living of Jesus in your mortal body. Indeed, you can't give life to others unless you are prepared for death yourself. So death is at work in me, life in you, meaning: as Jesus died that we might live, if you are going to serve Jesus you will know this death that others might live.

Now the third and last discouragement: *contempt*, preaching said to be useless. I remember a successful businessman saying that if I dropped the ministry he would take me into the business, he would give me quite a part in it, introduce me to the freemasons' lodge, and really see that I had a good career. It was an offer he made to me during my first year of ministry. He said, "You know, you're going to waste your time and talents in that. Why go into that?" I found out later he also had designs on someone else, but nevertheless this was his offer. He just saw the ministry of the gospel as an utter waste of a life. How futile, just spouting words! You see, the tools of my trade are words; I was ordained to the ministry of the Word. The main thing I do for people is to speak – that is my calling. God told me to do this. I suppose I filled the ears of my congregation with about eight thousand words every service! People might say, "What good does it do? What comes of it all? Isn't it just words?" That is the discouragement that can come. "Why go on in such a useless role?" Well, I will tell you why.

First, because it is the kind of faith that can't keep silent:

"I believed and so I spoke," said the psalmist. There are certain kinds of faith. There is the kind of faith that you don't need to share with anybody else, it is a private thing, you never talk about it, and it is not real. It is not the Bible faith. The only faith the New Testament knows is the faith you have got to speak. If you believe in your heart and confess with your mouth, you will be saved. Not: if you believe in your heart you will be saved, but if you believe in your heart with the kind of faith that comes out – that is saving faith.

Every preacher speaks because he has got to. He believes it so firmly, so deeply. He believes that unless people listen they are going to hell so he has got to speak. How could you stand and see a lot of people walking over a cliff and not shout after them and say, "There's danger. Don't go a step further. Stop, listen to me." You would do that, wouldn't you? "We believed and therefore we speak." You can't tell a man to stop preaching the gospel. He has believed it and therefore he has got to speak it.

But there is more to it than that. It may be that he would be frustrated if he didn't preach. I would be very frustrated if I said I would speak no more of Jesus and make no mention of his name. It would be as if there were, "A hidden fire shut up in my bones, and I'm weary with forbearing and I cannot contain." I am quoting Jeremiah there. He said that when he was a boy in his teens. Even if it produced no result we would have to go on preaching – even if nobody listened. But, thank God that is not the case.

The second reason why we go on preaching is that we believe. We know that one day, in the day of resurrection, we will see people there because we preached. Because the God who raised up Jesus from the dead will raise us also with others in his presence. That is what I am after: to get people to glory, to get them to heaven, and to believe that some word of mine, by the grace of God, will ensure that somebody will be there that day. Isn't that worth it? Of course it is. That is the biggest thing you could ever do for another human being: to get them into the resurrection morning standing in the presence of Christ. Oh well, someone says, "That's way in the future, what's happening now today? What good is preaching doing now?" Well, I'll tell you in three words: grace, gratitude, glory. There they are in the last verse.

Number one: spreading grace. I once noticed some girls in uniform on Guildford High Street, giving out free gifts, a soap product I think. I thought, "There they are. What a job going down that street, giving people something free. Lovely job." Yet, even so, you find some people will say "No!" They are suspicious. They think there is a catch. I am in the free gift business! I am in the business of saying to people, "The gift of God is eternal life and it is free." Grace means free gifts, and I am in the business of giving utterly free gifts to people – you can't buy them, you can't work for them, you can't be good enough for them – it is free – so that grace may spread to more and more people; so that I may give a free gift of God for anybody who will take it.

What will that produce? The grace or free gift of God, produces *gratitude*. What a lovely thing it is to do for the world in which we live – to produce grateful people. There is so much grumbling, complaining, covetousness and greed that just to be able to see people become thankful, grateful, content – what a lovely thing to be doing for people. I remember a lady who came to Christ and I went to see her in her home, and she said, "I've told my husband I don't want a dishwasher. You have no idea how lovely it is to be out of the rat race. I'm content with everything I've got." She had been just the opposite before. Grace, the free gift of God, produces this gratitude and this contentment. What a lovely thing to be doing for such a discontented world.

Now it comes full circle. What does the gratitude lead to?

It leads to *glory to God* – to the praise of his glory. I am using my lips to preach, to help others to use their lips to praise, and that is the object of the whole exercise. I am not doing it only for people. It is true it is for your sake, as Paul says, but it is ultimately for the glory of God. If I can increase the number of people who want to say thank you to God and give him the glory, then my living has not been in vain. This is how God operates through human lips preaching his grace to people. The whole thing comes from heaven and goes back to heaven again. That is what it is all about and the key word in this chapter comes in every paragraph: the word "God".

It begins: by the mercy of God we have this ministry. It is preaching Christ who is the likeness of the Father. It is commending ourselves to every person's conscience in the sight of God. It is an earthen vessel that does it, so that the transcendent power might be seen to be of God. It is all that the gratitude of men might give glory to God. It is God, God, God – no wonder those who can only see the human side of reality think that it is a waste of time. No wonder that they can be indifferent to the preaching of the gospel. No wonder they can be hostile to it. No wonder they can treat it with contempt – they can't see God, and yet God is in it all. It comes from God and it goes to God. Isn't that thrilling?

FUTURE
Read 2 Corinthians 5:1–11

A. NEW BODY (1–5)
1. FRAME
2. FEELINGS
3. FOUNDATION

B. NO BODY (6–11)
1. OBSERVATION
2. OUTLOOK
3. OBJECTIVE

Many religions of the world are concerned with souls and how to get the soul free from the "prison house" of this body. Christians don't talk like that. Christians take bodies very seriously indeed for three reasons.

The first reason is Creation. God made my body – therefore, let me never treat it as something that can be despised, something that doesn't matter. Anything that God created is good and something he wanted to make.

Secondly, I take bodies seriously because of *the Incarnation of the Son of God*. When he himself wanted to help men and women, how did he do it? He took a body and the Word came flesh. He did not only take a body for thirty-three years, he took a body forever. He still has a body in the unseen world. I worship a Lord with a body. The heart of my faith is belief in the resurrection of Jesus' body.

Thirdly, Christianity takes bodies seriously because of *salvation*. The word "salvation" is the same as our word "salvage" – it means to take something that is perishing, which is going to be thrown away as useless, and make it useful again. According to the New Testament, salvation includes my body. God is going to salvage not only my soul, but the whole of me. In the Bible the word "soul" doesn't mean something spiritual inside you, it means body plus breath. Whenever you see the word "soul" in the Bible that is what it means. Body + breath = soul.

God took the dust of the earth and he made out of it a shape, a corpse, but it had no breath, so it was not a soul – it was just a body. But he breathed life into it and it became a soul. Therefore, Christianity is concerned with bodies. This passage from beginning to end is concerned with your body. Paul tells us that the body is wasting away, that, "You will be judged by what you have done in your body" – and in between we learn about getting a new body. It is about bodies, but live ones, not dead ones.

Why does Paul write about bodies? Because if you get the right view of the body you will not be discouraged in the Christian life. Again Paul is saying we do not lose heart. You almost want to say, "Paul, you've said it once before, are you trying to convince yourself?" No, Paul is saying that there is no life that is so discouraging as the Christian life, but we don't lose heart. The Christian life is a tough life, it can be a lonely life, it can be a frustrating life, especially since it has to be lived in a world that is not Christian but is indifferent and antagonistic.

Paul has been through all this in chapter four—the frustration of having the truth and trying to teach it to spiritually blind people, the suffering that comes from antagonism and opposition. We don't lose heart – but why? Because of what God is going to do for our bodies. That is why we may be knocked down but we are not knocked out.

Let us look at what God is going to do. At the end of chapter four we had a paragraph about our natural body, the one we have got now which we have to use to live in this life. Then 5:1–5 is concerned with the new body which we are one day going to possess. Then 5:6–11 is concerned with the interval between the two when we will literally have no body. We have a natural body now, we will one day have a new body, but there is an "in between" when we shall have no body.

Take first the natural body. The simple fact is that you don't go to heaven the day you are converted. We often wish we could, but the simple fact is that when you are converted you have got to stay on earth. You are not given a new body straight away, you have to go on using the old one. To be utterly practical, the chin I shaved the day after I was converted was the same chin I shaved the day before. Wouldn't it be lovely if we went straight to heaven when we were converted – if as soon as we met Jesus we jumped straight into glory, saw his face and lived there happily ever after?

But how would we ever get anybody else there? Can you not see that God just has to leave you on earth when he has begun to save you? Then why didn't he give me the new body straight away? Why doesn't he give me a new body instead of leaving me in this one that gets old, tired and diseased? The answer again is very simple. Can you imagine how many people we would have to pack into churches if it was seen that as soon as you were converted you got a brand new body? You would never need a doctor again; you would never need to go to bed again. Can you imagine the queues we would have? People would be coming for quite the wrong reason. I can see that in his mercy, when Jesus had his resurrection body in this world, he never showed it to anyone who didn't believe in him. Why? Because he wasn't going to force them to accept his gospel for the wrong reason. So the simple truth is that when you become a Christian you are left on this earth in your old body until the Lord comes or calls and that is a bit of a frustration. You have got new life inside you, but it has got to be lived in an old packing case outside, and it doesn't seem to match. It is like new wine in an old wine bottle – it just doesn't line up. There is a tension between the inside and the outside of you, the inner nature and the outer nature. One is getting better every day, the other is not. One is getting stronger, the other is getting weaker. A Christian is in this tension.

Furthermore, a Christian is likely to have more physical strain than other people. Not only does he suffer the normal wastage of the human body – growing old, more and more grey hairs. We are all getting older! Not only do we have that, and we share that with everybody else, but as believers we also have the extra physical strain of doing God's work. It is a physical strain, and let us be quite frank with Christians about this. It is going to take from you your physical resources. There will be times when you are worn out in the Lord's service. There will be times when you feel all in. Paul says, "It's a slow death to serve the Lord. It is bearing in the body the dying of the Lord Jesus."

One wonders if Christians should plan for a nice sort of happy, peaceful old age with nothing to do. One wonders whether the Lord wants that, or whether he isn't asking for people who are prepared to wear themselves out in his service. I think of John Hunt, the Lincolnshire ploughboy who went out to Tonga and Fiji at the age of twenty-six to the cannibal infested islands they were. He died of old age when he was thirty-six, worn out for the Lord. But those are the "Friendly Islands" on the map now because John Hunt went there. Henry Martyn was another. One could go through life after life, remembering people who wore themselves out for the Lord.

Paul knew about this and his body was wasting away,

not only because he was getting older, but Paul was an old man before his time. He was roughly middle-aged when he wrote this, but if you had met him you would have thought he was an old man. He was worn out for the Lord. He had been in prison, beaten, stoned, left for dead, shipwrecked. He was worn out and yet he says: "I don't lose heart." Now the word "heart" in the Bible doesn't mean the organ that pumps blood around you. The word "heart" means the inside of you. It is the same as the word we use when we talk about the heart of a lettuce or the heart of a problem. We mean the inside. "We don't lose heart" – why not? Because though the outer nature is wasting away, though it's being worn out, the inside is being renewed.

The Bible says that even young people can get weary. Even young men shall faint. We old ones wear out much more quickly and we marvel at the youngsters. Even young men shall faint and grow weary, but they that wait upon the Lord shall renew their strength. It is not just a good night's sleep that puts us back on top, it is to wait on God in prayer. It is to be renewed in the Spirit; it is to have a fresh dose of life every day. To be renewed means to have your soul restored. That doesn't mean the spiritual part of you. "He restores my soul," said the psalmist, and he means, "He gives me back my life; I can breathe again." The Christian is someone who has discovered the secret. Even though the body is wearing out in a slow death, the Christian has discovered how to keep going.

I think of a dear little lady who in her mid-eighties was still in full-time Christian service. She was up at dawn, and from then until she went to bed she was winning people for Christ. At around the age of twenty-six she had been sent to my home town of Newcastle-upon-Tyne, to her relatives, to die, because she had been given one year to live by the doctors. She said, "Lord, if I've only got one year, then I'm going to use every minute to win others." So she went out into the slums of Newcastle and Gateshead, and she just talked to anybody about Jesus. She had over fifty years of doing that work. She was so tiny you might have thought a breath of wind would have blown her away, but Sister Winifred Laver, as everybody called her, was one of the great examples of the outer man wasting away – just skin and bones! Once I was preaching in Newcastle at the City Hall, and I looked up in the gallery and there was this little lady and she had a pew full of leather-jacketed boys. She was sitting at the end, holding them in. She had literally been on the streets before that meeting. She was then turned eighty and she just brought them in. She had sat them down and said, "You're going to listen to this."

This is the secret. Your outer man may waste away, may look worn out, and the physical strain of being a Christian today is going to be colossal, it is a battle, but when the inside can be renewed every day, it doesn't matter about the outside. Somebody can say to you, "How are you?" You can say, "Well, the body's in a dreadful mess, but I'm great. I'm fine." That is the inner man being renewed.

The second thing Paul says is this: not only do we have this *present renewal*, we have a *future reward* for the physical strain. There is a contrast between what we are going through now and what is waiting ahead. This physical strain, this affliction, is just momentary. It is so brief compared with the eternal glory that we are going to enjoy. One day, all the physical strain of serving Christ will seem just like a bad dream after you have woken up. It will seem so short when you have been there a thousand years in eternity. You will look back and think, "Those few years of physical tension and strain in serving the Lord – what was it? Nothing; momentary."

Furthermore, you'll say, "It's slight, it's a light thing

compared with the eternal weight of glory." Not only is this a comparison between now and then, but Paul is saying that the affliction now actually *produces* the glory then. It is not just a comparison, it is a production. The physical strain and suffering of serving the Lord here are working for you an eternal weight and glory. You will be glad you went through it; you will be glad it was a strain, because of the glory that it produces. That is the second thing that Paul talks about. We can face affliction now. If you do not bear a cross, you cannot wear a crown says the song, and this is true. If the Christian life is no strain to you; if you don't feel this pressure of bearing in your body the dying of the Lord Jesus, if your Christian life is one smooth picnic, then I pity you, there is not going to be the weight of glory. But those who have been through, and those who know the strain of serving the Lord, say: "We look to the things that are unseen."

Let us go further. What do we really look to? On what do we rely for our life? We live in a world in which people are looking to the things that can be seen. We all know this is a visual age. Advertisers know that the lust of the eyes is the best thing to get hold of, and behind that lies the pride of life. So look at it, see it, want it – and Paul says we don't look to the things that are seen. You can't tempt us that way. We look to the things that are not seen. Why? Everything that you can see is temporary. Everything that you can see with these eyes is going. There isn't a thing you can see that hasn't got its days numbered. Therefore, if you live for the things you can see, you are pinning your life on things that are going to vanish. Everything visible is going to disappear. How terrible to have lived and looked to the things that you can see, and see your whole life vanish.

Even the clouds in the sky, the hills and trees that you looked at this morning, are going to disappear. "The heavens will be rolled up like a tablecloth," says the Bible, "and put away." They will be rolled up like a great curtain, and it is all going to disappear. You look at people and they are looking at things they can see and saying they are looking to this, that and the other. Paul says, "I look at the things that you can't see." It is a contradiction; it is a paradox to look to the things that are unseen. But we rely on the things you can't see. Let us get this straight. We don't mean that Christianity is vague and nebulous. These things are real and one day we will see them. The only reason that they are unseen is that they are future. We have got to live by faith, not by sight. We have got to believe in a new heaven and a new earth. It is invisible now, but one day it won't be. We have to believe in a new body, and I have not seen a new body yet but I believe in it. It is not something intangible. I will shake hands with those new bodies one day. They are real, but I can't see them yet so I've got to *believe*.

If you can look to the things you can't see, then you are no longer worried about the physical strain. When you look in the mirror in the morning and you see the grey hairs, and you see the lines, and you see the signs of age, you don't look at the things that are seen, you look in the mirror of God's Word and you look at that new body you are going to have. You say, "Lord, I don't mind wearing out this one if there's a brand new one coming along," and you have a different attitude. You don't lose heart and you realise that the things you can't see are the things that will last forever. The things that are coming, the things that God is going to make, are the things worth pinning your life to. Otherwise, you are going to live the kind of life that will just see things disappear.

Let me be very practical in this: if you pin your religion to a minister or a church building, you are pinning it to something that will vanish. But if you pin your faith to the unseen Lord, you don't care whether a church building comes or goes. Your faith isn't dependent on being surrounded by gothic archways; you don't look at the things that are seen. You don't need a lot of paraphernalia in a service for your eyes. It can so easily become idolatry if you have got to have special things to look at to worship the Lord. You are becoming tied to things that are going to vanish. But when you look to the things that are unseen, then you are no longer tied. You are free, and that is a lovely freedom.

Even if the outer nature is wasting and the inner one being renewed, what will happen when the outer nature finally gives up? It is going to. The days of my body are numbered, and God knows how many birthdays I am going to have in the future, and he knows how many you are going to have. You only know how many you have had, but he knows how many you are going to have. This outer nature is going to finish altogether one day – what is going to happen then? Paul has a lovely phrase now, he says, "We know...." We are absolutely sure this is what's going to happen. I'm going to take this body off and put another one on. Isn't that tremendous? The contrast between the two bodies is the contrast between camping in a tent and living in a house. It is lovely to go camping in reasonable weather, but when the wind blows and the storm comes it is not such fun. There is not much between you and the elements. The thing can blow down, and even then there comes a day when camping is over. Who wants to live in a tent forever? So you pull the tent pegs up, you pull the tent down, and you pack it up. Do you realise that dying is no more than pulling your tent pegs up? Dying is just taking the tent down – because what we live in here is just a tent – temporary. It isn't very good protection. It's just a temporary home for me. I'm just living in it for the few years God puts me here. I'm just camping on earth. I'm on the move and the tent is going to be taken down.

The tent will be replaced one day by a building. There is

something permanent about the building that God is making for you to live in, a building which is a body but a permanent one – a healthy, whole body, a perfect body that is a building eternal in the heavens which God is making for you. We know that we have this. What a temporary frame we have got now, but we will get a permanent one.

How do we feel about this? We groan and we sigh. Wouldn't you just love to have that new body now, especially if you are finding this present body a trial? We want to be off and to get that new body – so that what is mortal can be swallowed up by life. That phrase just struck me as I read it, "swallowed up by life" (5:4). Do you know that everybody else is swallowed up by death? Everything mortal is swallowed by death until you know Jesus, and then everything mortal is swallowed up in life. That is the promise of the future.

I notice that it is God who prepares us for that. It doesn't say he prepares that for us. Let us get it the right way round. God is not preparing a new body for us, he is preparing us for the new body. He will make that new body in a moment, in the twinkling of an eye. No long process of evolution is needed. Just shut your eyes, open them, and there is the new body. It will be as quick as that. It is we who take such a long time to prepare. The new body will only take a moment but God is preparing us for that very thing. Do you think he wants to put me as I am in that new body right now? He wants to get me ready for it.

Now we come to the foundation of our hope. How do we know? Is it not just wishful thinking? Speculation? Guesswork? How can a man say we know that when this tent is pulled down we have a building eternal in the heavens made by God? We know this: we have got the guarantee. The guarantee is his Spirit. When you have received his Spirit you have got the guarantee because the Spirit comes as the first instalment of God's future for you.

The word translated "guarantee" means "the deposit", "the down payment". This is God's down payment to us, the guarantee that he will complete the job; the guarantee that he who began a good work in us will continue it until that day when it is all finished. The Holy Spirit is the guarantee. We already have a little foretaste of heaven. Already we know what heaven is going to sound like. Already we know what heaven is going to feel like. We have got the foretaste, the down payment. If God gives us the first payment, do you think he doesn't keep up his payments? No – men may not, but he will.

There is another reason why the presence of the Spirit guarantees a new body. Let me give it to you in Paul's own words, "If the Spirit of him who raised up Jesus from the dead dwells in you, then the Spirit who raised Jesus from the dead will quicken also your mortal bodies" – that is the promise. The same Holy Spirit who got Jesus out of the grave and gave him a resurrection body, which he still has and always will have, is the same Spirit dwelling in my heart, so I know I have got a guarantee of a new body.

Finally, Jesus Christ, the Son of God, was three days without a body at all, for he died and his Spirit became naked, unclothed. His body was put in a tomb, his spirit he commended to his Father, and three days later, the Spirit of Jesus and a resurrection body were united and came out of the tomb. Jesus had a gap between his natural body and his new body. Every Christian who dies before Jesus comes back will have a gap between this body and the new one.

At first sight, we tend to react against that and say, "Oh, I don't want to be naked, I don't want to be unclothed." Paul had that feeling. He said: I hope I'm still alive when Jesus comes back and then I'll just, in the blinking of an eye, put off this tent and put on my new body, go straight from one to the other. Every Christian hopes that. I hope that it may be within my lifetime that Jesus returns. If it is, I will never have to go through the business of pulling up the tent pegs. Isn't that lovely? I would just step straight out of one into the other and never go through the process we call death. But it may not be – it may be that I will pull up the tent pegs before Jesus comes back.

Why can't I have my new body then? Why can't I have it the moment I die? Let me tell you God's lovely purpose. It is that all people should have their new bodies at the same time; that those who have died in the Lord are waiting for the rest of us so that we can be made perfect together, so that we can all go into that one at the same time. But now comes the question: what is it going to be like waiting? I am not sure that I want to go into that second part. I want to hang on to this body. I know what it is like being in this body. Paul now deals with this question.

When the natural body is gone and the new body has not yet come, it will be away from the body, but it will be at home with the Lord. Here are two lovely words, "home" and "away" and to football fans that will mean something else! But I wept for joy when I realised what this was saying: that as long as I am in this body, I can't see the body of Jesus – I have to walk by faith, not by sight. But the day I lose this body, that day I see his. These words must mean that. To be at home in the body is to be blind. I can't see Jesus – why not? I am too far away from his body. His body is in the highest heaven and I am not near enough to him to see it. While I am at home in the body, in that sense, I am away from the Lord. Not spiritually, the Lord is very near to me, in my heart, but physically I am away from the Lord. As far as my body is concerned and his body is concerned, while I am in this body and he is in that one, I am away from the Lord and I can't see him. But the day that I can no longer see my own face, that day I will see his. I would rather be away from the body and at home with the Lord. Whose face would you rather see first thing in the morning in the mirror: your own or that of Jesus? This puts a completely different complexion on it.

The thief who died on a cross next to Jesus was a man of faith. He was probably brought up by godly parents. He knew religion, he knew truth, and he believed it deep down. I don't know how he had got into the bad ways he had got into – probably through wrong company. But he was a man who knew what was right. He was a man who knew that one day there was going to be a day of resurrection, and one day the kingdom would come, and he said to Jesus, "Lord, when you come into your kingdom would you remember me?" He would have thought that was going to be a long time in the future. But Jesus said, "Today you will be with me in Paradise." That was even before Jesus got his new body! To be absent from the body and at home with the Lord – to be with the Lord is all you want.

I know that death means you have got to say goodbye to people you love, and they have got to say goodbye to you. But there is one thing that takes the sting out of a goodbye, that the one you are saying goodbye to is going to be with someone they love most. That is why a wedding is rather like a funeral in emotions, and why there are tears at a wedding. Why? Because you are saying goodbye then – "A man shall leave his father and mother and cleave to his wife." There is a break. Ah, but why are the parents happy to let go? Even if they are not going to see as much of them? If the couple are going to live somewhere else – why are the parents happy to let them go? Because they are going to be with someone they love most.

That is why in parts of Africa if you stand outside a church and listen through the open gaps they have instead of windows, you would not be able to tell whether it were a wedding or a funeral going on, because it is the same atmosphere. What are we doing at a Christian funeral? We are letting someone go to be with someone they love. They are going to be with the Lord. If they are absent from us they are present with him. That is why Paul taught that we would rather be away from the body and at home with the Lord. If you give me the choice of staying in this body or to go into that second stage unclothed and without a body, every time I would long to depart and be with Christ for it is far better. Then I will be finished with all the tiredness and the weariness, and the aches and pains of this body. I will be with the Lord – the one I love the most.

Therefore, a Christian doesn't fear death. Even if it happens before the day of resurrection, he doesn't fear it. He is of good courage. Twice Paul says, "We are of good courage. We face this future." Why? "Because we would rather be absent from the body and at home with the Lord."

One final word comes out now: when we meet the Lord he will ask us what we did in the body. The last word about the body in this passage is just this: that we Christians (for this is addressed not to the world but to Christians) will appear before the judgment seat of Christ to receive what we deserve according to the things done in the body.

We want to be able to look him in the face and hear him say just one thing, "Well done, good and faithful servant." We want to see his face, but we want to hear that from his lips.

So, far from losing heart, what we believe about the body spurs us on to live for Jesus, driving us to give our very best for him, and to go on wearing ourselves out. Who cares? We are only here to serve God. There is only one thing that matters: whether you are in the body or out of it, you want to please Christ. It is not *where* you are, it is *what* you are that matters. It is not what body you have got, it is what you are doing with it that really matters. So whether we are at home or away, what occupies our whole attention is that we want him to be pleased with us.

EVANGELISM

Read 2 Corinthians 5:11 – 6:2

A. OUR MOTIVE (11–15)
1. RECOGNITION (11–13)
2. REVOLUTION (14–15)

B. OUR MESSAGE (16–2)
1. REGENERATION (16–17)
2. RECONCILIATION (18–2)

One of the things some people find objectionable about Christians is that they will not keep their religion to themselves. They insist on everybody else coming the same way, which is why people dread moving into an office with a Christian or having a Christian family move in next door. They are quite sure that sooner or later they will be "got at", and this is offensive to them. Why do Christians do this? Why can we not rest content with having our own faith? Why do we insist on trying to persuade men and women to accept Christ? Why are we always going outside our churches instead of staying inside them? Why are we all the time trying to turn everybody into our sort of person? This kind of thing is frequently said.

Paul gives two reasons, two motives: the fear of the Lord and the love of Christ. That is why we do it. If people ask us, "What do you get out of all this? What are you in it for? Do you think you're going to gain something by converting us?" The answer is no, we are not in this for what we get out of it. We are in it because of the fear of the Lord and the love of Christ. These two things go together. Just to go out and seek to persuade people through love of Christ is not enough and just to do it through fear of the Lord is not enough.

By "fear of the Lord" we don't mean that we cringe with terror of God that he will pack us off to hell if we don't go out and preach to others. A lady who knocked at my door some time ago did believe that. She belonged to a sect, which I will not name, but she was going around from door to door giving one hundred hours a month to this. Or was it one hundred visits a month? She was doing it because she was terrified that if she didn't, God would turn her out of heaven. That is not the fear of the Lord that makes us go out and persuade others. The one thing that we aim to do in life is to please Christ, and we are afraid of displeasing him. People may say, "Well aren't you afraid of displeasing people?" Yes we are. Every normal person is sensitive at this point. Nobody wants to offend others, upset them, disturb them. Yes, we are afraid of displeasing other people by talking to them about Jesus, but we are more afraid of Jesus – of displeasing him by not telling them. This is the motive that overrides all others. We would hate to break the heart of the one who loves us so much. The only reason he has left us in this world after we became Christians was so that we might do a job, which was to tell the whole world about him. We are afraid of facing him one day and having to say, "Jesus, we didn't do the job you gave us to do."

That is the fear we have, but if it were the only motive for our wanting to persuade everybody to become Christian, it would be a wrong, distorted motive, but it is matched by the motive of the love of Christ constraining us. We know the fear of the Lord, therefore we persuade, and the love of Christ controls us. It is both – we don't want to break his heart because he loves us, and his love constrains us to go out and love others. That is why we do it. Now of course, God knows why we do it – we are known to him.

God judges our lives and therefore we are quite happy to do it for the right motive in his sight. But we are worried lest other people think wrongly about our motives. Paul mentions appearing mad or sane. Well if we are mad, we are doing it for God and if we are sane we are doing it for people, but neither way are we doing it for ourselves. If you go out and talk about your religion, people will say straight away, "You've got religious mania." It is not the "done thing" in England to talk about your religion or your politics in polite society. So you will be considered to be just a little crazy if you try to persuade others to adopt your faith. Paul is telling the Corinthians: I don't mind if you think I'm mad; I'm mad for God. At one point Jesus was thought to be mad. His own family came after him one day to lock him up. They thought the kindest thing to do with Jesus was to put him away quietly where nobody would know that he had gone right off his head – a carpenter thinking he was going to convert the world.

Paul had the same difficulty. When he was on trial for his life he stood in the dock and he started talking to a king on a throne and he said, "King Agrippa, I want to talk to you about Jesus. You know these things are true, don't you? You've heard about Jesus." The whole scene in the courtroom is reversed: here is the man in the dock telling the judge all about Jesus. King Agrippa said, "Paul, you've studied too much. You're mad." Paul stated, "Whether I'm mad or not I wish that everybody were just like I am."

The fear of the Lord and the love of Christ will lead you to do things that some people may say are mad, but we do them because the love of Christ and the fear of the Lord compels us to do them. The love of Christ controls us because we discovered that love at the Cross – and everybody discovers the love of Christ there. If you really want to know if Jesus loves you, then go to the Cross and look at it and say, "He

371

did that for me." The love of Christ constrains us because when we look at the Cross we see that not only was I involved but that he died for all. When you seek to persuade someone else to be a Christian, you remember that they are already involved with Christ because he died for all. We judge that if one died for all, then all died. What does that mean? It means that when Jesus died on a Cross, mankind died; that everybody was involved in that death; that something happened at the Cross which has already changed the entire situation for every human being.

I am going to come back to that in a moment and tell you what it means. I am just underlining now that Paul is saying that if you have got the love of Christ in your heart, the person you go to is already involved in the Cross. You love them because you want them to realise that Christ's Cross already concerns them. You are not interfering; you are seeking to help them to realise what is already true – that something happened far away two thousand years ago that has changed the circumstances of their life. They now live in a world in which Christ was once crucified and life can never be the same again.

Before we come back to the explanation of how everybody is involved, why did Jesus die on a Cross? To promote a personal revolution in everybody's life so that the centre of their thinking, feeling and behaviour is no longer the capital "I" but is Jesus. Since Jesus died, the purpose of every human life on earth is to live for him, not for self. By nature I am self-centred. I can extend that self into my family, my country, my political party, my school, my college. I can extend my "self" but it is still an enlarged great big "me". By nature I am self-centred and so are you. You may do good things for your children, for other people, for your neighbours, but deep down the centre of your life is number one—the big "me". It is significant that God says, "I am the

I am" – you are not. Your life is now intended to be lived not for self but for Jesus.

Of course, if Jesus just died on a Cross and that was the end of it, you couldn't live for Jesus. How can you live with someone at the centre of your life who is dead and gone? Which is why he says, "One died for all, therefore all died." He died for all, that those who live might no longer live for themsclvcs but for him who for their sake died and was raised. He is alive. Now that is why we persuade people. The purpose of life for your next-door neighbour is that they should live for Jesus who died and rose again. They are already involved with Christ though they don't know it; they are already people for whom Christ died and they don't know it.

So when you go to persuade them, when you seek to talk to them about Jesus, you are not speaking of someone with whom they have no connection. You are saying to them, "Did you know that Jesus loved you, and that when he died something quite revolutionary happened to the circumstances of your life; that you are already living in the shadow of the Cross?"

Now let us go a little further. Having explained what the motive is and why Christians just will not keep their faith to themselves and, why they keep talking to others about Jesus, let us now look at the message. Let us turn from other people's attitude to Christians, to the attitude of Christians toward other people. How do we feel about them now that we understand that Jesus died for all? I will tell you. We no longer regard any person from a human point of view. Human beings are always judging others. We look at each other and we judge at the human level and we say, "He is good, he is bad; she is normal, she is strange." We say all these things, but when you have been to the Cross you don't judge people from a human point of view any longer. You look at that man and you don't look at his clothes and you don't look at the length of his hair and you don't look at the size of his house and you don't look at his education and you don't listen to his dialect or accent – you don't look at any of these things. You see someone for whom Jesus died. You no longer regard them from a human point of view. All distinctions, all those differences of wealth, culture and religion. You don't see that any longer. You see someone for whom Jesus died – as simple as that. You see them from Christ's point of view. It is a revolution in your outlook when you can look at people this way. You just see sinners for whom Jesus died, which is the thing that makes all human beings equal – not equal in dignity but in depravity, yet with potential dignity. There was a time when, perhaps, you judged Jesus from a human point of view. Paul said that he used to. He looked at Jesus and he said, "What kind of a man was he?" – and he came to certain conclusions.

There were people who looked at Jesus when he was on earth and they judged him from a human point of view and they said, "He's just a carpenter," and they were wrong. They were judging from a human point of view. A carpenter can't raise the dead; a carpenter can't heal the sick. He can only make coffins for the dead and beds for the sick. Is not this the carpenter? They were judging from a human point of view.

You can look at Jesus and just judge him as a human being. I am sure you will come to the conclusion that he was a great human being, but that wouldn't change your life. We no longer look at Jesus or anyone else from a human point of view. We look at Jesus now and see in him the universal Saviour and Lord of the human race – now that he has died for all. Because he has died for all and he is the universal Saviour, we see no-one as too far gone for Jesus to save. We see nobody disqualified from repenting and believing. You can go to anyone at all and you can say, "Jesus loved you enough to die for you," and that person is capable of becoming a new man, a new creature in Christ Jesus. That is what sent missionaries to a primitive tribe of people who had no written language, no civilisation; people who filed their teeth and ate their enemies. What did the missionaries hope to do with such people? I have met some of those tribesmen. I have shaken hands with murderers (which they were). I looked into their faces and they had only been a year or two in Christ and now I would trust them to babysit my children! Did you think you need a long period of civilisation before a sinner can become a saint? Oh no – don't look at people from a human point of view. Don't say, "What an ignorant savage." See a potential new creature in Christ, someone who has already been died for and therefore someone who could now live no longer for himself but for him who died and rose again. You see the potential of a saint. That is what sent missionaries all over the world. They didn't go to civilise. They didn't go to put people in trousers and shirts. They went to make new creatures. It is the kind of transformation that God is good at. Therefore Paul is challenging us: how do you look at people now? If any man is in Christ, he is a new creation. This is all of God because only God can create; only God can make something brand new. The only thing we can do is to take something old and renovate it and reform it. But God does much more than reform a person. He re-creates the person, makes a new man so that there is a new person inside that body who never was before. A new life has been created.

That is my definition of a Christian: a person who is *in Christ*. You may go to church, you may sing hymns, you may sing your prayers from time to time, you may even read your Bible and try and be kind to everybody, but that does not make you a Christian. You are still the old person trying to do better. You are still the old man. But when you step into

Christ, when you live in Christ, when he is the air that you breathe, when he is the dwelling you live in, when he is the life you live, when he is the ambition you have, when he is the affection you have, when you're in Christ – it is the same thing as saying when Christ is in you it is just so much one that you are in him and he is in you – when that happens, you are a new creation. Old things, the old affections, are gone. They have passed away.

How does it all start? How does God create a new life in me? It begins by being *reconciled to God*. That is a funny word to use: "reconcile". That implies that I am an enemy of God. It implies, even worse, that God is an enemy of me. Is that true? I'm afraid I must tell you that until you come to be in Christ that is true – that God is your enemy and you are his enemy. There is a double reconciliation needed. The word "reconcile" simply means to turn enemies into friends, to bring two people who have been alienated and estranged together in harmony – and that is what God in Christ was doing; connecting up enemies.

Let us look first at the enmity in our own hearts. The proof of it is that by nature we don't like God. We don't love him by nature. We might go to church out of a sense of duty but not because we love him. We are basically an enemy. We dislike him telling us what to do. We want to make our own decisions. We don't like his Word, we find it boring, or if we understand it we find it challenging and disturbing and we don't want it. Mankind is in a state of enmity towards God. It is so very difficult to persuade men and women to accept the love of God – when all that he wants to do is to love them better – so when you desperately want people to be loved and they need to be loved, why won't they pay attention to the gospel? Why is it they won't come and listen to the Word of God? The answer is: they are enemies of God. Deep down there is a resentment against him, a dislike of him, and of his Word, and of his people. Indeed that would be one indication that a man is an enemy of God – that he doesn't like God's children and there is this enmity. But what about God? Is there enmity on God's side? A God who loved the world? Is he an enemy of man? No, but he is an enemy of sin. He hates it and he is very angry with it. It is as if you spent a lot of loving care creating something extremely beautiful and then, when you had created it, some thoughtless vandal maliciously came and smashed what you had made and spoilt it all. How would you feel?

When God finished creating this lovely world of ours, he sat back as you sit back after a good day's work and said, "That's good." Then look what we have done to it. We have created a world in which we are frightened to live. We've created a world in which none of us is sure when we'll pollute each other to death or blow each other to death, a world in which we can't live together and in which we are at each other's throats; a world of hunger in which there would be enough food to feed everybody adequately if we learnt to share it with each other. That is what we have done to God's world and he hates it, and his wrath shows. It shows in the permissiveness of our society. It shows in the sheer blatant evil that becomes more and more open. It shows in homes and families that are broken up; in people living under one roof not talking to each other. It shows in little kids being corrupted from their earliest years and growing up with mistrust, angry with their elders. It shows in all these ways and it is God's anger, his wrath. Now somehow that had to be dealt with. The glorious good news I have got for you is this: God found a way to take away the enmity in his heart against our sin. He found a way, and that way was the Cross. Therefore we are ambassadors sent from a royal throne, telling you: this is an offer of peace with God. God need no longer reckon up the wrong things you have done.

It was shattering when someone once said this to me when I was thirty years old: "If you have just done or said one wrong thing per day (who could keep it down to that?) do you realise that God has reckoned up ten thousand sins against your name already?" You may have forgotten the wrong things you had done, but God never did. He doesn't forget until he forgives. So whether you have remembered all the wild oats you sowed in your youth or not, God has. He has a way of bringing out things you had forgotten. Do you remember when those men brought to Jesus the woman taken in adultery? They said, "We got her in the very act," and they were seen gloating over her. It is a horrible scene. Jesus said that the first one to throw a stone must be one who had not sinned. Do you notice that it was the eldest who felt guilty first? Somehow, when you are young you will brazen it out. You will put a good face on it, you will excuse it, but the older you get the more ashamed you get at life; the more you realise how far you have fallen short and how you have missed the target. Beginning at the eldest, they disappeared one by one until Jesus looked up and said, "Are they all gone?" Yes, the Lord has a way of just bringing out things that you have hidden and showing them to you. He has not forgotten.

Here I am told that God has found a way of dealing with us in peace so that he does not reckon our trespasses against us – so that he doesn't count them up; so that he doesn't have a long list and face me with it. He says we can forget all that now, I am offering you peace. I want to be your friend. This word "ambassador" is a lovely word, but unfortunately we tend to think of a splendid figure presenting his credentials at some foreign court. However, in the Roman Empire, an "ambassador" meant a man appointed by the emperor to go to a conquered nation and offer them terms of peace. If they accepted them, he was to come back and say, "That nation has now joined the Roman family." Therefore, we are ambassadors for Christ, saying: "On behalf of the King of kings we come and we offer you peace. Come and join the family." That is what an ambassador is to do.

My role as an ambassador is to say: be reconciled to God. Accept the offered friendship; the barrier on his side is gone at the Cross. He can now overlook everything wrong you have done; he can now forgive and forget it. All his anger against you for the wrong things you have done has been taken away now, and you can accept his love.

How can he do such a thing? We now come to the heart of our passage: 5:21. We should write this in gold letters in our Bible if we could. It is the most wonderful verse and it tells us three simple things.

Firstly: Jesus was perfect. He knew no sin. That was the verdict of everyone who met him and if you study his life with a view to finding fault with him, you will be disappointed. At the end of your search you will have to say as they said at his trial, "I find no fault in him."

It was the verdict not only of men; it was the verdict of Satan. Even the devil who tried to slander him couldn't find anything to pin on him, and the devil will pin something on you if he can. It was the verdict of his enemies as well as his friends. It was, surprisingly enough, the verdict of Jesus on himself. He said, "Which of you convicts me of sin?" Above all, it was the verdict of God the Father on Jesus, "This is my Son in whom I am well pleased." For the first time in all history God looked down from heaven and he saw one perfect life lived on earth from beginning to end, in Jesus.

Secondly, Jesus was put to death as the worst criminal on earth. What was happening? Why did God allow such a perfect life to end like that? Was it simply an assassination? No. It wasn't anything like that because it was Jesus who chose to go to Jerusalem and die. He wasn't struck down unexpectedly with the equivalent of a sniper's bullet. No, he deliberately went to die. Why? At the cross you see two things – sinlessness and sin in the same person. "Him who knew no sin was made sin by God."

God the Father treated Jesus his Son like a sinner. Jesus was going to have to face God's wrath, anger and condemnation. I want you to understand that God the Father was treating Jesus as God's holiness must treat a sinner. He who knew no sin, he made to be sin—why? Fact number three: *that we might become the righteousness of God*. It is a totally unfair exchange but it is as though Jesus now says to us: "I took your sin, will you have my righteousness? I took all your badness, will you have my goodness? I took all God's anger, will you have his love? I have removed the barrier that there was on God's side, will you take away the barrier there is on your side? Will you stop mistrusting me? Will you come and believe and I'll give you my goodness."

There is a world of difference between trying to have a goodness of your own and accepting the goodness of Christ; between trying to live a good life in order to get to heaven and accepting the love of God that he might give you the goodness that belongs to heaven. It is a completely different approach to living the good life, and this is the heart of the Cross. That is why everybody in your town or city was involved in the cross – because he died for all. There is no one overlooked at the cross, he died for all, but it doesn't work automatically. A person needs to remove the enmity in their heart and accept this reconciliation, this peace with God. That is why, working together with God, we entreat people: Get right with God now. There is an urgency about this.

The book of the prophet Isaiah says that now is the acceptable time, the day of salvation. Paul takes up that theme and gives it a new meaning: the *now* of God today. The word "now" means to me two things: a positive thing and a negative thing—a positive thing that is beautiful and a negative thing that is dreadful. Here they are. Positively, "now" means this: since Jesus died, you can get right with God. So *now* is the day – we are living in it. We don't need to wait as they had to wait in the days of the Old Testament for the promises to come and be kept and fulfilled. Now is the day of salvation. Nobody need have any unforgiven sin on their conscience – and that relates to the *past*. But there is a negative side in relation to the *future*. If now is the day of salvation, then there will come a day when it will be too late. We live in the day when people can get right with God and love him as he loved them. That day has dawned with Christ. It is a "day" that will come to an end and we could be too late, therefore there is an urgency. There are people who think there is plenty of time to get right with God. There isn't plenty of time. I don't know if I will have a tomorrow and neither do you. You don't know if you'll be able to go and listen to the gospel preached next Sunday and neither do I. For life is a very uncertain thing and a drop of water or a gust of wind can take your life from you.

So there isn't all the time in the world. Even if you are going to live a healthy life for many years yet, there is still a matter of urgency and I will tell you what the urgency is: that there are moments when God steps into your life and speaks to you. At other times you are too busy to listen. There are moments of quiet, and God says something to you. He is not speaking all the time, and sometimes when he does speak the television is on or there is other background noise to distract, and it is too noisy to hear his voice. So when he does speak, how important it is to listen.

Now is the day. He is talking; he is speaking to you now. Even if he goes on speaking to you and giving you opportunity after opportunity, one thing is quite certain in your life and mine, and that is that one day this life will end, and that for us personally is the end of the day of salvation. It is the end of the acceptable day when God can accept you for the Day of Jesus Christ. God has appointed a day even beyond that for every man to stand before his judgment seat, and after that – no hope. Now – *this* is the day when God would say to you: "I have removed the enmity on my side by providing the Cross. My anger has all been directed at my Son on your behalf. You were involved. He died your death, not his own. He didn't deserve it but he died your death and you are involved." Therefore, as an ambassador for Christ, I plead with you, accept the peace offer now while it is being offered.

EXPERIENCE
Read 2 Corinthians 6:3–13 and 7:2–16

A. REJECTING WORLD (6:3–13)
 1. ATTACK – our reliability
 2. DEFENCE – our righteousness
 3. ATTACK – our reputation

B. REJOICING CHURCH (7:2–16)
 1. JOY – your response
 2. SORROW – your repentance
 3. JOY – your reverence

One of the false cults that is gaining many new adherents today is the cult of the easy life. You can see it in advertisements; you can see it in the gambling fever, you can see it in the constant demand for shorter working hours. You can see it in the increasing emphasis on creaturely comforts in furniture design and so much else. If you want the easy life then I beg of you not to follow Jesus because he has nothing to do with that false cult. He didn't live an easy, comfortable life himself nor did he ever promise that a disciple of his would find that life would be easy, smooth, comfortable and safe. Indeed, he promised exactly the opposite. He said, "In this world you will have big trouble." Nor did he ever say that there would come a point in your Christian life where you could say, "I've done my bit, I'm going to retire now and leave it to the younger folk. I'm going to take it easy. I've fought the good fight all these years and I'm just going to ease up now." There is no discharge in that war. Not until we are dead will we be released from the battle that the

Christian life presents.

This passage underlines very clearly that Paul had been called by Christ not to a picnic but to a battle, not to a bed of roses but a crown of thorns. There are two areas in which he experienced real trouble and tension in the Christian life. These are the two areas in which you will too. One is the world and the other is the church. It comes as a surprise to some people, but the world makes it difficult for Christians. Those who have a naïve view of human nature and believe that everybody in the world is basically good, and that everybody really, if told the truth, would respond to it, and that everybody really wants to love God have never really exercised a ministry of the gospel.

When you do, you find it is tough. You find that people are not basically by nature good. They are not eager for the truth. They are not wanting to love God. Those who go to them with the truth will be called imposters and hypocrites. Those who go to share with them the riches of the world will be treated as those who are beggars. This is part of the battle that comes. Those of us who know what our own nature is really like and therefore what other people's nature is really like are not surprised that it is tough to be a Christian in the world. But what may come as a surprise to you as a Christian will be the discovery that Paul found it tough to be a Christian *inside* the church.

If you ask any missionary they will tell you that one of the greatest problems they face is that of relationships with other missionaries. Indeed it is in this second area that Paul found most of his deepest sorrows. His deepest emotions, griefs and burdens came to him not through the world's antagonism but through the church. We are going to look at these two areas in which you will find the Christian life tough. It will be tough in the world; it will be tough in the church. It is full of joy, victory and triumph but it will be a battle. Let us look utterly frankly and honestly, as Paul does, at these two areas of battle and how they contribute to this tough side of the Christian life.

Before describing the troubles that his Christianity had got him into, Paul makes an amazing claim which, quite frankly I could not make. He is saying: I am in no way responsible for the troubles that I have suffered; I've never brought these on myself; I have put no obstacle in people's way – there is no fault in my ministry that others could use to blame for the troubles that I have seen. He could say: Look at my ministry. We commend ourselves in every way. The troubles we have seen are due to what we have said, not what we are. Herein lies a very important principle: when we suffer as Christians, when we run into trouble, the first question must always be: "Have I caused this, or has the message caused this?"

It is vital that we should come to the right answer. If I have caused it then something must be put right. If the message has caused it then I have to face the battle and leave it there. Now Paul is saying, we have put no obstacle ... there is no fault in our ministry and yet in spite of that: trouble, trouble, trouble. He just ran out of one trouble into another. We are going to look first of all at the troubles he ran into in the world. He first makes the claim that he is utterly reliable as a minister of the gospel. No matter what discouragements, what troubles he goes into, he goes on. No matter how often he is knocked down, he gets up again and goes on. He is utterly reliable in all the troubles. Now look at the list – through thick and thin. It is an amazing list: afflictions, hardships, calamities, beatings, imprisonments, tumults, labours, watchings, hunger.

That is a very interesting list. It includes things that I have never known in the service of Christ and I daresay you have not known them either. What a life! The day that Paul met Jesus, he was committed to a life like this. He had not suffered before. He had had a career; he had gone to the top of that career. If there had been any suffering in connection with Paul it was the suffering he caused other people. He had not suffered himself, but the day he met Jesus, one thing Jesus told him was this: "I am going to tell you now how many things you must suffer in my name."

Now that is honesty which can be conspicuous by its absence from our evangelism today if we say: "Come to Jesus and all your troubles are over. Come to Jesus and life's going to be lovely and smooth and happy all day. Come to Jesus and life is just one glorious experience" – and a testimony can give that impression. One speaker, talking about how to give your testimony, said: "The Christian life is like mountaintops and valley bottoms on a graph. Somebody asks us to give our testimony so we draw a line mentally just below the top of those peaks. We string together all the things that are cut off by the line above the line, and then we give our testimony, and people get the impression life has just been wonderfully smooth and beautifully sweet ever since we came to know Jesus. That is not honest."

When that same speaker was asked to give his testimony in a cathedral, he mentally did that – he drew the line, put it all together, and asked the Lord to help him to make a real impression in the cathedral. The Lord said, "Whatever do you want to do that for?"

"Well I want to help these people to know you and to love you."

The Lord said, "Well that's not the way to do it."

"Well what do you want me to do?"

The Lord said, "I just want you to be honest."

The speaker replied, "But that's not the place for that."

An astonishing remark! But Paul is honest and Jesus was honest and the day that Paul came to Jesus, Jesus said, "You're going to suffer an awful lot. You are really going to go through it." How many things you must suffer – it is there in Acts 9:16 if you want to look it up. Paul knew from the very first day of his Christian life that it was going to be very tough. He went into it with open eyes, knowing that it was going to be a greater battle than he had ever had in his life. I think if we are absolutely honest our testimony ought to be that all of us who have come to know Christ have had more troubles since we came to know Jesus than we had before. But we face that trouble *with* Jesus and that is the difference. The troubles have been greater but the victories have been greater and therefore the joy has been deeper. This is an honest approach to the Christian life.

Paul knew all about these things before he experienced them, but that doesn't make it any easier to bear. When I look through this list I notice a number of things about them. First of all, most of them are physical suffering: strain of the body. Time and again he found himself worn out. The little word "watchings" – do you know what that literally means? I would prefer to translate it *insomnia*. Have you ever spent a sleepless night over the work of the Lord? Do you know what it is to lie awake at night wondering how the work of the Lord can go forward? What is going wrong with it? That is what is meant by "watchings". Doing without meals – hunger. It is nearly all physically something that the body had to suffer, and we are living in the flesh. We are in bodies and there is a physical strain in the Christian life, a physical toughness is needed.

Paul was not very strong physically. We know this from various descriptions of him – from outside the Bible as well as within it. He is described as a little man of poor physique, bow-legged, bald. He says in a letter in the New Testament, "My physical appearance is not very impressive, I know that." This little man was put through this kind of strain, finding himself in the middle of public riots. He found himself carried and dragged by the crowds, stoned and left for dead outside the city time and again – beaten with rods, whipped, put in prison with chains. This poor little man had to go through that.

I notice that all this did not break his reliability. He commended himself in much endurance – a man who can get up and go on. A man who doesn't do one of two things that would be very human. If Paul had done one of these two things I would have understood him and so would you. First, he was a man who didn't retire early. He could have said: "Look, I've done my bit. In the last ten years I've really been through it. I'm going to leave stronger, younger men to go on with the gospel now," but he never did. "I have fought the good fight, I have kept the faith, I've finished the course. I've got there" – that is what he said just before he died, a man who is utterly reliable no matter what physical strain he goes through. That is a man who is a minister of the gospel.

The other thing that human nature would do is to retaliate. It is human in us to hit back: when we are knocked down, to knock someone else down; when we are under strain, to pass that strain back to those who put us under it. When we are hit, to hit back. Did Paul retaliate? Let us turn now to look at the weapons of his defence. How did Paul fight this thing?

It is a sad reflection on human nature that battles usually tend to make us use the same weapons that the enemy has used first. A simple illustration of this would be the Second World War. The Germans first blitzed London and Coventry. There was outcry from correspondents in British newspapers at this inhuman, barbaric, cruel approach. Those letter writers were strangely silent two and three years later when we sent a thousand bombers to blast a German city off the map. It was the allies, not the axis, who first wiped out two Japanese cities. By the end of the war, we were doing things to the enemy for which we had condemned the enemy at the beginning of the war. Battles tend to have this effect on human nature. How did Paul defend himself? What weapons did he have in his right hand and in his left in this battle? He tells us now. The Christian approach to a battle is this: the best way to obtain victory is to fight with opposites. You will never overcome evil with evil; you can only overcome evil with good. Paul chose out of the armoury of God everything that was the opposite of what made people attack him. He was attacked because he went into a world of impurity, so he defended himself with purity. He was attacked because he preached in a world of ignorance, so he defended himself with knowledge. He was attacked because he lived in an impatient world and so he defended himself with forbearance. He was attacked because of unkind people so he defended himself with kindness. He was attacked because evil spirits possessed men so he defended himself by the Holy Spirit. He was attacked because people hated him, so he defended himself with genuine love. He was attacked by slander and false accusations so he defended himself with true speech. He was attacked by the power of men so he defended himself by the power of God. What a statement that is. Here is the way to fight the battle. When you are being pressed on all sides: fight with opposites, choose to defend with the very opposite of that which is attacking you – and these are the weapons for the right hand and the left.

In a Roman battle, in personal warfare, the right hand is used for attack and the left hand is used for defence. One hand was for the spear or sword, the other for the shield. Paul is saying that in this battle, whether attacking or defending, use the weapon that is the opposite to that which is being used against you. In other words the best weapon of all in the battles of life is sheer goodness, righteousness. A saint is invincible. You can't win a battle against sheer goodness. You may throw at a saint all that you have got and yet that saint cannot be beaten. This is the weapon to use and Paul says he is attacked on every side, but these were his weapons – sheer goodness to defeat the evil.

But we must now go on to realise that the world does not recognise sheer goodness. A man who is a saint walking through this world will not find everybody saying, "What a saint!" The reputation of a saint will vary tremendously. A saint will make enemies as well as friends. Beware of universal popularity. Jesus said, "Woe unto you when all men speak well of you." He knew this from hard experience. Jesus had a way of leaving people infuriated or loving him. They either thought highly of him and they dropped everything, fishing included, and followed him, or else they immediately began to plot and to hate him. He left enemies and friends instantly. He divided people down the middle. You couldn't be neutral in relation to Jesus. A saint who walks with Jesus will find the same thing.

John Bunyan called his autobiography *Grace Abounding* and underneath the title he wrote this text: "All who would live a godly life in Christ Jesus will suffer persecution." If you really want to be a saint, expect misunderstanding. Your reputation will be thrown around from one extreme to another in ill-repute and good repute, you will find both. Some people will think the world of you and some people will think just the opposite.

The one thing a Christian needs to be free from is any desire to have a reputation. How will the world treat us? In the opposite way usually to that which is really deserved – treated as imposters, we are true. People say, "He must be a hypocrite. He must be in it for something else. What does he get out of it all? The world will treat us as imposters, yet we are true. The world will treat us as unknown. "Who are these people? They're nobodies, no reputation." Yet in God's sight they are well-known. Here was Paul, this little

Jew wandering around the Roman Empire; the emperor at this stage had no idea that he existed. The public world had little knowledge of Paul. He was just a travelling preacher, yet he is now one of the most famous people in the world: as unknown, yet well known. Look at the next contrast: as dying, and behold we live. Whenever they looked at Paul they said, "There's a dying man, he's finished, I give him a few more months. Look at him." Yet Paul says, "Behold, we live."

The world will treat people as criminals, as those who ought to be cast out of society, as those who disturb and upset, and yet says Paul, "They can't kill us." A sad people? It is amazing how many people in the world think that if you become a Christian you will become miserable. To them, we are miserable. You put a Christian in the middle of a drinks party and see how happy he looks. To the world we are miserable. They can't share the joy and we can't laugh at their jokes. We are miseries, we are wet blankets – and yet always rejoicing.

The world says, "Look at you, you poor people. You are not big, powerful, mighty, rich." Yes, they were mostly slaves in those days – yet you have got enough wealth to make another a millionaire, making many rich. I can give people the earth, for the meek shall inherit the earth by the grace of God; I could preach a gospel that could make somebody a joint heir with Christ – as poor and yet making all rich. Then there is that lovely final contrast—the world will say, "You've got nothing that I want. You've got nothing to offer me." The world says you've got nothing and yet you are possessing all things. The word "possessing" means possessing things you will never have to let go. You really have got them forever.

The world opposed, the world misunderstood, the world attacked – but Paul did not care what people thought of him.

The real situation is that he was true, rich and rejoicing. You may think I am a miserable wet blanket but I rejoice. You may think that I have nothing to give you but have got everything to give you. You may think I am poor but I could make you a millionaire. It is this reliability of ministry and much endurance that can go on facing a world like that, which really wins through in the end.

Why does Paul write about all this? Why does he lay bare his heart? Why does he say, "Look into my heart, see how I feel." Why is he being so frank about the troubles he has been through? I'll tell you why: because his greatest burden was not the response of people of the world to him but the response of people of the church to him. There was reserve. He could put up with antagonism in the world – but suspicion in the church? No, that was hard. So he has told all this to the Corinthians because, he says: "Look my mouth is wide open. I'm talking about myself. I'm sharing my innermost feelings with you. Why? Because I want you to open your heart to me." Even if I don't have many friends in the world I want you to be my friends. You see, Christians need affection and love and they are not going to get it in the world. They need it so badly. Where can they find it? The answer is that they have got to get it in the fellowship of the church. If you don't find it there, then that is a great burden. What a sorrow. You can face anything in the world if you can get among Christians and find affection and love flowing, because our hearts cry out for affection. Nobody likes going through all these troubles. Nobody likes being disliked and misunderstood in the world. The only thing that can keep you going in that is the fellowship of Christians who love you.

This is a human thing. We can't just survive with the love of God. I don't want to be irreverent here, but the love of God is mediated to us through the love of Christians. If you feel that no Christians love you either, then you just can't face the battle outside. We are human and God wants us to have human love. Otherwise what happens is that all the troubles in the world makes us hard, bitter. We become a kind of self-imposed martyr. We get hard and we lose affection. Paul is saying that there is no reserve, no barrier on his side. He would go through earth, air, fire and water for them. He wanted them to open their hearts to him. Let's love each other; let's get rid of the restricted affections. You see, a group of Christians who are reserved, shy and withdrawn is a contradiction in terms. Paul was saying: don't receive the grace of the Lord in vain. That is at the beginning of the chapter. If you can receive the grace of God and remain closed in your heart and restricted in your affections, you have received it in vain – emptily. The grace of God is meant to liberate our feelings, our affections, and open our hearts. Paul had opened his mouth because his heart was wide. He wanted to get his feelings across because he wanted to have theirs. So let's have this mutual unrestricted affection. He hasn't told them all this to get their sympathy. Paul is a man in whom I can never find any trace of self-pity. He is not telling them about his feelings to get sympathy but to get their affection, so that they may love him as he goes through this battle.

So we move on to the second great difficulty of the Christian life, and that is relating to other Christians in warm affection – not respectable relations but warm affection, so that there is a flow of love; so that it goes from one to another.

Now this is particularly poignant here because Paul is talking to those who are his own children. There is something horrible about a family in which the children have no affection for parents. It has been my privilege to go into so many homes, and I don't think anything moves me as much as seeing a home in which children spontaneously show affection and love for their parents. Is there anything more tragic than to go into a home where the children don't have affection – don't have love? Paul is speaking as to his children. He had led them to the Lord so they were his children, and yet he felt that they were not giving him the affection that the parent should have. There was no barrier on Paul's side but there seems to have been a barrier on theirs.

So he plunges into this difficulty. We need to deal with the question of separation. It fits because Paul's message is: widen your affections, widen your hearts – but he is going to say there are limits to what your hearts should do. Your affections must not be unlimited. Your heart must never rule over your head. Widen your affections to believers, but be careful about relationships with unbelievers. We now jump to 7:2ff.

To recap a little history will help here. Paul had led a group of Corinthians to Christ, started a church and left them to it. Then he heard that things were going badly wrong. There were cliques in the church. They were openly allowing sin in the church. Men were getting drunk at the Lord's Table. Women were behaving in a way unfitting to their sex. Speaking in tongues had got out of hand and was turning services into bedlam. Members were doubting the physical resurrection of Jesus, and Paul was so unhappy he wrote a letter to them, which we call 1 Corinthians. That letter didn't put it right, so he went to them and he spoke to them – to their faces – and it was a painful visit. He came away very sad. They had opposed him to his face. They told him not to meddle in the church, they told him they no longer recognised his authority over them. He had a rough time at the hands of his own converts. Is anything sadder than that? Imagine someone you have led to the Lord turning around and treating you like this, and remember these were Christians. Paul came away from that painful visit and wherever he went to preach he couldn't get on with the preaching. His heart was heavy. He had confidence but was anxious about them. So Paul sent Titus. Paul had a heart that locked people inside it but he knew that he was not in the Corinthians' hearts at that moment. They were in his heart but he was not in theirs. That is something that shouldn't be among Christians. Titus went and came back and could then say to Paul that it was all right now. They were hurt. They were offended. They were grieved by what Paul said, but they had put it right and they were longing to see him.

Can you imagine Paul's heart? It was full before, but now it was bursting. Let me summarise what I am trying to say here. I don't think there is any sorrow known to Christians which is as deep as the sorrow stemming from lack of affection in the fellowship. Therefore there is no joy so deep at the human level known to Christians as the joy of unreserved fellowship. The Christian life is a life of deep emotion, deep feelings. The deepest joy you find is that of restored fellowship. Here then are the heights and depths of Christian emotion and we get all of them now.

Paul had been depressed. He realised that his visit, his letter, had hurt. Now he knew that the grief that was caused was God's way of bringing them all closer to himself. There are two sorts of unhappiness: there is a worldly unhappiness that leads to death, and there is a divine unhappiness that leads to repentance and reconciliation. These two sorts of happiness are totally different. Let me just draw that out.

First of all, what is worldly sorrow? Worldly sorrow has regrets, remorse and even resentment – but no repentance, no change. It leads to either despair or defiance but both kill. They kill love, they kill relationship. Despair and defiance are the products of worldly grief. Someone has said that every sinner will be sorry one day. But their sorrow will not lead to salvation. What is worldly sorrow for sin? It is either sorrow for being found out – the sorrow over exposure – or it is the sorrow over consequences. Hell is going to be a very, very sad place. Everybody in hell will be sorry that they have sinned. There will be weeping and wailing and gnashing of teeth, but all of that sorrow will not lead to salvation because it is worldly sorrow. It's being sorry about the consequences.

The godly sorrow that Paul mentions is the sorrow about the thing that was wrong. Just a sheer sorrow that something was not in God's plan or in his will. That kind of sorrow leads to a change. Again, there is a common misunderstanding that repentance is feeling sorry. Do you notice that it is the sorrow that *leads* to repentance? It isn't repentance in itself but godly sorrow produces repentance, which is a change of outlook, of behaviour, of attitude. It is that which brings salvation. Paul is saying: I wrote to you and I said certain things to you which hurt and I regret it hurting you at the time. But he knew it was God's way of producing a sorrow that led to a change of heart and a change of attitude and a change of mind to repentance. So – and this is the most paradoxical statement in this letter, "Your mourning means that I rejoice the more."

What a remarkable statement: I am happy because you're unhappy. He's happy because they were unhappy in a way that led them to God. It is part of his ministry. He was in a sense their pastor – not their pet lamb. Therefore from time to time what he said hurt, but it was God's way of bringing them into his perfect will. Their mourning made him rejoice the more because it was soon over. It had no regrets, they lost nothing, and it was soon over – and that is godly grief. Worldly regret is the exact opposite. It is full of regret and you do lose a lot and it is not so soon over. It goes on smouldering. Praise God for godly grief. There is a place for sorrow that leads us nearer to God and therefore nearer to one another.

Finally Paul says, "Titus told me wonderful things." Titus came back and said to him: Paul everything you said about the Corinthians is true – you said they'd come through it, you said you believed in them, you said you had confidence in them – well, you are right, they've come through it and they've just captured my heart. What a lovely church, what a fellowship. Paul finishes by saying: "I have perfect confidence in you." That is what makes for unrestricted affection. That is what makes for the joy of the Lord – unrestricted affection is due to perfect confidence. Everything that destroys confidence destroys affection. If you wrong someone, if you corrupt someone, if you exploit someone, they can't trust you any more and therefore your heart closes. But when you have got confidence in them, your heart opens and the affection flows.

Here then is Paul's tough Christian life. Let me finish by affirming this: love is a warm thing as hatred is a cold thing. I understand from my lessons in physics when I was a schoolboy that heat expands. If a heart is filled with love then it is going to get bigger. Widen your hearts, let them warm up and expand a bit.

A Christian can't live without emotions. To give the impression that the Christian life must get rid of feelings is utterly wrong—that is stoicism, not Christianity. Christianity is a life of deep feeling – it is not a purely intellectual thing. As a Christian you know mountaintops of great happiness and you may know very deep, dark valleys of depression. Not because of self-pity, for that kind of depression has no place in the Christian life, but the kind of depression that comes from concern for other people, and that concern will carry you down to the depths of sleeplessness.

But when it is put right, you will be on the mountaintop of joy. You'll say, "My heart's bursting again." There is no sorrow like the division of Christians, and no joy like the coming together again. So we can't live without emotions – intense joy and deep unhappiness are the lot of every Christian. But let me add that you can't live by your emotions. How fatal to link your faith to your feelings in such a way that your faith goes up and down. Let your feelings go up and down, but let your faith be constant and let it grow. It is this rightful relationship between faith and feeling that enabled Paul to be a faithful minister of the gospel. His feelings in the church and the world went up and down, but his faith remained absolutely firm and it was this that held him. So let us not be ashamed of emotion; let us not be reserved. Let us not allow sorrow to dictate what your fellowship should be like. Let us widen our hearts to each other – open them. Trust each other and let the affection flow as befits brothers and sisters in a family who are going to live together in heaven.

SEPARATION

Read 2 Corinthians 6:14 – 7:1

A. FROM OTHERS (6:14–16a)
 1. RESTRICTION
 2. REASON
 3. REVERENCE

B. TO GOD (16b–18)
 1. PREMISE
 2. PRECEPT
 3. PROMISE

C. IN OURSELVES (1)
 1. APPEAL
 2. APPLICATION
 3. APPREHENSION

At first sight this passage seems a real interruption in this letter to the Corinthians and the atmosphere is so different from what immediately goes before and what follows that some commentators have said that it doesn't belong here at all. Some would go so far as to say that it can't have been written by Paul himself and that it has been pushed in later by someone with a narrower mind than he had, just to try and get it into the Bible. Others have not gone quite as far. Some have said that this was not written by Paul the Christian, but is a throwback to Saul the Pharisee. I suppose the mildest suggestion is that this doesn't belong to this letter but is a little misplaced paragraph from what he called his painful letter, his severe letter which he wrote telling off the Corinthians roundly for certain wrong things they were doing. I want to say, not because I am perverse or I hold prejudice, that I think all these scholars are wrong. This little paragraph belongs squarely in the middle of this chapter.

Back at 6:11 Paul has just written: "Our mouth is open to you Corinthians. Our heart is wide, you are not restricted by us but you are restricted in your own affections. In return I speak as to children, widen your hearts also." Now go on to 7:2 – "Open your hearts to us...." You see, there is no break. It seems to go straight on. Is there any possible explanation why, in the middle of an appeal to open their hearts, to be unreserved in their affection and love, Paul should suddenly butt in with such a strong warning about human relationships? I think there is. I think I can see exactly why he put it in at this point and interrupted his appeal with this warning. There is a desperate need among Christians to widen hearts, to be unrestricted in affection, to love one another fully. They will not get a lot of love in the world but they should get a lot of love in the church. This is the divine compensation for the troubles of the Christian life – to support you in those troubles with the love of Christians whose hearts are wide open to you.

He is pleading for more emotion in religion. He is pleading for more feeling, more love and affection flowing not from the mind but from the heart. Indeed, to be quite literal, he uses the word "kidneys". But he means open your deep feelings to one another. Why then does he suddenly interrupt like this? It is because there are limits even to Christian affection. There are limits beyond which your heart must not carry you. There is always a danger when love is released, when affections are flowing freely, for Christians to get entangled in relationships that are not going to help them. There is always a danger when the heart is free that the heart takes over from the head, and this is an unscriptural balance. The head must always keep the heart in place. Let the heart be wide open but let the head keep control, for your head is meant to keep the control. Your heart is a vital part of your life. You can't live without feelings, you can't be a Christian without feelings, but they must never run away with you into a wrong relationship. Or I could put it this way: Paul is pleading for an open affection among believers and he is now going to say: but watch your affections for unbelievers.

This is why he puts this little warning in and, having given it, he goes straight back to the appeal to open wide their hearts. It is in little sandwiches like this that Paul keeps the balances in his teachings. It is so easy to get unbalanced in the Christian life; to get one-sided, lopsided, either over-emphasising the intellectual parts or over-emphasising the emotional side so that you run away with feelings into all kinds of highways and byways that you shouldn't be treading. Balance – keeping the thing together. So he interrupts his appeal for more feeling and affection with a warning about the wrong relationships that your heart can lead you into.

He is going to deal with the thorny question of separation. It is not a subject I would choose to preach on, but I find the discipline of working through the Bible very good for me. It is a subject that has got out of balance again and again in Christian fellowship. On the one hand there have been those who have carried the doctrine of separation to such extremes that Christians won't even eat with the members of their own family or have any link at all with people who are not Christians. That is just not practical. If Paul had meant that, he would never have said in 1 Corinthians 5:9, "I did not mean that you must not associate with men of the world." To do that you would have to go out of the world altogether, he says. You can't dissociate yourself from unbelievers and it would be utterly wrong to do so. My milk is delivered every morning as far as I know by an unbeliever, but I am happy to drink it. It gives me a link with him; we are in association.

My postman as far as I know is an unbeliever, but I have an association. Everywhere you go you must associate with unbelievers. This doctrine of separation is carried to an illogical and impractical extreme if it is taken to mean that you cannot associate with people who are not Christians.

That is the extreme to which the Pharisees took religion, and the word "Pharisee" means "separated one". It was a nickname given to those who, if they brushed up against someone in the marketplace, ran home, changed their clothes and had a bath. That is the extreme of separation to which the Pharisees carried their religion and that is the reason why Jesus ran up against them. They hated him and he condemned them. His words to them meant: whited sepulchres, you're so keen to get separated from people that you don't get separated from unclean things. He didn't get on with the Pharisees at all and they didn't get on with him because they said, "Look he's a friend of sinners. He goes into their houses and has meals with them."

So Paul, following Jesus, is not here going back to his Pharisee days by not having any association with those who are not Christians. If you don't befriend sinners, however will they get saved? If you are not prepared to associate with the ungodly, what hope is there for them? Let us avoid this extreme. But I would think that the greater danger among Christians today is the opposite extreme of thinking that you can go anywhere and mix with anybody and do anything now you are a Christian. I think that is the greater danger and I have got to try and walk a knife-edge – not treading on corns on either extreme but trying to guide you into the real meaning of this text.

There are three dimensions to the true doctrine of separation. There is a "from" and a "to" and an "in", and any one without the other two is inadequate as a real doctrine of separation. The Pharisees were separated from others but they were not separated *to* and they were not separated *in* and that is what made their separation *from* so offensive. The first three verses talk about the separation *from* and I dare not overlook this side. Even if it raises loads of questions in your mind, if it causes you to feel uncomfortable, I have got to say that here is a sentence which is not good advice but a command from the Lord: "Do not be mismated with unbelievers," that is a literal translation.

Having given a plea that the hearts of Christians should be wide open to each other and that they should have affection for each other and him, Paul now says, "But don't let your affections lead you into a mis-mating with a person who is not a Christian." Now let's look at this word. It is a restriction, a very definite limit to the affections of a Christian. There are two words in it that need defining. The first is the word "unbeliever". Now what does that mean? It does not mean someone who doesn't believe in God. Most people in the world believe in God. I would think that probably some seventy to eighty percent of the British people believe there is a God. If that is what is meant by a believer then really there is not much difficulty. It is only a minority of at least the British people that you have to worry about. But the word "unbeliever" in the New Testament means someone who doesn't know Jesus. Jesus said to his own disciples, "You believe in God, believe also in me." It is that plus that makes the difference between what the New Testament calls a "believer" and an unbeliever. A believer in the New Testament is someone who knows that Jesus is the Son of God and knows that Jesus is that person's Saviour. An unbeliever is someone who doesn't know Jesus like that. Therefore, this text is about relationships with those who don't know Jesus.

The word we have really got to look at carefully is "mismated". I think perhaps the Authorised Version is a little misleading at this point where it says "unequally yoked". People go back in the Old Testament to a law in Leviticus that says something about an ox and an ass being used to plough together with a wooden beam over their shoulders, with two smaller sticks down at each side resting on their necks in front of their shoulders. That is forbidden by God as cruelty to animals because one will pull harder than the other and the other will chafe and be sore. It is interesting that God himself is concerned with cruelty to animals and puts it in the Law of Moses. He says, "You must never plough with an ox and an ass together." I have been to the Middle East and I have seen an ox and an ass yoked together. They are still cruel enough to their animals today to do it, but Jews are forbidden to do it and they don't do it.

People have got the idea that Paul is saying, "Don't get unequally yoked. Trying to pull with someone will chafe you and it will make it difficult for you." It's something much, much deeper than that. The word is actually a sexual word and it is rightly translated, "Do not be mismated." It refers to a very intimate relationship, much more than working together, something much deeper than this. There are certain laws in the Old Testament, which talk about being mismated. There are some pretty frightening references to horrible vices such as sexual relations between men and animals. There are other laws which absolutely prohibit God's people from trying to breed across species. What God has put asunder, let no man put together is the gist of the law in the Old Testament about cross-breeding different species and trying to produce something else that is a hybrid – that is not what God intended to be bred. Now it is this word that is used here: don't crossbreed different creatures. That is something very much deeper than is traditionally seen in this text. Quite clearly, it does not forbid association with non-Christians. That is not crossbreeding with them. Indeed it allows a very deep level of friendship with those who are not Christians, the kind of level that Jesus had when he went into their homes and mixed with them and they liked him and he was known as the friend of publicans and sinners. But what does it refer to? Clearly, it is an intimate relationship. Secondly, it is a relationship that is going to affect quite profoundly both parties involved. Thirdly, it is a relationship that is going to involve a surrender of individual will and freedom and a surrender of conscience. It is also a relationship which is going to produce something that is less than pure, that is less than distinctive of either party. It is going to produce a mixture which is a dilution of both.

Now we begin to see the kind of relationship that Paul is getting at. It is the kind of relationship in which a Christian is entering into such a deep relationship with someone who is not a Christian – that the ultimate end product is going to be something that is a mixture between the two; in which the distinctively Christian character of the Christian species is going to be diluted and lost. It is going to produce something that is not clearly Christian. Now what relationships could do this? There are four at least that I want to mention. First of all and the most obvious is the one that includes this word "mate", namely the relationship of marriage. There can be no doubt at all that Paul would include the relationship of marriage. Here a Christian is absolutely forbidden to marry someone who is not a Christian. That is a hard command for a number of reasons. It comes particularly hard when the heart feels natural human affection for someone who has no affection for Jesus. It is a very difficult situation and it is not lightly spoken about. But the fact remains that here is a relationship when two species are being crossed, two completely different kinds of people are mating, and the result of that marriage is a hybrid that is not a true Christian home but a watered down version of the real thing. As one preacher used to put it: if you will choose to have the devil for your father-in-law, expect trouble from him. I'm afraid that is not a joke; it is only too true. The marriage may be fine for a number of years and then the devil begins to control the marriage. Well now, that is the first relationship and I have got to say that or I wouldn't be true to the word of God. Throughout the Old Testament, Jew was forbidden to marry Gentile, and throughout the New Testament, Christian is forbidden to marry unbeliever.

The second relationship that might do this (in fact which would) would be a relation in the religious sphere. Let me now be a bit of a prophet. One of the things that I can see coming on the world scene is a very strong pressure for all religions to get together to save the world. Already the first signs of it are here. Already there is the suggestion that if we are ever going to save the world, we have got to give it one religion and that one religion must be made up of all the religions relating together. That would be the crossbreeding of species. It would produce a hybrid that lacked the distinctive qualities of Christianity and it would be unable to save the world. We are going to have to resist that kind of relationship. However much affection at the human level we feel for sincere believers of other religions – and I have met Muslims in Arabia and my heart was warm to them – however much we feel drawn towards the heart, we must not let the head lose control here. It would be a hybrid thing.

A third area in which this could happen is in business. A church member once came to see me to ask whether he should go into business partnership with someone who was not a Christian. We looked at this deeply together. We looked at what would be involved in the partnership. We prayed about it, and finally we came to the conclusion that it was right for him to go into that partnership. It proved to be a right and a good thing. At no point was that Christian's conscience, character or testimony compromised. But there are some business relationships in which it would be. Undoubtedly, some partnerships would make it difficult to give a clear Christian testimony.

The fourth area that we have to look at is the area of friendship. We are called to be the friends of sinners. Our friendship is for all. A lovely notice seen in a church porch read: "A stranger is just a friend we haven't yet met." The word "friendship" appears in the letter of James: friendship of the world is enmity with God. We want to be a friend of everybody but we must let our head guard us against our heart leading us into being a friend of the world. By "the world" is meant that godless society which is an organised resistance army against God. Jesus loved sinners. He mixed with them, he befriended them, but at no point did he become a friend of the world in which they lived. Nobody could ever accuse him of compromising with the society of sin in which people lived. It is this delicate line that has to be trodden. We have given a good deal of attention to the first half of v. 14, which is a very important verse.

Now let us look at how Paul develops it. He appeals to the reason so that the heart will be kept in its place – with a series of rhetorical questions to each of which there is only one answer. He argues the point. Why should you not get into this kind of relationship with a person who doesn't love Jesus? Well, how much is there in common between good and evil? Now the answer to that one is utterly clear— nothing. There is no point of contact between good and evil. Another question: how much is there in common between light and darkness? Can you mix those two? The answer is: nothing. You can't mix them. You can never have light and darkness in the same place at the same time. It is either light or it is dark. How much in common have Christ and the devil? In the temptations, the devil thought he could make a partnership with Jesus, but how much have Jesus and Satan in common? – nothing at all. They are both in this world but they have nothing in common.

Now these are not just illustrations, these are the real situation. A believer is someone who has received the righteousness of God. Before that, he or she was basically evil in nature. Now he is basically good. But you say, "I can't accept that. People are not good or evil. They are a mixture; they are not black or white, they are grey." That is how man sees it but not how God sees it. Two people may behave rather similarly and appear to be in the middle of the moral range. Yet those two people may be like this: one may be a righteous man who has been dragged down by the world, the flesh, and the devil; the other may be a sinner who has been pulled up by a Christian home, by the influence of a Christian country. Their behaviour may look the same but if you remove the restraints in both cases, one would go to one extreme, and the other would go to the other. According to God's Word, human nature is basically evil. It is lifted up and restrained by so many influences that people who aren't Christians can behave well. "If you then being evil know how to give good gifts to your children...", said Jesus. When you come to know Jesus you receive a new nature that is perfect, that is good. The seed of God is in you, "That's why you can't go on sinning," says John. The sperm of God is in you and there is a new nature being born within the womb of your soul. That is a good nature.

So the difference between an unbeliever and a believer is between someone who is basically righteous and someone who is basically evil. Or put it another way, what happened when you came to know Jesus? He took us out of the kingdom of darkness and translated us into the kingdom of the Son of his love where we walk in the light. The difference between when you were not a Christian and when you are is the difference between midnight and midday. You are now in the light. The light has shone. You can see. You were once blind and dark. What is the difference between a believer and an unbeliever? A believer belongs to Christ. An unbeliever belongs to Belial. You see that these are not just rhetorical questions, they are expanding the difference between a believer and an unbeliever. It is not too strong to say that a believer and an unbeliever are different species on earth. For on the same page on which this is said: if any man is in Christ, there is a new creature. A new creation: the first man was from the earth – earthy; the new man is from heaven. As we have borne the image of this species of Adam, so we shall bear the image of the new species, Christ. Therefore, to get into the relationship that is going to try to produce something together is to mismate; it is to crossbreed species. This is the real, tragic truth. You may rebel against this, you may resent this horrible truth and yet here it is: there are only two kinds of people in the world, believer and unbeliever, and there is a gulf fixed between those two that literally means that in the last analysis they have nothing in common. I know they may catch the same train to work in the morning. I know they may go to the same shops for their food. I know that they may go to the same bank for their money. I know all that, but everything they have in common is temporary. As soon as those two die, there will be a great gulf between them that can't be bridged and they will have nothing in common at all. Now that is the difference.

How can we take two species that have nothing in common and try to crossbreed them to produce something good? It can't be done, and there is the mental argument. But Paul now brings in another note and he writes: "Would you bring an idol into a temple of God?" The Jews had a beautiful temple. It had magnificent furniture, stonework and carpentry. God had said that this was where he was going to live among them. But there was one thing which must never come in: an idol. It was a complete contrast to all the other temples of the ancient world and of many temples today where you can go in and you can see idols – squat little statues, ugly figures that people kiss and bow down to. An idol would pollute the altar of God and his temple. Pontius Pilate was the first slave ever to be made a Roman governor and it went to his head. He marched into Israel and brought the image of Caesar and set it up in the temple. He caused a riot and the blood of Galileans flowed through the streets of Jerusalem. This was the most horrible thing – the abomination of desolation in our temple. Paul is saying here: we are the temple of the living God. Were they going to bring an idol into that temple? Applying this: you may feel that you love this person so deeply that you have such human affection for them, but be careful. If you bring them into your life in this way, you have brought someone you idolised into the presence of God, someone who doesn't love him. Keep God's temple clean.

Now Paul goes on to the second part: if we need to separate from unbelievers or from this kind of relationship with them, it is only in order that we may have a closer relationship with God. To be separate *from* is only in order to be separate *to*. It is only holding one relationship back that another one might follow. When you put a ring on your finger you are saying, "I'm leaving other people for this deep relationship so that I can be with this one." You will still be friends with others but what would you think of a girl who said to her fiancé, "Do you mind if, after we get married, I stay engaged to that other boy?" That might sound ridiculous but it is what you are doing if you are a Christian and you want to keep a deep relationship with someone who isn't. It is ridiculous – you are freeing yourself from deep relationships with others that you might give yourself to the one who loves you.

Paul, quoting from the Old Testament, makes three things quite clear. First of all, the basic premise on which he argues is this: God says: "I will live among you. I will be your God. You will be my people." That is the basic premise from which we start, but now comes the precept from that premise. Therefore: away every person and every thing that would spoil that; come out. I am thrilled with the word "come". God didn't say get out. He did to some – he said to Abraham, "Get out" into a country. He said it to Moses – "Get out." But here God says, "Come out." Which means, "I'm not there; I'm here – come." It means: come closer to me; and that will involve coming further from them but come closer to me.

There is a glorious promise here: your relationship with him will then not just be "I will be your God and you will be my people," it will be, "I will be your Father and you will be my children." In other words there is an intimacy with God that is directly related to our separation. You can say, "I am God's person and he is my God." But when you have learned the balance of real separation then you will know God in the intimacy of a family circle. Do you see the change to being sons and daughters?

How well do you want to know God? How near do you want to get to him? Do you want just to say, "I believe in God and I'm among his people," or do you want to say, "Dad, I am your child"? You cannot have this intimacy with God unless you are prepared to say no to certain people and things. You cannot say yes to him until you have said no to all that keeps you from him. This is a promise. It is not a demand, it is an offer. God is not trying to take anything away from you, he is trying to give something to you. Give yourself to me and I can love you in a closer way, I can be more intimate with you – you can be with me. What a lovely promise. Well, which do you really want? Intimacy with an unbeliever or intimacy with God? That is what it boils down to. Oh, you could get entangled with an unbeliever and you could still believe in God and you could still belong to his people, but the intimacy will not be there; that loving family relationship will suffer.

Sometimes, of course, this happens at a human level where a family profoundly disapproves of someone a son or a daughter has chosen to marry – sometimes quite wrongly, but it can happen. Do you notice that when the family disapproves, something happens to the family intimacy? When God looks at his children and they start getting entangled with people who don't love him, something happens to the relationship, something goes wrong and God says no. Let me make it quite clear if you are already in a relationship that is compromised. Let me say that this passage does not tell you to break the relationship if it is marriage. I must put that in, because even though we tackled it in 1 Corinthians 7 it needs repeating: if you were married before you became a Christian, don't break it up on that account. That is very important. Stay in the marriage because the literal translation of v. 14 is this: do not begin to be mismated with unbelievers—do not *begin*.

In other words, now that you are a Christian, don't choose to go into that. A Christian, for the same reason, is forbidden in 1 Corinthians to sell himself into slavery. He may be a slave when he becomes a Christian, and then he should stay in that relationship. But he should never sell himself into it if he was free when God called him. In other words, after you come to Christ don't enter of your own choice into any relationship that will spoil your relationship with God.

We finish this section with the appeal for the third kind of separation: separation from unbelievers, separation to God, and *separation in ourselves*. If this is to mean anything it has got to be carried the whole way right into my life. It is no use my just separating from sinful people if I don't separate from sin here. Since we have such a lovely promise, let's go the whole way and separate ourselves inside from anything in body or spirit that taints or spoils or dirties the relationship that we have with God. It is hypocrisy to separate from others and not to separate from sin, and that is what the Pharisees were doing.

Jesus said that they were white on the outside – but look inside. Why didn't you separate from hatred, envy and all the things that are in your heart? Why didn't you separate from those? The deepest separation in the Christian life is not from sinners but from sin, and that has to be done cleanly and quickly. I notice that all the verbs in this passage are in a special tense of the Greek language which means, "do it quickly, straightaway; don't linger." Don't let time dull your conscience in this. I have noticed that when a Christian gets involved in this kind of relationship, the more time they play with it, the less they see it as wrong. The longer they delay cutting the relationship the more they convince themselves that it is all right. These verbs say, "Cut now, cleanse yourself now, get it done straightaway, cut it clean and quick and get it out" – and that is what we are to do.

It is no use praying, "God cleanse my life..." – it is our job to do the cleansing. The Bible says: let us cleanse ourselves. We can't shove the responsibility. We can't say it's God's job to make us clean – it isn't. Let us cut these things out – it is our job. Let us see that we will never rest content with less than perfect holiness. What a target! I have often quoted this little piece of doggerel but it is so appropriate that it is coming up again: "When I was young I set my goal as far as I could see; but now I'm nearer to my goal, I've moved it nearer me." Every Christian set off to be a saint. Every

Christian in their early days wanted to be perfect for the Lord. Every Christian wanted to be holy in every part of their being. Is that not true? I just couldn't believe it if you said, "I'm a Christian but I've never wanted to be perfectly holy." You have wanted to.

But how many go on wanting it? How many press on toward the mark and say, "I'm not going to rest content with anything less than perfect holiness"? What then is the one motive that will help us to go on seeking perfect cleanness? I will tell you: it is the fear of God. Now this is a phrase that is much misunderstood. People say, "But surely it's all love now. It's loving God." Is it? You read through the book of Proverbs – a wonderful book. Again and again: the fear of the Lord is the beginning of wisdom. Read through the Psalms too. But am I just quoting the Old Testament? No, let me quote the New Testament—again and again the fear of the Lord. Paul says it here, "Let us cleanse ourselves from every defilement of body and spirit and perfect holiness in the fear of God."

What does that mean? It doesn't mean frightened, it doesn't mean phobia. I have often used the illustration of the traffic on the roads. I know people who are afraid to begin to learn to drive because of the traffic, and that is a phobia. But I know people on motorbikes on those roads who have no fear of the traffic, and they are a menace! I wanted my children to grow up with a fear of causing an accident that might hurt or even kill someone else. That is a healthy fear, isn't it? Take the fear of heights. The fear of heights is a phobia and I suffer from it to a degree. I don't like heights and it tends to keep me away from the edge of a cliff. What the fear of heights does is that it makes you look down. But woe betide a mountaineer who has no fear of falling. The fear of falling will make him look up because that is the way you overcome that fear.

414

In this height of holiness, this mountain of sanctity that we are called to climb in the Lord Jesus, there should be no fear of heights that would stop us climbing. But the fear of falling should keep us looking up to Jesus. That is the fear: the fear of hurting God, the fear of hurting someone else wrongly; the fear of putting an obstacle in someone else's way. That is a healthy fear. Let us go on to perfect holiness in the fear of God.

My last word on this passage is a very practical one. Supposing you are in a situation now and you are not sure whether it is a mismating with an unbeliever or not, how do you tell? Because it is not always easy to tell when that kind of relationship is coming up. Marriage I think is quite clear – but in the other relationships I have mentioned, how do you tell when a friendship is stepping over this borderline into something wrong? How do you tell when a business colleague is stepping over the line? How do you tell when a religious unity is stepping over this line? Well I will give you just three little practical words.

Here is the first: consult other Christians. Don't trust your own heart or head because your heart can tie your head in knots. It is deceitful and desperately wicked. Ask other Christians if it is going to be an unequal yoke. Second: always give God the benefit of the doubt, never yourself. If you have any doubt at all, give God the benefit and cut it. Third, ask yourself: "Who means more to me, God or this person? Who do I want to be closest to?"

GIVING
Read 2 Corinthians 8 – 9

A. EXCELLENCE (1–7)
 1. MACEDONIANS
 2. CORINTHIANS

B. EQUALITY (8–15)
 1. CHRIST
 2. CHRISTIANS

C. EARNESTNESS (16–24)
 1. TITUS
 2. BRETHREN

D. ENTHUSIASM (1–7)
 1. RELUCTANT
 2. CHEERFUL

E. ENRICHMENT (8–15)
 1. GIVER
 2. GOD

The Victorian preacher C H Spurgeon used to say, "If you're going to give a tract to a starving man, then wrap it in a sandwich first." Behind that remark lies a fundamental principle: to treat people as whole beings and not just to treat parts of them. There are those who treat man purely as a body and think that when they have given him food, clothes and shelter that they have served him adequately. But they have ignored that man does not live by bread alone but by every word that proceeds from the mouth of God.

Then there are those who believe that if they have given people the gospel they have done all that God wants them to do, and they have just treated them as souls. It is this principle of meeting all needs of people, whether physical, mental, or, in our Western world now, emotional – or spiritual. The gospel includes preaching the whole grace of God to the whole man and serving people in all their needs, which is just an introduction to the fact that emerges in these chapters: that the great missionary Paul was not only concerned about preaching the gospel but he had started a famine-relief fund. This went alongside his preaching because he knew that people have bodies and that while we are in this world our bodies need food.

He was particularly concerned about the Jewish Christians in Jerusalem. A famine had struck that land, and they were suffering more than elsewhere because the world was sharing out its bread among its own and was not sharing it with the Christians. Therefore there was a group of Jewish believers in the city of Jerusalem where it had all begun who were going hungry. Paul, who had once thrown them into jail and persecuted them, now raises a famine-relief fund for them. Everywhere he went and preached the gospel, after he had got people converted he would then present to them the need to help others materially. That was part of the working out of their salvation.

As he talks to the Corinthians about this famine-relief fund, some principles of Christian giving emerge. Many Christians feel that money is a kind of dirty subject, something that should be swept under the carpet among true believers – that we should never mention it. I do not believe that, because the Bible frequently mentions money. Jesus said more about money than about any other subject. If you doubt that, then go through his teaching and mark every verse that mentions money – you will be shattered!

In our study of 1 Corinthians 16, we saw that there are two extreme attitudes to money among Christians, neither of

GIVING *2 Corinthians 8–9*

which is biblical – that you should never talk about money or you talk about it too much.

Now here are principles of Christian giving in chapters 8–9. First, the principle of *excellence*. In v. 7, Paul uses the word "excel" twice. He says, "I want you to excel in giving." Here is the first basic target for Christian giving, that it should not be a minimum target but a maximum, not "How little need I give?" but, "How much can I give? Can I go beyond what is expected? Can I excel?" The word means, "to surpass, to go beyond, to exceed, to go beyond what others would give, to excel in this virtue, not just to give what is expected or what is right but to go as far as possible." That is the first principle in Christian giving. It is the difference between mini-Christianity and maxi-Christianity. Not looking in my purse and saying, "Now, what's the smallest coin that would be a decent tip on this occasion?" but saying, "How much could I give of what I have?"

Many years ago a girl was selling flags for charity in the city of Oxford. People were giving her coins. But she stopped a rather seedy-looking gentleman and asked him if he would like to give to this worthy cause, and he asked her a bit about it. This man took out his cheque book and he wrote the figure "one" and then more and more zeros after that until her eyes were like two big noughts looking at this! He wrote out a cheque for one million pounds and gave it to her and squeezed it into the tin. She thought it was a hoax, but in fact it was Lord Nuffield! It certainly exceeded her expectations that day. She came back with this tin full of a million pounds and more! But the Bible, when it says, "excel in giving", never uses a rich man as an illustration, it always uses a poor person to show what excelling really is. Christ used a widow with a tiny amount to show what excelling is – to go beyond what is expected – and he said, "Look at that woman." So Christ used illustrations, and Paul does

419

here to encourage those who are poor to excel. Not to leave it to the rich but to encourage all of us out of our slender resources to excel in this gracious work also. Paul doesn't use the widow's mites, but he does use the Macedonians. Ancient Greece was divided into two provinces: Macedonia in the north and Achaia in the south. He is writing to Achaia about Macedonia. Do you notice that Paul often praised one church to another? He never criticised one church before another; he never carried tales of weakness. But he would say: you Corinthians, listen to what the Macedonians are doing – stimulating one lot of Christians by telling them what another lot were doing, and that is a valid thing to do. It is one of the great joys of hearing the news of what the Lord is doing elsewhere; it stimulates you to more prayer. Over half a century ago in Korea there was tremendous revival and thousands were being converted. Shall I tell you how it happened? Because the church members got up at five o'clock every morning in the week to gather for two hours of prayer. No wonder revival followed! When we are prepared to do that, we shall see revival too.

Paul says a number of things to the Corinthians about the Macedonians which show that they excelled in giving. They were in extreme poverty. Someone has said that it is the poor who know how to give because they know what it is to want, and they gave out of extreme poverty; they had gone through affliction. Many of the Christians had lost their jobs because they were Christians, and the few that managed to keep their jobs were keeping the rest in that little church. They were extremely poor, and yet it was out of the extreme poverty that they gave liberally. The second thing he says about them is that the reason behind their giving was their *abundant joy*. He says that certain things produced a wealth of liberality. Poverty plus joy equals wealth because it produces liberality. Notice Paul's phrase, "a wealth of liberality" – that is true riches. Not a wealth of possessions, but a wealth of getting rid of them. What a wealthy person a giver really is! The third thing he says about them is: they gave *according to their means*. Now people hate a "means test". We don't like somebody else knowing about our means, and we resent it, but the Bible teaches us that every Christian should apply the means test to themselves. They gave according to their means, and they even went beyond it. In other words, they only checked up on their income in order that they could be sure they were giving beyond their means. Some of us, perhaps, might do well to check up on our means and we may discover to our surprise we are not giving according to our means. But they checked up to go beyond their means, and they gave beyond.

Next we are told that the Macedonians *begged to give*. Now that word "beg" we usually reserve for receiving. But people who beg to give have really had a touch of the grace of God on them. They were begging for the favour of giving. That makes it an act of worship.

How did such excellent attitudes come about? How do you get this way? How do you get this wealth of liberality? I will tell you two simple steps. Step number one: give yourself to God. That is what the Macedonians did. Before they thought of giving money, they gave themselves. God would rather have you than your money. If he gets you, he will get your money anyway, but he would much rather have you first. They gave themselves to God. Therefore, having given the biggest thing to God, the other things came easily. When you haven't given yourself to God, to give anything else comes hard. But when you have given yourself to God, it comes easy for the very simple reason that you have no desire left to spend the money on yourself – because you have given yourself. It is logical and sensible.

The second thing is, therefore, that having given

themselves to God, *their free will was replaced by his will*. You notice that earlier in this paragraph Paul says, "I testify, they gave of their own free will," but then he says, "They gave themselves to God and then to us in his will." So that now instead of a self will, they had his will telling them what to do with their money. This is the secret of the wealth of liberality, to give yourself first and then say, "Lord, what is your will?" Then you can be like the Macedonians.

Having mentioned all that, Paul is teaching the Corinthians to excel as the Macedonians did. Their church was noted for many things. They excelled in faith, they were great believers, they excelled in utterance and were great speakers, they excelled in knowledge and were great learners. They excelled in earnestness, were very energetic and enthusiastic, and they excelled in their love for others. Those are great things, and any church with excelling virtues like that could well sit back and say, "We've arrived." But Paul is teaching them that you can have all those things and still be reluctant to part with your money – so excel in this, too. In other words: balance. Don't just excel in this or that, excel in all. Seek to go beyond in everything. Excel in this virtue, too. Just go beyond all human lines of expectation and excel.

Notice the word *grace* and the word "gracious". Paul writes of how the grace of God is shown in Macedonia: I want you to excel in this gracious work. Grace is a word that you hardly ever hear outside Christian circles. Move on to the next paragraph and you see what it means. The next principle in giving is the principle of *equality*. What kind of equality is in Paul's mind? Is it political equality or sexual equality? Look at what he says (see 8:13).

Remember that Jesus was wealthy beyond comparison, and he became poor – why? So that he could lift people up to his wealth. Some people think this refers to the poverty of his earthly life – that he left his carpenter's trade and wandered around dependent on charity. I think it is something much bigger than that. The poverty started at his birth. Look at the servants he had in heaven. He had literally myriads upon myriads of servants. He had twelve thousand private servants. He says that: twelve legions of angels that he could tell what to do. Yet he became a little baby, helpless, and his servants looked down in amazement at their Lord. Oh, how rich he was! The glory he had! I don't know what he wore in heaven before he came to earth, but it was glorious. He left it all behind and he was stripped naked, and he who was rich became poor.

But notice that it was not a grand gesture. He wasn't one of those who was just saying, "I'm going to align with the poor, and I'm going to be poor." No, he did it that they might be rich. It wasn't that he just might become poor like them; it was that they might become rich like him. That is a very different thing, it is not a gesture; it is an achievement. He wanted to lift people until they, too, had all the angels as servants. One of the things I am promised is that in heaven I will have angels as my servants. Think of that! Just think of the wealth that will be ours. We are lower than the angels at the moment, but we are going to be above them in glory. They will do our bidding and come and say, "What do you want?" – angels serving us. But that was the wealth he had, and it is the wealth that he wanted to share to make us joint heirs with him of all that he had.

There are two things that come out of this illustration about your giving. Firstly, how poor does it make you? Secondly, how rich does it make the person to whom you are giving? Aren't those challenging questions? First, how poor does it make you? I don't know how poor Lord Nuffield became as the result of writing that million pound cheque. I know that the widow gave everything she had. How poor does your giving make you? The Lord Jesus became poor.

The other question is: how rich does it make the people you are giving to? Our giving to the needy should not just meet their immediate need but help them to rise to the kind of level they should have. That involves very deep thinking about their need and asking, "How can I best help that person to get a job, to lift themselves, to rise to the level that they ought to be living at?" – in a world in which so many are well below even survival standards.

Paul comes to Christians in this matter of equality, and we are shown three stages in Christian giving to those in need: desiring to help them; actually doing it; completing it. Most people get twinges of feeling for the needy when they see them. Some people do something about it at the time, but to complete it, and see it through until the people are really helped – that takes grace. Most of us can respond quickly to an appeal but how many of us can see it through until the person we are trying to help is on their own two feet with adequate support?

Paul quotes from the book of Exodus. Here again is a very interesting little comment on what Christians think equality is. It is not that everybody should have the same wage. Let it be quite clear that this is not the equality that the Lord has in mind. When the Lord gave manna in the wilderness, some collected a lot and some collected a little. They had different amounts but – here's the but – they all had enough. The equality God wants to see among his children is not necessarily a mechanical equality in which everybody has identical income.

Now we move on to the principle of *earnestness*. The word "earnest" is used three times in 8:16–24. This section is very practical and is concerned with administration – the handling of funds. This must be right, not only in the sight of God, but in the sight of men. It is so easy to be suspicious. It is easy for people to say, "Well, that famine fund, most of it goes into the office here." You need to know the facts. Therefore, there must be published audited accounts. This is sensible.

Two principles emerge in this paragraph that remove criticism and suspicion. First, Paul did not handle this money by himself – he had three others to help him. The principle of a team handling Christian finance is very clear. Second, that they must be men of the right qualities. Integrity is taken for granted, but the lovely quality mentioned here is earnestness. Thank God when earnest men handle money. It means somebody who will go out of his way to help people in their giving. Titus is coming to Corinth of his own accord to collect the gift that could have been sent.

So we have here the principle of earnestness – meaning people who have confidence in the givers. It is a lovely thing when those who are responsible for a fund have the confidence that people will give, and say, "I know that if I present the need, they will give," and that is the earnestness that there was in Titus and the brethren. You notice that these men were tested and then appointed by the churches. How sensible, how wise, how practical – no suspicions, no criticisms, no talk about what these men did with the money, but tested, appointed teams of men handling the money for the relief of the saints – utterly practical. It is a thoroughly necessary passage, very down-to-earth. Christians are not fools, and they know the weaknesses of their own hearts so they see that their business administration is right.

Now we come to another principle that does liven us a bit more, the principle of *enthusiasm*—words like "readiness", "zeal" and "willingness". Paul contrasts two kinds of giver: the reluctant and the cheerful.

Some people I know even have a few hesitations about passing a plate around in a service, lest anyone feel that they are under some kind of compulsion to give. Congregations should feel entirely free, but the collection plate is usually the most convenient way of collecting gifts from a number of people. Christian giving should never have about it the idea that, "I must give because somebody's pressurising me, because somebody's telling me to give." No, the Lord loves a *cheerful* giver. To be a cheerful giver means that when the time comes in the service for the collection you enjoy it. The Lord loves a cheerful giver – not someone who grins and bears it – it is something much deeper than that. He loves to give to us; he is the Father who loves giving good things to his children. Therefore, let us be cheerful when we give.

The final principle here is that of *enrichment*. In v. 6, Paul has stated one of God's laws, and it operates on giving. Giving is sowing, and sowing always leads to reaping. I remember once when working on a farm I got into serious trouble with the farmer. He told me to sow a field with corn. I remember – it was still in my early days – I filled up the seed drill, climbed on the tractor, and drove up and down that field all day. I found that I had a lot of seed left over at the end, and I should have checked this earlier. I assumed that the seed drill, having been used before that season, was set for that kind of corn but it was not set correctly. In fact, it was only letting a little bit of seed out where it should have let out much more, and I realised afterwards. I remember when that field came up, the farmer was a good farmer, and he said he would wait and see what happened first before he did anything about it. It began to come through, and neighbouring farmers were commenting about a "bad field". It was right next to the main road where all the cars passed by, and it was a shocking field. I had to see it every day. So he finally cross-drilled it with some more seed and hoped to overcome my mistake that way.

It is a law of nature – it is always a law of giving. Sow sparingly – little harvest; sow bountifully – much harvest.

What kind of a harvest comes from giving? Three harvests are mentioned here which come to the giver, and a fourth one is mentioned which comes to God. So we are not talking now about the enrichment of the receiver, though of course they will be helped. First of all: *materially*. Here is the Word of God to promise two things to you. If you learn generosity, God will see that you have enough, and he will give you more than enough so that you can give. God loves a cheerful giver, and when anybody wants to be a cheerful giver he will give them the means to be a giver. He won't frustrate a desire like that.

At the beginning of a church building fund, I once suggested that each member think of raising fifty pounds. One dear lady didn't know how to get it, but she wanted to give it. She was the first in the church to give fifty pounds, and then she gave many more gifts of the same amount because the Lord gave her the means to give. That is all that God asks. He doesn't ask you to have the resources, he asks you to have the attitude. He says, "Will you want to give? Then I'll give you enough to give. If you want to meet the need, then I'll help you to do it." What a promise of material enrichment. It is fulfilled in those who want to give. You try it!

A lady listened to me preaching who had been on a fixed wage for twelve years and looked like being on a fixed wage for the rest of her life. She wanted to give to the Lord, but the rising cost of living was beginning to make it impossible to give what she had been giving to the Lord's work. I suggested that night that you can pray for a rise if your motive is right. She went home on the Sunday night and did so, and on the Monday morning at eleven o'clock, the boss called her into the office and gave her a rise of the exact amount that she had been giving to the Lord. You try it! There is a promise here that if you really want to give, he will give you the means to do so.

The second harvest is a *social harvest* – a harvest of friendship. There will be people who will pray for you because you were generous. It is not spoiling giving to say that there is an enrichment like this to follow. Thirdly, there is a *character enrichment*. Paul quotes from the psalms here, describing a righteous man – and a righteous man is one who scatters abroad and gives to the poor. He says there is a harvest of righteousness. Generosity brings righteousness of character.

The harvest for God is that *glory, praise and thanksgiving ascend to him* because of that generosity. It causes people to stop grumbling about God and to be grateful to him instead. What a lovely thing to be doing for other people. What a harvest!

No wonder Paul gets so excited he bursts out in praise to God and says, "Thanks be to God for his indescribable generosity, for his grace!" Now scholars have discussed and debated whether the gift he refers to is the gift of Christ or the gift of Christian generosity. I would say it is both. You don't need to argue that one. It is the gift of Christ in God's generosity that stimulates the gracious work of generosity in our hearts. The grace produces what is gracious. Thanks be to God for his inexpressible gift.

BOASTING
Read 2 Corinthians 10:1 – 12:13

A. FAULTLESS (10:1–18)
 1. DEADLY WEAPONS (1–6)
 2. FORCEFUL LETTERS (7–11)
 3. MISSION COMMENDATION (12–18)

B. FALSE (11:1–15)
 1. DIFFERENT GOSPEL (1–6)
 2. NO CHARGE (7–12)
 3. SATANIC MASQUERADE (13–15)

C. FOOLISH (11:16–33)
 1. MISGUIDED TOLERANCE (16–21a)
 2. EXTRAORDINARY RECORD (21b–29)
 3. HUMILIATING BEGINNING (30–33)

D. FATEFUL (12:1–13)
 1. HEAVENLY VISIT (1–6)
 2. PHYSICAL HANDICAP (7–10)
 3. APOSTOLIC MARKS (11–13)

The last four chapters of this letter stand out as quite different from the rest. It comes almost as a shock and a surprise to feel the personal sadness and hurt here. Paul seems to be back against the wall and defending himself against critics in an alarming way. The key word in these last four chapters is the word "boast". In chapters 10–11 it occurs sixteen times. Now what has got into Paul, that he is boasting? What an extraordinary attitude for him to adopt! Surely a Christian should never boast? Surely he shouldn't be worried about what other people say about him? Surely his self is crucified and people can criticise him as much as they like and it won't hurt, so why is Paul defending himself like this?

Well, behind these four chapters is a very sad truth, which you will experience if you seek to obey Christ and spread the gospel. It is this: every messenger of Christ will come in for slander and criticism, and I will tell you why in a moment. Some of the criticisms that were being made about Paul were dreadful. They accused him, for example, of being cowardly. They said, "When he's with you he's all meek and charming and gentle. As soon as he gets a few hundred miles away he writes letters really tearing a strip off you. He is humble when he is with you and he is very bold when he is away. He can really write a stinging letter, but meet him face to face and say, 'Say those things to my face,' and he won't."

Then they charged him with being worldly. They said his motives and his methods were of the flesh, were human, and he was doing this for what he could get out of it, and the methods he used were manipulative methods – forcing people to go his way.

Then there was the third charge, that he was a man of unpleasant appearance. Well, as far as we know, he was. They took this line because the Romans and the Greeks worshipped men who were strong and big and handsome and could be worshipped as demi-gods. But this ugly little man they said was uncouth in speech, that he didn't have a gift of oratory, that his words were not like the great Greek speakers, and he just put words together. Then they accused him falsely of being too independent – he wouldn't take money from them. They said, "It's pride, he doesn't want to depend on us. He doesn't love us, he's not willing to receive from us" – and they went on like this.

Now why did people criticise Paul? Wherever he went to preach, somebody came along afterwards and tried to poison the minds of his converts against him. One of the most difficult things he had to bear when he went to Galatia, when he went to Philippi, everywhere he went, someone came along afterwards and tried to detract from him. Why did they do it? Was it professional jealousy from other preachers and teachers? Was it their greed and ambition? Did they want to rob him of his converts so they could take them over and have a bigger congregation? What was it? Paul said, "It is Satan." The simple fact is that Satan hates the Word of God – he hates the message of the gospel. Since he can't attack the message because it is true, he will attack the messenger. If he can plant seeds of doubt in a person's mind about the preacher he has effectively neutralised the preaching. It is a method as old as the hills. If you don't like what a man says then criticise the man. I have known a little share of this from time to time and how horrible it can be.

I remember one time I received a real poison-pen letter. I had helped a young man to go to a Bible college. This poison pen letter accused me that I had helped him to get to Bible college because I had a homosexual relationship with him. Nothing could be further from the truth, and yet it came. It is horrible, it is of Satan, and the devil loves to do this. So the devil got hold of people who got hold of Paul, and criticised him, and slandered him as a coward, as a worldly man, as an uncouth man, as an independent man, and finally as a man who had not been authorised by Jesus to preach. It was horrible. Paul said, "I must defend myself against these charges." Not because he was defending himself, but because the message was at stake, and because the gospel was at stake.

This is why he went to the lengths of boasting "like a fool". It was a desperate measure for a desperate situation. His Corinthian church, this fellowship that he had started and led to the Lord, was going to be smashed by this, unless Paul re-established his authority.

431

Let us look at how he did it: I can't analyse this flow of passion. This is a flow of a human heart that is sore and sad, and that is seeking to re-establish the gospel of Christ. He just pours it out, saying that if they boast about themselves and criticise him then he is going to boast. He is going to meet that criticism so that they can once again come back to the truth.

The first criticism was when he was a long way away from them he was pretty bold, but when he was near to them he was soft. When he was far enough away he would write them stinging letters, and he had done that, but when he came to preach he didn't dare to say such things to their face. Here is a charge that no Christian must allow to stick. Every believer must be ready to say the things to a person's face that they are ready to say under other circumstances – to have the courage and boldness to talk directly to someone and not behind their back. Paul is saying: "I will come and I will be bold with you, if you insist. But I entreat you not to let me come like that. I could be bold; I could come into your very presence and say these things. But I entreat you, don't force me to. I don't like doing it. I would prefer to come with the meekness and gentleness of Christ. I know you say I'm gentle when I'm with you, I want to be, so don't force me not to be." He says, "I know that you accuse me of being human in this, of being a worldly man, and of using worldly methods of manipulating you, but I'm not. We fight a battle, but it's not a worldly battle and we don't use worldly weapons."

Here is the first great lesson I want to apply. This is the principle: we are not engaged in worldly warfare, therefore we must not use worldly weapons. No-one must ever accuse us of trying to manipulate human beings by human force. This has very far-reaching implications. We are not fighting against men and women – let it be known the world over. No

Christian is fighting a human being. That is not our warfare and we must beware of engaging in any activity that could easily be seen as fighting people. We wrestle not against flesh and blood, but against principalities and powers. What weapons do we use? Here is the kind of warfare we wage: we meet the attack of human reason not with argument but with divine revelation. We meet the attack of human taunts not with taunts in the reverse direction, but with testimony. We meet the obstacles of human pride with prayer. We fight with otherworldly weapons.

One mistake we can make is to think that in our warfare, numbers count, but how utterly foolish that is. Gideon thought like that, and God had to reduce him to three hundred men. It was not because he had a massive number of people with him that he was going to win the battle. It is not through numbers that you make your impact. Three hundred plus God can do it, where thirty thousand without God can do nothing. How important it is that Christians never give the impression that they think they can force other people to adopt the Christian way by sheer weight of numbers. It doesn't work that way. God chooses minorities.

When Paul walked into Corinth he said he had divine power to overthrow strongholds – and he came by himself. This is to be our trust; we must not use worldly methods to achieve the kingdom. We dare not, we cannot. We must put our trust in weapons other than those the world uses. The world will use any force it can – financial, military, psychological. Let us eschew all those forces and say that our kingdom is not of this world, else would we fight, but we have weapons that you know not. So Paul is saying, "I have divine power to deal with every human argument, to deal with every proud obstacle to the knowledge of God, to bring into captivity every thought in obedience to Christ."

Do you realise that this is the major moral battle that is

needed – which is to be fought in this country? Not to stop the deeds, but to bring every thought into captivity to Christ, because when you have captured a man's thoughts, you have captured his words, and you have captured his deeds. Here is the citadel that you are after: the mind of man. Not just his behaviour, so that you can say you have reformed his behaviour and limited his sinful acts. But to capture the stronghold of his intentions, to capture his mind for Christ, so that he is thinking of whatever things are pure, and lovely, and honest, and of good report – then the words and the deeds will follow.

How do you capture men's minds for Christ? Well certainly not by using worldly weapons, but by using divine power and divine revelation, and by prayer. The world needs to know that Christians are praying for this nation – that we are praying not because we blame flesh and blood or because we are saying, "You are evil," but because we are blaming ourselves as part of the human race for not being what God wants us to be, with every thought in obedience to Christ. Paul teaches us that you can only be ready to punish disobedience when your obedience is complete. What a challenge! In other words, the weapon that we can use to deal with disobedience is the weapon of obedience. What a powerful weapon that is – the weapon of obeying Christ.

Here then is a principle I draw from the opening verses of chapter ten. We are not in human warfare, but we use divine weapons. The principle is from vv. 7–17. Paul is asking the Corinthians to use their eyes, to look at the evidence. They were criticising him as not being fully authorised by Christ. They had been deluded by other preachers who had come. They commended themselves; they compared themselves with others. Here is the second great principle that Paul is going to enunciate. Just as we must turn away from human warfare and use divine weapons, we must turn away from human comparisons and use divine commendation. It doesn't matter how I compare to another man, it is whether God commends me or not that matters.

One of the awful dangers of the Christian life is that when God begins to sanctify you and make you more like Christ, you begin to feel a little better than someone else. You begin to make human comparisons. People outside the church make comparisons with people inside. They say, "I'm as good as those who go." Let us beware, lest we fall into the same trap and use comparisons the other way and say, "No you're not, we're better than you are." Paul says, "These men commend themselves, they compare themselves with one another—'I'm better than he is, I'm better than you are.'" But, he says, "I don't compare myself. I say what does God do with what I do?" There can be no comparison between what I do as a Christian and what you do as a Christian. The real commendation is: what does God do with what I do, and what does God do with what you do?

Paul is not ashamed to boast now of his authority: You say my personal appearance puts you off. You say I'm uncouth in my speech. I don't mind, it's what God does with what I do that matters. It's not what I do in comparison with what you do. And I'm a pioneer; I go places where nobody's heard the gospel. I boast of this, that I don't build on what other men have done; I do my own work. I don't grab other people's converts, I get my own and I'll go anywhere the gospel hasn't been. I want to go beyond you at Corinth to the west and pioneer for Christ.

May I say that that is something to boast about. It is nothing to boast about that you inherit the fruits of another man's labour. But it is something to boast about that you have provided something for others to build on, that you have launched out into the unknown, that you have broken fresh ground. There is a text in the Old Testament: "Break up the fallow ground, it is high time to seek the eternal." Break up the fallow ground; go where there isn't anything growing. Go to people who have not heard the gospel. Go and do something yourself that is new and let God bless it. It is his commendation that you can boast about. So Paul is saying: Let's have done with human comparison, and let's seek divine commendation. This is what is going to do it, when God blesses what we do.

I think now of a man who was a professor of English walking through Hyde Park Corner. He heard an open-air speaker at Speaker's Corner – a man with a text on a little soapbox stand. This speaker's English was hopeless. He split every infinitive, he mixed every metaphor; he did everything he shouldn't have done with English grammar. This professor of English was so upset by this that he felt that he would wait until he had finished speaking and then he would take him to task and tell him he shouldn't be getting up to speak in public. So he waited while this man went on, but before the end of the man's speech the professor was converted! At the end of the talk he didn't criticise the speaker and he realised that this man, uncouth as he was, murdering the Queen's English as he did, was a man whom God was blessing and using. This is the divine commendation. By human comparison that man ought not to have been speaking in Hyde Park. By human comparison he wasn't fit to speak – but by divine commendation there is now a professor who is a Christian. The Lord used the uncouth language to attract that man to listen. Maybe he came in a critical spirit, but the Lord can deal with that too.

The first comparison was: not human warfare but divine weapons. The second comparison is: not human comparison but divine commendation. Paul now meets his critics in a third way. By this time he is feeling very uncomfortable. He hates this kind of talk, he hates defending himself – he feels silly. He is saying: "I'm a fool for doing this, bear with me in my foolishness. I'm going to go on, and I'm going to go on saying these things. But I'm sorry I seem a bit silly, do bear with me." Then he unburdens his heart. He says, "Within my heart I feel jealousy." Professional jealousy, that other preachers were replacing him? No – jealousy for his converts. If you love someone you will feel jealous for them; if you really love someone you are bound to be jealous. Jealousy is the other side of love. Now, jealousy can be a bitter thing that is self-centred, or it can be a lovely thing that is unselfish.

Can you see what lies behind this? Paul is jealous because he betrothed the Corinthians to Christ. It was his job to keep them away from all others, so he had a holy jealousy. He wanted to present them pure to their one husband, Jesus. He was afraid he was not going to manage it but they were going to be led astray, and that something would come between them and Christ, as it came between Adam and Eve when Satan beguiled Eve. Now what is he afraid of? The next verse tells you: that they will turn to another Jesus, receive another spirit, and accept another gospel. The tragedy is that there isn't only one Jesus being preached in the world today, there are many. I have read book after book about Jesus claiming that he was a hippie or a communist or something else. There is only one true Jesus, and he is the Jesus that Paul preached. There were things disturbing us in the Baptist Union some years ago on precisely this question. Are there those among us who are preaching another Jesus? Because there is only one. There is only one Holy Spirit but there are many other spirits abroad and it is possible to get another one. There is only one gospel, and yet there are many others being preached.

The first time that Satan got hold of Eve, the very first effect was that Adam and Eve drifted apart. They had things to hide from each other. They could no longer share everything; it was no longer pure devotion. That is the tragedy, and Paul didn't want that to happen to Christians. So he is teaching that it is not the manner of speaking that you must listen to, it is the matter of what is said. It is not a man's brilliant eloquence or oratory; it is whether he is speaking the truth. It is not how impressive a person is – it is whether it is the same Jesus and the same gospel. How easy it is at the human level to be impressed with the speaker because of his personality or persuasiveness and not ask whether what he says is true. So here is the third principle that I draw from this: *it is not a matter of human oratory, but of divine oracles* – that is what we need to look for.

In 11:7–15 a funny criticism is mentioned. Paul had deliberately not taken any money for preaching at Corinth. He did at Macedonia and he did in other churches, but not at Corinth. They offered him money but he didn't take it. Now why did he not take it? I will tell you why. Corinth and Athens in Achaia, southern Greece, were the centres of public speaking. Everybody who was anybody would get up and speak in public and then send the hat round. It was understood. They were the pop stars of their day. Just as some celebrities today get massive sums of money, the people who did it in those days were the public speakers at Corinth and Athens. They were the "pop stars", and they were considered great if they got a lot of money.

Of course Paul didn't get anything. The church at Corinth felt rather inferior because of this. You can get the feeling, can't you? Paul was telling them: I didn't take any money from you. I didn't want anybody to think I was in this for the money. I even "robbed" poor churches up in the north by accepting support from them so that I could come and preach to you.

If you are in a critical mood you can find something

wrong with anybody. So when Paul didn't take money do you know what they said? They said, "He doesn't love us. If he loved us he would take our money. He's independent, he's proud, he doesn't like us so he won't have our cash." Paul is saying: I'm not going to take your money and I never will, and I'll tell you why. Because I don't want you to class me with these men who will take every penny you've got. I don't want to be thought of like them. I want to dissociate myself from them.

He then says something about these men who grumbled because he wouldn't take money, because they themselves took it: "They are deceitful, false, disguised servants of Satan." I want you to realise that Satan is a past master at disguise. Have you read Bunyan's book *The Pilgrim's Progress*? What a marvellous book! You must read it. In it, every time Satan appears he is dressed as somebody different: Apollyon, Beelzebub and a host of others – and do you know the most subtle? Flatterer.

I read a little sentence that really stuck with me, "Beware of the man who flatters you, because the man who flatters you can also slander you; he is a stranger to the truth, both ways" – and Flatterer was one of the disguises. Satan doesn't come to you dressed up as a bad angel. He doesn't come to you dressed up as a demon. He doesn't come to you as a bad man. He comes to us as a good man – that is the tragedy. Satan is so subtle that he can dress up as an angel of light. You could see an angel of light and think it was from God, but it might be Satan himself. Oh, how you have got to be on your guard. If he came as a prowling lion we would soon run. I love the story of two lions walking up Oxford Street and one saying, "I thought this place was supposed to be crowded!" Well, if you really saw a prowling lion come in through your door, you would get away quickly! Now Satan is a prowling lion but he has never yet appeared as one. He disguises himself and he comes in subtle disguise and you just don't recognise him. That is part of the horror of it, and you just don't realise when he is getting at you. Therefore his servants also look like good people, and look like nice people, and look like kind people. How do you tell them? Not by the disguise. But, Paul says, by their deeds and by their destiny – what they do and where they go to, and their end, their destiny, will fit their deeds, not their disguise.

Here is the next comparison that Paul gives to these people. Don't judge by human appearance, judge by divine achievement – their deeds.

Finally we come to the last part of this chapter. I am as uncomfortable preaching this part of 2 Corinthians as Paul was writing it. It is not a very nice part to read. He is fighting, he is boasting, he is being a "fool". Once again, he says, "I repeat, let no one think me foolish. But even if you do, accept me as a fool. I'm going to boast again. I will boast, and boast, and boast if I can preserve your belief in the message I brought to you. I will boast." What are the limits to which a Christian can boast? I will tell you. A Christian can boast to the limit of what God has done to bless his work – no more than that. He mustn't boast of what he has done. But he can boast of what God has done through him – that is boasting. Let him who boasts, boast in the Lord. Paul is saying: "I'll boast of what God does through me. Not of me, not of what I do, but of what God does in me. At this point he becomes thoroughly sarcastic. Sarcasm is not a very nice weapon, but it is a weapon that must be used occasionally. It is the besetting sin of some professions – I think perhaps preachers included, and certainly teachers, amongst others. It is easy to be sarcastic, but sometimes it is good. Paul says: You are so wise yourselves, I'm sure you'll bear with a fool like me. Talk about sarcasm! Then he goes on to say something like this: For of course, you put up with it when a man takes advantage of you, and makes a slave of you, and hits you in the face, and preys on you. Oh you can put up with fools can't you – fine. I must admit we were too weak to do that to you. Now it is sheer sarcasm and he is trying to get across through irony. The fact is that these men who have come have come for what they can get – they have come to make slaves of people, they have come to be tyrants. They have come to manipulate and control.

Paul is saying: I'm going to match my ministry against theirs – not by their standards, nor even by mine, but by God's. He says, "Anything they can say, I can say better. Are they Hebrews? I'm a Hebrew. Are they Israelites? I'm an Israelite. Do they claim to be descendants of Abraham? So do I. Do they claim to be servants of Christ? I'm a better one."

Under what circumstances can anyone say, "I'm a better servant of Christ?" It is when you have suffered more than anyone else. These are the only circumstances in which you can claim to be a better servant. The proof: the scars in your own body.

Then follows the catalogue of Paul's better qualifications to the allegiance and loyalty of the Corinthians than those others. He says, "Five times I've received thirty-nine lashes." Do you know what that was? A man was stripped, tied, bent double, and then a great leather thong with separate lashes at the end was brought. It had to touch both sides of his body and leave weals both sides. A man was there to count them because if it actually went over the regulation forty, the man who had done it had to be lashed. So for safety's sake they never did forty, they always did thirty-nine. But another man had to be there to witness the death of the lashed man so that it cleared of the guilt of murder the man who had lashed him. Invariably, a man died of that. Five times this little Jew had had it. Three times he had had the rods. Have you seen that symbol of Roman justice? A bundle of rods with a kind of axe stuck through? The axe was for beheading but the rods, the bundle of rods with a crisscross string on them, were the rods that were used for corporal punishment.

Paul was a Roman citizen – it was illegal to beat him with rods, but three times he had had that too. He had been shipwrecked, he had been without food, he had been stoned, and left for dead. This poor little body had been beaten black and blue and it had scars all over it, literally. Paul was telling them: "I'm a better servant of Christ. They prey on you, they take advantage of you, they exploit you, they strike you in the face. I'll tell you what makes me a better servant of Christ – they have struck me in the face, I've suffered." This is the honour of being worthy to suffer for the name of Jesus. There is a dignity of suffering in the cause of Christ that lifts a man to the roll of honours, and Paul was saying that he had got that.

On top of all this, he had the "anxiety for the churches." It is almost as if he said the last straw, the last burden of all – on top of all the beatings, shipwrecks, imprisonments and famine – he had to worry about this church and that church. When they are weak, he feels weak. When somebody knocks them down, he is angry. His feelings are tied up with his people. So at night he lies sleepless, thinking about them after he has had a beating, and he is praying for them. This is Paul, the great missionary. Do they claim to be servants of Christ? He is a better one.

Then he begins to think that he's painting himself a bit of a hero so he says, "If I must boast, I'll boast of the things that show my weakness. I'll tell you of something terribly undignified that happened to me – I got let down in a basket." He is guarding against anybody looking up to him. He tells of how he went to Damascus. He came out in a basket at night, let down from a window because they were after his blood. Can you see this little Jew sitting in his little basket, coming down the wall? Paul is deliberately getting them to laugh at him. He is boasting of his weakness because the strength that he has to go through all this is not his. He himself is a little man in a basket – but a servant of Christ. Therefore the final comparison he makes is this: the real test of a man of God is not a human tyranny that he exercises over a congregation, but the divine tribulation that you see in his life. Paul has defended himself against these dreadful criticisms made by his enemies.

When I read these words I looked at Paul, and I looked through Paul and I could see another person called Jesus. I could see someone who said, "My kingdom is not of this world, else would my servants fight." He never once tried to force people or manipulate them with any kind of force, but waged warfare with spiritual power. I saw a man who never compared himself with others but allowed God the Father to commend him. I saw a man who did not rely on human appearance. We have no description of the appearance of Jesus. I say it reverently, but he probably looked very ordinary. He has no form nor comeliness that we should desire him, but he relied on what the Father did. When it came to the great crisis, Jesus didn't exercise any tyranny over men. He who had twelve legions of angels at his disposal said, "Father, forgive them, they know not what they do." He allowed them to spit on him, flog him, scourge him, laugh at him, mock him, and dress him up and take it off again, and nail him to a cross. You can see there the mark of the true suffering servant of God, the man of sorrows, and acquainted with grief. Paul in defending himself was inviting them to use their eyes. Could they not see Christ in him? That is the final defence that any man can ever make to his critics.

We are going to look at an example of supernatural discipline, of God humbling one of his servants – a servant who is humble enough to tell the story to other people. It concerns an amazing spiritual experience and the aftermath of it. Paul is still boasting—he has been forced to do so. Those who should have been commending him are doing just the opposite, so he must defend his apostleship. The key word from chapter 10 right through to the end of this letter has been the word "boast." It comes sixteen times in just two chapters. But what is Paul boasting about? His greatness? No, he boasts about his suffering and everything that brings him low, because in spite of that, God has used him to perform miracles for other people. Indeed, one of the most humbling things in Paul's life is that what he was able to do for others by the power of God he was not able to do for himself. He is going to speak of something that was a sore pain to him, and that kept him humble. He is going to boast about that because in spite of that humbling of God, the Lord used him as a mighty apostle.

Somebody once said to me, "How does anyone know what heaven is like? No-one has been there." That is not true – some have had a trip to heaven and come back. Paul was one, John was another. Of course, Jesus was the one who said that he had descended from heaven, so he knew what it is like.

Paul said, "I couldn't put into words what I saw and heard. I heard things that no man could utter." John came back and told us that the Spirit had enabled him to write of what he saw. The book of Revelation is the result.

Paul said "fourteen years ago" – and that should be about seven years after his conversion. He had a spiritual experience the like of which he had never had before, and he had not had since. It was the high peak of his spiritual experience. He didn't know whether God took his body up to heaven or whether his body stayed unconscious on earth and his spirit went up alone – that doesn't matter. You notice that a body or a spirit can see and hear. Whether it was in the body or out of the body he didn't know, but he said, "I know a man..." – and he turns it into the third person. He was caught up to heaven. Of course it is himself but he is talking in a way that takes attention away from himself so that we see the experience and its wonder.

Now what does this phrase "the third heaven" mean? The Jews had a phrase – "the seventh heaven" – meaning the very highest point at God's throne. I think we still use the phrase in popular language. We have a wonderful time of happiness and we say, "Oh, I was in the seventh heaven." That was their phrase. When Paul says "the third heaven" he means two things. First of all he means: I didn't get right up; there is still more beyond what I saw, much more, but I saw something – some of it." He means, secondly, that he got beyond space, because the Jews call the universe "space" – the first heaven. Where the stars and the planets are is only the first.

Space is limited. People ask, "What's beyond space?" I'll tell you – God. When Paul says "I got to the third heaven," he means: I was aware of vast spaces; I got right beyond the heavens; I got right beyond the planets; not just beyond – that would have been the second, I got even further beyond, I got as far as that into infinity and I saw things and I heard things. God told me things and I can't put them into words. Paul indicates that it was the most wonderful experience of his life. He could remember, yet fourteen years had elapsed and it was still vivid. He went to heaven and he came back again.

Fancy having such an experience – but he is not boasting of that, though even if he did he would be telling the truth. He is not boasting of it because he said no-one else witnessed it. He wanted people only to think of him by what they could see and hear in him. It was private to him and nobody could share it. But he mentioned it because they could see the result of that experience in him. For when he came down to earth, God brought him down to earth with a big bump. He was so elated, so thrilled, so excited that he needed an anchor to hold him down on earth. I can understand that, I have never had an experience like this. I have never seen heaven. But I think that if I had then I would be a very difficult person to live with on earth. I would walk around so big-headed, so full of myself, "I've been to heaven!" Can you imagine it? God would have to tie me down in some way. Paul is saying that he has told them this because God gave him something that tied him right down and stopped him getting too elated, too proud of such an experience. I don't think Paul had ever mentioned it for those fourteen years until the Corinthians forced him to boast like this.

Now here we come from the rapture to heaven to the "thorn in the flesh" which tied him down to earth. I realise that this is one of the most controversial phrases in the New Testament. It has been used, I think wrongly, in two ways. First of all, it has been used of every sickness, as much as to say that if a Christian is sick he must simply call it a thorn in the flesh and repeat, "My grace is sufficient for you." I think that is an abuse of this text. We must not call every sickness a thorn in the flesh that God has put there. Otherwise we shall be prevented from believing that God can take it away, and we may be guilty of refusing to believe in the healing power of Christ.

On the other hand, there are those who have taken this phrase and tried to make it mean something that is not physical. It is very difficult to take it in any other way. Some people have said it was a spiritual temptation or an awkward colleague. I have heard people use the phrase "thorn in the flesh" of another Christian who was just a bit difficult to get on with. It has been used for all kinds of metaphorical meanings like that, but I must say that the more I study this, the more I am convinced that for Paul it was a physical thing. The context in which he speaks is physical. He has just been writing of all his physical sufferings – stoned, beaten and shipwrecked. He has just been writing of his body being let down in a basket from the Damascus wall. He is writing of weakness.

When Paul uses the word "weakness", invariably he is using it of physical weakness. Furthermore, the word "flesh" in a context like this usually means his body. Above all, the word "thorn" is never used in the Bible except of something that can prick you physically—something that tears, that cuts; that causes agony and pain. You know what a thorn does. The word can also mean a "stake" – meaning the sort of thing that was driven through the hands of our Lord, a dreadful, sudden agony that goes through a body. Now this is what Paul, I believe, is meaning. He is saying that after this trip to heaven that lifted him up so high, he was given something that gives him agony in the flesh. It is like a thorn pricking; it is like a stake tearing his body, and this has held him down to earth, and it has humbled him, it has made him weak from time to time. Clearly, from the way he writes, it was an intermittent thing.

What was it? Some people have thought it was his physical appearance, and we know that that wasn't impressive. But I don't think that would give him a savage, tearing agony. Some people have guessed it was epilepsy but I don't think it is that. Some have pointed to that virulent malaria which is common in the eastern Mediterranean, which feels like a red-hot iron searing the brain when it comes on and leaves a man incapable of doing anything.

Whatever it was, I believe that God in his wisdom did not want us to know, and I can see why. Because if we did know, anybody suffering from that would begin to be too elated that they were like Paul and say, "I've got this special thorn in the flesh." Suffice it to say that Paul said he was given this. He recognised it as something of Satan, something that Satan had caused, yet he said that it was given him, and there is no doubt that he was saying that God gave it to him. God can allow a man to be buffeted by Satan physically, as in the case of Job, for a purpose of his own.

The important thing is this: Paul said that his prayer to have it removed was answered. There is a world of difference between praying and having no answer, and having the answer no, and we must never get these confused. Let us never use this scripture until God has given us a direct answer "no". Let us not use it to cover unanswered prayer for sickness. Paul said he prayed three times, but he got a direct answer, and therefore the pain had become purposeful.

The purpose was two-fold. Firstly it was to keep Paul down, and secondly to lift God up. If those two purposes are fulfilled then the pain was worth it. So Paul is saying: He gave this to me to keep me down, it was his discipline, it was his humbling of me. It was to keep me from getting too big-headed that I had been to heaven, and I thank God that he has kept me humble through it. He may have kept me weak from time to time, but he has kept me down. The other purpose was this: if God kept Paul down and those who didn't see his trip to heaven saw his pain on earth, they would say, "Isn't God strong, that he can use a man like this." Paul: God's grace is going to be all that you need, and when you are weak and when you are prostrate, I am strong.

Paul is therefore able to go on to say that he is content with things that happen to him and knock him down, because he knows that when he is knocked right down, God is lifted up, because he goes on. It may humble Paul, but it exalts the Lord. Paul is weak, but God strong. Therefore, when I am weak, I am strong, because people can see that my strength comes from him and not from me. When we are physically fit and strong and full of energy, people can say, "Isn't he full of energy, isn't he strong, isn't he a wonderful man of God?" But when you are weak, people say, "God's wonderful, God's strong. He can use a person like that for his power and glory."

So Paul is telling us that he has been disciplined, he has been humbled, he has been brought low by pain – physical pain – which God gave him to keep him down. Therefore, he is able to go on to say that they ought to be commending him, he oughtn't to be boasting like this, because they knew that even when he was prostrate, even when he was knocked down, even when he went through this agony, he could perform signs and wonders and miracles on them. That is the proof that it was of God, because if a man had the healing gift, and not God, then that man would be able to heal himself.

I remember a fine preacher from overseas preaching in London. God was using him to heal other people in a lovely way. People were going and receiving God's gift of healing. But in the middle of his visit he was struck down himself. The chief critics said, "Healed others; can't heal himself." But, you see, that criticism implies that *he* has the power of healing. But that man was being so wonderfully used that people were beginning to think too highly of him, and God humbled him. While he was sick he was able to heal others by the grace of God, and people knew it was God and not him; they began to think less of him, and more of God.

I believe that God can heal today. I would not be preaching or writing now if he couldn't – quite literally. But I believe too, that the ministry of power, signs and miracles is a dangerous ministry for the person who exercises it, and he needs to be kept humble, and kept low. God can do it in his own way—Paul, I'm going to keep you down, but I'm going to use you to lift me up. So Paul is able to say to the

Corinthians that they had seen his weakness, they knew his pain, they knew that he was prostrate, that he himself was just a poor human being. But they saw the signs, the wonders and miracles. They ought to be commending him. God had disciplined him. I think every mature saint has known what it is to be disciplined by God, and humbled and brought low, so that people don't think so much of them.

I heard a well-known Christian speaker tell of how he had confessed to another preacher that he was envious of this other preacher, that he felt God was using him more. This other preacher looked at him and said, "Have you been feeling like that too?" He'd been feeling it about the first preacher. Then he said, "You just came right down off your pedestal in my mind." The first speaker, honest man that he was, said to himself, "Perhaps I've been too humble. Perhaps, I would have liked a little pedestal – just a little one." But then he was humble enough to say that God took him right off his pedestal.

Paul could have been on a pedestal: he had been to heaven, he had performed miracles, but God is going to keep Paul down here – just a poor human being in whom God's grace and strength is seen. Let us discipline ourselves here, lest God have to bring us low; lest he have to say, "You're getting a bit too big for your boots – just come down a bit."

DISCIPLINE
Read 2 Corinthians 12:14 – 13:14

A. SOCIAL (12:14–13:4)
1. NOT TAKING BUT GIVING (14–18)
   a. Himself
   b. His colleagues
2. NOT PRIDE BUT CONCERN (19–21)
   a. Mental
   b. Moral
3. NOT WEAKNESS BUT POWER (1–4)
   a. Fair
   b. Firm

B. SELF (13:5–14)
1. TESTING YOURSELVES (5–10)
   a. Faith
   b. Works
2. LOVING EACH OTHER (11–13)
   a. Mental
   b. Physical
3. ENJOYING THE LORD (14)
   a. Grace
   b. Love

The word "disciple" and the word "discipline" are the same word, and you cannot be a disciple of Jesus without discipline. There are two kinds of discipline in the Christian life and both are needed to produce mature spiritual men and women.

"Whom the Lord loves he chastises," and he humbles those who are his children. He disciplines. He is a Father, not a grandfather. It is the privilege of grandfathers to have the joy of children without the responsibility of disciplining them, but it is the privilege and responsibility of a father to discipline a son. There is nothing soft or indulgent about the holiness of God. The first kind of discipline is *social discipline*, the discipline of other people. For the Christian, the community that disciplines him is the church. They are his family. If the church really is a family then there will be mutual discipline within it. The second kind of discipline, and the very best of all, is *self-discipline* – when a person is mature enough to examine themselves, and test themselves to see whether they be in the Lord. Indeed, if you learn the secret of the second discipline you don't need the first.

Now the first sort of discipline is *social* – the discipline that Christians exercise over one another. It is a note or mark of the church that is dying out in England though it is found in some parts of the world – the mutual discipline of a Christian family. Now there are some who believe that a church ought to exercise no discipline at all, that if someone wants to join they should be able to do so; if someone wants to leave, they should be able to leave but that the church should say nothing about either. They believe that the church should never consider an application for membership, and never take anyone off the roll. Above all, while they are on the roll the church should not make any comment on any member. That is not the New Testament.

The New Testament church is a family and therefore discipline begins when someone says, "I'm a Christian, I want to be part of the fellowship." The first step in discipline is for the fellowship to decide whether that profession is real and fruitful. There come moments when the church also has to decide that a person who is either not fulfilling their responsibilities or is disregarding the honour of the Lord Jesus in their life, has reached the point where as an act of discipline the church says, "We cannot identify with you until this is put right." In between, there are times when the church as a family has to say to each other, "This is wrong and you must put it right for the sake of the honour of Christ in this fellowship." That takes an awful lot of doing.

The first thing is, of course, that those who do the disciplining must be in the right kind of relationship with those who are disciplined. Here we have Paul talking to the Corinthians about his relationship to them. He is saying that he is going to come and discipline them; he is going to put right what is wrong, and will not spare any of them. But let us get the relationship right. First of all, they think he is taking advantage of them. They seem to be hurt in their pride that he didn't take any money from them. But he wanted them, not their money. He wanted to spend himself and be spent for their souls. He did not want to take things from them, he wanted to give to them. That was all he was trying to do – to build them up, not break them down. If he disciplined them it was not taking advantage of his position, but because he wanted them for the Lord.

Here is the first requirement. If you are going to discipline someone it must be in a spirit like this: you must never take advantage of them and never exploit them. But rather you must say, "I am willing to be spent for you – to spend my time, my money, my energy, everything for you" – and for them to say, "We want you, not your money, not your presents," and that is the really deep concern. We must make it quite clear too, as Paul does in 12:19–21, that in saying this no-one is defending themselves but rather being concerned about someone else.

Paul is afraid that when he arrives he will be humbled by weeping in front of them, for two reasons. On the one hand: mental sins of malice, gossip, jealousy, disorder, rivalry, competition – sins largely of the tongue, you notice; and the other thing, sins of their past life that were creeping back into their life now – of immorality, impurity and licentiousness.

453

These are the two major things that need mutual discipline in a church. We shrink, don't we, from dealing with them both? On the one hand is the gossip and the things said behind backs, and the slander and the "clique-ishness". That must be dealt with in discipline, because we are a family and families don't wash dirty linen in public, and families don't go talking about each other elsewhere.

Therefore, if we know within the fellowship of things being said about one another and about the fellowship in a wrong way, and in a wrong place, there is need for discipline. We don't do that. On the other hand, there is always the problem that those who have lived in sin, which means all of us, allow those habits to creep back into our life and spoil the honour of Christ who has saved us from these things. So Paul is telling them that he going to come, and it will not be in weakness but in power and strength to deal with these two kinds of sin. He is going to deal with them firmly, with justice, fairness and strength.

We need to be fair and absolutely firm – "fair" meaning that there must be nothing said or believed that isn't in the mouth of two or three witnesses. A church must never be less fair than a law court. We must seek the witnesses who will tell us of what is wrong, and put that right. Then, Paul is saying, he is going to deal with them firmly, as Christ is in power and not in weakness. Look again at 13:4, "For he was crucified in weakness, but lives by the power of God. For we are weak in him, but in dealing with you we shall live with him by the power of God." Now what does that mean? One of the commonest misunderstandings of the Christian life is that Christ is soft, that he is meek, that he is indulgent, that he doesn't mind sin; that Christ in his love overlooks things, that Christ allows sin to do its worst to him and just says nothing back, and says, "Father, forgive them," and that's all. May I say that in his death, sin piled on top of him – the Cross – and he was weak; he did nothing back, but having been crucified in weakness, he is now in the power of the resurrection. When he comes again, people will be astonished to see him in power to judge the quick and the dead. In his risen power he is strong in how he deals with sin. Therefore, we have got to be too. Oh, we don't like to be—it's hard to be, it is easier to be indulgent and tolerant with one another. But Paul is saying: Even though I don't want to do it, when I come a third time to see you again I will come in the power of the risen Christ and not in the weakness of the crucified Christ. We will not let sin ride over the fellowship any more, we are going to be strong and firm. I shrink from this and so does a congregation – it is part of the being a family together that is hard, to know the power of Christ in dealing with sin, and yet we are called to do this in mutual discipline.

Let us move on to the other kind of discipline: self-discipline. You can save all this, you can save the discipline of God, you can save the discipline of the church, by being self-disciplined. By examining yourself and testing yourself, and putting it right before others notice, before they can come and talk to you about it – put it right. Discipline yourself. Test yourselves to see whether you be in the faith, to see whether you are a Christian at all.

I want to mention some very searching questions written by some Africans in Uganda. A synod there, worried about the declining life of the churches, sent round a questionnaire to every Christian saying, "Test yourselves by these four questions." Number one, do you know salvation through the Cross of Christ? Number two, are you growing in the power of the Holy Spirit, in prayer, meditation and the knowledge of God? Three, is there a great desire in you to spread the kingdom of God by example, and by preaching and teaching? Four, are you bringing others to Christ by individual searching, by visiting and by public witness? They sent that out, saying, "Test yourselves brethren, to see if you're in the faith." I would like to add one or two more questions to that! Do you love Jesus now more than you did a year ago? Do you love your fellow-Christians more than you used to? Are you bursting with a desire that everybody should know about Jesus? Can you look on the world in which you live, and weep for it? These are the kinds of tests to apply, the kind of self-discipline that gets alone with God and says, "God, show me myself; help me to see me as I really am." Test yourselves, brethren! Not just to see whether you are in the faith, but whether that faith is being translated into works.

Paul is teaching: I don't want you to be testing me – we may fail the test in your eyes. It is easy enough to test public preachers. Test yourself, look at yourself; we want you to be doing what is right. Even if you think we fail, we want you to do what is right. So test yourself.

The second part of self-discipline is this: love one another. Ask yourself, "Do I really love the people who are worshipping with me? Will I want to stay behind afterwards and speak to them, or do I rush off home by myself as fast as my legs can carry me? Do I love the people by living in peace and harmony with them? Paul is saying: agree with one another; live in harmony and peace – have a mental attitude to each other, and an emotional attitude to each other, which will express itself physically.

We thought about this at the end of 1 Corinthians and let us address it again now: Greet one another with a holy kiss. In a family, you can express your love physically. I can kiss my wife; we can both kiss the children. They could kiss each other, though when they reach their teens they may think that is beneath their dignity. But a real family is not afraid to express family love physically. Do you love shaking hands with people after a service? Do you like putting your arm around someone when you are talking to them in love? Now let us keep it holy, of course. That goes without saying – well, no, Paul says it. There are always dangers, but let us live dangerously – in the sense that if the world outside sees a church that is disciplined in love, then they will see something that they will never see anywhere else.

One day, many decades ago, we stood in Trafalgar Square when a public demonstration was under way. A girl came up and was attacking a group of Christians, and we began talking to her. She said that there was racial discrimination among Christians. Just by my side was a black girl and she responded, "Oh no, there isn't." I noticed immediately Christians came right up close by her – a demonstration for that girl that in Christ there is no such a thing. This is the discipline of love. You can only discipline each other when you are close enough in love. Otherwise, discipline becomes an inquisition, a hard thing, a thing that hurts more than it should, and a thing that has no love in it.

It is only in a family of love that you can get discipline. I have been into homes where there has been no discipline of the children at all, and I have seen a home without love. Love is discipline, and you have got to learn the love first before you can rebuke and discipline one another. This then is the message I have for you. It is a message of discipline, it is a message of God keeping us humble, it is a message of us keeping each other humble, and it is a message of our keeping ourselves humble. But the whole thing must be in love, drenched with love, or else it would harm or break down.

So Paul's message as he closes means this: I beg you, I'm coming to see you a third time, practise self-discipline before I get there so that I can come in love and we can greet one another; I don't want to find what I may not wish in you, so that you may not find in me what you don't wish for in me. Let us discipline ourselves that we may be free in love. What will help us to do this? An experience of three things: the grace of our Lord Jesus, the love of God, and the fellowship of the Holy Spirit. Without those three you could never have such discipline, without that you can never have such love. But this is the order: I become a Christian by discovering the grace of our Lord Jesus; then, as I discover Jesus, I begin to love God, and the love of God begins to be poured into my life, and I know what it is; then that love of God is to be translated into fellowship, and the Holy Spirit sets me free to pass on the love to the fellowship. That is not a formula – it is an experience. It is not a creed, it is something that you know. *The grace of the Lord Jesus Christ, and the love of God, and the fellowship of the Holy Spirit be with us all. Amen.*

For more of David Pawson's teaching,
including DVDs and CDs, go to
www.davidpawson.com

FOR FREE DOWNLOADS
www.davidpawson.org

Lightning Source UK Ltd.
Milton Keynes UK
UKOW06f2121040416

271531UK00001B/4/P